Market Expansion and Social Dumping in Europe

The term 'social dumping' regularly appears in public debates and in policymaking circles. However, due to its inherent ambiguity it is used by differing proponents in the manner that best suits their particular argument, thus opening the door for misconceptions and ill-grounded accusations.

This book systematically examines social dumping in the context of the European integration process. It defines social dumping as the practice, undertaken by self-interested market participants, of undermining or evading existing social regulations with the aim of gaining a competitive advantage. It also shows how the two major EU integration projects – the creation of the Internal Market, and EU enlargement to the east and to the south – have provided market actors with new incentives and opportunities to contest existing social 'constraints'. The empirical chapters examine social dumping practices accompanying labour migration, employee posting and cross-border investment distribution. In addition, they outline the process of formation of social standards and trace initiatives at EU and national levels that contribute to the spread of social dumping in Europe.

This book will be of interest to scholars and students of employment relations, EU studies, international political economy, globalization studies, welfare studies, social policy and migration studies.

Magdalena Bernaciak is Researcher at the European Trade Union Institute, Brussels.

Routledge advances in European politics

1 **Russian Messianism**
Third Rome, revolution, Communism and after
Peter J.S. Duncan

2 **European Integration and the Postmodern Condition**
Governance, democracy, identity
Peter van Ham

3 **Nationalism in Italian Politics**
The stories of the Northern League, 1980–2000
Damian Tambini

4 **International Intervention in the Balkans since 1995**
Edited by Peter Siani-Davies

5 **Widening the European Union**
The politics of institutional change and reform
Edited by Bernard Steunenberg

6 **Institutional Challenges in the European Union**
Edited by Madeleine Hosli, Adrian van Deemen and Mika Widgrén

7 **Europe Unbound**
Enlarging and reshaping the boundaries of the European Union
Edited by Jan Zielonka

8 **Ethnic Cleansing in the Balkans**
Nationalism and the destruction of tradition
Cathie Carmichael

9 **Democracy and Enlargement in Post-Communist Europe**
The democratisation of the general public in fifteen Central and Eastern European countries, 1991–1998
Christian W. Haerpfer

10 **Private Sector Involvement in the Euro**
The power of ideas
Stefan Collignon and Daniela Schwarzer

11 **Europe**
A Nietzschean perspective
Stefan Elbe

12 **European Union and E-Voting**
Addressing the European Parliament's internet voting challenge
Edited by Alexander H. Trechsel and Fernando Mendez

13 **European Union Council Presidencies**
A comparative perspective
Edited by Ole Elgström

14 **European Governance and Supranational Institutions**
Making states comply
Jonas Tallberg

15 **European Union, NATO and Russia**
Martin Smith and Graham Timmins

16 **Business, The State and Economic Policy**
The case of Italy
G. Grant Amyot

17 **Europeanization and Transnational States**
Comparing Nordic central governments
Bengt Jacobsson, Per Lægreid and Ove K. Pedersen

18 **European Union Enlargement**
A comparative history
Edited by Wolfram Kaiser and Jürgen Elvert

19 **Gibraltar**
British or Spanish?
Peter Gold

20 **Gendering Spanish Democracy**
Monica Threlfall, Christine Cousins and Celia Valiente

21 **European Union Negotiations**
Processes, networks and negotiations
Edited by Ole Elgström and Christer Jönsson

22 **Evaluating Euro-Mediterranean Relations**
Stephen C. Calleya

23 **The Changing Face of European Identity**
A seven-nation study of (supra) national attachments
Edited by Richard Robyn

24 **Governing Europe**
Discourse, governmentality and European integration
William Walters and Jens Henrik Haahr

25 **Territory and Terror**
Conflicting nationalisms in the Basque country
Jan Mansvelt Beck

26 **Multilateralism, German Foreign Policy and Central Europe**
Claus Hofhansel

27 **Popular Protest in East Germany**
Gareth Dale

28 **Germany's Foreign Policy Towards Poland and the Czech Republic**
Ostpolitik revisited
Karl Cordell and Stefan Wolff

29 **Kosovo**
The politics of identity and space
Denisa Kostovicova

30 **The Politics of European Union Enlargement**
Theoretical approaches
Edited by Frank Schimmelfennig and Ulrich Sedelmeier

31 **Europeanizing Social Democracy?**
The rise of the party of European socialists
Simon Lightfoot

32 **Conflict and Change in EU Budgetary Politics**
Johannes Lindner

33 **Gibraltar, Identity and Empire**
E.G. Archer

34 **Governance Stories**
Mark Bevir and R.A.W. Rhodes

35 **Britain and the Balkans**
1991 until the present
Carole Hodge

36 **The Eastern Enlargement of the European Union**
John O'Brennan

37 **Values and Principles in European Union Foreign Policy**
Edited by Sonia Lucarelli and Ian Manners

38 **European Union and the Making of a Wider Northern Europe**
Pami Aalto

39 **Democracy in the European Union**
Towards the emergence of a public sphere
Edited by Liana Giorgi, Ingmar Von Homeyer and Wayne Parsons

40 **European Union Peacebuilding and Policing**
Michael Merlingen with Rasa Ostrauskaite

41 **The Conservative Party and European Integration since 1945**
At the heart of Europe?
N.J. Crowson

42 **E-Government in Europe**
Re-booting the state
Edited by Paul G. Nixon and Vassiliki N. Koutrakou

43 **EU Foreign and Interior Policies**
Cross-pillar politics and the social construction of sovereignty
Stephan Stetter

44 **Policy Transfer in European Union Governance**
Regulating the utilities
Simon Bulmer, David Dolowitz, Peter Humphreys and Stephen Padgett

45 **The Europeanization of National Political Parties**
Power and organizational adaptation
Edited by Thomas Poguntke, Nicholas Aylott, Elisabeth Carter, Robert Ladrech and Kurt Richard Luther

46 **Citizenship in Nordic Welfare States**
Dynamics of choice, duties and participation in a changing Europe
Edited by Bjørn Hvinden and Håkan Johansson

47 **National Parliaments within the Enlarged European Union**
From victims of integration to competitive actors?
Edited by John O'Brennan and Tapio Raunio

48 **Britain, Ireland and Northern Ireland since 1980**
The totality of relationships
Eamonn O'Kane

49 **The EU and the European Security Strategy**
Forging a global Europe
Edited by Sven Biscop and Jan Joel Andersson

50 **European Security and Defence Policy**
An implementation perspective
Edited by Michael Merlingen and Rasa Ostrauskaitė

51 **Women and British Party Politics**
Descriptive, substantive and symbolic representation
Sarah Childs

52 **The Selection of Ministers in Europe**
Hiring and firing
Edited by Keith Dowding and Patrick Dumont

53 **Energy Security**
Europe's new foreign policy challenge
Richard Youngs

54 **Institutional Challenges in Post-Constitutional Europe**
Governing change
Edited by Catherine Moury and Luís de Sousa

55 **The Struggle for the European Constitution**
A past and future history
Michael O'Neill

56 **Transnational Labour Solidarity**
Mechanisms of commitment to cooperation within the European Trade Union Movement
Katarzyna Gajewska

57 **The Illusion of Accountability in the European Union**
Edited by Sverker Gustavsson, Christer Karlsson, and Thomas Persson

58 **The European Union and Global Social Change**
A critical geopolitical-economic analysis
József Böröcz

59 **Citizenship and Collective Identity in Europe**
Ireneusz Pawel Karolewski

60 **EU Enlargement and Socialization**
Turkey and Cyprus
Stefan Engert

61 **The Politics of EU Accession**
Turkish challenges and Central European experiences
Edited by Lucie Tunkrová and Pavel Šaradín

62 **The Political History of European Integration**
The hypocrisy of democracy-through-market
Hagen Schulz-Forberg and Bo Stråth

63 **The Spatialities of Europeanization**
Power, governance and territory in Europe
Alun Jones and Julian Clark

64 **European Union Sanctions and Foreign Policy**
When and why do they work?
Clara Portela

65 **The EU's Role in World Politics**
A retreat from liberal internationalism
Richard Youngs

66 **Social Democracy and European Integration**
The politics of preference formation
Edited by Dionyssis Dimitrakopoulos

67 **The EU Presence in International Organizations**
Edited by Spyros Blavoukos and Dimitris Bourantonis

68 **Sustainability in European Environmental Policy**
Challenge of governance and knowledge
Edited by Rob Atkinson, Georgios Terizakis and Karsten Zimmermann

69 **Fifty Years of EU–Turkey Relations**
A Sisyphean story
Edited by Armagan Emre Çakir

70 **Europeanization and Foreign Policy**
State diversity in Finland and Britain
Juha Jokela

71 **EU Foreign Policy and Post-Soviet Conflicts**
Stealth intervention
Nicu Popescu

72 **Switzerland in Europe**
Continuity and change in the Swiss political economy
Edited by Christine Trampusch and André Mach

73 **The Political Economy of Noncompliance**
Adjusting to the single European Market
Scott Nicholas Siegel

74 **National and European Foreign Policy**
Towards Europeanization
Edited by Reuben Wong and Christopher Hill

75 **The European Union Diplomatic Service**
Ideas, preferences and identities
Caterina Carta

76 **Poland within the European Union**
New awkward partner or new heart of Europe?
Aleks Szczerbiak

77 **A Political Theory of Identity in European Integration**
Memory and policies
Catherine Guisan

78 **EU Foreign Policy and the Europeanization of Neutral States**
Comparing Irish and Austrian foreign policy
Nicole Alecu de Flers

79 **Party System Change in Western Europe**
Gemma Loomes

80 **The Second Tier of Local Government in Europe**
Provinces, counties, départements and landkreise in comparison
Hubert Heinelt and Xavier Bertrana Horta

81 **Learning from the EU Constitutional Treaty**
Democratic constitutionalism beyond the nation-state
Ben Crum

82 **Human Rights and Democracy in EU Foreign Policy**
The cases of Ukraine and Egypt
Rosa Balfour

83 **Europeanization, Integration and Identity**
A social constructivist fusion perspective on Norway
Gamze Tanil

84 **The Impact of European Integration on Political Parties**
Beyond the permissive consensus
Dimitri Almeida

85 **Civic Resources and the Future of the European Union**
Victoria Kaina and Ireneusz Pawel Karolewski

86 **The Europeanization of National Foreign Policies towards Latin America**
Lorena Ruano

87 **The EU and Multilateral Security Governance**
Sonia Lucarelli, Luk Van Langenhove and Jan Wouters

88 **Security Challenges in the Euro-Med Area in the 21st Century**
Mare Nostrum
Stephen Calleya

89 **Society and Democracy in Europe**
Oscar W. Gabriel and Silke Keil

90 **European Union Public Health Policy**
Regional and global trends
Edited by Scott L. Greer and Paulette Kurzer

91 **The New Member States and the European Union**
Foreign policy and Europeanization
Edited by Michael Baun and Dan Marek

92 **The Politics of Ratification of EU Treaties**
Carlos Closa

93 **Europeanization and New Member States**
A comparative social network analysis
Flavia Jurje

94 **National Perspectives on Russia**
European foreign policy in the making
Maxine David, Jackie Gower and Hiski Haukkala

95 **Institutional Legacies of Communism**
Change and continuities in minority protection
Edited by Karl Cordell, Timofey Agarin and Alexander Osipov

96 **Sustainable Development and Governance in Europe**
The evolution of the discourse on sustainability
Edited by Pamela M. Barnes and Thomas C. Hoerber

97 **Social Networks and Public Support for the European Union**
Elizabeth Radziszewski

98 **The EU's Democracy Promotion and the Mediterranean Neighbours**
Orientation, ownership and dialogue in Jordan and Turkey
Ann-Kristin Jonasson

99 **New Democracies in Crisis?**
A comparative constitutional study of the Czech Republic, Hungary, Poland, Romania and Slovakia
Paul Blokker

100 **Party Attitudes Towards the EU in the Member States**
Parties for Europe, parties against Europe
Nicolò Conti

101 **The European Union and Occupied Palestinian Territories**
State-building without a state
Dimitris Bouris

102 **Portugal in the European Union**
Assessing twenty-five years of integration experience
Laura C. Ferreira-Pereira

103 **Governance and European Civil Society**
Governmentality, discourse and NGOs
Acar Kutay

104 **The EU, Migration and the Politics of Administrative Detention**
Edited by Michela Ceccorulli and Nicola Labanca

105 **Political Representation in the European Union**
Democracy in a time of crisis
Edited by Sandra Kröger

106 **New Approaches to EU Foreign Policy**
Edited by Maciej Wilga and Ireneusz Pawel Karolewski

107 **Democracy, Law and Religious Pluralism in Europe**
Secularism and post-secularism
Edited by Ferran Requejo and Camil Ungureanu

108 **Contemporary Spanish Foreign Policy**
Edited by David Garcia and Ramon Pacheco Pardo

109 **Reframing Europe's Future**
Challenges and failures of the European construction
Edited by Ferenc Miszlivetz and Jody Jensen

110 **Italy's Foreign Policy in the Twenty-first Century**
A contested nature?
Edited by Ludovica Marchi, Richard Whitman and Geoffrey Edwards

111 **The Challenge of Coalition Government**
The Italian case
Edited by Nicolò Conti and Francesco Marangoni

112 **The Nordic Countries and the European Union**
Still the other European community?
Edited by Caroline Howard Grøn, Peter Nedergaard and Anders Wivel

113 Mediating Policy
Greece, Ireland, and Portugal Before the Eurozone Crisis
Kate Nicholls

114 The European Parliament and its International Relations
Edited by Stelios Stavridis and Daniela Irrera

115 Market Expansion and Social Dumping in Europe
Edited by Magdalena Bernaciak

116 The Diplomatic System of the European Union
Evolution, change and challenges
Edited by Michael Smith, Stephan Keukeleire and Sophie Vanhoonacker

Market Expansion and Social Dumping in Europe

Edited by
Magdalena Bernaciak

Routledge
Taylor & Francis Group
LONDON AND NEW YORK

First published 2015 by Routledge

2 Park Square, Milton Park, Abingdon, Oxon OX14 4RN
711 Third Avenue, New York, NY 10017, USA

Routledge is an imprint of the Taylor & Francis Group, an informa business

First issued in paperback 2017

British Library Cataloguing in Publication Data
A catalogue record for this book is available from the British Library

Library of Congress Cataloging-in-Publication Data
Market expansion and social dumping in Europe / edited by Magdalena Bernaciak.
pages cm. – (Routledge advances in European politics)
1. Labor market–Europe Union countries. 2. Labor laws and legislation–European Union countries. 3. Free trade–European Union countries. 4. Foreign workers–European Union countries. 5. European Union countries–Social policy. 6. Competition, Unfair–European Union countries. 7. Marginality, Social–European Union countries.
I. Bernaciak, Magdalena, editor.
HD5706.M237 2015
331.2'2–dc23 2014048891

ISBN: 978-1-138-78714-8 (hbk)
ISBN: 978-1-138-71667-4 (pbk)

Typeset in Times New Roman
by Wearset Ltd, Boldon, Tyne and Wear

Contents

List of figures xv
List of tables xvi
Notes on contributors xvii
Acknowledgements xxii

Introduction: social dumping and the EU integration process 1
MAGDALENA BERNACIAK

PART I
Intra-EU labour and service mobility: threat to labour standards? 23

1 **Large-scale migration in an open labour market: the Irish experience with post-2004 labour mobility and the regulation of employment standards** 25
TORBEN KRINGS, ALICJA BOBEK, ELAINE MORIARTY, JUSTYNA SALAMOŃSKA AND JAMES WICKHAM

2 **Breaking the law? Varieties of social dumping in a pan-European labour market** 43
LISA BERNTSEN AND NATHAN LILLIE

3 **The politics of migrant irregularity: social dumping in the French construction industry** 61
MARCUS KAHMANN

4 **Varying perceptions of social dumping in similar countries** 80
JENS ARNHOLTZ AND LINE ELDRING

5 Socioeconomic cleavages between workers from new member states and host-country labour forces in the EU during the Great Recession 97
MARTIN GUZI AND MARTIN KAHANEC

PART II
Social dumping pressures in manufacturing sectors 123

6 Marketization and social dumping: management whipsawing in Europe's automotive industry 125
IAN GREER AND MARCO HAUPTMEIER

7 Social dumping with no divide: evidence from multinational companies in Europe 140
VERA TRAPPMANN

8 Coordinated interest representation along the automotive value chain as a response to social dumping practices 157
VOLKER TELLJOHANN

PART III
The deregulation agenda at the EU and national levels 171

9 EU economic freedoms and social dumping 173
JAN CREMERS

10 Have your competitiveness and eat it too: the pull and limits of cost competition in Hungary and Slovakia 190
VERA ŠĆEPANOVIĆ

11 Tracing the competitiveness discourse in Spain: social dumping in disguise? 210
MÒNICA CLUA-LOSADA

Conclusion 226
MAGDALENA BERNACIAK

Index 235

Figures

1.1 Total employment of Irish and non-Irish nationals aged 15 years and over 27
1.2 Irish and non-Irish employment in the construction sector 30
1.3 Irish and non-Irish employment in the hospitality sector 35
3.1 The evolution of employment of salaried and temporary agency workers in the French construction sector, 1996 to 2012 69
5.1 The share of immigrant population from EU-15 and EU-12 in the 15 old EU member states 105
5.2 Labour market participation of EU-15 natives and EU-12 immigrants in the 15 old EU member states 109
5.3 Unemployment rates of EU-15 natives and EU-12 immigrants in the 15 old EU member states 111
11.1 New employment contracts in Spain, 1985 to 2005 218

Tables

2.1 Savings made by companies through strategic posting 55
3.1 Legal entities in the French construction industry by number of salaried workers (2012) 68
5.1 Descriptive characteristics of EU-12 migrants and EU-15 native populations 106
5.2 Labour market indicators for EU-12 migrants and EU-15 natives over time 107
5.3 Decomposition results: labour market participation rate 110
5.4 Decomposition results: unemployment rate 112
5.5 Decomposition results: self-employment rate 114
5.6 Decomposition results: incidence of over-education among workers 116
5.7 Decomposition results: incidence of elementary occupation 117
5.8 Decomposition results: temporary contracts 119
9.1 Social policy fields relevant for the free movement of workers 175

Contributors

Jens Arnholtz is an Assistant Professor at the Employment Relations Research Centre (FAOS), University of Copenhagen. His research interests are labour migration and posting of workers within the EU, and EU labour market regulation more generally. His PhD thesis dealt with the regulation of posted work following the *Laval* ruling, and he has published articles on post-enlargement labour migration in journals such as the *European Journal of Industrial Relations* and *Economic and Industrial Democracy*.

Magdalena Bernaciak is a Researcher at the European Trade Union Institute, Brussels. She completed her PhD studies in Political Science at the Central European University, Budapest. She was also a visiting fellow at the Institute for Economic and Social Research (WSI) in Düsseldorf and at the University of Warwick's Industrial Relations Research Unit (IRRU). Magdalena's research interests lie in the political economy of the EU's eastern enlargement, transnational cooperation among trade unions, the socioeconomic impact of foreign direct investments, and labour migration. Her articles have appeared in the *European Journal of Industrial Relations*, *Industrielle Beziehungen*, *Transfer* and the *Industrial Relations Journal*.

Lisa Berntsen completed her PhD in early 2015 at the Department of Sociology of the University of Jyväskylä, Finland, and at the Department of Global Economics and Management of the University of Groningen, the Netherlands (double degree). Her research focuses on intra-EU migration, migrant employment, migrant practices, migrant organizing and labour relations. Since January 2015, she has been a Postdoctoral Researcher at the University of Tilburg, researching undocumented migrant workers in the Netherlands.

Alicja Bobek is a Research and Teaching Fellow at the Department of Sociology, Trinity College Dublin. She previously worked on the 'Learning from Poland' project funded by the Irish Research Council. Her research interests include migration, labour markets, social networks, and ethnic and cultural studies. She holds a PhD in Sociology from Trinity College Dublin, an MA in Sociology, and an MA in Migration and Ethnic Studies from the Jagiellonian University in Kraków.

Mònica Clua-Losada is a Lecturer in Political Science at the Department of Political and Social Sciences of the Universitat Pompeu Fabra in Barcelona. She completed her PhD in Politics (2010), MA (2006) and BA Hons (2004) at the University of York (UK). In her research she examines the critical political economy of crisis dynamics, particularly in relation to subaltern groups in society and their ability to disrupt and resist the political, economic and social manifestations of capitalist accumulation. She is the Vice-Chair of the Critical Political Economy Research Network of the European Sociological Association.

Jan Cremers is a Senior Researcher at the Amsterdam Institute of Advanced Labour Studies (AIAS). He has worked as a European trade union leader and as General Director of the Dutch works council training fund. He was also a Member of the European Parliament. His book *In Search of Cheap Labour in Europe* was published in 2011 by International Books. He has also published *A Decade of Experience with the European Company* (ETUI, March 2013) with Sig Vitols and Michael Stollt, and *The Long and Winding Road to an Asbestos Free Workplace* (International Books, June 2013) with Rolf Gehring. In November 2013, he received the Doctor of Letters award (D.Litt.) from Westminster University 'in recognition of his services to European Social Policy'.

Line Eldring is a sociologist and Senior Researcher at the Fafo Institute for Labour and Social Research in Oslo. She has been involved in a broad range of projects in the fields of labour mobility, EU enlargement and industrial relations, and has published widely on these issues. Since 2012, she has co-authored three articles in the *European Journal of Industrial Relations* and a chapter in an edited volume published by Ashgate.

Ian Greer is Professor of Comparative Employment Relations at the University of Greenwich. He directs the Work and Employment Research Unit and is principal investigator on a four-year project funded by the European Research Council on marketization and its social effects. His articles have appeared in the *British Journal of Industrial Relations*, *Industrial Relations*, the *European Journal of Industrial Relations* and *Politics and Society*.

Martin Guzi is a Postdoctoral Researcher at Masaryk University in Brno. He obtained his PhD in Economics from CERGE-EI (Prague) in 2013; he also holds an MSc in Mathematics from the Comenius University in Slovakia and an MA in Economics from CERGE-EI. From 2009 to 2013 he worked at the Institute for the Study of Labor (IZA) in Bonn as a Resident Research Affiliate. Martin is also a CELSI Research Fellow and since 2009 has been a team member of a scientific research group on the Wage Indicator project. Martin has published in the *International Journal of Manpower* and the *Czech Journal of Economics and Finance*. His research interests include labour economics and applied econometrics, focusing on migration, income adequacy, social welfare programmes and subjective well-being.

Marco Hauptmeier is a Senior Lecturer and Co-Director of the Employment Research Unit at Cardiff University. He holds a PhD from Cornell University and his research interests include comparative employment relations, comparative political economy and institutional theory. He is currently working on an Economic and Social Research Council Future Research Leaders project that examines employers' organizations in the United Kingdom. He has published in leading academic journals such as *Human Relations*, *Industrial Relations* (Berkeley) and the *British Journal of Industrial Relations*. He has recently edited the book *Comparative Political Economy of Work* (Palgrave, 2014) with Matt Vidal.

Martin Kahanec is an Associate Professor at Central European University in Budapest and a Co-Founder and Scientific Director of CELSI, Bratislava. He is also a Visiting Research Fellow, Deputy Programme Director on 'Migration' and former Deputy Director of Research at the Institute for the Study of Labor (IZA) in Bonn, and a Visiting Research Fellow at Harvard University's Labor and Worklife Program. His research interests are labour and population economics, ethnicity, migration, and reforms in Central and Eastern European labour markets. He has published in peer-reviewed academic journals, contributed chapters to collected volumes, and edited several scientific books and journal special issues.

Marcus Kahmann is a political scientist and sociologist based at the Institut de recherches économiques et sociales (IRES) in Noisy-le-Grand near Paris. He has also worked at the European Trade Union Institute, Warwick Business School and the University of Hamburg. He has published on trade union mergers in Britain and Germany, immigration policies, industrial relations in France and Germany, and the relationship between trade unions and migrant workers.

Torben Krings is an Associate Professor at the Department of Economic and Organisational Sociology, Johannes Kepler University of Linz, Austria. He previously worked as a Postdoctoral Researcher at the Employment Research Centre, Trinity College Dublin, following the completion of his PhD thesis on trade unions and immigration at Dublin City University. His research interests include migration, industrial relations, work and employment, and European societies. He has published in the *European Journal of Industrial Relations*, *Economic and Industrial Democracy*, the *Irish Journal of Sociology* and the *Journal of Ethnic and Migration Studies*.

Nathan Lillie is a University Lecturer in Social Policy at the University of Jyväskylä, Finland. He has previously been an Associate Professor in Global Economics and Management at the University of Groningen, the Netherlands, and a Research Fellow at the Helsinki Collegium, and he holds a PhD in Industrial and Labour Relations from Cornell University. He has published articles on transnational collective bargaining, labour migration and European Union labour politics. He is currently running a project on 'Transnational

Work and the Evolution of Sovereignty' funded by a European Research Council Starting Grant (TWES #263782), focusing on the regulation of posted migrant work in the EU.

Elaine Moriarty is an Assistant Professor at the Department of Sociology, Trinity College Dublin. Elaine's teaching and research interests include mobility and migration, employment and labour markets, qualitative research methods, and race and ethnicity. Her current research focuses on European mobility and the portability of social protections.

Justyna Salamońska is a Research Associate at the Migration Policy Centre (Robert Schuman Centre for Advanced Studies, European University Institute, Florence). She holds a PhD in Sociology from Trinity College Dublin. Her teaching and research interests include labour market integration, mobility, intra-European migration and mixed methods research.

Vera Šćepanović is a Visiting Lecturer in the Department of Public Policy at Central European University, Budapest. Her research interests include the role of the EU in the development of transition countries and the impact of foreign direct investment on industrial development and labour relations in Central-Eastern Europe. She has participated in several EU-funded research projects: ICaTSEM ('Institutional Changes and Trajectories of Socio-Economic Models', FP7), RECWOWE ('Towards an Employment-friendly Welfare State', FP6) and MAXCAP ('Maximizing the Integration Capacity of the European Union'). Her articles have appeared in the *European Journal of Industrial Relations* and *Industrielle Beziehungen.*

Volker Telljohann is a Senior Researcher and Head of the European Policies Department at IRES Emilia-Romagna, Italy. He holds a DSocSci degree in Social and Economic Sciences. He also lectures on the sociology of work and EU social policy at the University of Parma. His research focuses on new trends in employment relations, restructuring processes, work organization and working conditions. He has coordinated several national and European projects on company-level interest representation, new models of participation in the context of restructuring in the private and public sectors, public policies and work-oriented innovations, labour market policies and new tendencies in collective bargaining. He has published in the *European Journal of Industrial Relations*, *Transfer*, *La Revue de L'IRES*, *WSI Mitteilungen* and *Sociologia del lavoro*.

Vera Trappmann is an Associate Professor of Employment Relations at Leeds University Business School. Her comparative research deals with labour relations, welfare and corporate social responsibility in Western, Central and Eastern Europe. Her recent books include *Business Leaders and New Varieties of Capitalism in Post-Communist Europe* (Routledge, 2013); *Fallen Heroes in Global Capitalism. Workers and the Restructuring of the Polish Steel Industry* (Palgrave Macmillan, 2012); and *Das Erbe des Beitritts. Europäisierung in Mittel- und Osteuropa* (Nomos, 2006).

James Wickham is a Professor and Fellow Emeritus of Trinity College Dublin, where he directed the 'Migrant Careers and Aspirations' project on Polish migrants in Dublin. He researches the relationship between employment and different forms of mobility, ranging from migration to business air travel. As well as academic journal articles, his publications include *Gridlock: Dublin's Transport Crisis and the Future of the City* (New Island, 2006).

Acknowledgements

This volume originated from the research project 'Social Dumping in the Enlarged EU: Concepts, Challenges and Policy Options', which was carried out at the European Trade Union Institute (ETUI) and coordinated by the editor. We are grateful to the ETUI for financial and administrative support for our work.

The editor would like to thank Svetoslav Salkin for his critical remarks and suggestions concerning the concept of social dumping. She is also grateful to the chapter authors for their active contribution to project discussions and for their comments on earlier versions of the Introduction.

We would also like to thank Niamh Warde for her professional work as language editor.

Introduction

Social dumping and the EU integration process

Magdalena Bernaciak

In his Toulon speech on 1 December 2011, President Sarkozy of France expressed his discontent with 'social and fiscal dumping' in Europe and condemned EU member states' 'disloyal competition' practices (*The Economist*, 2011). At about the same time, the European Trade Union Confederation (ETUC) launched consultations with its member organizations in preparation for a pan-European drive 'against wage and social dumping'. Among the initiatives envisaged in the campaign, the ETUC intended to publish a black book revealing instances of social dumping in EU member states, which could then be used as a shaming device in the battle against attempts 'to destroy national social and labour standards' (ETUC, 2011). The business community seems equally concerned about the issue, albeit for a different reason: in its 2012 Annual Report, the European Construction Industry Federation maintained that preventing social dumping was crucial for the preservation of the sector's competitiveness (FIEC, 2012). None of these actors, however, provides a definition of social dumping, which is symptomatic for broader trends in Europe: even though the term appears regularly in the public discourse and in policymaking circles, it is usually used by differing proponents in the manner that best suits their particular argument, thus opening the door for misconceptions and ill-grounded accusations.

In a similar vein, social dumping has so far received limited scholarly attention. It seems that the normative clout and emotional load accompanying the term's popular use has discouraged scholars from addressing the issue in more detail, leaving unclear both the mechanism behind the notion and its relation to socioeconomic changes in Europe – in particular, to the process of EU integration. Despite the vagueness of the term, however, it is still capable of influencing actors' strategies and government policies. The introduction of transition periods temporarily restricting the access of the workforces of candidate countries to the labour markets of the old EU member states, as well as the failure of the French and Dutch EU Constitutional Treaty referenda, may be largely seen as resulting from the presence of real or perceived social dumping concerns within European societies.

In view of the high political resonance of social dumping in Europe on the one hand and the term's ambiguity on the other, there is a need to systematize the concept and to analyse specific instances of social dumping pursued in the

EU context. These two tasks are taken up in this volume. Building on recent contributions in the fields of economic theory, economic sociology and institutional political economy, we define social dumping as the practice, undertaken by self-interested market participants, of undermining or evading existing social regulations with the aim of gaining a competitive advantage. We then show how the two major EU integration projects – the creation of the Internal Market, and EU enlargement to the east and to the south – have provided market actors with new incentives and strategic opportunities to contest or circumvent transnational and national social regulations. Subsequent chapters examine social dumping practices that have developed in the course of EU economic integration, outline the process of formation of social standards and document trade unions' reactions to social dumping threats. The concluding chapter reflects on the long- and short-term effects of social dumping. It argues that, in the short run, social dumping exerts downward pressure on wages and working conditions in Europe. If pursued by a large number of actors over a long period of time however, it could considerably weaken the beneficial social effects of economic growth, threaten social cohesion and even lead to the disintegration of the market order.

Social dumping in popular and academic discussions

Popular debates on social dumping have accompanied various initiatives towards trade liberalization and advances in economic integration between 'high-' and 'low-wage' countries. Cross-national differences in wage levels and extents of social protection, as well as the different degrees to which labour market regulations are actually implemented, have often been a source of concern among high-wage country actors about the potential negative consequences of integration processes. The fear is that as the liberalization agenda progresses, differences in social standards could be used by low-wage country actors to gain a higher market share, which would hurt the job prospects and earnings of the actors in high-wage settings. These arguments featured in debates on the World Trade Organisation's social clause and were also raised in the discussions that preceded the conclusion of the North American Free Trade Agreement and the EU's enlargement to the south and to the east.

However, to regard low-income countries' wages and social standards as 'an illegitimate export subsidy and a form of social dumping' (Van Roozendaal, 2002, p. 170) is problematic for at least three reasons. First, the label 'cheaper and thus more competitive' is often applied on the basis of comparisons of raw wages and GDP per capita without taking into account productivity gaps between high- and low-standard settings. In reality, productivity tends to be lower in the latter case, which often compensates for real-wage differentials (De la Dehesa, 2007). Second, such claims disregard the fact that social dumping practices are not pursued exclusively by actors from low-wage environments. In particular, the role of high-wage country companies in exploiting the differences in socioeconomic conditions between domestic and foreign locations is rarely a subject of public debate. Third, the choice of high-wage country standards as the point of reference in international comparisons is a normative choice that can give a protectionist flavour to accusations of social dumping (Bhagwati, 1995).

An analysis of the scientific contributions that have taken on the task of conceptualizing social dumping also reveals a number of problems. Some definitions follow the popular understanding of lower wages and inferior employment standards as being equivalent to social dumping and 'unfair' competition. For instance, the 2012 edition of the European Industrial Relations Dictionary compiled by the European Foundation for the Improvement of Living and Working Conditions (Eurofound) defined social dumping as 'a practice involving the export of goods from a country with weak or poorly enforced labour standards, where the exporter's costs are artificially lower than its competitors in countries with higher standards, hence representing an unfair advantage in international trade' (Eurofound, 2012).[1] According to this definition, virtually all developing countries' exports would fall into the social dumping category. In addition, it is unclear on what basis one can label the price of developing country exports as being 'artificially' low. Just like the participants in the public discourse, Eurofound seems to implicitly refer to the standards of developed/high-wage countries. As pointed out above, however, the decision to adopt the latter's standards as the benchmark is an arbitrary, normative choice.

Other studies consider states as 'social dumpers' using counterfactuals that, by definition, cannot be verified or supported by empirical evidence. Alber and Standing's (2000, p. 99) analysis of global trends in social protection and welfare spending conceptualizes social dumping as 'situations in which standards in one country are lowered relative to what they would have been because of external pressure from all or part of the global economic system'. The authors further specify that the decline can take the form of erosion of the existing levels of social protection or the so-called arrested development of social regulation, which refers to situations where social standards do not advance at a pace proportional to economic growth as a result of external competitive pressures. The notion of arrested development of social policies is problematic, however, because it is difficult to determine what the exact level of social standards would be had it not been for the alleged activity of social dumping. Moreover, the authors seem to impose a universal benchmark for social protection that should be reached by countries at a certain level of development, which is hardly justifiable in view of the considerable variation among developed countries in terms of the degree of social protection they offer. Similar objections may be formulated in relation to Sinn (2003, p. 3), who defines social dumping as the practice by less developed states of 'maintaining an underdeveloped welfare state to create a competitive cost advantage for their industries'. Again, it is unclear what 'underdeveloped' welfare state means exactly. In addition, similar to the popular understandings of the notion, Sinn's focus on the actions of poorer countries' governments ignores the possibility that social dumping initiatives may also be pursued by actors in high-wage environments.

Yet other authors construct their definitions of social dumping in an inductive manner, listing risks related to the notion with regard to a concrete political-economic setting. Discussing the EU Internal Market, for instance, Pochet

(1990) warns against social dumping in the form of: (1) production relocations; (2) fragmentation of national regulatory environments as a result of intra-EU labour mobility; (3) state reforms increasing labour market flexibility that are designed to boost a country's competitiveness; and (4) multinational companies' pressures for further flexibility of employment conditions. Similarly, Mosley (1995) argues that social dumping in the EU may involve: (1) the displacement of high-wage country producers by their competitors from low-standard countries; (2) company relocations; and (3) states' low-wage and anti-union policies. Both accounts are interesting in that they point to possible manifestations of social dumping in different policy fields. At the same time, neither may be regarded as a comprehensive catalogue of dumping threats. Because they fail to identify the mechanism underlying the dumping behaviour, they are of relatively little use outside of the specific contexts to which they refer.

An important contribution to the scholarly debate on social dumping is Vaughan-Whitehead's (2003) study on the potential impact of EU eastern enlargement on Western European labour markets and social protection systems, which links the issue of social dumping to its counterpart in trade. The author claims that trade dumping and social dumping share a common goal, given that they are both pursued in order to gain a higher market share on the basis of lower prices. The author subsequently defines social dumping as:

> any practice pursued by an enterprise that deliberately violates or circumvents legislation in the social field or takes advantage of differentials in practice and/or legislation in the social field in order to gain an economic advantage, notably in terms of competitiveness, the state also playing a determinant role in this process.
>
> (Vaughan-Whitehead, 2003, p. 325)

Vaughan-Whitehead's definition is supplemented by a set of criteria that help determine a company's degree of intention in violating social norms. A significant gap between home- and host-country legislation, for instance, allegedly proves a firm's willingness to enhance its competitive position by investing in the low-standard environment. Similarly, if the economic condition of an enterprise enables it 'to progressively assimilate working conditions in the host country to those prevailing in the home country', but the firm nevertheless pays its foreign workers wages that are 'well below what is the norm at home', its social dumping motivation is evident (Vaughan-Whitehead, 2003, pp. 327 and 326). Vaughan-Whitehead's conceptualization is interesting because it goes further than any other definition in outlining the possible motivation behind social dumping and in specifying the actions it may entail. Nonetheless, it is still ambiguous about the role of governments and does not address the issue of employee involvement in dumping practices. On closer scrutiny, the two criteria put forward by the author are also problematic. According to the first, all foreign direct investment flows to low-wage countries could be viewed as 'dumping driven'. Vaughan-Whitehead fails to distinguish between efficiency- and market-seeking investments and neglects to account for the company practice of transferring the majority of labour-intensive operations to worker-rich countries and concentrating the higher value-added activities at home, which might enhance a company's competitiveness and, in consequence, benefit both the home- and the host-country units. The second criterion, on the other hand, recalls Eurofound and Alber and Standing's benchmarks: it is impossible to assess how much a firm should pay its employees, or at which point exactly host-country wages are 'well below' those in the home country.

To conclude, the available scholarly definitions of social dumping suffer from considerable flaws. They either confuse lower wages and inferior employment standards with social dumping and 'unfair' competition, or mix positive and normative elements, arbitrarily designating the social standards of high-wage countries as the universal criteria. Moreover, most studies take the form of single-case studies and focus on a particular regulatory context, which creates the impression that the term is applied to unrelated phenomena. In a bid to avoid normative traps and to bring different manifestations of social dumping under a common analytical umbrella, we construct our definition of social dumping on the basis of recent theoretical literature on the role of regulation in capitalist economy, and that on current trends in market expansion. We lay out our concept in the following two sections and subsequently move to the analysis of recent trends in European integration through the prism of opportunities and incentives for social dumping that they have provided.

Competition and regulation in capitalist markets

In the simplified reading of neoclassical economics embraced by contemporary market libertarians, the market mechanism is considered the most efficient instrument for allocating scarce resources. In line with Adam Smith's 'invisible hand' paradigm, the benevolent effects of free market exchanges and unbridled competition are not limited to those involved in concrete transactions. Insofar as the rivalry between profit-maximizing actors drives innovation and pushes down the prices of goods and services, it benefits consumers, stimulates economic and technological progress, and thus serves wider societal interests.[2] This seemingly positive feature of the free market is often invoked to justify the laissez-faire approach to economic regulation and policymaking. According to its proponents, any form of intrusion into free market operations is harmful because it skews the self-regulatory potential of the system, leading not only to reduced economic performance but also to suboptimal aggregate outcomes.

Arrow and Debreu's general equilibrium model demonstrated that the neoclassical notion of benevolent markets rests on assumptions that are impossible to find in practice. Since then, the catalogue of recognized market failures (i.e. situations where the pursuit of individual self-interests does not lead to efficient outcomes) has been steadily growing. However, whereas traditional accounts of market failures have focused on mechanisms that undermine the 'invisible hand' mechanism, recent contributions to the field of economic theory assert that the very logic of market competition may in itself constitute a market failure. Drawing upon earlier work by Schelling (1978) and upon insights from Darwin's natural selection theory, Frank (2011) observes that human attainment is often assessed not in terms of one's *absolute* performance but according to how well one fares *relative* to others. In the case of so-called positional goods, whose value is measured in terms of their relative rather than their absolute consumption, people have an incentive to build up advantages over their rivals.[3] If left uncontrolled, however, this process can lead to wasteful spending and underinvestment in non-positional goods. Positional struggles rarely translate into the expansion of the common good and may actually prove harmful to individual and community interests.

Positional competition features in many everyday situations and is also one of the principal mechanisms guiding the behaviour of self-interested market participants. Business success does not depend on the absolute levels of investment or costs incurred by market participants but on their relative performance vis-à-vis their competitors. In an effort to outcompete its rivals, a company may invest excessively in a certain area, far beyond what would be considered optimal if the absolute and not the relative performance mattered. Alternatively, it might cut expenditure, in a domain that does not directly affect its market position, down to a level that adversely affects its general performance. The problem is that once a firm makes a move of this kind, it gains a merely temporary advantage over its competitors, who soon follow a similar course. According to Frank, unbridled competition results in 'expenditure cascades' (Frank, 2011, p. 61), while in other contexts it leads to a 'race to the bottom' among self-interested market participants. Even though, at the end of the day, the relative position of the competing firms has not changed in terms of market shares, they have all wasted resources that could otherwise have been used in a more productive way, or they have engaged in unnecessary cost-cutting that has not only reduced the efficiency of their own operations but may also have harmed broader societal interests. All in all, then, in the case of positional competition actors' pursuit of individual gain does not translate into a common good. In most instances, the benevolent effects of the 'invisible hand' fail to materialize because it is more the exception than the rule that individual and group interests coincide.

To illustrate the above argument, let us consider a firm that seeks to outcompete its rivals by lowering its expenditure on wages and reducing the quality of its employees' working conditions. Employee compensation is a non-positional good because, at least at face value, a wage scale is an internal company affair that does not influence the company's position relative to its market competitors. By contrast, a company's performance is highly positional: it is subject to financial market discipline and is reflected, for instance, in share prices and the CEO's remuneration. Initially, the cut in employee compensation or a shift towards poorer employment conditions gives the enterprise an advantage, which soon disappears, however, as other firms follow suit and reduce wages and social protections to a comparable level. Moreover, seeing their wage levels drop and working conditions deteriorate, workers may lose their motivation and work less productively, which will impact negatively upon the company's business results. Furthermore, as a result of the reduced income, employees' purchasing power may decline and translate into lower levels of demand. At the end of the day, it may turn out that nobody benefits from the 'race to the bottom': while the relative positions or market shares of the companies implementing the cuts are similar to their values at the outset, they may be suffering from decreasing sales and plummeting corporate profits. The social and economic implications of the salary slash may be even broader and involve deteriorating living standards and lower levels of economic growth.

It would undoubtedly be in the interest of market participants not to engage in wasteful rivalries of this kind. However, none of them has an incentive to unilaterally change his or her behaviour and withdraw from the race because they would lose out vis-à-vis those competitors who nevertheless decide to increase (or reduce) their spending in order to improve their relative position, irrespective of the negative consequences. Unfettered competition can therefore be a destructive force – a specific form of market failure. It creates collective-action problems that may threaten economic efficiency and long-term market sustainability and hinder the provision of public goods.

How can the negative effects of positional competition be eliminated or at least reduced? This cannot be achieved by relying on the self-regulating market, which, far from offering a solution, is actually the very source of the problem. Instead, competition-driven collective-action problems similar to those described above can be solved by means of market regulation. Well-designed rules prohibit harmful activities or remove the incentives that encourage individual actors to participate in wasteful spending. Health and safety regulations are a case in point: by setting standards for employee protection, they prevent companies from endlessly reducing their spending on safety measures – a non-positional variable that would otherwise be a likely target of cost-cutting schemes. Moreover, thanks to their universal character, they induce a change in the behaviour of market participants that would not be initiated through individual actions.

Beyond the effects of positional competition, regulation is also used to correct other failures associated with the unfettered functioning of markets. It makes up for informational asymmetries and the resulting lack of trust, and thus encourages actors to enter long-term contractual arrangements. It also prevents the abuse of market power by limiting the scope for predatory and rent-seeking behaviour, and protects the state and other non-market institutions from being captured by particularistic interests (Bruszt, 2002). Importantly, the rules governing markets are not limited to written laws and statutes, but rather also encompass informal codes of conduct and 'ways of doing things' that structure and guide the behaviour of actors in a given political-economic setting (Berntsen and Lillie, Chapter 2, this volume). These rules may also be enshrined in the procedures that govern the collective bargaining process, or take concrete shape through the deliberations of the social partners (Arnholtz and Eldring, Chapter 4, this volume). All of these formal and implicit norms provide a framework within which private market relations – contractual exchanges between self-interested actors – take place (Streeck, 2010). Rather than being shaped by pure market forces, then, well-functioning markets are actually constructed. Not only their long-term efficiency, but also their very existence depends on the presence of rules that establish rights and enforce obligations enabling market participants to maximize their profits in a predictable, ordered and closely supervised environment.

Social constraints and the appeal of social dumping

Social regulations constitute an important element in the construction of capitalist markets. As observed by Polanyi (2001, p. 75), people are not commodities in the same sense as goods: even though a worker's work in the capitalist system has its market price referred to as 'wage', labour constitutes a field of activity that has 'not [been originally] produced for sale'. For this reason, human beings cannot be fully subjected to market forces; the extension of market principles into all areas of societal life would destroy the very substance of society. In order to prevent the devastating effects of universal commodification, society needs to retain the ability to limit the exposure of its members to untamed market mechanisms. To use the term coined by Polanyi, it has to embed the market by subjecting it to a system of regulatory checks and controls. At the same time, society also needs to preserve those institutions governed by non-market logic that assist the weaker or more vulnerable members of the community and decrease their dependence on the market as the principal provider of goods and services. In practice, market embeddedness may take different forms, and its extent varies across specific political-economic settings. Most measures, however, fall within one of the three categories identified by Polanyi: 'factory laws', workers' representation structures and social legislation. Labour laws and industrial relations institutions protect employees from abuse and exploitation, enabling them to defend their interests and to co-shape market and corporate governance processes. Social and welfare policies, on the other hand, are based on the principle of redistribution and 'decommodify' certain members of the community, allowing them to maintain decent living standards by relying (fully or partially) on non-market income sources and provisions (Esping-Andersen, 1990).

It is not only society that has to be protected from excessive exposure to 'bare' market forces, however. Social controls and bridles are indispensable for ensuring the undisturbed operation of capitalist markets. This is because, as argued during our earlier discussion of Frank's (2011) volume, competition often tends to channel actors' behaviour into inefficient or wasteful activities. The wide spread of such practices would not only undermine the viability of individual business ventures, but could also lead to the decline, or even the disintegration, of the economic system as a whole. From this perspective, welfare policies cushioning the effects of market forces, as well as regulations preventing or discouraging actors from undertaking socially harmful activities, may be viewed as market-sustaining devices. As argued by Streeck (1997), social restrictions on self-interested rationality may even go beyond this protective function and enhance firms' economic performance. Employment protection and minimum-wage regulations may seem restrictive because they prevent companies from cutting wages below a certain level and from 'hiring and firing' as they see fit, but, at the same time, they encourage long-term planning and continuous investment in human capital. Similarly, collective bargaining and co-determination rules limit managerial autonomy but also help build trust between management and workers, boost a sense of responsibility for company performance among employees and stimulate productivity increases. Over time, social constraints may lead to the redefinition of corporate identity, inducing a shift from low-cost to high-quality, capital-intensive production. In this new market segment, a highly motivated, skilled workforce and an ability to innovate constitute key competitive advantages, and thus what used to be viewed as 'constraints … can open up as yet unknown [business] opportunities' (Streeck, 1997, p. 203). Certain welfare institutions can similarly serve as a 'productive factor' (Ferrera *et al.*, 2001) by contributing to social cohesion and leading to a more efficient utilization of human capital. Universal social security schemes, for instance, create an expectation of temporary relief in the event of job and income loss, stimulating more efficient job–skill matches and benefiting both the jobseeker and the economy.

Despite their beneficial aggregate effects and positive long-term impact, however, the arrangements set up to protect society from the adverse effects of unbridled competition clash with capitalist markets' tendency to expand and subsume those elements of societal activity that do not operate in line with their logic. This process of market expansion, or marketization, may be defined as the introduction or intensification of price-based competition in areas that in the past were sheltered from market pressures (Greer and Doellgast, 2013). It might involve the *spread* of markets and their self-regulating logic into new geographical regions or new fields of activity, or the *increasing depth* of commodification, resulting from the growing exposure of societal actors to the market mechanism (Streeck, 2010).

In the academic literature, the recent phase of market expansion is viewed as the result of policy decisions at the national and supranational level inspired by neoliberal ideology (see van Apeldoorn and Horn, 2007; Standing, 2009; Crouch, 2013). It must be remembered, however, that marketization is not synonymous with deregulation, which is the dismantling of regulations and institutions orchestrated and implemented by policymakers. As argued by Greer and Doellgast (2013, p. 2), marketization is 'institutionally thick' in the sense that alongside the gradual elimination of legal and institutional barriers to the market, it involves the creation of a brand-new set of bodies that, unlike the protective institutions in the Polanyian tradition, are geared towards supporting the market-based logic of exchanges. Against this background, the authors identify major directions of the current wave of marketization. The increase of contractual, price-based relations and the creation of internal markets of goods and services within what previously used to be a single organization or company both signify the growing spread of markets. Marketization unfolds through the disintegration of corporate value chains, the privatization of public assets, the practice of outsourcing and the creation of semi-independent subsidiaries; it can take place not only within a single economy but also at the cross-border level via foreign direct investments and international trade in goods and services. As markets expand and actors who are external to the company's core become asset holders, subcontractors and suppliers, price mechanisms and uniform criteria for quality and expenditure calculation are adopted. The resulting standardization of goods, services and production processes enables performance comparisons between individual establishments or service providers, stimulating rivalry within the value chain. By contrast, the increasing reliance on active labour market policies (ALMPs) testifies to the increasing depth of the market and to the growing exposure of society to market mechanisms. By imposing stricter conditions for benefit distribution, ALMPs seek to steer the unemployed back into the market. Moreover, much as they aim at increasing jobseekers' employability, they often lead to their commodification at the lower end of the wage scale. Finally, the liberalization of labour migration regimes in combination with policies promoting cross-border labour mobility simultaneously extends and deepens international markets for labour. As previously sheltered national labour markets are opened up to new entrants, job competition intensifies, affecting not only demographic and employment structures, but also the prices and wage levels in a given political-economic setting.

The above examples suggest that market expansion not only proceeds in a 'top-down' fashion through deregulation drives and the establishment of market-enabling institutions, but also follows directly from the strategic choices of self-interested market participants. Since the beneficial effects of regulatory constraints materialize only in the long term, rational actors forced to act according to the short-term market logic will view them as barriers to profit maximization. In a similar vein, despite the positive aggregate impact of regulation, from the point of view of a profit-maximizing individual it would nevertheless be optimal if he or she could undercut or evade the existing norms at the same time as his or her rivals are abiding by them. As argued by Frank (2011), market actors will primarily be interested in improving their position vis-à-vis their competitors and, in the course of this rivalry, they are likely to sacrifice non-positional goods such as wages and working conditions. As a result, instead of internalizing social norms and constraints imposed upon the market, individual market participants will have an incentive to ignore them or to adjust them to serve their own needs. In the words of Streeck (2010, pp. 15 and 21), 'a typical rule taker' may be rewarded with a higher profit or a larger market share 'for undercutting public or private regulatory institutions'.

It is in the context of actors' pressures on the regulatory framework that the notion of social dumping comes into play. We view social dumping as a specific subcategory of marketization – market actors' rebellion against social norms and obligations that may negatively affect their profit margins and market position in the short term. We accordingly define it as the practice, undertaken by self-interested market participants, of undermining or evading existing social regulations with the aim of gaining a short-term advantage over competitors.

The actor-driven social dumping and 'top-down' marketization initiatives discussed earlier in this section do not take place in isolation, but rather are mutually reinforcing. The spread of certain forms of social dumping may induce legislative changes that de-penalize or even encourage such practices, or may prompt the creation of institutions ensuring the further expansion of the market mechanism at the cost of social regulation. This may also have an impact upon social conventions and those elements of the regulatory structure that are not formally enshrined in law: by affecting the societal perception of what constitutes a social norm, the spread of social dumping may lead to societal approval (or, conversely, to a more categorical rejection) of a given behavioural pattern. On the other hand, social dumping practices are encouraged by national and supranational initiatives to expand markets. Insofar as deregulation and the establishment of market-making institutions expose previously sheltered actors to competition, or increase their exposure to competitive pressures, they provide them with incentives to disregard or contest the social constraints that still remain binding for their rivals. In the next section, we apply this logic to the process of EU economic integration to demonstrate how the excessive focus on market-expanding measures in Europe has encouraged market actors to engage in social dumping.

Europe: from social model to social dumping?

In the first three decades after World War Two, the countries of Western Europe developed at an unprecedented speed. Alongside high levels of economic growth and substantial productivity increases, the post-war 'miracle' brought about a spectacular rise in living standards across all societal groups. The speedy recovery and the balanced economic expansion that followed were by no means accidental, however. They relied on rules and institutions put in place by European governments to contain market forces and to channel the behaviour of individual market actors for socially desirable outcomes. Together with basic social laws enacted at the level of the European Economic Community (EEC), this set of values, norms and policy instruments constituted a uniquely European approach to socioeconomic policymaking or, to use the term popularized by the former President of the European Commission Jacques Delors, added up to the 'European Social Model' (Jepsen and Serrano Pascual, 2005, p. 234). According to Ferrera *et al.* (2001), this paradigm's common features encompassed basic universal social security systems, collective bargaining institutions and structures for the representation of socioeconomic interests, as well as high levels of income equality. In a similar vein, Vaughan-Whitehead (2003) identified substantial elements of the 'model', which included labour law and public services; policy principles guiding its creation (such as non-discrimination and equal opportunities); and various forms of social activism that it stimulated – in particular social dialogue, collective bargaining and civil society's involvement in the policymaking process.

To be sure, the existence of common traits by no means implied that national varieties of regulatory systems ceased to exist. European countries continued to exhibit considerable variation with regard to their welfare and industrial relations institutions, the extent of social protection provided and the degree of institutionalization of specific governance instruments. These differences could be traced back to institutional legacies, national values, and power relations between major socio-economic and political groups (Ebbinghaus, 1999). Nor did the existence of such a model mean that the national systems, once established, remained intact; on the contrary, they were constantly evolving as a result of internal deliberation and external pressures (see e.g. Pierson, 2001; Streeck and Thelen, 2005). What was important, however, was the shared logic behind the post-war social systems. By embracing the European Social Model, Western European governments had committed themselves to protecting their citizens from the negative effects of exposure to market forces by providing them with social safety nets and non-market-based income sources. At the same time, they had given organized interest groups an opportunity to co-shape the course of social and economic policies, creating a space for necessary market corrections and interventions for the sake of the common good. The effect of this regulatory effort was a two-track policy course combining the goal of economic efficiency with that of social cohesion, which distinguished Europe from other developed parts of the world. While the US and East Asian countries exhibited equally impressive levels of economic growth, Western Europe fared much better in terms of equality and social justice (Vobruba, 2001).

Over time, however, the balance between market expansion and social protection began to change. The first cracks in the European Social Model appeared in the early 1970s. Following the oil crisis, economic growth in most Western European countries slowed down or stalled completely. In an effort to bring down rapidly growing unemployment figures, Europe's governments resorted to new policy remedies inspired by the neoliberal ideology. At the same time, increased competition from other regions of the world, in particular from the US and the expanding East Asian economies, forced European leaders to seek new ways of raising economic efficiency and forging growth opportunities for domestic businesses. To an extent, the solutions adopted to tackle the economic stagnation and external pressures remained country-specific and mirrored the existing differences in the countries' institutional set-ups and political-economic interest constellations. The general trend, however, was one of increased reliance on markets and a growing belief in their efficiency-enhancing impact. These ideas have also made their way to the supranational level and thus influenced the two major European integration projects implemented since the 1980s: the launch of the EU Internal Market and the enlargement of the EEC (EU) to the south and to the east.

The EU Internal Market: liberalization and regulatory stalemate

The creation of the Internal Market featured in the Treaty of Rome as one of the goals of the EEC. In a nutshell, it entailed the gradual consolidation of EEC member states' markets into a common market space. By allowing goods, capital, labour and services to move freely across national boundaries, the Internal Market was expected to boost international trade and investment, enabling companies to benefit from increased specialization, higher economies of scale and foreign demand. The first step in this direction was the elimination of tariffs and quantitative restrictions on intra-EEC trade, followed by the establishment of customs union among the member states in 1968. The process gained new momentum in the 1980s, not least as a result of vigorous lobbying by international business representatives (Van Apeldoorn, 2002). The Single European Act signed in 1986 set 1992 as the provisional deadline for the completion of the Internal Market process. The integration of European service markets advanced at a slower pace, with two landmark acts – the Posted Workers Directive (PWD) and the Services Directive – being introduced in 1996 and 2006, respectively.

The process of building a unified European market space has been a large-scale exercise in marketizing. It has involved the removal of constraints on cross-border business operations and the introduction of the market mechanism in domains that had traditionally been sheltered from competitive pressures, such as utilities and certain public services (Clifton *et al.*, 2003; Keune *et al.*, 2008). The speed and vigour of the Europe-wide liberalization drive, however, has not been matched by the development of joint norms and regulations aimed at protecting market actors and society from excessive exposure to competition. As argued by Scharpf (1996), this has largely been a result of the EEC/EU's institutional set-up. The two institutions charged with furthering the Internal Market agenda – the European Commission and the European Court of Justice (ECJ) – have a supranational character and are not subject to the control of national constituencies. As a consequence, they were able to act relatively promptly and pursue the Internal Market agenda 'without much political attention' (Scharpf, 1996, p. 15). The principle of supremacy of EU law over national legislation, enshrined in the Treaty of Rome and subsequently confirmed by the ECJ's rulings, legitimized their market-making efforts. It has only been in the context of recent ECJ decisions which explicitly put economic freedom before fundamental social rights that the wide scope of these institutions' mandate and the lack of democratic accountability have come under criticism (Höpner, 2012). In contrast, joint social regulations at the Community level needed to be based on a compromise within the intergovernmental Council of Ministers. Such agreement was difficult to reach, however, because cross-national differences in factor prices and factor productivity translated into diverging preferences with regard to the extent of social protection that should be provided. Countries adhering to lower standards feared losing their competitive advantage and thus preferred to abstain from joint regulation or to set European standards as low as possible. At the opposite end of the spectrum, states characterized by high levels of social protection were reluctant to accept the logic of 'lowest common denominator', fearing the subsequent pressure on standards in their own jurisdictions. The resulting stalemate was sometimes solved by means of compensation (e.g. in the form of social funds) offered by richer countries to the poorer ones in exchange for the latter's acceptance of a more stringent Community regulation (Leibfried and Pierson, 1995). More often than not, however, conflicting preferences within the Council precluded the development of joint social rules, resulting in a 'fundamental asymmetry' between negative and positive integration in Europe (Scharpf, 1996, p. 15; see also Crouch, 2013) and the reduction of the Internal Market's *raison d'être* to its liberalizing function.

Neither could the expansion of the European market be counterbalanced by protective social regulations at the national level. As argued by Pelkmans (2012), the Internal Market regime guaranteed actors unconditional access to other member states' markets and thus went beyond the provisions of standard agreements on trade liberalization. Potential restrictions on these freedoms needed to be well grounded and applied only in strictly defined situations. But even if regulatory interventions were allowed, European governments would have little incentive to impose more stringent rules. Once the scope of the market ceased to overlap with state boundaries, any attempt at the national level to introduce additional restrictions or to enact regulations stricter than those in other EU countries could result in capital flight and the shift of productive activities towards other, more permissive environments. In this respect, the creation of a Europe-wide market space has not only limited EU member states' regulatory capacity but has also opened the door to 'regime shopping' and a 'race to the bottom' in relation to market, social and environmental norms (Leibfried and Pierson, 1995).

EU enlargement: diversity and growing competitive pressures

Tensions between social regulations and the market-making agenda became particularly pronounced with the extension of the European market to the Southern (in the 1980s) and the Central-Eastern European (CEE) countries (in the 2000s). From the point of view of high politics, the rationale for the two enlargement rounds was never called into question. The former round was viewed as a major factor in stabilizing the three newly democratized Mediterranean regimes; it also had geopolitical importance in that it expanded the Western European capitalist camp (Wallace, 1979; Verney, 2006). Similarly, EU eastern enlargement was regarded as an important step towards the reunification of the continent, marking the CEE states' 'return to Europe' after several decades of the East–West divide. In both instances, however, economic disparities between 'old' EEC/EU member states and the newcomers became a matter of concern. In a report issued in the 1960s, the European Commission still referred to Greece as a country 'in the course of development' (quoted in Siotis, 1981). In 1975, Spain's GDP per capita was 71 per cent, and Portugal's only 49 per cent of the EU average (Hutsebaut, 1979).[4] In the early 2000s, the East–West gap was even wider, with CEE candidate countries' GDP per capita amounting to only 45 per cent of the EU average (Krings, 2009). As regards earnings, gross annual wages across the post-communist region remained far below EU-15 standards: in 1999, Slovenia arrived at 71 per cent and Bulgaria at only 22 per cent of the EU average (Kunz, 2002). The statistical differences were supplemented by qualitative reports pointing to the fragility of tripartite structures in CEE, politicized industrial relations systems and half-hearted adoption of the already meagre EU social *acquis* (Meardi, 2012).

The post-enlargement European market offered fertile ground for the evasion of social regulations. With regard to cross-border service provision, Greek, Portuguese and Spanish firms initially posted their workers on the territories of other member states and paid them in line with their home-country rates. In view of concerns over low-wage competition, the ECJ ruled, in the 1990 *Rush Portuguesa* case, that EEC member states could extend certain (and potentially even all) employment regulations to posted workers. However, the focus on basic rules later established by the PWD and subsequent ECJ rulings made it possible for companies to exploit the difference between minimum and standard levels of protection. Combined with weak enforcement, the minimum-protection approach has made employee posting particularly prone to social dumping. In manufacturing sectors, the extended Internal Market has enabled companies to move production to cheaper or less regulated locations in Southern and, later on, Central-Eastern Europe, or to use the threat of exit to extract concessions from employees in more stringent regulatory settings. Large multinational companies have also found it easier to play off national governments against one another, making investments conditional upon generous subsidies and labour market reforms, which has sometimes led to regulatory 'races to the bottom' (Bohle, 2008). Finally, the prospect of labour migration from new, low-wage EU member states has increasingly become an object of concern. In the aftermath of both southern and eastern enlargement, most 'old' member states temporarily imposed labour market restrictions. While the transition periods admittedly reduced migratory inflows into certain jurisdictions, they also encouraged bogus self-employment that often amounted to social dumping (Galgóczi *et al.*, 2012). As shown by Guzi and Kahanec in Chapter 5 (this volume), migrants are more likely than native workers to work in precarious jobs, which enables the firms employing them to cut costs spent on wages and social contributions. Moreover, the growing pool of foreign workers has decreased companies' dependence on local workforces, putting pressure on wages and working conditions in the host countries.

Scharpf's (1996) account of regulatory traps in the context of the heterogeneous Internal Market may be applied both to the southern and the eastern EU enlargement rounds. In the context of debates on the PWD in the early 1990s, the divide between Northern European countries (pushing for a wide catalogue of social standards applicable to posted workers and shorter grace periods during which posted companies could still apply home-country regulations) and Southern European and Anglophone states (demanding less stringent regulations) was particularly apparent (Eichhorst, 1998). Following EU eastern enlargement, CEE governments became vocal defenders of EU economic freedom. They supported the original Commission proposal for the EU Services Directive and the so-called country-of-origin principle, which stipulated that an individual or a company was allowed to provide services in the territory of another EU member state on the basis of the laws and regulations of his or her country of origin or the country of establishment of the business, and not those of the host state (Gajewska, 2009). Even though the final version of the Directive did not follow the country-of-origin logic, the discord continued. In written observations submitted to the ECJ in the context of the *Laval* and *Viking* cases, CEE governments, together with the UK and Ireland, advocated the primacy of economic rights over social protection – at a time when the remaining EU member states were arguing the opposite (Lindstrom, 2010). More recently, the majority of CEE countries suggested that only a limited catalogue of national control measures be included in the planned PWD Enforcement Directive. These examples point to the existence of deep political cleavages in the enlarged EU and dash hopes for a more balanced development of social and market-making regulation in the foreseeable future. Particularly with respect to the EU eastern enlargement, then, one can speak of a double-negative effect: the process has simultaneously 'exacerbate[d] the scope and nature of regime competition within Europe's integrated market, and threaten[ed] to stall further Europeanisation of the institutions and processes of labour market regulation' (Marginson, 2006, p. 12).

By focusing more closely on the EU Internal Market and EEC (EU) enlargement, we do not wish to claim that social dumping has been unique to these two processes. As shown by Frank (2011), the very logic of competition provides market participants with powerful incentives to avoid or circumvent regulatory constraints, including social regulations. Tensions between the existing constraints and the possible short-term benefits of evading them are inherent in the capitalist system of production and accumulation; as a result, social dumping is practised by different groups of actors in a variety of market settings. In the European context, however, these two instances of 'top-down' marketization inspired by the neoliberal ideology have been particularly relevant. They have simultaneously extended both the scope and the depth of the European market, leading to the unprecedented intensification of price-based competition. In effect, not only have they made micro-level rule evasion more prevalent, they have also provided market participants with new strategic opportunities to contest or 'bend' the existing social constraints. As the threat of social dumping has become more imminent, it has grown into one of the most pressing political and social concerns in Europe. It has also emerged as an important topic of popular and policy debates.

Outline of the book

This volume is divided into three parts. The first focuses on social dumping practices pursued in the context of cross-border employee posting and labour migration. In Chapter 1, Torben Krings and his co-authors assess the impact of post-2004 enlargement migration upon Irish labour standards by examining the construction and hospitality sectors. They argue that the specific repertoires of social dumping actions they found in their study mirror the differences in the regulatory settings of the two industries. In construction, where social partnership traditions were strong, social dumping was synonymous with the breach or circumvention of collective agreements, whereas in hospitality – a traditionally low-wage, bargaining-free sector – it involved non-compliance with the country's employment legislation. The chapter also presents migrant workers' attitudes towards social dumping, showing that the longer they stayed in Ireland, the more actively they demanded better pay and working conditions. The theme of different social dumping strategies is continued in Chapter 2 by Lisa Berntsen and Nathan Lillie, which examines the activities of companies employing migrant and posted workers in the Dutch and Finnish construction and distribution sectors. Exploring the different ways in which the firms engage with the two countries' regulatory frameworks, the authors identify three forms of social dumping: regulatory evasion, defined as the violation of existing norms; regulatory arbitrage, which involves the strategic choice of the applicable regulatory regime; and regulatory conformance, in which norms are formally respected but at the same time are manipulated for cost advantage. Chapter 3 by Marcus Kahmann extends the scope of the social dumping debate beyond recent EU enlargement rounds and looks at the working conditions of irregular third-country (i.e. non-EU) migrant workers in the French construction industry. He shows that this group is assigned to the most physically demanding jobs, is deprived of basic social rights and is permanently threatened with dismissal. These abusive practices pursued by temporary work agencies have been driven not only by the increased use of outsourcing in the construction sector, but also, paradoxically, by government policies aimed at preventing migration and at combating illegal employment, which have pushed irregular third-country workers outside the boundaries of the regulatory system. In Chapter 4, Jens Arnholtz and Line Eldring examine how social actors define what are regarded as 'normal' standards and what constitutes a deviation from the norm. They point to the different understandings of social dumping in the two Nordic countries Denmark and Norway: while the Danes define it as non-conformance with the principle of equal treatment, in Norway it is understood as a breach of the minimum standards. The authors conclude that these varying definitions of social dumping have emerged as a result of differences with regard to the two countries' labour market models, the numbers of CEE migrants they have received and the composition of their governments during the EU eastern enlargement. In the final chapter in this part of the book, Martin Guzi and Martin Kahanec explore whether CEE migrants are disadvantaged vis-à-vis otherwise comparable native workers in the host countries with regard to employment or occupational status. They identify gaps in outcome variables that remain unexplained by differences in the characteristics of immigrant and native populations. These gaps point to the existence of a labour market cleavage that may result from migrants' conscious strategy of undercutting local labour standards, from discrimination or from other unobserved factors. The chapter demonstrates the limited applicability of quantitative approaches to the analysis of social dumping. At the same time, it makes it clear that the cleavage between migrant and domestic workers seriously threatens social cohesion in the host countries.

Part II examines social dumping practices that are related to cross-border investment flows and production organization. Drawing on evidence from the

European car industry, Ian Greer and Marco Hauptmeier (Chapter 6) show that the process of investment distribution among company units involves the extraction of labour concessions through so-called 'whipsawing', whereby individual locations are played off against each other. The authors identify different forms of whipsawing and discuss how it undermines collective bargaining norms and industrial relations arrangements. They conclude that the large-scale imposition of market relations in Europe has provided the business community with an incentive to use competition as a lever to extract concessions from labour and from the state, and that only encompassing regulation at the level of the market as a whole would limit the scope of social dumping in this industry. The theme of interplant competition is continued by Vera Trappmann in Chapter 7. Focusing on multinational companies in the steel and IT sectors, the author depicts a variety of strategies employed by central managements to lower labour costs at individual locations, such as the use of the disinvestment threat to extract wage concessions, the replacement of permanent workforces with agency workers, outsourcing, and production relocations to cheaper or less regulated environments. Trappmann argues that labour's capacity to counteract management pressures depends on the creativity and engagement of local employee representatives. These localized responses, however, often involve concession bargaining that is also a form of social dumping. Chapter 8 by Volker Telljohann examines the impact of outsourcing on wages, working conditions and industrial relations within automotive supply chains. He shows how carmakers use outsourcing as a cost-cutting strategy, replacing unionized workers on open-ended contracts with low-paid, unorganized labour. This leads to the disintegration of plant and sectoral structures of interest representation, especially at lower levels of the automotive supply chain. Telljohann also describes workers' efforts to minimize outsourcing-related social dumping threats via the coordination of employee interest representation beyond company and sectoral boundaries, organization at lower levels of the production chain and the strategic use of transnational agreements to enforce labour standards at supplier companies.

Part III focuses on the effects of the 'top-down' marketization advocated by EU and national actors, with a particular emphasis on the deregulatory measures implemented with a view to boosting the economic performance and 'competitiveness' of EU member states.[5] In Chapter 9, Jan Cremers argues that in view of the primacy assigned by EU institutions to economic freedoms, the Internal Market legislation might pose a threat to national labour standards. Using evidence from the international road transport and construction sectors, the author documents instances of rule circumvention accompanying the application of EU social security regulations and cross-border employee posting. He also points to the abuse of the EU's freedom of establishment through the creation of letter-box companies. The author argues that the existing ambiguity regarding the applicable laws impedes efficient rule enforcement and opens the door to social dumping. The final two contributions focus on national-level deregulatory drives. Vera Šćepanović (Chapter 10) examines patterns of competition over foreign direct investments in Hungary and Slovakia. In an effort to attract investors, the governments of the two countries have reduced corporate taxes and made labour markets more flexible, which has benefited the business community but had a negative impact on the welfare of broader social groups. The author accounts for the states' choice of the social dumping road to economic growth by highlighting the role of pressure from investors and intraregional benchmarking. However, she also points to the limits to this approach as stemming from CEE societies' desire to catch up with 'European' living standards and from the inability of the states in question to stand up to the cost-based competition posed by even cheaper locations in post-Soviet Eastern Europe. In Chapter 11, Mònica Clua-Losada reconstructs the Spanish path towards the lowering of employment standards in the period 1986 to 2008. The author argues that successive Spanish governments adopted the rhetoric of 'competitiveness' to justify their attacks on the country's regulatory framework. She also shows that although labour market protections were dismantled during this period, social policies largely remained intact, which may suggest that the Spanish welfare state was used as a buffer to mitigate the negative effects of the narrower scope of labour market protection.

On the basis of the evidence presented in the empirical contributions, the concluding chapter reviews different forms of social dumping and reflects on its short- and long-term effects. It also dispels popular misconceptions about the notion and discusses prospects for limiting the extent of social dumping in Europe.

Notes

1 Eurofound has recently withdrawn this definition from its dictionary and replaced it with a review of popular and academic uses of the term.
2 Smith himself remained rather sceptical about the notion of the 'invisible hand'. In particular, he did not argue that the pursuit of self-interest always leads to outcomes that are beneficial for society as a whole (Sen, 1987; Frank, 2011).
3 For a detailed discussion of competition for positional goods, see Hirsch (2005).
4 All figures are at purchasing power parity.
5 Krugman (1994) discusses the pitfalls of applying the microeconomic concept of competitiveness to macroeconomic phenomena.

References

Alber, J. and Standing, G. (2000) 'Social Dumping, Catch-up or Convergence? Europe in a Comparative Global Context'. *Journal of European Social Policy*, 10(2): 99–119.

Bernaciak, M. (2012) 'Social Dumping: Political Catchphrase or Threat to Labour Standards?' *ETUI Working Paper*, No. 2012.06. Brussels: European Trade Union Institute.

Bhagwati, J. (1995) 'Trade Liberalisation and "Fair Trade" Demands: Addressing the Environmental and Labour Standards Issues'. *The World Economy*, 18(6): 745–759.

Bohle, D. (2008) 'Race to the Bottom? Comparative Institutional Advantages? Competition of Capitalisms in the Enlarged EU'. Paper presented at the Political Economy Research Group seminar, Central European University, Budapest, 26 March.

Bruszt, L. (2002) 'Market Making as State Making: Constitutional and Economic Development in Post-communist Eastern Europe'. *Constitutional Political Economy*, 13(1): 53–72.

Clifton, J., Comín, F. and Díaz Fuentes, D. (2003) *Privatization in the European Union. Public Enterprises and Integration.* Dordrecht: Kluwer Academic.

Crouch, C. (2013) 'Europe and Problems of Marketization: From Polanyi to Scharpf'. *Lectio Magistralis*, 4. Florence: Firenze University Press.

De la Dehesa, G. (2007) 'Are Developing Countries Engaging in "Social Dumping"?' *VOX.* Available at: http://voxeu.org/index.php?q=node/213 (accessed 15 October 2011).

Ebbinghaus, B. (1999) 'Does a European Social Model Exist and Can It Survive?' In Huemer, G., Mesch, M. and Traxler, F. (eds), *The Role of Employer Associations and Labour Union in the EMU.* Aldershot: Ashgate, pp. 1–26.

Eichhorst, W. (1998) 'European Social Policy between National and Supranational Regulation: Posted Workers in the Framework of Liberalized Services Provision'. *MPIfG Working Paper*, No. 98/6. Cologne: Max-Planck-Institut für Gesellschaftsforschung.

Esping-Andersen, G. (1990) The *Three Worlds of Welfare Capitalism.* Princeton, NJ: Princeton University Press.

ETUC (2011) 'Proposal for an ETUC Campaign against Wage and Social Dumping in Europe'. Available at: www.etuc.org/IMG/pdf/Supplementary_Report.pdf (accessed 29 November 2011).

Eurofound (2012) 'Social Dumping' [Online]. Available at: www.eurofound.europa.eu/areas/industrialrelations/dictionary/definitions/SOCIALDUMPING.htm (accessed 16 January 2012).

Ferrera, M., Hemerijck, A. and Rhodes, M. (2001) 'The Future of the "European Social Model" in the Global Economy'. *Journal of Comparative Policy Analysis: Research and Practice*, 3(2): 163–190.

FIEC (2012). 'Annual Report 2012'. Available at: www.fiec.eu/en/library-619/annual-report-english.aspx (accessed 11 October 2013).

Frank, R.H. (2011) *The Darwin Economy. Liberty, Competition and the Common Good.* Princeton, NJ: Princeton University Press.

Gajewska, K. (2009) *Transnational Labour Solidarity: Mechanism of Commitment to Cooperation within the European Trade Union Movement.* Abingdon: Routledge.

Galgóczi, B., Leschke, J. and Watt, A. (2012) *Labour Migration in Troubled Times. Skill Mismatch, Return and Policy Responses.* Farnham: Ashgate.

Greer, I. and Doellgast, V. (2013) 'Marketization, Inequality and Institutional Change'. Unpublished working paper. London: University of Greenwich Business School.

Hirsch, F. (2005 [1977]) *Social Limits to Growth.* New York and London: Routledge.

Höpner, M. (2012) 'Usurpation statt Delegation. Wie der EuGH die Binnenmarktintegration radikalisiert und warum er politischer Kontrolle bedarf'. *MPIfG Discussion Paper*, No. 08/12. Cologne: Max-Planck-Institut für Gesellschaftsforschung.

Hutsebaut, M. (1979) *Enlargement of the European Community Following the Accession of Greece, Spain and Portugal. Socioeconomic Aspects.* Brussels: Günter Köpke.

Jepsen, M. and Serrano Pascual, A. (2005) 'The European Social Model: An Exercise in Deconstruction'. *Journal of European Social Policy*, 15(3): 231–245.

Keune, M., Leschke, J. and Watt, A. (2008) *Privatisation and Liberalisation of Public Services in Europe.* Brussels: ETUI.

Krings, T. (2009) 'A Race to the Bottom? Trade Unions, EU Enlargement and the Free Movement of Labour'. *European Journal of Industrial Relations*, 15(1): 49–69.

Krugman, P. (1994) 'Competitiveness. A Dangerous Obsession'. *Foreign Affairs*, 73(2): 28–44.

Kunz, J. (2002) 'Labour Mobility and EU Enlargement – A Review of Current Trends and Debates'. *ETUI Discussion Paper*, No. 2002.02.01. Brussels: European Trade Union Institute.

Leibfried, S. and Pierson, P. (1995) 'Multitiered Institutions and the Making of Social Policy'. In Leibfried, S. and Pierson, P. (eds), *European Social Policy. Between Fragmentation and Integration.* Washington, DC: The Brookings Institution, pp. 1–40.

Lindstrom, N. (2010) 'Service Liberalization in the Enlarged EU: A Race to the Bottom or the Emergence of Transnational Political Conflict?' *Journal of Common Market Studies*, 48(5): 1307–1327.

Marginson, P. (2006) 'Between Europeanization and Regime Competition: Labour Market Regulation Following EU Enlargement'. *Warwick Papers in Industrial Relations*, No. 79. Coventry: University of Warwick.

Meardi, G. (2012) *Social Failures of EU Enlargement: A Case of Workers Voting with Their Feet.* London: Routledge.

Mosley, H. (1995) 'The "Social Dumping" Threat of European Integration: A Critique'. In Unger, B. and van Waarden, F. (eds), *Convergence or Diversity? Internationalization and Economic Policy Response.* Avebury: Aldershot, pp. 182–199.

Pelkmans, J. (2012) 'Mutual Recognition: Economic and Regulatory Logic in Goods and Services'. *Bruges European Economic Research Papers*, No. 24/2012. Brugge and Natolin: College of Europe.

Pierson, P. (ed.) (2001) *The New Politics of the Welfare State.* Oxford: Oxford University Press.

Planet Labor (2013) 'EU: Snatched Compromise on the Charged Issue of "Posted Workers"'. Available at: www.planetlabor.com/en/european-level/labor-law/eu-snatched-compromize-charged-issue-posted-workers/ (accessed 17 December 2013).

Pochet, P. (1990) 'Dumping social: un concept operationnel?' *Nota Bene*, 56: 1–4.

Polanyi, K. (2001[1944]) *The Great Transformation: The Political and Economic Origins of Our Time.* Boston, MA: Beacon Press.

Scharpf, F.W. (1996) 'Negative and Positive Integration in the Political Economy of European Welfare States'. In Marks, G., Scharpf, F.W., Schmitter, P.C. and Streeck, W. (eds), *Governance in the European Union.* London: Sage, pp. 15–39.

Schelling, T.C. (1978) 'Hockey Helmets, Daylight Savings and Other Binary Choices'. In *Micromotives and Macrobehavior.* New York: Norton, pp. 211–244.

Seideneck, P. (1993) 'Vertiefung oder Erweiterung? Zu aktuellen Problemen der Europäischen Gewerkschaftspolitik'. *Gewerkschaftliche Monatshefte*, 44(9): 543–552.

Sen, A. (1987) *On Ethics and Economics.* Oxford: Blackwell.

Sinn, H.-W. (2003) 'Social Dumping in the Transformation Process?' *NBER Working Paper*, No. 8364. Cambridge, MA: National Bureau of Economic Research.

Siotis, J. (1981) 'The Politics of Greek Accession'. In Minet, G., Siotis, J. and Tsakaloyanis, P. (eds), *The Mediterranean Challenge IV: Spain, Greece and Community Politics.* Sussex European Papers, No. 11/1981. Brighton: Sussex European Research Centre, pp. 85–120.

Standing, G. (2009) *Work after Globalization. Building Occupational Citizenship.* Cheltenham: Edward Elgar.

Streeck, W. (1997) 'Beneficial Constraints. On the Economic Limits of Rational Voluntarism'. In Boyer, R. and Hollingsworth, J.R. (eds), *Contemporary Capitalism. The Embeddedness of Institutions.* Cambridge: Cambridge University Press, pp. 197–221.

Streeck, W. (2009) *Re-forming Capitalism. Institutional Change in the German Political Economy.* Oxford: Oxford University Press.

Streeck, W. (2010) 'Taking Capitalism Seriously. Toward an Institutionalist Approach to Contemporary Political Economy'. *MPIfG Working Paper*, No. 10/15. Cologne: Max-Planck-Institut für Gesellschaftsforschung.

Streeck, W. and Thelen, K. (eds) (2005) *Beyond Continuity. Institutional Change in Advanced Political Economies*. Oxford: Oxford University Press.

The Economist (2011) 'The Euro Crisis. One Problem, Two Visions (Part II)'. Available at: www.economist.com/blogs/charlemagne/2011/12/euro-crisis-0 (accessed 5 December 2011).

Van Apeldoorn, B. (2002) *Transnational Capitalism and the Struggle over European Integration*. Abingdon: Routledge.

Van Apeldoorn, B. and Horn, L. (2007) 'The Marketisation of European Corporate Control: A Critical Political Economy Perspective'. *New Political Economy*, 12(2): 211–235.

Van Roozendaal, G. (2002) *Trade Unions and Global Governance. The Debate on a Social Clause*. London: Continuum.

Vaughan-Whitehead, D. (2003) *EU Enlargement versus Social Europe? The Uncertain Future of the European Social Model*. Cheltenham: Edward Elgar.

Verney, S. (2006) 'Justifying the Second Enlargement: Promoting Interests, Consolidating Democracy or Returning to the Roots?' In Sjursen, H. (ed.), *Questioning EU Enlargement: Europe in Search of Identity*. Abingdon: Routledge, pp. 20–44.

Vobruba, G. (2001) 'Coping with Drastic Social Change: Europe and the US in Comparison'. In Beck, W., van der Maesen, L.J G., Thomése, F. and Walker, A. (eds), *Social Quality: A Vision for Europe*. The Hague: Kluwer Law International, pp. 251–270.

Wallace, W. (1979) 'Grand Gestures and Second Thoughts: The Response of Member Countries to Greece's Application'. In Tsoulakis, L. (ed.), *Greece and the European Community*. Westmead: Saxon House, pp. 21–38.

Part I

Intra-EU labour and service mobility

Threat to labour standards?

1 Large-scale migration in an open labour market

The Irish experience with post-2004 labour mobility and the regulation of employment standards

Torben Krings, Alicja Bobek, Elaine Moriarty, Justyna Salamońska and James Wickham

Introduction

The Irish migration experience at the beginning of the twenty-first century was quite extraordinary. Within the space of a decade, the country's share of foreign-born population doubled to over 17 per cent (OECD, 2011, p. 385). In the context of an open labour market and an unprecedented economic boom, Ireland attracted large-scale migration from the new EU member states (NMS). Since EU enlargement in 2004, more than half a million citizens from the NMS, in particular from Poland, have arrived in the country. While this migration contributed to economic growth during the boom years, it also raised concerns about social dumping and a 'race to the bottom' in relation to employment conditions. Although the boom came to an abrupt end in 2008, compliance with wage agreements and employment regulations remains a significant challenge in the 'post-Celtic Tiger' era.

This chapter explores the impact of recent mass migration upon labour standards in Ireland. It focuses specifically upon two employment sectors – construction and hospitality – that have been major destinations for NMS migrants. Drawing upon qualitative interviews with Polish migrants and Irish firms,[1] the chapter shows that employers have frequently used migrant labour as a cost-cutting strategy in what may be classified as instances of social dumping. However, these practices have varied, depending on the regulatory environment and the role of unions in each sector. In construction, where unions are a powerful force, social dumping mainly involved the breach of collective agreements through subcontracting arrangements at the more informal fringes of the sector. In hospitality, by now largely de-unionized and characterized by an informal work culture, social dumping was often synonymous with non-compliance with existing employment regulations.

More generally, both sectors experienced growing casualization of employment in the context of social dumping practices. While this was primarily an employer-driven strategy, migrants did not necessarily perceive the casualized employment relationship as a disadvantage, especially when the job was seen as only transitional and comparisons were made to Poland. However, the longer they stayed in the country, the more assertive migrants became about their employment rights, sometimes assisted by the unions. While some migrants were able to negotiate better working conditions during the boom years, the 2008 recession fundamentally transformed the labour market situation in Ireland. In times of rising unemployment, the bargaining position of employers strengthens as domestic and foreign workers alike struggle increasingly to meet growing demands for more flexibility in pay and working practices.

The chapter proceeds as follows. It first outlines the context of mass migration to Ireland and subsequent attempts to re-regulate the labour market. It then presents evidence from the two sectors to illuminate the experiences of migrants and the strategies of employers at the micro level. The chapter concludes by discussing the future of labour standards in post-boom Ireland, which continues to host a substantial migrant workforce.

Mass migration in a 'gold-rush' labour market

The context of large-scale migration to Ireland from the NMS and elsewhere was the 'Celtic Tiger' boom in the 2000s. Whereas in the 1990s the upswing was driven by foreign direct investment and high-tech manufacturing (Barry, 2007), the main driving force in the 2000s was the construction sector. An unprecedented building boom not only created one of the worst property bubbles in recent history but also generated a huge demand for additional labour. In the later boom years, this demand was largely met by mass migration from Poland and other NMS as the Irish labour market effectively ceased to be a 'national' labour market in the context of EU enlargement.

Unlike the 'guest-worker' migration of the 1960s and 1970s, this East–West mobility was not an organized form of labour migration but a free flow of people and information. For potential migrants in Poland, Irish job offers were visible on the Internet or communicated through informal social networks (Komito and Bates, 2009). New transport technologies made Dublin easier to reach from Warsaw than Warsaw from many provincial Polish towns. New arrivals could be fairly certain to find employment, while employers could be quite confident to have access to new labour. In short, the Irish 'gold-rush' labour market was characterized by an apparently infinite demand for and a seemingly infinite supply of new labour, whereby demand and supply mutually reinforced one another and led to an explosion of new jobs.

As the territorial boundaries of the Irish labour market became permeable, the composition of the workforce changed. In the 1990s, the vast majority of new jobs were taken up by Irish nationals. Ireland's late baby boomers of the 1970s were entering the job market, more women were looking for work and Irish emigrants were returning. However, the picture changed in the 2000s. Especially from 2004 onward, two-thirds of new jobs were taken up by NMS nationals.[2] In other words, in the final years of the boom, employment growth was largely driven by mass migration coming mainly from Poland, but also from Lithuania,

Latvia and Slovakia. However, almost by definition, a 'gold rush' does not last forever. In 2008, the boom came to an abrupt end as Ireland was hit by a sharp recession and a concomitant decline in employment (see Figure 1.1).

At the time of EU enlargement in 2004, the unemployment rate in Ireland was quite low, at around 4 per cent, which is usually regarded as being close to full employment. The need for additional labour thus seemed self-evident in the light of a fast-rising number of jobs and vacancies in the 'gold-rush' labour market. However, it is worth bearing in mind that mass migration occurred at a time when the employment rate in Ireland was 'only' 66 per cent and as such below the 'Lisbon target' of 70 per cent set by the EU for its member states in 2000. In other words, for Ireland, importing labour was de facto preferable to mobilizing all the potential 'indigenous' workforce. This perhaps was not all that surprising given that liberal market economies are more prone to importing labour to compensate for skill and labour shortages (Menz, 2009). Whereas more ambitious active labour market programmes would have required more strategic and long-term planning, the boom years were characterized by instantaneous growth and short termism, which to some extent encouraged dumping practices, especially in the construction sector.

In relation to enlargement, there were particular concerns among many old EU member states that labour mobility from the NMS could lead to incidents of wage dumping and job displacement (Donaghey and Teague, 2006). However,

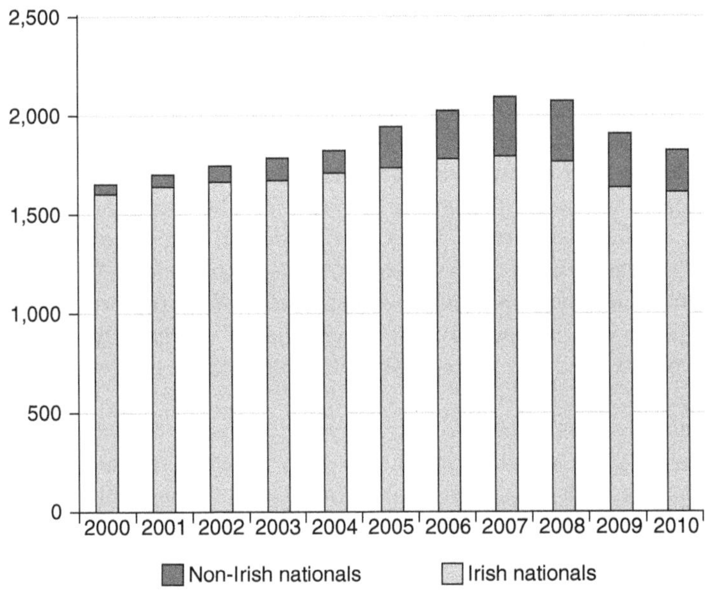

Figure 1.1 Total employment of Irish and non-Irish nationals aged 15 years and over (in '000s) (source: European Labour Force Survey (Eurostat, 2013); data compiled by authors).

in spite of the large-scale migrant inflows, Ireland did not experience major labour market dislocations. Its flexible labour market was able to incorporate the new arrivals to the workforce without undergoing major displacements or exhibiting the levels of segmentation that are characteristic of immigrant workforces in the Southern European countries (Schierup *et al.*, 2006; see also Kahmann, Chapter 3, this volume). While wage growth may have been moderated in some less skilled occupations, employment opportunities for the domestic workforce have not declined in the context of recent migration (Barrett, 2010).

The flip side of Ireland's flexible and fast-growing labour market was a weak enforcement of labour standards. Especially in the immediate aftermath of enlargement and Ireland's opening up of its labour market, non-compliance with labour standards was quite widespread (Flynn, 2006; MRCI, 2006). However, since many such incidents occurred in non-unionized workplaces, they were initially not an issue of major concern for the Irish trade union movement. This began to change in 2004 when a multinational construction company, GAMA Construction, was found to be paying its Turkish building workers wages that fell well below the industry rates. Eventually, the Services, Industrial, Professional and Technical Union (SIPTU), Ireland's largest union, became more actively involved and intervened on behalf of the migrant workers, many of whom were actually enrolled as members of SIPTU (Flynn, 2006).

If the GAMA case raised awareness about the plight of some migrants in Ireland, it was the 2005 Irish Ferries dispute (in many respects a paradigmatic example of social dumping) that captured the attention of Irish unions and the broader public. The decision of Irish Ferries to replace over 500 of its mostly unionized Irish staff with cheaper agency workers from Central-Eastern Europe in the name of 'competitiveness' sparked off huge public protests, culminating in a 'National Day of Protest' that saw around 100,000 people take to the streets in Dublin and other parts of the country. Although the protest marches organized by the Irish trade union movement had an inclusive outlook ('Equal rights for all workers'), resentment towards migrants increased among some segments of the Irish public. There was particular concern about the impact of mass migration upon employment conditions (Brennock, 2006). To counter such tendencies and to prevent a segmentation of the workforce along national lines, the unions responded with a rights-based approach to ensure that 'migrant workers have the same rights and protection as Irish workers' (SIPTU, 2006, p. 21).

For the unions, besides efforts to put a greater emphasis on organizing migrants (see below), the social partnership process became the main forum for addressing issues such as labour market compliance. In negotiations for the 2006 partnership agreement *Towards 2016*, the unions eventually succeeded with their demand for a stronger enforcement regime, not least because the employer bodies were keen to maintain industrial peace and the continuation of the partnership process. Among the measures agreed on by the social partners was stronger protection against collective dismissals (so as to prevent an Irish Ferries scenario 'on land') and the establishment of a statutory agency for employment rights. Although the proposed Employment Law Compliance Bill has yet to be enacted – because employer groups began to resist some of the agreed measures, especially following the onset of the economic crisis (Doherty, 2011, p. 378) – the National Employment Rights Authority (NERA) was already established as an enforcement body in 2007. Since its inception, NERA has revealed relatively high rates of non-compliance with employment rights in sectors such as construction and hospitality that have a high proportion of migrants (NERA, 2009, p. 8). This situation will be illustrated below at the micro level by presenting evidence from a two-year qualitative panel study with a group of Polish migrants complemented by employer interviews.

Migrant employment in the construction sector: subcontracting and agency labour

In the first decade of the twenty-first century, Ireland experienced an unprecedented construction boom. Its main driving force was the expansion of domestic credit, leading to rapidly rising asset prices – a classic property bubble. As the sector burgeoned, construction employment skyrocketed: between the second quarter of 2002 and the same quarter of 2007, employment in this sector rose from 170,000 to 270,000 (CSO, 2011). After 2004 and the opening up of Ireland's labour market, much of this increase came from mass migration (especially from Poland), which arguably contributed to sustaining the construction boom. Employment of Irish nationals also increased in those years, suggesting that inward migration was largely complementary to the domestic workforce (see Figure 1.2).[3] As many Irish workers moved into semi-skilled job positions, there was a particular demand for less skilled construction labourers. At the same time, NMS migrants were also recruited for skilled trades occupations and, in smaller numbers, for higher skilled engineering positions. Much of the recruitment was quite informal, often relying on migrant networks to meet the fast-rising demand for additional labour (Moriarty *et al.*, 2012). The rapid growth in employment was of only short duration, however. When the bubble burst in 2008, employment in the sector virtually collapsed.

The Irish construction sector is governed by industry-wide collective agreements known as Registered Employment Agreements (REAs), which are negotiated between employer bodies and trade unions. Although union density declined from 47 per cent to 27 per cent between 1994 and 2004 (CSO, 2005), unions remain an important player in the industry and are able to a considerable extent to enforce these agreements. However, at the fringes of the sector, informal employment is more widespread. This is linked to some broader structural changes in the industry: during the past two decades, large firms have transformed themselves into 'management firms' (Veiga, 1999, cited in Schierup *et al.*, 2006, p. 239) that increasingly outsource individual tasks in the work process to smaller firms so as to save on costs and acquire greater flexibility. Hence, the

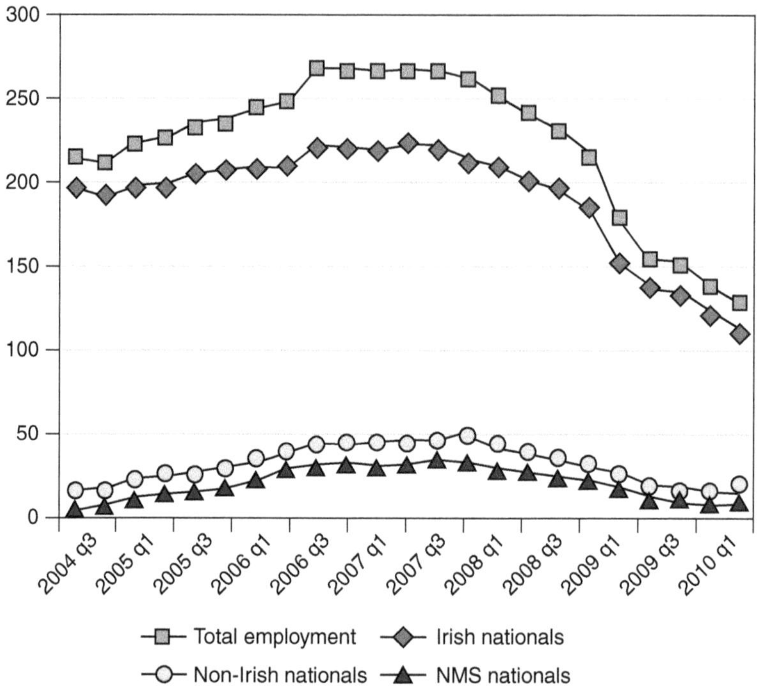

Figure 1.2 Irish and non-Irish employment in the construction sector (in '000s) (source: Quarterly National Household Survey (CSO, 2011)).

number of manual workers who are directly employed by these 'management firms' has diminished. While these firms retain a core of direct employees who have specialist knowledge and cannot be easily replaced, manual labour is increasingly sourced from subcontractors and recruitment agencies as the work process has become more fragmented.

This 'division of labour' has important implications for migrant workers. For many migrants, the main route into employment in the Irish construction sector was through subcontractors and recruitment agencies (Krings *et al.*, 2011). Although subcontractors are formally bound by REAs, further down the subcontracting chain the sector is less regulated and non-compliance with labour standards is more common:

> They were paying me cash through an envelope.... In addition to that I was getting a form that I am a subcontractor for him.
>
> (Bogdan, 24, painter, interview wave W1)

In the context of an informal work culture, migrants were less likely to receive the prevailing rates for the sector:

> When it comes to wages, these are not great because we don't even have the minimum [wage] for labourers.... In the beginning I was earning really small money ... 80 euros for ten hours. And then it was raised to 120 euros.
>
> (Wiktor, 29, metal fixer, W1 [the lowest hourly REA rate at that time was €14.88])

Hence, if 'it is legitimate to speak of social dumping ... when foreign or local companies employ their workers at conditions inferior to those laid down in the host country's employment regulations or collective agreements' (Bernaciak, 2012, p. 26), then social dumping was relatively widespread in Irish construction, especially in the immediate aftermath of EU enlargement in 2004, when the sector experienced rapid growth (Flynn, 2006). Indeed, it sometimes appeared as if such cases were part of the 'bargain of convenience' between migrants and employers. Especially in the early stages of a migrant's time in Ireland a salary just below the official rates still appeared to be reasonably good money, especially if comparisons were made to Poland (also see Anderson *et al.*, 2006).

Having said this, we are not suggesting that migrants were generally content with wages below the 'going rates'. Indeed, our interviews indicate that the longer they stayed in the country, the more assertive they became about their employment rights:

> In the beginning it was slightly illegal. But after two months of work I asked for my rights and I got a contract, and I got the salary in accordance with the laws.
>
> (Bogdan, 24, painter, W1)

> My colleague already went to the unions and they explained to him that our minimum wages should be €14.50. And we will simply fight with the company now to get our rights ... the Irish will always be the Irish, and the foreigner will always be the foreigner, but we didn't come here to work for nothing.
>
> (Wiktor, 29, metal fixer, W1)

A stronger insistence on employment rights is likely to be assisted by the fact that, as EU citizens, Polish migrants have the same labour market rights as Irish nationals. Further, the role of unions in the sector was of considerable importance. SIPTU, in particular, had raised the issue of employment rights among the migrant construction workforce through various information campaigns and a number of newly appointed Central-Eastern European organizers (Krings, 2007). Indeed, in construction, where SIPTU was particularly active through its new organizers, NMS migrants had a membership level of 17 per cent, which was well above their average union density level of 10 per cent. This suggests that union presence in the workplace in conjunction with duration of stay is the crucial variable in accounting for differences in unionization among migrants (Turner *et al.*, 2008).

Sometimes, however, migrants did not go to the unions or make use of the official industrial relations channels when they encountered violations of their employment rights. Instead, they tried to exert pressure on the subcontractor by threatening to inform the general contractor about his practices, thus engaging in a form of implicit regulation:

> We threatened them [the subcontractor] that we will send [the unions] to the main developers, those where they have the jobs from.... And the negotiations started. After two weeks everything changed, we have kind of normal wages now ... those lowest ones in construction, but it is much better anyway.
>
> (Wiktor, 30, metal fixer, W2)

The large construction firms were quite aware that cooperation with non-compliant subcontractors could generate negative publicity and have adverse consequences for their own business. However, in spite of their insistence that subcontractors adhere to the prevailing REAs, it appears that at least to some extent they insulated themselves from responsibility for employee rights and protection by making extensive use of subcontracting arrangements. This also amounted to an attempt to circumvent the traditional industrial relations institutions in the sector, given that there is less pressure to adhere to collective agreements in a non-unionized environment:

> The industry is very much unionized ... that's probably another reason why companies are not as keen to employ [people directly].... There is a tendency then to say 'well we push that on to a subcontractor, let him deal with the problem' ... the further down you go, it's unregulated.
>
> (Manager, large construction firm)

During the boom years, migrants viewed casual employment less problematically because there were plenty of job opportunities and they were sometimes able to negotiate better working conditions. However, the 2008 downturn dramatically changed the situation as employment sharply declined in the sector (Figure 1.2). While both Irish and non-Irish workers have been affected by this development, the latter have been hit the worst: employment of NMS migrants in construction declined by two-thirds between 2008 and 2010 (CSO, 2011). For those who remained in employment, work became more intense, especially at the informal fringes of the sector:

> They are trying to get more and more out of us.... Before we had a norm of installing 50 plates per day, and now it is 70 per day.... If you are asking too many questions ... then he [the boss] will simply tell you that you are [just] a fixer and you will get fired ... I don't know, to be honest ... I will be going to work on Monday, for how long I don't know. They could fire me after the lunch break.
>
> (Wiktor, 31, metal fixer, W4)

Not only were job losses quite severe, but a certain amount of occupational downgrading also occurred in the sector. Whereas Irish building workers largely abandoned the less skilled labourer positions during the boom years (Bobek *et al.*, 2008), some of them have now returned to these jobs. In other words, natives and migrants are increasingly in competition for the same jobs, which has led to growing tensions in the sector:[4]

> You can simply feel when somebody is treating you as a foreigner and you can see that with this crisis now, you still work and, for example, his friends don't ... you can feel that he doesn't tolerate you here.... When there are some tensions or redundancies in the company, then everybody is trying ... one nation is trying to get rid of the other.... The Irish were only the foremen, nothing apart from that, but ... I saw that three or four of them are working with us, two general operatives and one who screws the plates.
>
> (Wiktor, 30, metal fixer, W3)

Predictably, the crisis exerted downward pressure on wages. Whereas wages rose continuously during the boom, the recession has reversed this trend as the bargaining position of employers has strengthened:

> There are 20 men looking for every job now, pay scales have gone down. There are crane drivers who now work for us for X amount, whereas two years ago they wouldn't have imagined doing that ... they got €250 a day, now if they get €150 a day, they are lucky.
>
> (Manager, recruitment agency)

Subcontractors and recruitment agencies were the most likely to lay off people in the crisis. This does not mean, however, that such rather precarious employment arrangements are likely to disappear. Previous research has indicated that non-standard forms of employment actually become more widespread in the context of a downturn (Peck and Theodore, 2007). Indeed, some employers stated their intention to increasingly utilize agency labour should they resume recruitment in the future. This may offer greater flexibility in the light of possible future ups and downs in the industry.

In their quest for greater flexibility, some employers went even further and began to challenge the system of industry-wide wage agreements. In May 2013, a group of electrical contractors succeeded with a legal challenge against the REA system, which was declared 'unconstitutional' by the Irish Supreme Court (Burke-Kennedy, 2013). At the time of writing (December 2014), the implications of this ruling are still unclear. So far, most construction firms appear to be adhering to the REA system.[5] One likely reason for this is the role of unions in the sector, which, in spite of the recession, remain a powerful force and have made it clear that they will not accept any deviation from existing agreements. Moreover, employers may still have an interest in retaining a system of basic wage rates so as to avoid a 'race to the bottom' in which they would have to compete with domestic and foreign service providers on costs. Hence, the main employer body, the Construction Industry Federation (CIF), has so far not advocated abolishing the REA system but has instead pushed for a reduction of rates. Ultimately, and against the background of rapidly rising unemployment, the CIF and the unions agreed in 2010 to a pay reduction of 7.5 per cent for all wage agreements in the sector (which was substantially lower than what employers had initially sought) (Farrelly, 2011).

To summarize, the Irish construction sector experienced growing casualization of work at its more informal fringes, where employers used subcontracting and migrant labour as a cost-cutting strategy that often involved the breach of collective agreements and employment regulations. However, the core of the sector remained broadly regulated through the governance of the REA system and the role of unions. In the end, it was the collapse of the construction bubble, and not migration, that brought about serious labour market dislocations. While employers might push ahead with further wage cuts and make use of more precarious work arrangements such as agency labour in the future, it appears unlikely that the sector will be completely deregulated.

Migrant employment in the hospitality sector: informality and casual work

The hospitality sector in Ireland, as in many other countries, has traditionally been a low-wage sector with comparatively low trade union density and a relatively large share of less skilled occupations. Collective bargaining is largely absent, although – until recently – Joint Labour Committees (JLCs) comprising employers and worker representatives set the terms and conditions of employment for a number of low-wage sectors, including catering and hotels. Much of the work in hospitality is casual and seasonal, often involving long working hours and atypical work arrangements (Wickham *et al.*, 2009). From the 1990s onward, employment almost doubled as the number of hotels, restaurants, fast food outlets and coffee shops soared.

After 2004 and Ireland's labour market opening, the employment structure of the sector changed. Whereas the share of Irish employees declined somewhat, the share of migrant employment increased substantially (see Figure 1.3). This raises the question as to whether Irish nationals were displaced by migrants. The most likely scenario is that Irish nationals were replaced and possibly moved into better jobs during the boom years, given that overall unemployment did not increase (NESC, 2006, p. 45). Interestingly, however, since 2008 and the recession, the number of Irish employees in hospitality has increased, which suggests that at least some Irish nationals are returning to jobs that would previously have been regarded as 'migrant jobs'.

Although casual work was always a feature of the hospitality sector, there is little doubt that the fast expansion of low-wage jobs reinforced a trend towards casualization and informalization. Many new employees had a short-term orientation towards work, and there was a high rate of job turnover because 'the

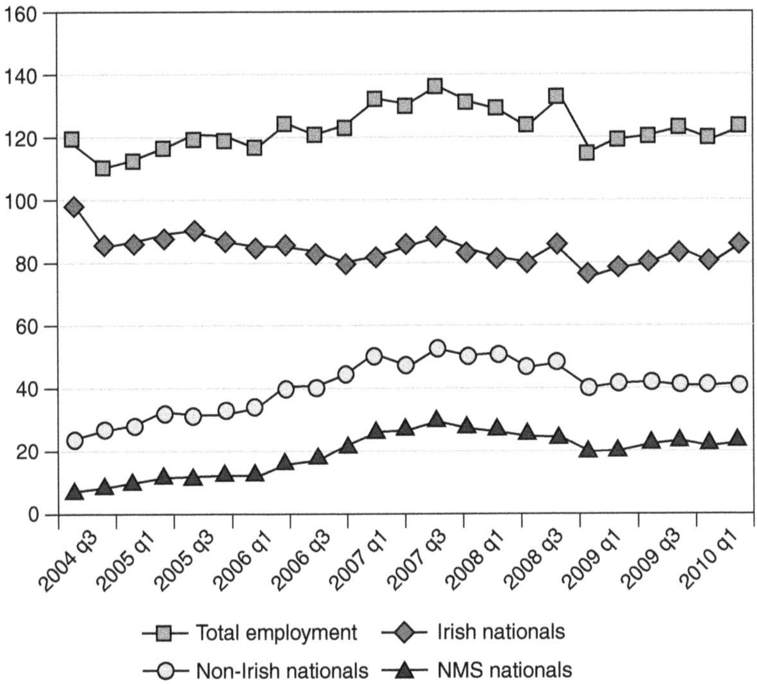

Figure 1.3 Irish and non-Irish employment in the hospitality sector (in '000s) (source: Quarterly National Household Survey (CSO, 2011)).

workplace [was] not governed by any strong set of accepted social rules and the customary practices that govern established jobs [were] substantially absent' (Wickham *et al.*, 2009, p. 88). During the boom years, employers appear to have taken on virtually everyone regardless of qualification or experience:

> She [the manager] didn't even know where I had worked, what my name was! I mean, I noticed that they hire everybody there. Well, unless during an interview, I don't know, somebody punched her in the face … in general they hire everybody.
>
> (Olga, 21, waitress, W1)

Many migrants initially took on hospitality jobs that were below their qualifications. As also observed in research on Central-Eastern European migrants in the UK (Anderson *et al.*, 2006), they sometimes 'traded off' a lower status job for short-term economic gains:

> I am struggling with it a lot as I am a very ambitious person and I didn't graduate from so many courses to work as a waitress, I am aware of that.…

> For the moment I have said to myself: 'take it easy, work in the hotel, earn some money, do what you need to do, and then … we will see what's going to be next'.
>
> (Iza, 28, hotel waitress, W1)

Many hospitality workplaces were characterized by high levels of informality and non-compliance with labour standards. For instance, in 2008 the National Employment Rights Authority found breaches of employment legislation in 85 per cent of inspected contract cleaning businesses, 78 per cent of hotels and 73 per cent of catering businesses (NERA, 2009). While this was primarily an employer-driven strategy, Polish migrants did not necessarily perceive the casualized employment relationship as a disadvantage, especially when the job was seen as only transitional:

> I didn't have any job contract there [restaurant], I was working there illegally. And all in all I didn't know that I was working illegally … I didn't get any pay slip, and I wasn't asked my account number, they simply paid me in cash. But that suited me because I worked there many hours, let's say 50 hours per week, or even 60 when I wanted and I was not charged any taxes … that suited me at that time, because I cared only about the money.
>
> (Olga, 21, waitress, W2)

Employers were well aware that many migrants had a different orientation towards work than Irish workers. After all, a 'bad job' in Ireland may not appear as 'bad' if comparisons are made to Poland (also see Waldinger and Lichter, 2003). Initially, employers hired migrants because of labour shortages. However, they soon began to see them as a more hard-working and acquiescent workforce:

> The Eastern Europeans … are more willing to take jobs that are probably not as glamorous as what the Irish people would want. It is hard work, being a chef, it is just a horrible, stressful, very sweaty [job].… Cheffing [and] especially waiting is not really a career path in Ireland … I can't imagine a business without some [migrants]; having Irish people, I think … would be a lot more expensive, like wages, definitely, a lot more demand by Irish people.
>
> (Manager, restaurant)

It may thus be only a small step from hiring migrants because of vacancies to preferring them, especially in times of ample supply of additional labour from abroad (Waldinger and Lichter, 2003). It certainly appeared that Irish employers were sometimes using migrant labour to push ahead with organizational change, as in the case of the following upmarket Dublin hotel. Not unlike the Irish Ferries case, management replaced one workforce with another in the context of organizational restructuring:

> With the hotel opening under completely different terms and management … we don't have union representation and we haven't had any request for it

> … our workplace is structured in a completely different way to what it was before. Before we closed, we had quite a lot of long-service employees who were with the hotel for 20 years, 15 years, and the average age was probably 40 to 45; and we had 75 per cent Irish. Now it's [the] opposite, our workers are 25 to 35 years old, and it is only about 25 per cent Irish.
>
> (Manager, hotel)

Between 1994 and 2004, union density had declined from 21 per cent to 10 per cent in hospitality. In other words, the decline preceded the arrival of large-scale migration from Poland and elsewhere. As a result, migrants usually entered a union-free workplace. In contrast, our research suggests that there was a relatively broad awareness of the statutory National Minimum Wage. Indeed, migrants were at times quite assertive about this entitlement, which is likely to reflect the fact that as 'free movers' (Favell, 2008) they were less dependent on a single employer:[6]

> On payday, when everybody was given their money, everybody was getting the money in an envelope as usual. So everybody was there somewhat illegally.… And I didn't get my envelope so I went to the boss … he said, 'OK, I'll count it for you'. And he said, 'so what, 8 euros, isn't it?' And I said 'No', because I worked there for 9 euros. So then he said, 'OK, OK' … well they paid me the minimum [wage], the same I was paid in the previous restaurant.
>
> (Olga, 21, waitress, W2)

Thus, the National Minimum Wage appeared to be a relatively effective threshold in low-wage sectors such as hospitality that received a huge inflow of migrants and where trade unions no longer possessed the organizational strength to prevent a 'race to the bottom'.

Unlike the construction sector, the hospitality sector did not experience large-scale job losses in the 2008 recession. However, laying people off is not the only option that employers have in a downturn. Other responses may include pay cuts, an increase in unpaid overtime and redeployment of existing staff (Rogers *et al.*, 2009, p. 7). As a result, work may become more intense:

> I can feel I am more exploited at work, really … the manager is on quite long leave and … they showed me his work and they promised to give me higher position, which never happened. But I got his duties now, so besides [my work] there are added responsibilities like checking financial reports from the previous day from the whole hotel.
>
> (Ewa, 24, hotel receptionist, W4)

As in construction, there was a growing preference among management for more flexible work arrangements in the crisis. Indeed, it sometimes appeared that the recession provided employers with a pretext to push through with organizational change:

> If we are bringing in anybody now, we may change that a little bit because we have too many being on full-time contracts … anybody who is brought in right now is going to be on a part-time contract. It just means that there is more flexibility anyway … anybody brought in now, it is more cost-effective for us now to bring them in as part time.
>
> (Manager, hotel)

Such practices do not constitute a formal breach of labour market regulations. However, because they represent attempts by employers to push for ever more 'flexibility' and to undermine the existing regulatory environment, they may still be regarded as social dumping (Bernaciak, Introduction to this volume). There is no doubt that such practices contribute to a further casualization of work. Pressure on employment standards increased to an even greater extent in 2011 when the High Court declared the wage-setting mechanisms of the Joint Labour Committees to be 'unconstitutional'. This case was brought by a group of fast-food businesses with the tacit backing of larger employer groups such as the Irish Hotels Federation and the Restaurant Association of Ireland. In 2014, the JLC system was reformed and reinstated by the Irish government, much to the displeasure of employer organizations which would have preferred abolishing the system altogether (Prendergast, 2014). Thus, as unions do not wield much influence in hospitality any more, the Irish government, which includes the Labour Party, appears to be jumping in to prevent a lowering of social standards as employers pursue a more confrontational approach in a dramatically changed business environment.

How workplace relations will develop in the sector remains to be seen. As already mentioned, a growing number of Irish nationals are returning to employment in hospitality. However, it appears unlikely that there will be a return to the status quo ante when tourists in Dublin were usually greeted by an Irish person at the hotel reception or coffee bar, since the Irish workplace has irrevocably changed in the context of mass migration from Poland and other NMS.

Conclusion

This chapter has examined recent inward migration from Poland to Ireland by focusing specifically on two employment sectors: construction and hospitality. It has shown that, in both sectors, practices of social dumping were quite widespread after 2004, when rapid job growth and mass migration mutually reinforced one another. Social dumping practices differed, however, depending on the regulatory environment in the two sectors. In construction, where unions remain an influential actor, employers often used migrant labour to circumvent the institutions of collective bargaining. In the by now largely de-unionized hospitality sector, in turn, social dumping mainly involved non-compliance with employment regulations.

In the context of such social dumping practices, a casualization of work occurred in both sectors. While this was mainly an employer-driven strategy, during the boom years casual employment was not necessarily experienced as a disadvantage by migrants because it offered some flexibility. Moreover, some migrants were able to negotiate better working conditions, sometimes with the help of unions. However, negotiating better conditions became less of an option when Ireland was hit by a sharp recession. In this changed labour market situation, the power imbalance of casual employment was exposed as migrants struggled increasingly to meet employer demands for greater flexibility in the workplace.

The recession not only triggered an employment crisis in Ireland but also brought an end to social partnership. After 30 years, the distinctive Irish system of social partnership collapsed as the government, employer associations and the Irish trade union movement diverged increasingly in their analyses and prescriptions as to how to remedy the country's dire economic situation (Doherty, 2011). While it appears unlikely that Ireland will experience full-scale labour market deregulation, a possible scenario is that the country is moving towards a more liberal system of employment relations. Certainly employer bodies are less inclined than before to negotiate wage agreements with unions. Much will depend on the future role of the Irish government and whether it will put in place a new framework for collective bargaining.

What are the implications of these developments for migration? So far, there is no conclusive evidence to suggest that recent inward migration impacted negatively upon the employment opportunities of domestic workers in Ireland. However, as shown above, employers frequently engaged in social dumping practices during the boom years, which contributed to an informalization and casualization of work in some employment sectors. There are already signs that this trend has become more pronounced in the recession. Especially in times of economic crisis, firms are increasingly tempted to resort to social dumping practices to save on costs. However, such a strategy would be quite short-sighted and detrimental to workplace relations, wider social cohesion, and indeed to long-term economic development.

In 2014, six years on after the recession hit the country, migrants still account for 15 per cent of the Irish workforce. So far, the integration of migrants into Irish society has proceeded relatively smoothly, and even in the recession Ireland has not experienced a backlash against immigrants, unlike, for instance, Greece (Margaronis, 2012). To ensure that it remains so, a rights-based integration of migrants in the workplace is of paramount importance to prevent a segmentation of the labour market along ethnic lines. In this regard, especially unions and enforcement bodies such as the National Employment Rights Authority have an important role to play in ensuring continuous compliance with wage agreements and labour standards, including the National Minimum Wage, which has provided a threshold against a 'race to the bottom' in some low-wage sectors with a large share of migrants. It may be true that the 'beneficial constraints' (Streeck, 1997) of labour market regulations only become visible in the long term (Bernaciak, Introduction to this volume). In any case, more effective labour market compliance coupled with more long-term labour market policies, including a greater investment in human capital, offer a more sustainable path to recovery for Ireland than a reliance on social dumping practices.

Notes

1 The research originated in the Migrant Careers and Aspirations project at Trinity College Dublin (2007–2010). The core of the project was a Qualitative Panel Study involving six interview waves with 22 Polish migrants over a period of two years, which were complemented with employer interviews (Krings *et al.*, 2013). The study focused altogether upon four employment sectors: construction, hospitality, financial services and IT. For the purposes of this chapter, we confine ourselves to the former two sectors.

2 For reasons of data availability, the nationality variable will be used henceforth as a criterion when presenting migration figures. Because much of the migration to Ireland has been quite recent, 'nationality' may be regarded as a reliable indicator for migrant inflows.

3 It is likely that in the construction sector especially, the official figures from the Irish Central Statistics Office represent an underestimation of the migrant workforce because many of the latter were employed under informal arrangements.

4 Whereas, pre-crisis, Irish attitudes towards immigrants were comparatively favourable, this has changed somewhat in the context of rapidly deteriorating economic circumstances. A survey carried out by the *Irish Times* in 2009 found that over two-thirds of Irish people wanted to see a reduction in the number of migrants, with almost 30 per cent preferring most migrants to leave (O'Brien, 2009).

5 However, there is anecdotal evidence that, especially outside of Dublin, firms are increasingly paying below the 'going rates' as the informal economy has expanded in the context of the crisis.

6 In fact, research by the Migrant Rights Centre Ireland found that the single greatest reason why restaurant workers from outside of the European Economic Area did not make a complaint about employment rights violations were concerns about their job and the renewal of their work permit (MRCI, 2008).

References

Anderson, B., Ruhs, M., Spencer, S. and Rogaly, B. (2006) *Fair Enough? Central and East European Migrants in Low Wage Employment in the UK*. Oxford: Centre on Migration, Policy and Society.

Barrett, A. (2010) 'EU Enlargement and Ireland's Labor Market'. In Kahanec, M. and Zimmermann, K. (eds), *EU Labor Markets After Post-enlargement Migration*. Berlin: Springer, pp. 145–162.

Barry, F. (2007) 'Foreign Direct Investment and Institutional Co-Evolution in Ireland'. *Scandinavian Economic History Review*, 55(3): 262–288.

Bernaciak, M. (2012) 'Social Dumping: Political Catchphrase or Threat to Labour Standards?' *ETUI Working Paper*, No. 2012.06. Brussels: European Trade Union Institute.

Bobek, A., Krings, T., Moriarty, E., Wickham, J. and Salamońska, J. (2008) *Migrant Workers and the Construction Sector in Ireland*. Dublin: Trinity Immigration Initiative.

Brennock, M. (2006) 'Growing Anxiety over Migrant Labour'. *Irish Times*, 23 January.

Burke-Kennedy, E. (2013) 'Supreme Court Ruling Casts Doubt on Wage Agreements'. *Irish Times*, 10 May.

CSO (2005) *Quarterly National Household Survey: Union Membership 1994–2004*. Cork: Central Statistics Office.

CSO (2011) *Quarterly National Household Survey 2004–2011*. Cork: Central Statistics Office.

Doherty, M. (2011) 'It Must Have Been Love … But it's Over Now. The Crisis and Collapse of Social Partnership in Ireland'. *Transfer*, 17(3): 371–386.

Donaghey, J. and Teague, P. (2006) 'The free Movement of Workers and Social Europe: Maintaining the European Ideal'. *Industrial Relations Journal*, 37(6): 652–666.

Farrelly, R. (2011) 'Court Ratifies Construction Industry Pay Cut' [Online]. European Industrial Relations Observatory Online. Available at: www.eurofound.europa.eu/eiro/2011/02/articles/ie1102019i.htm (accessed 3 December 2013).

Favell, A. (2008) *Eurostars and Eurocities: Free Movement and Mobility in an Integrating Europe*. Oxford: Blackwell.

Flynn, G. (2006) 'Mobile Worker Disputes Jolt Ireland's "Social Partnership" Model'. *Transfer*, 12(2): 267–272.

Komito, L. and Bates, J. (2009) 'Virtually Local: Social Media and Community Amongst Polish Nationals in Dublin'. *Aslib Proceedings: New Information Perspectives*, 61(3): 232–244.

Krings, T. (2007) 'Equal Rights for all Workers: Irish Trade Unions and the Challenge of Labour Migration'. *Irish Journal of Sociology*, 17(1): 43–61.

Krings, T., Bobek, A., Moriarty, E., Salamońska, J. and Wickham, J. (2011) 'From Boom to Bust: Migrant Labour and Employers in the Irish Construction Sector'. *Economic and Industrial Democracy*, 32(3): 459–476.

Krings, T., Moriarty, E., Wickham, J., Bobek, A. and Salamońska, J. (2013) *New Mobilities in Europe: Polish Migration to Ireland Post-2004*. Manchester: Manchester University Press.

Margaronis, M. (2012) 'Fear and Loathing in Athens: The Rise of Golden Dawn and the Far Right'. *Guardian*, 26 October.

Menz, G. (2009) *The Political Economy of Managed Migration*. Oxford: Oxford University Press.

Moriarty, E., Wickham, J., Krings, T., Bobek, A. and Salamońska, J. (2012) '"Taking on Almost Everyone?" Migrant and Employer Recruitment Strategies in a Booming Labour Market'. *The International Journal of Human Resource Management*, 23(9): 1871–1887.

MRCI (2006) *Harvesting Justice: Mushroom Workers Call for Change*. Dublin: Migrant Rights Centre Ireland.

MRCI (2008) *Exploitation in Ireland's Restaurant Industry*. Dublin: Migrant Rights Centre Ireland.

NERA (2009) *Review of 2008*. Dublin: National Employment Rights Authority.

NESC (2006) *Migration Policy*. Dublin: National Economic and Social Council.

O'Brien, C. (2009) 'Lack of Jobs Brings Change in Attitudes to Migration'. *Irish Times*, 24 November.

OECD (2011) *International Migration Outlook 2009*. Paris: Organisation for Economic Cooperation and Development.

Peck, J. and Theodore, N. (2007) 'Flexible Recession: The Temporary Staffing Industry and Mediated Work in the USA'. *Cambridge Journal of Economics*, 31(2): 171–192.

Pendergast, A. (2014) 'Pay-Setting Powers of Joint Labour Committees Curtailed'. European Observatory of Working Life. Available at: http://eurofound.europa.eu/observatories/eurwork/articles/working-conditions-other/pay-setting-powers-of-joint-labour-committees-curtailed (accessed 12 March 2015).

Rogers, A., Anderson, B. and Clarke, N. (2009) *Recession, Vulnerable Workers and Immigration: Background Report*. Oxford: Centre on Migration, Policy and Society.

Schierup, C.-U., Hansen, P. and Castles, S. (2006) *Migration, Citizenship and the European Welfare State: A European Dilemma*. Oxford: Oxford University Press.

SIPTU (2006) *Diversity in the Workplace: A Guide for Shop Stewards*. Dublin: Irish Trade Union Trust.

Streeck, W. (1997) 'Beneficial Constraints. On the Economic Limits of Rational Voluntarism'. In Boyer, R. and Hollingsworth, J.R. (eds), *Contemporary Capitalism. The Embeddedness of Institutions*. Cambridge: Cambridge University Press, pp. 197–221.

Turner, T., D'Art, D. and O'Sullivan, M. (2008) 'Union Availability, Union Membership and Immigrant Workers: An Empirical Investigation of the Irish Case'. *Employee Relations*, 30(5): 479–493.

Waldinger, R. and Lichter, M. (2003) *How the Other Half Works: Immigration and the Social Organization of Labor*. Berkeley: University of California Press.

Wickham, J., Moriarty, E., Bobek, A. and Salamońska, J. (2009) 'Working in the Gold Rush: Polish Migrants' Careers and the Irish Hospitality Sector'. In Bolton, S. and Houlihan, M. (eds), *Work Matters: Critical Perspectives on Contemporary Work*. Basingstoke: Palgrave Macmillan, pp. 81–96.

2 Breaking the law?

Varieties of social dumping in a pan-European labour market

Lisa Berntsen and Nathan Lillie

Introduction

Intra-EU labour mobility has become a major structuring factor in certain occupational labour markets. Firms engage in transnational hiring and, in doing so, consciously strategize across sovereign sites and arenas of regulation in order to take advantage of lower cost structures and less strict regulatory environments. These practices are part of a pervasive dynamic of labour-cost competition that is integral to the growth of capitalist markets (Bernaciak, Introduction to this volume). They are embedded in the process of 'creative destruction' that inherently threatens social standards but, in mainstream economic thought, is also fundamental to the logic of capitalist accumulation. According to Schumpeter (1942), who coined the concept of creative destruction, capitalism progresses by destroying old social and production structures and replacing them with new, presumably more efficient ones. Schumpeter argues that, in the end, creative destruction will make society as a whole better off, although there will be winners and losers in the process. While the underlying necessity of creative destruction is rarely contested, the limits of what can be done to achieve it are. Defining these limits is the focus of the social dumping debate.

When firms transgress certain normative boundaries as a way to make themselves more competitive, they often trigger accusations of social dumping. In Europe, such accusations usually refer to normative structures inherited from the post-war national industrial relations systems of Western Europe, which sought to ensure income stability for workers, humane treatment and due process in the workplace, as well as rights to workplace representation and collective action, reasonable notice prior to dismissals, and similar worker protections (Bernaciak, Introduction to this volume). However, business actors are constantly testing the boundaries of what is acceptable and what they can get away with (Streeck, 2009), and increasing numbers of employers reject the existing norms – if not in principle, then certainly in practice. Some companies play a double game in which they appear to support and conform to the traditional normative frameworks of industrial relations while in fact operating in ways that allow them to remain price competitive in unconstrained markets. For unions and society as a whole, the challenge is to enforce normative constraints upon such 'unruly' employers (Streeck, 2009, p. 75).

Much has been written about the conditions and downward labour market pressures created by recent intra-EU labour mobility (Lillie, 2012; Meardi, 2012; Wagner, 2014). The term 'social dumping' may be politicized and ill defined, but the basic premise that wages and employment in Western Europe have come under pressure as a result of migration in certain occupational labour markets is indisputable (Meardi, 2012). Labour mobility in the EU is creating a more competitive labour market environment – as indeed is the intention – as EU institutional actors such as the European Court of Justice (ECJ) and the European Commission have made clear in public documents (see e.g. European Court of Justice, 2007). A premise behind EU policies and ECJ rulings is that market-making and market expansion will lead to efficiency increases. In practice, this means the removal of barriers to the free movement of workers and services, and the intensification of competition – including wage competition.[1] Regulatory regimes, and firms' ability to interact with them, have become a competitive parameter that tends to favour less restrictive and cheaper regulatory environments. Similarly, the regulation of employee posting has created new windows of opportunity for labour-cost competition by defining posted workers as those remaining partially outside the national regulatory scope of the receiving country, given that they come from different legal, social and organizational contexts (Wagner and Lillie, 2014).

This chapter focuses on strategies for regulatory engagement that firms employ when they have the option of choosing between different national regulatory regimes. Drawing on examples from Finland and the Netherlands, we examine how firms hire and manage foreign labour, and how they strategize between the regulatory frameworks of various national industrial relations systems. We show that workers from low-wage countries are employed in high-wage countries under conditions that in certain respects refer back to the labour standards of their country of origin (posted work), or under contracts conditioned by host-country regulations (agency work). On the basis of our research, we identify three categories of firms' cost-saving regulatory engagement strategies, which may also be viewed as different types of social dumping. *Regulatory evasion* refers to the violation of formal and informal national industrial relations rules, and to the concealment of these violations, presumably to avoid enforcement. *Regulatory arbitrage* is defined as strategizing about the regulatory treatment of a transaction in the selection between two (or more) alternative regulatory regimes from different sovereign territories (Fleischer, 2010, p. 4). It involves conformance to formal rules (and possibly informal ones) but makes a claim for exception from the normal local rules on the basis of adherence to an alternative set of foreign rules. *Regulatory conformance* means conforming to the formal industrial relations system but potentially manipulating the rules for cost advantages. Regulatory conformance does not involve breaking industrial relations rules directly, but it may put them under pressure as employers access foreign workers who may accept worse treatment than natives on an informal level.

All three practices presented in this chapter involve strategizing between rule systems – even regulatory conformance is a decision *not* to take advantage of foreign regulatory systems and to stick with the local regulatory regime. It is important to note that we are not making a strict differentiation between legal and illegal practices, because social dumping is not just about the legality or illegality of actor behaviour; rather we are talking about violations of social and industrial relations norms in ways that create a certain kind of competitive dynamic (Bernaciak, Introduction to this volume). Interpretations of what is legal and what is illegal can vary, especially between unions and employers (see Arnholz and Eldring, Chapter 4, this volume), given that there are conflicts between legal frameworks resulting from EU regulation and overlapping national jurisdictions. Industrial relations practices and legal rules are often applied in national contexts where they conflict with formal and/or informal industrial relations norms and laws. This patchwork of EU and national regulations results in 'grey zones' where actors do not necessarily know the rules or feel invested in them.

This chapter draws upon case studies from the Dutch and Finnish construction and distribution sectors. It is based on qualitative interviews with unionists, employers, employer associations and government officials about firm practices of recruiting and managing international personnel, as well as interviews with foreign workers about their jobs and working conditions. The interviews were conducted between 2005 and 2012 in Finland and from 2011 to 2013 in the Netherlands.[2] Interview data are supplemented with media searches and reports, as well as discussions and meetings in Brussels with EU actors.

The use of the term 'social dumping'

In the public discourse, the term 'social dumping' is applied pejoratively and strategically as a way of condemning firms that seek to access the lower cost structure of labour in another country or within a country or firm. In this respect, social dumping is used as a politicized label in conflicts about who gets what work and how much they should be paid. It may also invoke a competitive aspect concerned with the way in which firm practices erode existing social and labour standards through 'regime competition' (Streeck, 1992) or cost-based competition founded on the characteristics of social systems, collective bargaining agreements or welfare regimes.

The fundamental premise of the social dumping frame is that it is normatively wrong for firms to make a competitive advantage out of seeking out the lowest social- and wage-cost structures they can find. The logic of free movement and economic liberalization in the EU, however, leaves no room for the normative evaluation of firms' practices as potential sources of social dumping. This is because labour standards are regarded as a potential source of competitive advantage, and the exploitation of such advantages is judged as a fundamental right. There is also an explicit outcome-focused reasoning in recent ECJ decisions (commonly referred to as the Laval quartet)[3] concerning the relationship between national industrial relations and EU free movement rights, which justifies the setting aside of national rules in order to boost regime competition. In the *Laval* decision (*Laval* Case C-341/05), the ECJ concludes that:

> the right of trade unions of a Member State to take collective action [designed to raise the pay and conditions of posted workers above legal minimums] … is liable to make it less attractive, or more difficult, for undertakings to provide services in the territory of the host Member State, and therefore constitutes a restriction on the freedom to provide services within the meaning of Article 49 EC.

The Latvian firm Laval un Partneri had won its contract in Sweden on the basis of being able to offer services at a lower cost; therefore union (industrial) action that served to erase this cost advantage could be considered a restraint on free movement. The Court has made it clear that any attempt to interfere with strategies based on labour costs constitutes an a priori restriction on free movement. Restrictions on free movement can be justified, but the reasons for such restrictions must be substantiated, and the means used to achieve them should be proportional (*Viking* Case C-438/05).

Following the ECJ's reasoning, if firms observe legal minimum wages and legally extended collective agreements, and abide by the framework for intra-EU posting, they are not involved in social dumping, or at least are not doing anything that would provide grounds for unions or governments to apply sanctions. Following the ECJ, then, 'social dumping' refers to existing minimum-wage laws and legally extended collective agreements: firms that violate legally mandated standards for labour–cost advantage are engaging in social dumping, while firms that uphold legal standards are not. If one follows this legalistic definition, social dumping becomes impossible in countries or industries where there are no minimum wages or legally extended agreements because there are no standards to violate.

In a broader view, however, social dumping is any competitive strategy which relies on accessing labour supplies that are cheaper due to looser regulatory frameworks or differences in wage levels or wage expectations. This is closer to the way the term has been used in academic discussions and political debates. Belgian politicians, for example, accuse the German meat-packing industry of social dumping precisely because there is no minimum wage in this sector and so posted workers from Central-Eastern Europe (CEE) can work there for very low wages (Debroux, 2013). German-based firms, however, are simply making a competitive advantage out of the looser regulatory framework in the German meat-packing industry. This game of creating and exploiting 'regime competition' (Streeck, 1992) is one of the core ways in which many scholars have tried to define precisely what social dumping is (Erickson and Kuruvilla, 1994; Alber and Standing, 2000; Kvist, 2004; Donaghey and Teague, 2006): that is to say, an economic dynamic that puts pressure on the regulatory framework to allow lower standards. This is also in line with the conceptualization developed by Bernaciak in the Introduction to this volume.

The term 'social dumping' has also been applied to governments seeking to use lower social security or labour standards as a way of attracting capital (Alber and Standing, 2000; Šćepanović, Chapter 10, this volume). Although governments' market-making efforts and companies' social dumping strategies are not synonymous, these two aspects are connected because firms react to government incentives when they engage in social dumping. Low standards for workers in one context can also affect conditions for workers in other settings if the latter have to compete with the former. Growing competitive pressures create incentives for market actors to undermine or circumvent social regulations, which may lead to the erosion of the existing standards. By the same token, social dumping is encouraged by EU institutions. Kvist (2004) points out that the EU has brought about a 'dual development' in which the EU puts pressure on national social standards via competitive mechanisms, but at the same time provides EU citizens with access to EU- and national-level rights through EU legislation and jurisprudence. As observed by Höpner and Schäfer (2012), however, the dynamic created by the interaction of these two developments erodes national welfare states. The market-making agenda of the EU continuously pushes national consensus norms down the liberalization path, and social aspects are increasingly less important than market norms.

Posting, subcontracting, agency work and social dumping

Labour mobility in Europe may occur either as posting – when an employer sends an employee abroad to perform a job – or as individual migration. These different forms occur under different regulatory frameworks (the free movement of services and the free movement of workers, respectively) and activate different sets of worker rights and protections (Dølvik and Eldring, 2008). Specifically, as we discuss below, certain aspects of the host-country social security systems and labour rules do not apply to posted workers, but they do to migrants who move on the basis of the free movement of workers (also see Cremers, Chapter 9, this volume). However, whether workers come as posted workers or as individual migrants, they are most often employed via temporary work agencies (TWAs). Posting of workers also occurs via subcontractors or between subsidiaries of multinational enterprises. The difference between a subcontractor and a TWA is that, in the latter case, the customer firm has a much greater role in organizing the work. Subcontractors provide their own management and micro organization of production, while TWAs perform only recruitment, payroll and human resource functions (MacKenzie and Forde, 2005).

Firms employing foreign workers in host countries strategically situate themselves in particular regulatory regimes or industries. In the Netherlands, for example, the benefits applicable to posted workers in the construction sector are more extensive than in the metal sector, allowing for cost savings when firms post workers under the conditions for the metal industry. TWAs can choose between situating themselves in the host country and employing the foreign workers under agency contracts or posting the agency workers from the home country, or even a third country where social security contributions are lower. With the first option, employment conditions have to be regulated in line with the host-country framework; in the second and third option, there will be a combination of host- and sending-country regulations.

Over the past decade, temporary agency work has increased significantly throughout Europe (Markova and McKay, 2008) and is considered to be one of the most rapidly growing forms of atypical work (Schmidt, 2006). In the Netherlands, TWAs are the most important providers of foreign workers (Fellini *et al.*, 2007). TWAs play an important facilitating role in the migration process by offering workers 'all-inclusive' packages arranging travel, accommodation and food. Going for short tenures abroad is very much simplified through the transnational agency sector.

The Temporary Agency Work Directive (TAWD), passed in 2008, puts forward the principle of equal treatment for temporary agency workers compared with direct hires at a client firm from day one of their assignment. The TAWD establishes that the basic working and employment conditions applicable to temporary agency workers should be at least those that would apply if they had been recruited directly by that undertaking to perform the same job. The level and scope of implementation of the TAWD is left to EU member states to decide upon and the impact thus depends on each EU member state's own labour institutions and traditions (Wynn, 2014).

The Posted Workers Directive (PWD), passed in 1996, establishes that posted (construction) workers are entitled to the statutory minimum conditions of either their host state or sending state, whichever is better from the worker's perspective, thus extending national regulation of employment to transnational subcontractors. The Laval quartet of ECJ decisions, however, redefined the list in the PWD as a comprehensive limit to what national regulators are allowed to regulate, making it clear that governments and unions cannot seek to enforce any standards for posted workers that are not both explicitly mentioned in the PWD and set down in national law. Therefore, the full range of benefits accorded to native workers and individual migrants cannot be mandated for posted workers, but only the more limited set in the directive. Furthermore, minimum-wage laws (or the legal extension of collective agreements) and not collective bargaining per se must be the mechanism to enforce wage levels. Therefore, even when the legal wage minimums and extended collective agreements are fully applied, it is still possible that posted workers can end up being cheaper than domestically recruited workers (Lillie, 2012). In Finland and the Netherlands, national labour law and collective agreement systems in principle provide for host-country regulation of wages, even under the constraints of the Laval quartet decisions, although, as we will see from the cases, it is still possible to circumvent certain wage provisions and employment conditions.

The Netherlands and Finland are characterized by strong market regulations and high degrees of cooperation and coordination between state, capital and labour. In both the Netherlands and Finland, wages for most workers are regulated via extended sectoral collective agreements. The Netherlands also has a minimum wage, which is lower than collectively agreed wages; Finland does not have a minimum wage, but most workers are covered by legally extended collective agreements. The way pay is regulated in the Netherlands and Finland – in contrast to Germany, for example – sets a lower boundary on working standards, meaning that foreign employers employing posted workers must maintain a certain minimum-wage level set by the host country, even given the constraints of the Laval quartet. As we will show, this does not mean that there is no legal room for labour–cost savings, but it does mean that the room for legal cost savings on wage payments through the use of posted workers is limited. In effect, in these countries there is a sharper line between legal and illegal behaviour than in national contexts where wages are not regulated by law, because norm-conforming firm behaviour tends to be legal, and norm-violating behaviour illegal. In contexts where the legal protections are weak but worker protections are effected through other channels, it is common to see norm-violating behaviour that is perfectly legal.

The share of foreign workers in the Dutch agency workforce was 35 per cent in 2003, compared to 16 per cent in the workforce at large (Tijdens *et al.*, 2006). More recent estimates indicate that 50 per cent of Central-Eastern Europeans working in the Netherlands are employed via TWAs (Tweede Kamer, 2011, p. 33). Three types of TWAs were identified as active in the Dutch market: law-abiding agencies; agencies operating in a grey zone; and the so-called 'mala fide', law-evading agencies (Tweede Kamer, 2011). It was estimated that around 5,000 to 6,000 law-evading agencies were active in the Dutch market, supplying an estimated 100,000 CEE workers (De Bondt and Grijpstra, 2008). In Finland, labour migration occurs through posting by subcontractors, agency work and individual migration. The tax office noted that in 2012, 53,000 foreign construction workers were issued tax numbers (Mäkelä, 2012). This would indicate that legally employed foreign labour constitutes about one-third of the Finnish construction labour force (Rakennusteollisuus, 2012).

Even though conditions for migrant posted and agency workers are relatively well regulated by Dutch and Finnish law, in practice the enforcement of these regulations to fight social dumping practices remains problematic. As a Dutch labour standard enforcement agent told us in an interview in 2012:

> It is well regulated. Only, it is so well regulated to the smallest details that it becomes very unclear. It is not simply, oh this person comes from Germany and these are the employment conditions that apply. No. So I think it needs to be made much simpler so that it is clear for everybody which regulations apply. I think that that is very important.

Effective enforcement requires extensive research into firm behaviour and gathering evidence of malpractices. For example, even just determining whether the collective labour agreement for the construction sector should be applicable to a firm's business practices is a time-consuming exercise. Another issue with foreign workers is the difficulty of cross-border enforcement because labour inspectorates from different countries collaborate very little, even though firms' cross-border practices often fall under the scope of both the sending and receiving countries' regulations regarding social security (the former) and taxes (the latter), for instance, in the case of posted work.

Varieties of social dumping

As the application of regulation across spaces – whether geographical or social – has become more fragmented and contingent (Martinez Lucio and MacKenzie, 2004), firm compliance with regulation has become strategic. The ability to strategize successfully between regulatory frameworks has turned into a competitive parameter, and companies have different approaches to this issue. Based on the evidence from the Dutch and Finnish construction and distribution sectors, we have identified three distinct categories of firms' cost-saving strategies in engaging with regulatory frameworks: regulatory evasion, regulatory arbitrage and regulatory conformance.

Regulatory evasion

Regulatory evasion involves the violation of formal national industrial relations rules, and implies the concealment of these violations from regulatory authorities. Quite often, this is done by obscuring a firm's practices or by increasing the level of legal uncertainty about whether a firm's practices are illegal by means of regulatory arbitrage. For example, by hiring employees in another national jurisdiction than the one in which the work is performed, regulatory evaders make it difficult for regulatory authorities to check whether the employment conditions meet the existing standards. Control and enforcement by compelling client firms to avoid using subcontractors who practise regulatory evasion is indeed a challenge:

> There can be highest managers, they can give the orders that we have to control this way, but lower in the organization there can be some manager who can get some benefit, he can even get bribes from illegal subcontractors when he's using them.... We can't show anything, but we know that, and even this middle management's organization, they admit that among their members, these rakennusmestarit [master builders], they even admit that there are some men who are taking bribes.
>
> (Finnish trade union official, 2009)

Much of the public attention given to posted work has been due to the very poor labour conditions of some posted workers and the illegal activities of their employers. The growth of posted work has been associated with the appearance of numerous 'fly-by-night' TWAs supplying cheap labour at substandard conditions (Finnish union official, interview, 2005). These are so-called shell firms that disappear as soon as regulatory authorities take too close an interest; they often simply change their names and move elsewhere. Many of these firms appear to be only small entrepreneurs using their personal contacts to deliver workers to job sites; one Finnish shop steward at a shipyard referred to them as 'the guys with lots of chains, a mobile phone and an SUV' (Finnish shop steward, interview, 2009). Employers rhetorically draw a line between themselves and unscrupulous grey-market employers. In this way, they make out the problem of regulatory evasion to be a technical issue of control and enforcement (interviews with Finnish construction employers, 2008; the Finnish Employers' Association, 2009; the European Construction Industry Federation, 2006). However, these types of labour suppliers nonetheless are often present on the production sites of 'respectable' core firms. Many 'respectable' firms play a political double game of rhetorically supporting high standards while actually obstructing the enforcement of labour standards on the fly-by-night operators where the most serious violations tend to occur (Lillie *et al.*, 2014). Therefore, while these agencies represent only a segment of the labour market, they are not a segment apart, as some client firms and employer associations would like to present them, but rather a part of a spectrum and an inevitable presence in the regulatory environment that permits and promotes their activities. For example, at the major power-plant construction sites of Olkiluoto 3, Finland, and at the construction of Avenue 2 in the Netherlands, they were an integral part of the production process. Some of these shady businesses operate on a larger scale, and, in the case of at least one well-known example, they have professionalized as well.

The case of Atlanco Rimec demonstrates that a thin professional veneer allows even persistently and strategically evasive agencies to access respectable client firms. Atlanco Rimec is a multinational manpower firm that has made a business out of hiring workers from low-wage EU countries for work in high-wage EU countries. It has also systematically utilized the legal uncertainty and enforcement difficulties created by the interaction of national systems and EU rules to violate national laws and industrial relations norms. While doing this hardly makes it unusual, what is unusual is that it operates on a large scale, in a systematic and apparently respectable way. Its clients are often well-known firms and household names. Atlanco presents a respectable public face, advertising itself as an 'expert in the mobilisation and management of teams of workers within the borders of Europe to meet the needs of our clients' (Atlanco Rimec website, 22 October 2012). It has offices around Europe and appears to be a firm of substantial size and resources; it reported €84.3 million turnover in its 2004 Annual Report. According to research conducted by Swedish journalist Anna-Lena Norberg (2013a), the company maintains a database with information about past and current employees. There are around 500,000 names in the database, including former job applicants. In addition, the database contains addresses, phone numbers, passport and tax identification numbers, information about current and previous job locations and field of work, as well as details about personal character and behaviour (attitude, skills, punctuality, and information concerning the premature termination of contract). For every person, the database specifies advice on possible rehiring: each worker is either recommended or blacklisted.

Atlanco Rimec consists of a network of companies, which appear in many cases to be shell firms created with the goal of avoiding legal responsibility.[4] Workers' employment can be moved from one company to another, as is illustrated by an excerpt from an Atlanco Switzerland employment contract of

2012: ‘The company reserves the right to transfer the employee at any time to other companies of the group of which the company is a member on similar terms within the period of the agreement’ (Norberg, 2013a). This is similar to the strategy used by certain kinds of firms in the maritime shipping business where, as in the case of Atlanco Rimec, complex multinational networks of shell companies shield owners from liability (Stopford, 1997).

Workers who have worked for Atlanco or one of its subsidiary firms, as well as unions that have dealt with them, accuse them of not paying regularly, of dismissing workers who complain, and of using double contracts and paying wages in violation of the relevant collective agreement and/or less than what was originally agreed. One former office staff member of Atlanco who successfully sued the company and was quoted in a Swedish news article related:

> I have worked for a long time for Atlanco and some of the workers see me as part of the company. With this judgment, I can show that I have nothing to do with Atlanco’s tricky business. That is the most important thing for me.
>
> (Norberg, 2013b)

By employing workers via Cyprus, sometimes without their knowledge and without workers having ever been there, Atlanco prevents its temporary staff from acquiring social security and pension rights in their home or host countries. This seems to be a side effect of locating in Cyprus rather than a deliberate action, however. At the same time, Atlanco has been at the centre of several industrial and legal disputes. Misconduct by Atlanco has been reported at the construction of the nuclear power plant in Flamanville, France, at Olkiluoto in Finland, at the Eemshaven and Avenue 2 construction sites in the Netherlands, and at several sites in Sweden. At Olkiluoto, Atlanco Rimec’s behaviour resulted in a major work stoppage (Lillie and Sippola, 2011).

At the building site in Eemshaven, several Atlanco employees did not receive the collective agreement wages. An Atlanco Rimec worker whom we interviewed when working in Eemshaven (2011) explained the firm’s practices as follows:

> Atlanco Rimec is a dangerous firm because it abuses people.... It abuses the law, in this case the Dutch law, by stretching it to find ways to circumvent it, only to rob us. It is a criminal agency. This is the first and last time that I work with them.

Atlanco often lumps all social security deductions together so that workers cannot detect what kinds of payments have been made on their behalf. This is something our interviewee also discovered when he received his first payslips:

> When the first payslips arrived, they did not provide us with any information, except for my last name, the company name and a mysterious logo.

> The agency's address is not on there, nor my personal identification number. There are no separate entries for pension or social security or tax payments. There is only a general sum. This is very secretive.

This worker contacted Atlanco about this matter, but they did not provide him with any explanation. The firm is known for not being forthcoming with information and has a reputation for threatening legal action to prevent its activities from being disclosed.

Regulatory evasion is made possible by the existence of the formally, legally legitimate strategy of regulatory arbitrage. The Atlanco Rimec case illustrates how legal ambiguity and enforcement difficulties mean in practice that it is difficult to draw a clear line between these two types of social dumping.

Strategic posting: regulatory arbitrage

Regulatory arbitrage is the exploitation of differences between national systems within the constraints set out by the Posted Workers Directive (PWD). Firms that engage in regulatory arbitrage follow EU rules and the appropriate national rules, but they remain partially outside the national industrial relations framework of the host country. Firms strategically locate themselves and post employees so as to benefit from the differences between national social security systems in Europe. The PWD ensures a minimum set of rights for posted workers, including minimum-wage standards in countries where these are present, but this list of rights does not concern social contributions. Social contributions are paid in the country from which a worker is posted (which is not necessarily the worker's home country). Tax authorities, but also trade unions in Finland, Sweden and the Netherlands, have noticed that over the past few years, Cyprus, Luxembourg and Slovakia have been increasingly used as places of residency by temporary employment agencies.

Many practices of regulatory arbitrage currently fall into a grey zone in EU legislation. Unions have campaigned against the opportunities for social dumping practices that the PWD creates. For example, the European Transport Workers' Federation (ETF) noticed, after interviewing around 1,000 professional drivers in the period 2008 to 2012, that it is common for firms in road transport to open letter-box companies in EU member states with lower levels of social protection and lower labour standards (ETF, 2012; also see Cremers, Chapter 9, this volume). This is the case even though a posting firm is formally required to have a genuine business activity in the posting state in order to be able to legally post workers. The European Commission (2012) has published explicit rules concerning this issue, but their enforcement is weak and thus letter-box posting has become widespread.

In our fieldwork we encountered many instances of strategic posting. One example was a Portuguese agency firm which posted Portuguese and Polish workers to work in the Netherlands. A Polish worker we interviewed in 2012 explained that he had been recruited in Poland but had received a Portuguese employment contract from a Portuguese subsidiary agency firm of the Polish firm that had recruited him. Since he worked as a posted worker via Portugal, he thought all social security payments were made in Portugal, but he was not sure:

> all such payments [pension, social security, etc.] go to Portugal. At least that is what they tell us.... Time will tell [if the TWA is being truthful].

A Portuguese posted worker (2012), also on a Portuguese contract, related:

> We are basically subcontracted. We have normal benefits, housing, food and travelling. The pension and social security is paid in Portugal and taxes in the Netherlands.

The practice of regulatory arbitrage is a known phenomenon among agency firms in the construction sector, as this Dutch trade union official (2011) elaborates:

> What they [agency firms] do is look for the countries with the lowest social contributions, in this case Portugal [put them under Portuguese contracts] ... and pay social fees in Portugal instead of in the Netherlands or Poland. And if you compare these rates, there is an easy difference of 25 per cent to be made.

Table 2.1 provides an overview of the cost savings that can be achieved through strategic posting. The example shows that even though the three nationals earn the same net income, posting a worker from Portugal (or Poland) saves an employer a significant amount on labour costs through the difference in social security payments.

Also in regard to wages, it is possible to make cost savings compared to firms complying with host-country regulatory frameworks. In Finland, wages are set through national-level collective bargaining, with uniform minimum standards across the whole country. In the construction sector, collective agreement wages are quite often the actual wage in rural areas, particularly in the north. In the Helsinki region, however, wages have commonly been much higher than the collective agreement wages. Firms practising regulatory arbitrage make cost savings by paying their workers exactly the collective agreement rate, employing their workers on home-country contracts and conforming to Finnish norms only in regard to the mandatory items mentioned in the PWD (Lillie, 2012). Finnish unions have de facto accepted employment on foreign contracts that comply with the PWD but not with the full range of standards to which Finnish workers are entitled – only because the workers are foreign. Furthermore, Finnish unionists and labour inspectors frequently voice suspicions that these workers are not actually receiving the wage levels they say they are, making the boundary between regulatory arbitrage and evasion difficult to define.

Table 2.1 Savings made by companies through strategic posting

Dutch worker		*Portuguese worker*		*Polish worker*	
Net salary	1,600	Net salary	1,600	Net salary	1,600
–/– soc. sec in NL	496	–/– soc. sec in Portugal	81	–/– soc. sec in Poland	350
–/– taxes in NL	81	–/– taxes in NL	81	–/– taxes in NL	81
Gross salary	**2,177**	**Gross salary**	**1,762**	**Gross salary**	**2,032**

Source: Wapening in Beton (2012, p. 7).

Regulatory conformance

Employers often make an argument that sourcing foreign labour is not about exploiting labour–cost differences but about finding workers for jobs for which there are no locals available, either because they do not have the skills or because no local person is willing to do that particular job. In the former case, certainly there is room for worker posting that would not trigger social dumping accusations, while the latter is in principle possible but may also be related to the ethnicization of labour markets or the redesign of jobs in ways that make them less desirable precisely because there is a cheap labour force available to do them. Even when firms comply with the regulatory framework, they can still set in motion a social dumping dynamic. We refer to this as regulatory conformance, which means conforming to the formal industrial relations system, but manipulating the rules for cost advantage. There is generally considerable room for achieving labour–cost savings in ways that bend but do not break the rules of the national social and industrial relations systems. Often firms find it cheaper or more convenient to follow local rules than to access foreign rule systems.

In the Dutch supermarket distribution sector, for instance, firms exploit loopholes in the TWA regulatory regime to segment the labour market into domestic core workers and contingent foreign workers in order to maximize their flexibility and achieve cost savings. There are two main groups of workers: the Dutch, who usually work on permanent contracts with the client firm, and the Poles, who generally work on temporary agency contracts with a Dutch temporary agency firm. In the Netherlands, the collective agreement for the agency sector provides for the 'contractual phase system' for agency workers. The system consists of phase A, phase B and phase C contracts. Phase A is the first phase, where there is no limit on the amount of temporary contracts an employer can sign with an employee, but the total duration is maximum 78 weeks (unless other arrangements are made in a company collective labour agreement). Phase A agency contracts can be terminated at any time and the worker usually has no guaranteed number of hours' work, as this Dutch agency worker explained (2013) when we talked about his employment contract:

> A phase A contract is a zero-hours contract.... But it is only one way. Because when you say one day in advance that you cannot come to work, it

> is not possible. But when they [the agency firm] say that you don't have to come, there is nothing you can do about it.

After 78 weeks, the firm must provide the employee with a phase B contract if the working relationship continues. The phase B contract gives an employee more job security because it provides a guaranteed number of hours, for example, which is not the case under phase A. However, when an employer sends the employee on a break that lasts at least 26 weeks, the worker's length of employment is reset and the worker can be rehired by the same firm on a phase A contract again. This is general practice for the Polish agency workers in this industry, as this Polish agency worker told us:

> I had been working for 1.5 years in phase A. Then I had a six-month break, well it was a forced break. Then I came back and I have been working for six months now.... In phase A they can sack you any time and it overall lasts for 78 weeks. Then you either receive phase B or you are sacked. There is a policy of almost never giving phase B. Once you have worked for that period, then you are simply kicked out.

The firms' practices comply with the letter of the regulatory framework for the agency sector. However, they do so in a way that undermines the intention of the collective labour agreement, which is to provide workers with a longer length of employment and more job security. In the sector examined here, the regulations are used in such a manner that Polish agency workers almost never attain this more secure phase of employment. As a result, even though firms do not violate the rules enshrined in law, they do violate the expectations that unions had when they concluded the collective agreement. Recent industrial actions organized in 2013 by the Dutch FNV union and Dutch and Polish distribution workers against this form of insecurity show that the unions consider this a violation of the spirit if not the letter of the collective agreement, protesting that this was not in line with the client firms' proclaimed corporate socially responsible behaviour. Their actions forced the client firms to change their policies; the latter agreed to stop this practice of resetting the length of employment of the Polish workers they hire via TWAs and instead to accumulate the total length of employment in the future.

Discussion

The different sectoral and national regulatory structures that are in place inform firm strategies. More lax regulation in one sphere attracts firms seeking cost advantages that subsequently employ workers under that particular regime. Countries with less extensive social security systems, such as Cyprus, attract letter-box posting companies that post workers all around Europe to save on indirect labour costs. For example, differences in industry arrangements make employing scaffolders for wages set by the collective agreement for the metal sector in the Netherlands a lucrative option because these are lower than the wages set in the construction collective agreement. Firms also strategize in terms of the way they operate and structure their firm: for example, do they operate as an agency firm, a posting subcontractor firm or a posting agency firm? For each type of firm, different regulations apply and provide the firm with different responsibilities towards their employees.

EU regulations on transnational employment relations are not yet well established and firms exploit existing legal uncertainties to their advantage. Firms often change appearances, using shell companies when it seems strategic to do so. Many workers we talked to in our research were unsure about where their contractual employer was legally based, given that many of these firms have branches in several European countries. The fact that EU law leaves room for firms to move between and exploit different regulatory regimes, makes legal abuses difficult to detect for the controlling and enforcing authorities.

The categorization presented in this chapter captures firms' social dumping practices using examples that we can clearly fit into one category or the other. In reality, of course, firms experiment and move fluidly between one strategy and another. Certain instances of regulatory arbitrage, such as the case of a Portuguese posted construction worker discussed earlier, seem to be legally sound. Others, such as the case of the Polish construction worker recruited in Poland but posted via a Portuguese agency to the Netherlands, represent an abuse of the posting regulations according to trade unions. Since enforcement remains ineffective and since jurisprudence on posted workers' employment rights remains slim, firms continue to operate via these channels and within these grey zones, pushing the boundaries of the regulatory system.

Conclusion

In this chapter we argued that due to its vagueness, the discursive use of the term 'social dumping' does not capture differing firm practices nor delineate the defining feature of social dumping: the norm-undermining and norm-violating tendency of this type of behaviour. The fact that firms involved in regulatory arbitrage operate in a legal grey zone where effective enforcement is lacking makes regulatory evasion hard to detect and control. As a result, firms experiment with cost-saving social dumping practices without having to run the risk of getting caught or punished. Furthermore, a dynamic is created where the ability and willingness to violate norms becomes a competitive parameter. In cases where the national framework itself offers opportunities for cost-saving, as in the Dutch distribution sector, firms can engage in social dumping while still complying with national industrial relations frameworks.

The term 'social dumping' may thus be used to label different forms of firms' strategic engagement with regulatory frameworks undertaken to achieve cost savings. Here, we propose a taxonomy of firms' social dumping practices that encompasses regulatory compliance, regulatory evasion and regulatory arbitrage.

The examples discussed in this chapter to illustrate the three types of behaviour are not limited to these countries, sectors or firms; rather, they are widespread in Europe. The EU market-making agenda creates opportunities for firms to continuously push and often transgress the boundaries of regulatory systems because the profits are high and the risks of punishment remain low due to inefficient enforcement.

Notes

1 Meier (2004), for example, argues that employee posting results in welfare gains for the EU economy as a whole, and that any application of minimum wages to such workers via the Posted Workers Directive can only have the effect of reducing these welfare gains.

2 This research was conducted in the context of the Transnational Work and the Evolution of Sovereignty project (European Research Council Starting Grant #263782), which studies posted work in the EU.

3 The 'Laval quartet' refers to four ECJ judgments: *Laval un Partneri* (C-341/05), *Viking* (C-438/05), *Rüffert* (C-346/06) and *Luxembourg* (C-319/06).

4 In 2004, Atlanco reported the following subsidiary companies: Atlanco Limited (Republic of Ireland), Atlanco UK, Atlanco Selecção Lda (Portugal), Atlanco South Africa Pty, Atlanco Poland, Atlanco Worldwide Limited (Republic of Ireland), Atlanco S.R.O. (Czech Republic), Rimec Limited (Republic of Ireland), Rimec B.V. (the Netherlands), Rimec SRO (Czech Republic), Atlanco Spain SL, Rimec Contracting (the United Kingdom), Rimec Poland and Rimec Hungary (Norberg, 2013b). In 2013, Atlanco's website reported company contact points in four countries: Ireland, the United Kingdom, Denmark and Portugal (Atlanco Rimec website, accessed 13 May 2013).

References

Alber, J. and Standing, G. (2000) 'Social Dumping, Catch-up, or Convergence? Europe in a Comparative Global Context'. *Journal of European Social Policy*, 10(2): 99–119.

De Bondt, H. and Grijpstra, D. (2008) *Nieuwe grenzen, oude praktijken: Onderzoek naar malafide bemiddelaars op de arbeidsmarkt.* Eindrapport. Zoetermeer: Research voor Beleid.

Debroux, M. (2013) 'Germany: Social Dumping of Flesh and Bone'. *Equal Times*, 25 March. Available at: www.equaltimes.org/allemagne-le-social-dumping-en-chair-et-en-os (accessed 23 August 2014).

Dølvik, J.E. and Eldring, L. (2008) *Mobility of Labour from New EU States to the Nordic Region*, TemaNord series, No. 537. Copenhagen: Nordic Council of Ministers.

Donaghey, J. and Teague, P. (2006) 'The Free Movement of Workers and Social Europe: Maintaining the European Ideal'. *Industrial Relations Journal*, 37(6): 652–666.

Erickson, C. and Kuruvilla, S. (1994) 'Labor Costs and the Social Dumping Debate in the European Union'. *Industrial and Labor Relations Review*, 48(1): 28–47.

ETF (2012) *Modern Slavery in Modern Europe? An ETF Account on the Working and Living Conditions of Professional Drivers in Europe*. Brussels: European Transport Workers' Federation.

European Commission (2012) *Practical Guide: The Legislation that Applies to Workers in the European Union (EU), European Economic Area (EEA) and Switzerland.* Available at: ec.europa.eu/social/BlobServlet?docId=4944&langId=en (accessed 24 March 2014).

European Court of Justice (2007) Judgment C-341/05, *Laval un Partneri Ltd* v *Svenska Byggnadsarbetareförbundet and Others*, 18 December.

Fellini, I., Ferro, A. and Fullin, G. (2007) 'Recruitment Processes and Labour Mobility: The Construction Industry in Europe'. *Work, Employment and Society*, 21(2): 277–298.

Fleischer, V. (2010) 'Regulatory Arbitrage'. *Texas Law Review*, 89: 227.

Höpner, M. and Schäfer, A. (2012) 'Embeddedness in Regional Integration: Waiting for Polanyi in a Hayekian Setting'. *International Organisation*, 66(3): 429–455.

Kvist, J. (2004) 'Does EU Enlargement Start a Race to the Bottom? Strategic Interaction among EU Member States in Social Policy'. *Journal of European Social Policy*, 14(3): 301–318.

Lillie, N. (2012) 'Subcontracting, Posted Migrants and Labour Market Segmentation in Finland'. *British Journal of Industrial Relations*, 40(1): 148–167.

Lillie, N. and Sippola, M. (2011) 'National Unions and Transnational Workers: The Case of Olkiluoto 3, Finland'. *Work, Employment and Society*, 25(2): 1–17.

Lillie, N., Wagner, I. and Berntsen, L. (2014) 'Posted Migration, Spaces of Exception, and the Politics of Labour Relations in the European Construction Industry'. In Hauptmeier, M. and Vidal, M. (eds), *Comparative Political Economy of Work*. Basingstoke: Palgrave Macmillan, pp. 312–331.

MacKenzie, R. and Forde, C. (2005) 'The Myth of Decentralization and the New Labour Market'. In Martinez Lucio, M. and Alonso, L.E. (eds), *Employment Relations in a Changing Society, Assessing the Post-Fordist Paradigm*. Basingstoke: Palgrave Macmillan, pp. 69–85.

Mäkelä, K. (2012) 'Suomessa kaksi kertaa luultua enemmän ulkomaalaisia rakennusmiehiä'. *YLE uutiset*. Available at: http://yle.fi/uutiset/suomessa_kaksi_kertaa_luultua_enemman_ulkomaalaisia_rakennusmiehia/6780866 (accessed 24 March 2014).

Markova, E. and McKay, S. (2008) 'Agency and Foreign Workers Literature Review'. London: TUC Commission on Vulnerable Employment. Available at: www.vulnerableworkers.org.uk/wp-content/uploads/2008/08/literature-review-final.pdf (accessed 15 May 2013).

Martinez Lucio, M. and Mackenzie, R. (2004) '"Unstable Boundaries?" Evaluating the "New Regulation" within Employment Relations'. *Economy and Society*, 33(1): 77–97.

Meier, V. (2004) 'Economic Consequences of the Posted Worker Directive'. *Metroeconomica*, 55(4): 409–431.

Norberg, A.-L. (2013a) 'Atlanco Rimec'. In *EFBWW Conference*. Brussels, European Federation of Building and Woodworkers, 23 January. Available at: www.stopsocialdumping.eu/downloads/0 (accessed 24 August 2014).

Norberg, A.-L. (2013b) 'French Judgment against Atlanco'. *Stoppafusket.nu*. Available at: www.stoppafusket.se/2012/10/08/french-judgment-against-atlanco/ (accessed 24 March 2014).

Rakennusteollisuus (2012) *Rakentamisen yhteiskunnalliset vaikutukset 2012*. Confederation of Finnish Construction Industries RT. Available at: www.rakennusteollisuus.fi/RT/Tilastot/Rakentamisen+yhteiskunnalliset+vaikutukset/ (accessed 24 March 2014).

Schmidt, V. (2006) 'Temporary Migrant Workers: Organizing and Protection Strategies by Trade Unions'. In Kuptsch, C. (ed.), *Merchants of Labour*. Geneva: International Institute for Labour Studies, pp. 191–206.

Schumpeter, J. (1942) *Capitalism, Socialism and Democracy*. London: Routledge.

Stopford, M. (1997) *Maritime Economics*, 2nd edn. London: Routledge.

Streeck, W. (1992) 'National Diversity, Regime Competition and Institutional Deadlock: Problems in Forming an European Industrial Relations System'. *Journal of Public Policy*, 12(4): 301–330.

Streeck, W. (2009) *Re-forming Capitalism: Institutional Change in the German Political Economy*. Oxford: Oxford University Press.

Tijdens, K., van Klaveren, M., Houwing, H., van der Meer, M. and van Essen, M. (2006) 'Temporary Agency Work in the Netherlands'. *AIAS Working Paper*, No. 06/54. Amsterdam: University of Amsterdam.

Tweede Kamer (2011) 'Arbeidsmigratie in goede banen, Eindrapport tijdelijke commissie LURA'. Vergaderjaar 2011–2012, *Kamerstuk* 32 680, No. 4. The Hague: Tweede Kamer der Staten-Generaal.

Wagner, I. (2014) 'Rule Enactment in a Pan-European Labour Market: Transnational Posted Workers in the German Construction Sector'. *British Journal of Industrial Relations*. Published online at: DOI: 10.1111/bjir.12053. Abstract available at: http://onlinelibrary.wiley.com/doi/10.1111/bjir.12053/abstract (accessed 24 August 2014).

Wagner, I. and Lillie, N. (2014) 'European Integration and the Disembedding of Labour Market Regulation: Transnational Labour Relations at the European Central Bank Construction Site'. *Journal of Common Market Studies*, 52(2): 403–419.

Wapening in Beton (2012) 'FNV Eemshaven: Ingeleend buitenlands personeel wordt onderbetaald'. *Wapening in Beton*, 01: 6–7.

Wynn, M. (2014) 'Power Politics and Precariousness: The Regulation of Temporary Agency Work in the European Union'. In Fudge, J. and Strauss, K. (eds), *Temporary Work, Agencies and Unfree Labor: Insecurity in the New World of Work*. New York: Routledge, pp. 48–69.

3 The politics of migrant irregularity

Social dumping in the French construction industry

Marcus Kahmann

Introduction

As intra-EU labour mobility has increased with successive waves of EU enlargement since the 1980s, industrial relations research has focused on the ways in which these flows have impacted upon the national wage systems and employment regulations of the receiving states (see Berntsen and Lillie, Chapter 2, Cremers, Chapter 9 and Krings *et al.*, Chapter 1, this volume). In such accounts, labour migration typically appears as a challenge or threat to the (usually well-developed) labour market institutions and regulations in the high-wage destination countries. The loss of sovereign control over borders in the EU Internal Market and the questioning of the territorial principle of labour law by European jurisdiction are often seen as fundamental to these issues (Bernaciak, Introduction to this volume).

What has caught researchers' attention to a much lesser extent is the fact that the erosion of obstacles to transnational flows of labour and capital within the EU and the spatial extension through enlargement have gone hand in hand with the hardening of frontiers to the majority of non-EU workers. EU regulations have played an increasingly significant role in these processes (Geddes, 2008). Externally, the creation of the Schengen zone has resulted in the 'fortification' of EU borders. EU member states have sought to restrict the access of family members, asylum seekers and refugees. The official demand for non-EU labour migration has been mainly satisfied through the proliferation of temporary labour migration schemes designed to impede settlement (Castles, 2006). Internally, the boundaries of civic membership have been tightened; access to more stable statuses, including nationality, has tended to become conditional upon diverse proofs of civic virtue (Chauvin and Garcés-Mascarenas, 2012). It is uncertain to what extent these changes have been successful in achieving their principal goal – the reduction of flows that are deemed undesirable and the 'moralization' of resident migrant populations. In any case, they have clearly affected the conditions under which people migrate, live and work.

This chapter addresses the link between third-country (i.e. non-EU) labour migration and social dumping by focusing on the implications of the legal status of a specific category of migrants, namely irregular migrant workers without a valid residence and work permit. Over the past two decades, European governments have become preoccupied with the growing presence of irregular migrants. In 2008, an estimated 1.9 to 3.8 million of them resided in the EU (Morehouse and Bloomfield, 2011, p. 6), representing between 7 and 13 per cent of the EU's foreign population and being concentrated mainly in the old EU member states. The majority of these migrants are in employment or are looking for a job. Public policy concerns about irregular migration range from worries about cultural cohesion, security and political stability, to the negative impact upon the employment of national workers. The primary response from the EU and member states has been to reinforce border controls, increase control pressures on resident irregular populations, facilitate their deportation and increasingly target their employers. Thus, irregular migration has changed from a phenomenon that was quietly dealt with and sustained by state administrations, or even encouraged during the post-war expansion (for France, see Blanc-Chaléard, 2001), into a major public policy problem.

Irregularity is first and foremost a 'juridical status that entails a social relation to the state' (De Genova, 2002, p. 422) and not a characteristic of individuals. It unifies an otherwise wide variety of people with regard to migratory trajectories, motivations, skills and (professional) situations.[1] Rather than providing a neutral frame that allows distinctions between 'legal' and 'illegal' migrants, the law constructs different statuses derogating from national citizenship (Anderson, 2010). In the case of 'illegals', the potential consequences generated by the contradiction between migrants' physical and social presence and their official negation are particularly blatant, ranging from unemployment, immobility and isolation, to death. Moreover, irregular migrants are the object of various policies, usually coming under the policy template of the 'fight against illegal immigration' and aimed at suppressing and preventing the phenomenon. Finally, laws and policies pertaining to irregularity are the object of strategies and tactics by actors such as employers and workers who try to circumvent and exploit them. This relates to the social fact that 'the existence of a legal prohibition creates around it a field of illegal practices' (Foucault, 1979, p. 280, cited in De Genova, 2002). As a complex tangle of regulations, practices and strategies, these elements constitute the 'politics of irregularity'.

Drawing upon evidence from a case study on the Parisian construction industry, this chapter seeks to identify norm-evading actor strategies and the ensuing patterns of social dumping. It argues that the fear of being dismissed without any notice represents the decisive mechanism that ensures irregular workers' loyalty in the face of violations of institutionalized (i.e. legally and collectively agreed) employment norms. Rather than promoting a radical departure from such norms, however, irregularity provides employers with leeway for modulating them, depending on the specific worker and market conditions. This situation highlights the normative strength of the National Minimum Wage and the dominant position of the subcontractor in an industry that has become increasingly characterized by the concentration of market power in the hands of large contracting groups.

French construction is a suitable field for an investigation into the politics of irregularity, given that the employment of (irregular) migrant workers, illicit or not, is a long-standing trait of this industry. Moreover, unlike sectors such as domestic services, it is particularly exposed to control pressures by public authorities. Methodologically, the study draws on ten semi-structured interviews with formerly undocumented migrant workers, with trade unionists and with labour inspectors, conducted between April and November 2013. Most of the interviewed workers had been employed as temporary agency workers by a demolition subcontractor (ABC) operating in the Greater Paris region. The findings of the study were supplemented with Jounin's (2006, 2007, 2008) ethnographic research on Parisian construction works.

The chapter proceeds as follows. First, it discusses the relationship between irregularity and social dumping. Second, it outlines recent developments in French policy with regard to irregular migration, focusing on the 'fight against illegal immigration'. Third, it describes structural changes in the French construction labour market. Fourth, building on case study material, it identifies specific social dumping practices in the sector. The final section discusses the evidence in the light of the mechanisms that are likely to sustain social dumping in the examined setting.

How does irregularity impinge upon employment relations?

Immigration scholars have sought to capture the relationship between immigration and labour market norms by recurring to the notion of 'cheap labour' (Portes and Walton, 1981). According to this view, the demand for labour migrants in the receiving countries is not so much driven by labour shortage per se, but by the need for a specific type of 'inferiorized' labour (Castells, 1975; Moulier Boutang *et al.*, 1986; Sassen, 1988). Migration policies reinforce the temporal aspect of the migratory process by limiting the length of stay, thus seeking to prevent migrants from making rights-based claims and proceeding to settlement. Thus, they construct certain types of workers – irregular, seasonal, posted, short-term – who correspond to certain types of precarious employment relations (Anderson, 2010). In this respect, irregularity represents a particularly powerful mechanism that undermines possible resources associated with citizenship, notably in asymmetric relations such as employment. Although national and international law and conventions provide irregular migrant workers with basic protection and elementary labour rights,[2] in practice the means to enforce employment regulations are limited by criminalization: at the workplace, employers may use the absence of migrants' legal status to threaten and control them. These conditions of 'institutionalized insecurity' (Anderson, 2010) create situations of over-dependence reflected by employers' reference to retention as an advantage of migrant labour (Waldinger and Lichter, 2003).

The above accounts point to a major effect of policies depriving workers of the right to stay and work: by seeking to protect one category of workers – citizens and non-citizens – they create the conditions for the exploitation of another category – (irregular) migrant workers. However, the regulatory approach has its limits in the sense that it is imprecise about the relationship between the employment of irregular migrants and institutionalized norms. Does irregularity of status intervene – as the generic term 'cheap labour' suggests – primarily as a means to ensure the acceptance of low wages? With regard to immigration more generally, economists tend to agree that if there are any negative effects on natives' wages at all, they tend be limited to the lower wage tiers (see Dustmann *et al.*, 2008). Or is irregular migration more closely interrelated with other provisions of the employment contract such as working time, health and safety, or rules on dismissal? Similarly, the limits of irregular migrant employment, both with regard to its scope and the extent of norm violation, remain unclear in such accounts.

Analytically, these shortcomings rely on the argument that irregularity 'fashions' migrants for certain jobs, exposing them to precarious employment and possibly social dumping. In order to contribute to a more thorough understanding of social dumping patterns, this chapter relates the strategies used by labour market actors regarding the constraints imposed upon them by irregularity to the characteristics of the labour market in which they are situated. Thus, it acknowledges that the demand for irregular migrant labour is inseparable from the global dynamics of regulation of the labour market in question (Moulier Boutang, 1991).

The 'fight against illegal immigration' in France

Over the past two decades, immigration and associated cultural and social phenomena, such as controversies over the use of Muslim headscarves and burkas, or suburban youth riots, have become a major subject of debate and legislation in France. They have culminated in the idea that immigrants and their offspring represent a threat to French national identity (Noiriel, 2007). Between 2002 and 2011, in an attempt to fend off party competition from the extreme right, successive conservative governments undertook four reforms of the immigration code. The main objective was to further limit migration for family reasons – the principal gateway to settlement in France – and to tighten regulations on residence and nationality for spouses of French nationals. Automatic access to the long-term resident card was successively abandoned in order to provide leeway for the authorities to refuse candidates on the grounds of ill-defined 'republican integration'. Instead, migrants remained on the one-year residence permit, subject to yearly administrative reconsideration of the applicant's personal situation (Morokvasic *et al.*, 2008). By redefining the boundaries and conditions of regularity, the authorities have multiplied the number of situations of irregularity.

Another element of French immigration policy has been the 'fight against illegal immigration'. According to estimates, the number of resident irregular migrants amounts to up to 400,000 (CLANDESTINO, 2009, p. 59).[3] Policies have focused on measures pertaining to resident irregular migrants, while also promoting minimum standards regarding irregular migration at EU level.

Nationally, deportations have been facilitated and possibilities for regularization have been further reduced. The 2006 immigration law eliminated the automatic granting of the (temporary) residence card to irregular migrants after ten years of proven continuous stay in France, replacing it with much less advantageous procedures. In 2007, for the first time, a government set official quotas for deportation: each year between 25,000 and 28,000 irregular migrants were to be deported. To achieve this ambitious goal, the government increased pressure on public bodies, and police agents multiplied identity checks in public places such as subway stations and streets.

At the same time, the government stepped up measures against the – illegal – employment of irregular migrant workers. Labour inspectors were joined by the police in industries such as construction that were considered to be heavily populated by irregular migrant workers. Since 2003, labour inspectors have been asked not only to check the conformity of the employment contract and working conditions, but also to verify work and residence permits. As a result, inspectors have found it increasingly difficult to sanction employers without endangering workers. Employers increasingly became part of the state's efforts to identify irregular migrant workers and prevent their hire. In July 2007, a government decree obliged them to transmit to prefectures the permits of the foreign workers they intended to employ. Employers risked fines of up to €15,000 and five years' imprisonment for the employment of workers without a work permit. Since then, the use of falsified permits with employers who seek to declare their workforce has become virtually impossible. As quickly as in 2008, however, the government provided an escape route from penalization by authorizing employers to propose their irregular workers for the official admission procedure by signing a binding offer of employment.

These measures were intended to erect new barriers to irregular migrants' employment and presence more generally. Lawmaking has allowed governments to signal to citizens that the state is still capable of protecting them against the forces of globalization (Sassen, 1996). To what extent the state apparatus has been able to enforce the norms is uncertain, however. The National Police struggled to meet the deportation targets (since officially abandoned) of the Sarkozy administration (2007–2012). The expansion of the competencies of the labour inspectorates did not result in an increase in resources. As a result, the number of enterprise checks has remained relatively stable over the past decade. Enforcement difficulties are not only caused by migrant strategies of evasion or legal hurdles; perhaps more fundamentally, they point to the ambiguous role of the state with regard to the phenomenon (Moulier Boutang, 1991). These observations suggest that the effectiveness of the 'fight against illegal immigration' resides, first and foremost, in the ways in which it stigmatizes migrants as undesirable (and therefore destined for deportation). It makes (rights-based) claims and collective organization appear illegitimate; it also divides migrant populations by proclaiming that the 'fight against illegal immigration' would be in the interests of regular migrant populations.

The transformation of the French construction industry

Economists analysing the political economy of irregular migration have identified temporal availability of labour and productive discontinuity as major drivers of employer demand for irregular migrant workers (Moulier Boutang *et al.*, 1986). Campinos-Dubernet (1984) highlighted the particularities of labour demand in construction by pointing to the variability of construction activity, which stems from the fact that most of its products are immobile prototypes. Spatial (geology, access) and meteorological conditions change with each site, and production itself is difficult to predict and to standardize as regards its start, duration and volume. These characteristics require a superior degree of flexibility in the deployment of labour, machines and logistics. Therefore, construction enterprises are confronted with a major dilemma: they have to make production capacities available without knowing if, when and for which object they will obtain a contract.

For these reasons, even during the heydays of Fordism, standard employment relations had difficulty emerging as the principal norm in construction. Between 1949 and 1970, the golden age of French capitalism, when employment in construction almost doubled to 1.7 million, there were many firms in construction, not all of which were necessarily large. 'Atavistic' (non-Fordist) types of employment, in particular the use of short-term contracts and remuneration in the form of piece wages, played an important role. Firms would regularly employ workers only for a single job and hire others for the next one (Jounin, 2008). Although profits were considerable, wages remained modest and working hours long. The construction labour market displayed the typical traits of job dualism, with one stable market segment characterized by clearly defined jobs and more or less clear systems of promotion, and the second tier marked by randomized promotion and unstable and lower paid jobs (Reich *et al.*, 1973; Piore, 1979).

The employment of immigrant workers in construction became important at the beginning of the 1960s in the context of wage rises and a massive flight of citizen-workers to better-paid industries. By the 1970s, immigrants represented one-third of the workforce in construction but 50 per cent of the low-qualified workers (Campinos-Dubernet, 1984, p. 276). Unlike in the industrial sector, however, the crisis of the early 1970s did not provoke their substitution. In urban centres – Paris, Marseille and Lyon – the second labour market segment became strongly marked by the presence of successive waves of foreign-born populations, from now on bearing the devaluating and auto-reproducing traits of an 'immigrant labour market' (Sayad, 2006). National data reveal that in 2007, 12 per cent of the immigrant population worked in construction, mostly in concrete works, bricklaying and non-qualified industrial construction jobs (Jolly *et al.*, 2012). Irregular construction workers – diverse in terms of race, occupation and nationality – form an integral part of this workforce. They are likely to work side by side with workers who, apart from their administrative situation, share the same characteristics, experiences and employment situations.

The steep economic downturn of the 1970s provoked a wave of bankruptcies in construction. By 1982, employment in the industry had fallen to 1.2 million. Many workers either left construction or became subcontracted bogus craftsmen who depended on their former employers to provide them with equipment. By 1986, the number of such subcontractors had risen to 310,000 (Jounin, 2008, p. 59). The employment of irregular migrants continued (Garson and Mouhoud, 1989), but the chances of obtaining a permit were greater – either through individual regularization or mass amnesty – and few workers were expelled. Besides its immediate economic consequences, the crisis of the 1970s triggered a number of transformations that contributed to the profound change of employment in the industry. Two decisive phenomena may be singled out. First, the gradual disappearance of medium-sized firms led to the dualistic organization of the market into an oligopolistic pole of large groups and a competitive pole of small businesses executing the work. Second, the strategic reorientation of the activities of large contractors resulted in the increasing externalization of their manual labour force. Associated with this transformation were declining job opportunities for racialized (migrant) workers, increasingly insecure migrant status and the decline of labour representation.

Growing concentration and polarization

From the 1980s onward, an important movement of economic and financial concentration set in. The market leaders initially began absorbing regional medium-sized companies and then, in a second step, absorbed and merged with other construction groups (Campagnac, 1996). Within 20 years, the number of major groups had fallen from eight to three: Eiffage, Vinci and Bouygues. In parallel, these financially and technologically powerful entities began to extend their activities to foreign markets. In order to become more independent of slumps in the business cycle, they started to diversify by developing new activities along the value-added chain, such as facility management, engineering and maintenance. Eiffage and Vinci, for example, expanded into the management of public infrastructures such as railways and motorways. Housing and property development, as an insecure market, was increasingly abandoned. The groups also extended into businesses that were not directly related to construction; Bouygues, for instance, became a major player in French television and telecommunications. The oligopolistic structure of the market and the diversification of their activities allowed these groups to cope with the contraction of construction activity in a period of economic crisis and austerity (Thireau, 2012). Because many medium-sized French construction enterprises were not able to withstand the process of concentration, the industry became increasingly polarized in terms of size, capital and technological equipment (see Table 3.1). High rates of enterprise creation and bankruptcy were particularly common among small-sized businesses.

Table 3.1 Legal entities in the French construction industry by number of salaried workers (2012)

0	*1–10*	*10–49*	*50–199*	*200–499*	*500–1999*	*2000 +*
290,559	166,183	26,688	2,162	266	135	24

Source: INSEE (2014a).

Increase in subcontracting and temporary agency work

In terms of employment patterns, instead of leading to a concentration of employment in the newly created conglomerates, main contractors – often belonging to construction groups – increasingly outsourced less specialized labour-intensive work to other contractors and concentrated instead on the coordination and supervision of sites. Between 1990 and 2000, the biggest construction companies (more than 500 employees) reduced the number of directly employed manual workers (*ouvriers*) by 60 per cent (Jounin, 2008, p. 59). The primary motivation for outsourcing was price and not specialization. By dealing with the subcontractors on a fixed-price basis for their services, they transferred to them the risks associated with the variability of production. In the competitive market for subcontracting, they could obtain services at prices they would ultimately not be able to sustain themselves – despite economies of scale and higher productivity – if these were to be conducted in accordance with the industry's applicable social norms. Working conditions in these often peripheral enterprises increasingly diverged from those of the remaining core workforce in these groups, who benefited from wages and conditions set in line with favourable company collective agreements. Main contractor liability was introduced in the 1970s, and penal and administrative sanctions for illicit employment (*travail illégal*) have continuously increased. However, liability has remained hard to establish in the courts of law.

The industry's quest for increasing external labour market flexibility did not stop here. New legislation offered opportunities for the development of temporary agency work (Jounin, 2008), and enterprises did not hesitate to make use of them. The number of temporary agency workers in construction rose considerably – from 56,613 in 1994 to 117,364 in 2013 – while overall employment has remained relatively stable (Figure 3.1). In 2009, some 7 per cent of the industry's salaried workforce were temporary agency workers. In the building trade (*gros œuvre*; *travaux publics*), both general contractors and subcontractors nowadays use temporary agency workers on a large scale. On construction sites, the proportion of temporary agency workers can amount to between 30 per cent and 40 per cent of the workforce.

The trend towards the concentration of employment in small and micro-enterprises as well as the rise of temporary agency work has also had an impact in terms of industrial relations. Many of these workers do not benefit from workplace interest representation and negotiation rights due to the characteristics of their employment (agency work) or the size of their enterprise. This is because

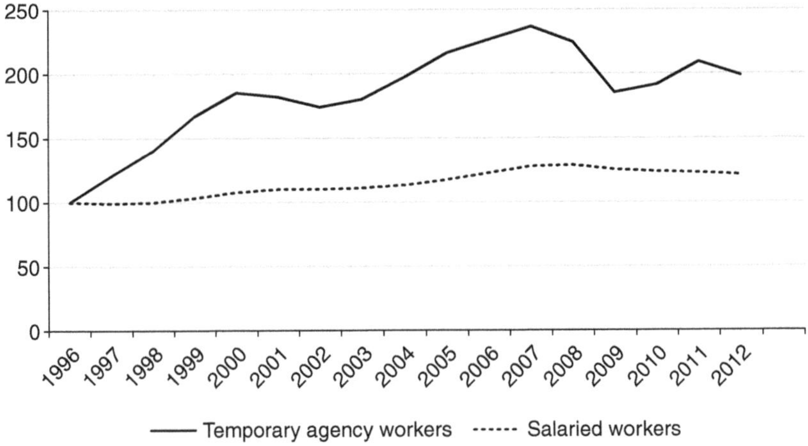

Figure 3.1 The evolution of employment of salaried and temporary agency workers in the French construction sector, 1996 to 2012 (base 100=1996) (source: DARES (2014); INSEE (2014b); author's calculations).

Note
Temporary agency employment in full-time equivalents.

the elections for workplace representatives (*délégués du personnel*) are held in companies with more than ten employees, while the threshold for the election of a works council (*comité d'entreprise*), the health and safety committee (*comité d'hygiéne, de sécurité et des conditions de travail*), and the nomination of workplace union delegates (*délégués syndicaux*) is 50 employees. Industry-wide union density has fallen below 5 per cent, and union delegates are now concentrated among the large contractors, where they represent the shrinking and increasingly professionalized core labour force.

The industry's generally binding collective agreement and the minimum provisions of the labour code constitute the backbone of employment regulation for the majority of workers in small and medium-sized enterprises. In such deserts of employee voice, the domination of contracting firms setting exceptionally low-priced contracts translates into pressures on workers that exceed those produced by the internal hierarchy of the enterprise (Jounin, 2008, p. 64). The system in place has allowed main contractors as well as private and public clients to keep in check labour costs, despite the industry's above-average national growth rates between 2000 and 2007.

The employment of irregular migrant workers in Parisian demolition works: the case of ABC

The market for construction in the Greater Paris region and in Paris, in particular, is characterized by demand for renovation works and for large-scale public and private infrastructure and construction works. In the latter sector, the major construction groups are well represented. In order to identify the strategies and patterns pertaining to the employment of irregular migrants in the industry, the remainder of this chapter focuses on a particular enterprise operating in this local market: ABC.[4]

ABC was founded in Paris in 1998 as a family-run enterprise specializing in demolition works. In 2008, it declared a turnover of €17 million. In October 2009, it requested the opening of a safeguard proceeding; this came about because for eight months, 59 of its workers had occupied a construction site in the Arc de Triomphe quarter of Paris. They had participated in trade union-led strikes of some 6,000 irregular workers claiming permits and legislative change in the criteria pertaining to regularization (Barron *et al.*, 2011).[5] In August 2010, ABC was declared bankrupt, but the owner appears to have set up another business in the same trade in the aftermath of these events. ABC regularly worked as a subcontractor for Eiffage, Vinci (through its subsidiaries SICRA and GTM) and Bouygues, which would contract the company directly. It was present on prestigious Parisian construction sites such as the AXA tower in the La Défense business quarter, the Lafayette department store, the OECD offices, the American Embassy and the National Parliament. All ABC workers were migrant workers hailing from Mali, Senegal and Mauritania. According to one interviewed worker, all were irregular. Their foreman was aware of the administrative situation of the workforce: when the workers announced that they could not work on a site where checks of identity cards were required on entry, he promised them he would find a solution.

Circumventing the dismissal rules: the role of specialized temporary work agencies

Apart from around ten fixed-term employees (accountant, supervisors, foremen, secretary), all ABC workers were employed through three small Parisian temporary work agencies. To obscure their status, they used the residence permits of regular workers. The profile of these agencies is particular insofar as they do not belong to the temporary agency industry's market leaders and are specialized in labour provision for small-sized construction businesses. Such agencies are concentrated in Parisian quarters such as the Boulevard Magenta, close to the Gare du Nord railway station. Workers looking for jobs in the building trade in these agencies are practically all male ethnic minority and migrant workers, mostly of West and North African origin; those identified as ethnic French left this local labour market a long time ago (Jounin, 2008). The number of workers employed by ABC through these agencies depended on the size of the contract it had concluded. During the two-year renovation of the AXA tower, for instance, it mobilized some 85 temporary agency workers.

A major role of these agencies is to provide using firms such as ABC with a way to circumvent dismissal rules. French temporary agency regulations stipulate that a worker's contract for a particular job (*contrat de mission*) has to be issued by the agency within 48 hours of the beginning of the job. In practice, however, the large majority of contracts were signed at the end of each working week or at the end of the entire job, or were not actually signed at all. The objective of this – illegal – practice is clear: if the worker does not hold a contract, he can be dismissed at any time. It is only under this condition that, for the using firm, temporary agency work is a profitable alternative to a fixed-term contract: under French legislation, the conditions for concluding and terminating a contract agreed directly with a company or with an agency are the same. In addition, workers receive a 10 per cent short-term contract bonus (*prime de précarité*) and the agencies also need to be paid. The threat of being dismissed by the ABC foreman from one day to the next functions as an efficient means to discipline the workforce: 'As soon as you show any weakness, the job is over. That is why they don't sign the contract before you start the job. It [the agency] gives you the contract after the job' (Idrissa).

Hollowing out collective wage norms

With regard to remuneration, French legislation stipulates that the wages of temporary agency workers should not be lower than those of the salaried workers of the using firm with the same level of qualifications and doing the same job. Since 1990, 'premiums and other wage components' must be included in the estimation of the wage of the temporary agency worker. According to the findings of Chauvin and Jounin (2010), the wages of workers employed through these temporary agencies would rarely be below the National Minimum Wage rate, which is close to the lowest wage bracket in the extended collective agreement.

However, infractions of the labour code and collective provisions do concern elements such as end-of-job compensation, holiday leave compensation, compulsory medical visits, bad-weather leave and refusal to provide safety footwear. The agency regularly imposes fictitious fees on the worker or transforms parts of the salary into premiums (Jounin, 2008). Such incidences of under-declaration to social security can appear negligible to the agency and irregular workers alike, as the latter do not benefit personally from the associated rights. As a rule, the more the worker appears inexperienced and vulnerable to the agency, the more he is exposed to fraud. Another means to lower wages is to ignore the qualifications of the worker. At ABC, agency workers' contracts would indicate specific jobs such as equipment driver or welder, but in reality they would be paid the unskilled workers' minimum rate (i.e. €350 a week).

All in all, irregular workers clearly experience pressure on wages, but the normative clout of the minimum wage appears sufficiently strong to play the role of a holding line in the (illegal) employment of these workers. The pressure on wages is part of a more general phenomenon associated with the increased use of outsourcing. Taking the example of concrete works, Jounin (2006) reports that iron benders in Greater Paris had seen their wages decline by some 30 per cent compared to the 1980s, when these jobs were still carried out by specialized contractors with a directly employed workforce. According to interviewed labour inspectors and Parisian trade union officers, lunch compensation or dressing/undressing time discounted off working time have tended to disappear, despite being collectively agreed. The same holds for more informal norms: in the 1980s, individually granted premiums were still an important part of the wage package (Dressen and Tallard, 1985). This fits into a larger picture in construction – in Greater Paris but possibly also elsewhere – according to which, in view of the growing role of subcontracting and temporary agency networks, the normative power of the collective bargaining agreement has been increasingly diluted to include merely the core wage norm.

Putting pressure on health and safety standards

The permanent threat of losing one's job and pay (irregular workers are not entitled to replacement income such as social assistance or unemployment benefit) from one day to the next underpins the brutal workforce management by foremen. Worker testimonies are unequivocal: cadences are high, and injuries and illness are often hidden because a slackening in pace may be punished by dismissal. Disrespecting health and safety standards can be a means to provide a competitive advantage for the using firm. At ABC, for instance, workers were asked to remove asbestos without observing the very strict regulations. The impact upon health would not be immediate, so the foreman would regularly close his eyes. According to Adama, he 'didn't give a damn. And me? I was an undocumented worker. If you say you won't do it, he will kick you out tomorrow.' However, work accidents put a significant strain on the employer who seeks to escape interference by authorities tasked with uncovering health and safety conditions on the site, just as does the employment of illegal workers. When a colleague of Adama, an undocumented welder, had to jump off his nacelle because a gas fire broke out, he was refused transport to hospital. Instead of declaring such incidences, ABC would pay certain injured workers sick leave for one week and even fund their medical treatment.

Health and safety is also related to the question of qualifications. Irregular workers would not only be asked to execute the most physically demanding tasks, often limited to preparation and finishing (e.g. chip hammering and cleaning). Permanent availability for all kinds of subaltern work also limited their prospects for informal qualification paths. The interviews reveal the potentially tragic consequences of this type of workforce management. In October 2007, during the renovation of the AXA tower, an unqualified ABC worker was killed by falling steel scrap when he was asked by the foreman to gas cut large tubes. 'He [the foreman] said: Take the burner, Mamadou [disrespectful generic name for African construction workers], he [the worker] cut it, was squeezed against the wall and died on the spot', recalls Adama.

Stabilizing the core 'temporary' workforce

The fact that agencies bypass contract regulations in order to lay off workers with minimum delay does not rule out workers being permanently employed. In reality, many of them work with a single agency and often even for a single user company over extended periods. In the case of ABC, some of the undocumented workers had been working for the company for ten years. Jobs can be very lengthy, too. Jobs on different sites can succeed one another, but no new contract is signed and the legal duration threshold for temporary agency contracts (normally 18 months, including renewal) is exceeded. In reality, only a fraction of ABC's workforce is recruited and selected by the agencies. Another part is imposed upon them by ABC and its supervisory personnel in particular: workers the company wants to keep but refuses to hire. The latter constitute a stable but extremely vulnerable workforce. In this context, the role of the agency is not so much to provide precarious (irregular) workers but to provide precariousness itself (Jounin, 2007, p. 41).

Idrissa's case is an example of this type of workforce management. As one of the core workers, ABC would send him to another site as soon as a job was finished. If there was no work left to give him, he would return home and wait for the foreman to call him. In the meantime, he would return to the agency to find an intermediate job. In order to manage the labour process on sites and protect informally acquired job skills, but also to counter the unintended consequences of precariousness (such as worker defection and sabotage), the using firm seeks to stabilize a core workforce – illegally, because agency work in France is temporary by definition. Informal but easily reversible 'favours' such as wage increases or promotions as well as personal ties become the principal means for employers to ensure worker loyalty (Iskander, 2007; Chauvin and Jounin, 2010).

Discussion: the reproductive mechanisms of social dumping

This chapter has sought to identify strategies and patterns of social dumping in the employment of irregular migrant workers. With regard to the case in question, what emerges first is that the heightened barriers to their employment have proven permeable. On the employer side, the use of specialized temporary work agencies by subcontractors may be seen as a means to deal with the consequences of the intensification of the 'fight against illegal immigration'; in other words, as a means to escape the administrative burden of verifying migrant status prior to hiring and to reduce the increased legal risks. In the event that the labour inspectorates should turn up on a site and discover irregularities (infractions against the labour code; employment of irregular migrants), it would be the temporary work agency and the irregular workers themselves who would be the primary object of inquiry, not the subcontractor and even less so the main contractor. The use of these agencies is a comparatively sophisticated response to the challenge of criminalization; typically, irregular migrant workers are directly employed. The migrant workers, for their part, have adapted to the changes both in employment and in their everyday tactics to avoid police controls in public places and transport. When the use of false permits became seriously restricted, workers were obliged to rent cards from regular migrants. This measure not only increased the costs associated with irregularity and created a new market in the 'migration industry', but also made undocumented workers more reliant upon employer acceptance of 'identity change' in case the lender should reclaim his or her card. Workers without such cards have been forced into undeclared employment, which has also seriously hampered their prospects for meeting the criteria for regularization. This suggests that the burden associated with the 'fight against illegal immigration' is primarily carried by the workers.

Second, in terms of the relationship between the employment of irregular migrants and social dumping, the case study evidence confirms pressures on wage norms and on health and safety rules. However, contrary to a vision of social entropy, according to which the employer 'does whatever he or she wants' and every irregular worker is seemingly easy to replace, basic institutionalized norms and personal ties continue to shape the behaviour of employers and workers. Selectively granted informal sick pay and the National Minimum Wage rates are a case in point. The latter appear to function if not as a holding line, then at least as an orientation mark for actors in the formal economy who are firmly rooted in the cognitive framework of the French economic system.[6] This suggests that irregularity intervenes in institutionalized norms by providing a leeway for employers in which employment and working conditions are modulated depending on the specific worker characteristics and market conditions more generally.

One could argue that the major derogation from institutionalized norms does not concern wage levels, as suggested by the popular notion of 'cheap labour', but the conditions of conclusion and termination of employment contracts. In the Parisian construction industry, specialized temporary work agencies have been instrumental in providing subcontractors with the possibility to free themselves from this crucial constraint of the labour contract. This technique not only follows a narrow economic rationale, namely to save on wages under conditions of variability of production and the impossibility of offshoring production. The threat of being (illegally) dismissed from one day to the next may be identified as the decisive mechanism that makes workers accept and sustain low wages as well as substandard and hazardous working conditions. Thus, the basic sentiment of social instability (Castels, 2003) – not knowing what tomorrow brings – due to irregular migrant 'deportability' (De Genova, 2002) is doubled at the workplace. Temporariness of presence, both imagined by the worker seeking to return at some point and imposed upon him or her by the state and the employer, is fertile ground for willingness to put up with hardship and stigma (Piore, 1979; Sayad, 2006).

The other side of the fear of unfair dismissal of workers confronted with illicit employer behaviour is the lack of alternative labour market prospects and the absence of institutions created to protect workers in the first place. In this respect, irregularity reveals its specific capacity for ensuring worker loyalty over exit or voice (Hirschman, 1970).

Being dismissed is a risk that has to be much more carefully considered by irregular migrants than by workers who are 'only' confronted with the ordinary selection criteria (notably gender and race) governing access to particular jobs and occupations (Waldinger and Lichter, 2003). The interviewed workers described more or less long periods of unemployment after they had lost a job. Without any state-guaranteed replacement income, they quickly lose autonomy.

During prolonged unemployment, they had to rely on networks of mostly kin solidarity and look for undeclared jobs on a day-to-day basis. Typically, they would move in with friends or family members, thus falling back into situations similar to when they arrived in France years previously. Beyond general market conditions, the difficulties of irregular workers in getting a job reflect the significance of employer criminalization as a specific barrier to their labour market entry. The number of employers prepared to take legal risks is limited; they have to carefully weigh those risks against the advantages that the employment of irregular workers provides over other workers with more or less stable statuses. Many employers may thus prefer other forms of illicit employment involving regular migrant workers, or they may respond to rising administrative pressures by dismissing their irregular workforce (Iskander, 2007). In 2007, when employers were obliged to transmit to prefectures the permits of the foreign workers they intended to employ, a wave of layoffs took place out of the public eye (Barron *et al.*, 2011). In other words, the scope of irregular migrant employment is not only limited by the availability of these workers in the local labour market but also by the 'fight against illegal immigration' itself. Such effects do not necessarily reduce illicit employment practices, but they tie irregular workers more firmly to employers.

Likewise, irregularity of status undermines basic labour protections that are normally available in the case of dismissal or other matters. Under conditions in which employment relations are de-collectivized, an appeal to the labour courts may appear to be the only chance to voice rights-based claims. According to an interviewed trade union officer, labour courts do not demand to see workers' permits. However, the union would discourage irregular workers from presenting their case in court because of the risk that the employer could denounce the worker to the police. Officers therefore seek arrangements by communicating directly with the employer. Interviewed workers, on the other hand, reject the idea of resorting to legal action as being too costly and too slow. Under these conditions, worker resistance occurs mainly through microscopic acts of sabotage and disobedience at work (Jounin, 2008). Cyclically occurring social movements (Siméant, 1998; Barron *et al.*, 2011) have been a breakaway from this bleak cycle of highly subordinate employment relations. Irregular migrants do not usually voice specific work-related claims; rather they mobilize for the regularization of migrants and a change in related policies. However, the movement in which the ABC workers participated declared itself a worker protest and thus objected to dominant representations of illegal immigrants. By occupying their workplaces and voicing their claim as *travailleurs sans papiers* (literally, workers without permits), they highlighted the contradiction between their social and economic integration as workers and their 'exploitation' resulting from their exclusion from formal citizenship.

The relationships of domination conducive to social dumping are intrinsically linked to the dualistic organization of the industry. They become apparent if we take into account the nature of benefits derived by employers from undermining institutionalized norms. These depend mainly on the employer's position in the industry's reinforced hierarchy of enterprises, in particular on its place in the contracting chain. Without being exposed to the legal risks associated with it, the shift to subcontractors of the economic uncertainty resulting from variability enables main contractors to maintain price agreements that are incompatible with institutionalized norms. This has also allowed them to escape the reputational stigma associated with illegalities related to migrant status and irregular employment. Seeking to protect their relationships with public clients and, perhaps more importantly, to secure activities they have developed outside the construction business, construction groups have carefully sought over the past 20 years to deconstruct this image by presenting themselves as spearheads of technological innovation and exemplary employers who are open to social dialogue. By contrast, for subcontractors, the hiring of irregular workers is a means to survive in the highly competitive market for labour provision. The fate of ABC during the 2009 strike events is revealing in this respect. In the course of the occupation of the Lafayette site, the Eiffage management informally convened trade unionists, striking workers and the ABC management. It urged the latter 'to bring things in order' by providing the workers with a binding offer of employment – the condition these workers had to satisfy in order to obtain a permit. Instead of meeting these demands, however, ABC shut down.

Conclusion

Over the past two decades, illegal immigration has become an increasingly important issue on the agenda of European policymakers seeking to safeguard citizens against the perceived risks of uncontrolled immigration. However, the analysis of the labour market effects of the politics of irregularity reveals that rather than protecting citizen-workers and preventing social dumping, these policies feed into deteriorating employment conditions in 'immigrant' labour markets. The workers with the weakest position in the labour market carry the major burden of the tacit alliance between forces driving the reorganization of the industry to the detriment of labour regulations, and state policies maintaining a highly regulated system of derogatory statuses of migrant labour. If irregularity is fundamentally justified by the criterion of not belonging to a civic community, the heightening of the barriers to civic status reveals another paradox of the politics of irregularity: it maintains the justification for irregularity deployed in the first place and thus tolerates the prolongation – and potentially the amplification – of the effects that irregularity may have upon institutionalized norms.

Notes

1 Irregularity is not only a status but also a process in the sense that a person becomes 'illegal' only from the moment when he or she has crossed the border, and often much later than this. Frequently, it is not an end state but one stage in a shifting range of statuses between which non-citizens move (e.g. from overstayer to legal resident to illegal resident). Status mobility can be an effect either of changing state policies or of individual choices and opportunities (Anderson and Ruhs, 2010).

2 French labour legislation stipulates that workers without a work permit are to be treated equally to other workers.
3 In absolute terms, this places France below neighbouring countries such as the UK, Germany or Italy (CLANDESTINO, 2009). Over the past decade this estimate has remained fairly stable, suggesting that the number of deported and regularized migrants roughly equals those entering into a situation of irregularity (overstayers and newcomers).
4 The names of the company and of the interviewed workers have been anonymized.
5 In the course of the strike, however, the responsible ABC boss refused to sign the promise of employment the workers needed to apply for a permit. Instead, he set fire to the building occupied by his workers in order to drive them out and then sealed the site entrance.
6 It is questionable whether this also holds for transnational service providers of posted workers (DGT, 2012).

References

Anderson, B. (2010) 'Migration, Immigration Controls and the Fashioning of Precarious Workers'. *Work, Employment and Society*, 24(2): 300–317.

Anderson, B. and Ruhs, M. (2010) 'Researching Illegality and Labour Migration'. *Population, Space and Place*, 16(3): 175–179.

Barron, P., Bory, A., Chauvin, S., Jounin, N. and Tourette, L. (2011) *On bosse ici, on reste ici! La grève des sans-papiers*. Paris: La Découverte.

Blanc-Chaléard, M.C. (2001) *Histoire de l'immigration*. Paris: La Découverte.

Campagnac, E. (1996) *L'implication des grands groupes de BTP dans la production urbaine*. Mimeo.

Campinos-Dubernet, M. (1984) *Emploi et gestion de la main-d'œuvre dans le BTP. Mutations de l'après-guerre à la crise*. Paris: CEREQ.

Castells, M. (1975) 'Immigrant Workers and Class Struggle in Advanced Capitalism: The Western European Experience'. *Politics and Society*, 5(1): 33–66.

Castels, R. (2003) *L'insécurité sociale. Qu'est-ce qu'être protégé?* Paris: Seuil.

Castles, S. (2006) 'Guestworkers in Europe: A Resurrection?' *International Migration Review*, 40(4): 741–766.

Chauvin, S. and Garcés-Mascarenas, B. (2012) 'Beyond Informal Citizenship: The Moral Economy of Migrant Illegality'. *International Political Sociology*, 6(3): 241–259.

Chauvin, S. and Jounin, N. (2010) 'L'externalisation des illégalités. Ethnographie des usages du travail "temporaire" à Paris et Chicago'. In Weber, F. and Barbe, N. (eds), *Les paradoxes de l'économie informelle. A qui profitent les règles*? Paris: Karthala, pp. 113–138.

CLANDESTINO (2009) *CLANDESTINO Project, Final Report*. Brussels: European Commission.

DARES (2014) 'Données annuelles sur l'intérim' database. Available at: http://travail-emploi.gouv.fr/etudes-recherches-statistiques-de,76/statistiques,78/emploi,82/l-interim,2285/l-interim,15028.html (accessed 16 October 2014).

De Genova, N.P. (2002) 'Migrant "Illegality" and Deportability in Everyday Life'. *Annual Review of Anthropology*, 31(1): 419–447.

DGT (2012) *Bilan du plan national d'action sur les contrôles de travail illégal effectués en 2011 dans les secteurs prioritaires*. Paris: Direction Générale du Travail.

Dressen, M. and Tallard, M. (1985) 'L'expression dans le BTP: Obstacles socio-économiques'. *Travail et Emploi*, 24: 31–42.

Dustmann, C., Frattini, T. and Preston, I. (2008) 'The Effect of Immigration along the Distribution of Wages'. *CReAM Discussion Paper*, No. 03/08. London: Centre for Research and Analysis of Migration.

Foucault, M. (1979) *Discipline and Punish: The Birth of the Prison*. New York: Random House.

Garson, J.-P. and Mouhoud, E.M. (1989) 'Sous-traitance et désalarisation formelle de la main-d'œuvre dans le B.T.P.'. *La Note de l'IRES*, No. 19. Paris: Institut de Recherches Economiques et Sociales, pp. 36–47.

Geddes, A. (2008) *Immigration and European Integration*. Manchester: Manchester University Press.

Hirschman, A.O. (1970) *Exit, Voice, and Loyalty: Responses to Decline in Firms, Organizations, and States*. Cambridge, MA: Harvard University Press.

Insee (2014a) 'Sirene' database. Available at: http://insee.fr/en/bases-de-donnees/default.asp?page=sirene.htm (accessed 16 October 2014).

Insee (2014b) 'Estimations d'emploi' database. Available at: www.insee.fr/fr/methodes/default.asp?page=sources/ope-estimations-emploi.htm (accessed 16 October 2014).

Iskander, N. (2007) 'Informal Work and Protest: Undocumented Immigrant Activism in France, 1996–2000'. *British Journal of Industrial Relations*, 45(2): 309–334.

Jolly, C., Lainé, F. and Breem, Y. (2012) *L'emploi et les métiers des immigrés*. Paris: Centre d'analyse stratégique.

Jounin, N. (2006) 'Les travailleurs immigrés du bâtiment entre discrimination et précarité. L'exemple d'une activité externalisée: le ferraillage'. *Revue de l'IRES*, No. 50. Paris: Institut de Recherches Economiques et Sociales, pp. 3–25.

Jounin, N. (2007) 'L'illégalité sous-traitée? Les conséquences du recours à des employeurs intermédiaires dans le secteur du bâtiment'. *Droit social*, 1(January): 38–45.

Jounin, N. (2008) *Chantier interdit au public. Enquête parmi les travailleurs du bâtiment*. Paris: La Découverte.

Morehouse, C. and Bloomfield, M. (2011) *Irregular Migration in Europe*. Washington, DC: Migration Policy Institute.

Morokvasic, M., Dinh, B., Potot, S. and Salzbrunn, M. (2008) 'Immigrant France: Colonial Heritage, Labour (Im)Migration and Settlement'. *IDEA Working Paper*, No. 2. Available at: www.idea6fp.uw.edu.pl/?strona=4 (accessed 27 August 2014).

Moulier Boutang, Y. (1991) 'Dynamique des migrations internationales et économie souterraine: comparaison internationale et perspectives européennes'. In Montagné-Villette, S. (ed.), *Espace et travail clandestins*. Paris: Masson, pp. 113–121.

Moulier Boutang, Y., Garson, J.-P. and Silberman, R. (1986) *Economie politique des migrations clandestines de main d'œuvre. Comparaisons internationales et exemple français*. Paris: Publisud.

Noiriel, G. (2007) *A quoi sert 'l'identité nationale'?* Paris: Agone.

Piore, M. (1979) *Birds of Passage*. Cambridge: Cambridge University Press.

Portes, A. and Walton, J. (1981) *Labor, Class and the International System*. New York: Academic Press.

Reich, M., Gordon, D.M. and Edwards, R.C. (1973) 'Dual Labor Markets: A Theory of Labor Market Segmentation'. *American Economic Review*, 63(2): 359–365.

Sassen, S. (1988) *The Mobility of Labor and Capital*. Cambridge: Cambridge University Press.

Sassen, S. (1996) *Losing Control? Sovereignty in the Age of Globalization*. New York: Columbia University Press.

Sayad, A. (2006) *L'immigration ou les paradoxes de l'altérité. L'illusion du provisoire.* Paris: Raisons d'agir.

Siméant, J. (1998) *La cause des sans-papiers*. Paris: Presses des Sciences Po.

Thireau, O. (2012) *Comment les majors européens du BTP traversent-ils la crise?* Paris: Mazars.

Waldinger, R. and Lichter, M.I. (2003) *How the Other Half Works: Immigration and the Social Organization of Labor*. Berkeley: University of California Press.

4 Varying perceptions of social dumping in similar countries

Jens Arnholtz and Line Eldring

Introduction

In the Nordic countries, 'social dumping' and labour migration have become highly related issues in public discourse since the EU enlargements of 2004 and 2007. As workers from the new EU member states have travelled in large numbers to the old EU member states, concerns have been raised about the effect this will have on the receiving countries. Large socioeconomic differences between Western and Central-Eastern European (CEE) countries, manifested in significant dissimilarities in wages and working conditions, have formed the background for these concerns. Terms like 'the Polish plumbers', 'welfare tourism' and 'social dumping' may be seen as part of a populist political discourse aimed at fuelling and exploiting these concerns. However, they also stand for some of the more broadly harboured concerns about the specific institutional arrangements that have been at stake in the debates on labour migration and social dumping. This has been particularly true for the Nordic countries, where both welfare and labour market institutions have been seen as potentially being put under pressure by the arrival of the new labour migrants.

In the academic literature, much attention has been paid to the pressures and challenges raised by EU labour migration since the recent EU enlargement rounds. The underlying assumption of many of the studies may be exemplified by Woolfson, who explicitly argued that 'labour standards in the EU-15 may be subject to increasing pressure occasioned, in particular, by the arrival of … labour from Eastern Europe' (Woolfson, 2007, p. 200). While this is a very general assumption, specific variations have also been detected. A number of studies have identified differences across sectors in the kinds of pressures exerted by the presence of labour migrants (Barrett *et al.*, 2012; Arnholtz and Hansen, 2013; Bengtsson, 2013), while other studies have tracked variations across types of employment (Friberg *et al.*, 2014). In particular, posting of workers has been seen as a strategy for 'circumventing national class compromises' (Lillie, 2010, p. 693), and as putting pressure on wages through the use of 'cheap labour' (Cremers, 2011).

However, while these studies have focused on what causes 'social dumping' and the mechanisms through which it manifests itself, they have been less concerned with defining what 'social dumping' actually is. In this respect, Bernaciak (in the Introduction to this volume) has called for a stronger effort to clarify the concept, and the aim of this chapter is to contribute to this endeavour. Our argument is that the phenomenon of 'social dumping' is not just a product of strategic actions by market participants but is also shaped by the efforts of other actors who define and try to uphold the social standards that 'social dumping' violates. That is, the concept of 'social dumping' is itself part of a political struggle revolving around the issue of distinguishing between acceptable, everyday competitive pressures of a market economy and unacceptable, extraordinary social problems engendered by 'unfair' competition.

To make this point, the chapter will show that the understanding of 'social dumping' can vary substantially depending on institutional and political differences. Taking two very similar countries, namely Denmark and Norway, we show how the debate on social dumping has differed in the two countries since EU enlargement. Analysing both public discourse and reform initiatives, we argue that Danish trade unions have struggled to maintain the principle of equal treatment between domestic and migrant workers as their standard for assessing what constitutes social dumping. In so doing, they have faced substantial problems in upholding labour market standards, with some migrant workers falling far below the minimum standards set by collective agreements. In Norway, on the other hand, there has been a gradual shift in the understanding of 'social dumping' – from a lack of equal treatment to a failure to abide by the minimum standards. This more pragmatic approach, and the legal initiatives it has prompted, has had some success in securing minimum standards for migrant workers compared to Denmark. However, it has also involved an acceptance of lower standards being good enough for migrant workers.

The analysis is based on data from a number of previous projects related to labour migration, posting and EU enlargement.[1] These data include an analysis of the statistical development of labour migration to the two countries (Dølvik and Eldring, 2008; Friberg and Eldring, 2013), survey data on the use of foreign workers and their wages and working conditions in the receiving country (Friberg and Tyldum, 2007; Arnholtz Hansen and Hansen, 2009; Friberg and Eldring, 2011), extensive knowledge of the regulatory reforms that have occurred as a response to the recent EU enlargements and the new flow of labour migration (Andersen and Arnholtz, 2013), and knowledge about trade union responses to the challenges posed by the inflow of CEE workers (Eldring and Arnholtz Hansen, 2009; Eldring *et al.*, 2012). In addition to this extensive background knowledge, the specific questions posed in this chapter have required us to revisit and reanalyse central policy documents and interviews with key actors, including a small-scale media analysis.

The chapter is structured as follows. In the following section, we outline the theoretical argument behind our analysis, stressing the importance of norms and norm formation for the understanding of social dumping. We then present some important similarities and differences between Denmark and Norway. We subsequently analyse how the concept of 'social dumping' has been used in the two countries and how it has been gradually given new content by regulatory reforms and discursive struggles. Finally, we discuss the findings and round off the chapter with a short conclusion.

Theoretical perspectives

As Bernaciak has aptly argued in the Introduction to this volume, providing a consistent and comprehensive definition of 'social dumping' is a difficult task. However, what stands out from her review of the literature is that violations or undercutting of more or less explicit norms is an essential part of the phenomenon called social dumping. This is clear in some of the more normative definitions she reviews that refer to '*artificially* low costs' or '*underdeveloped* social protection' (emphasis added), and it is equally true of Bernaciak's conceptualization, which defines social dumping as 'the practice, undertaken by self-interested market participants, of undermining or evading existing social regulations with the aim of gaining a short-term advantage over their competitors' (see Introduction to this volume). While the 'social regulations' referred to may have a very concrete manifestation in each specific situation (e.g. a certain wage level), they are nonetheless based on some kind of norm (e.g. that wages should not lie too far below the average wage). To understand 'social dumping', then, we need to understand the norms it violates and how they are shaped. Without these norms, 'social dumping' could simply be perceived as an expression of everyday market competition.

Such norms will typically vary from case to case (be they countries, sectors, educational groups or across time). In some countries, the relocation of jobs will elicit huge protests from workers, while in others it will simply be seen as part of everyday life. During certain periods, the opening of borders to foreign workers will be seen as direct aggression against local workers' rights, while in others it will be seen as a pragmatic solution to labour shortages or a natural part of the European integration process. In some sectors, working for the minimum wage will be quite normal, while in others it will be a clear expression of 'social dumping'. Thus, trying to determine (or even measure) 'social dumping' will always be an endeavour related to the categories of reference – that is, the 'social standards' or 'social regulations' considered to be under attack.

Social standards are seldom purely academic matters. More often than not, they are the result of political struggles involving both practical and discursive elements. To make our point more clear, we will draw upon Foucault (2007, pp. 83–87), who wrote about the interplay between 'normation' and 'normalization'. If 'normalization' is the process whereby practices are brought within the realm of the normal, then 'normation' is the process whereby the normal is defined. We find this argument valuable for understanding the concept of social dumping. While most studies – and the majority of the contributions in this volume – have focused on the mechanisms and strategies that lower social standards, and some have studied the responses of trade unionists and authorities trying to uphold social standards by 'normalizing' the conditions of migrant workers, few have focused on the processes which produce the norms that define these social standards. We want to home in on this kind of 'normation' process – in Foucault's sense – whereby actors gradual define and redefine the limits of what may be regarded as normal 'social standards' and thus, by proxy, the abnormal standards that should be regarded as 'social dumping'.

More specifically, we want to analyse how the definition of social standards is affected by the appearance of labour migrants. Social standards will often be the result of long-term historical developments and the functioning of institutions. However, one can hypothesize that they will be affected by pressures on these very same standards. Furthermore, we will argue that normation and standard-setting processes may vary across countries due to the variations in labour standards and regulatory systems, but also because of different political constellations and different relations between employers and trade unions, as well as finer institutional details. In this sense, the normation process is not just the result of discursive struggles but involves practices as well. Often the confrontation between the general norms and the specific practices will alter both of these – in other words, both the company strategies to use foreign labour to gain competitive advantages *and* the very understanding of what constitutes acceptable and unacceptable employment conditions will be affected by this interaction (Wagner, 2014). Rather than focusing on company strategies, our contribution to the debate on social dumping will consist in analysing the normation process in two very similar countries – Norway and Denmark – showing that their understanding of social dumping has come to differ somewhat despite very similar starting points.

Denmark and Norway: labour markets and migration

There are many similarities between the Danish and Norwegian societies and labour markets. Both countries have relatively small and open economies with well-developed welfare systems. High union density, extensive worker representation and centralized agreements embedded in social models based on close interaction between working-life policies, the welfare state and macroeconomic policies are central features of the two states (Dølvik, 2011).There are also similarities in the provisions for regulation of the labour market. Whereas most national European labour markets are heavily regulated through legislation, including minimum wages, this is not the case in Norway and Denmark. Although several aspects of work are regulated through working environment acts, minimum wage levels have traditionally been based on collective bargaining and have been binding only for workers who are covered by a collective agreement (Eldring and Alsos, 2012). Although coverage is lower in Norway, collective agreements often establish norms in enterprises that are not formally bound by them (Stokke *et al.*, 2013). In some sectors, local rates of pay are often well above the agreed minimum rates, making these minimum rates of limited importance for actual wage levels. Nonetheless, in these sectors the collective bargaining system contains some mechanisms that make this a form of 'organized decentralization' (Traxler *et al.*, 2007).

Furthermore, collective agreements in both countries cover not only minimum wage levels but also a range of other additional payments and rights.

These similarities give rise to a number of similar challenges with regard to labour migration and 'social dumping'. First, the fact that the minimum wage is not statutory presents the continual challenge of securing collective agreement coverage of migrant workers – something which is difficult because only few migrants are organized, while many are satisfied with wages below the usual standards. Without such collective agreement coverage, employers are formally free to pay their workers whatever they are willing to accept. This can put pressure on the standards for wages and working conditions of domestic workers.

Second, the sometimes rather large discrepancy between minimum wages and local rates of pay gives rise to problems because migrant workers will seldom enter local negotiations to increase their wages beyond the minimum level. In a sector like construction, the difference between the minimum rate of pay and the average wage amounts to somewhere between 30 and 40 per cent. This implies that the presence of foreign workers can put pressure on the wages of domestic workers even when they are covered by collective agreements. In addition, the migrant workers' lack of engagement with local bargaining can pose a challenge to the institution of local bargaining processes itself. Trade unions see this as a threat to the tradition of workers' active participation in the determination of wages and working conditions.

Third, there are problems with securing all the rights prescribed by collective agreements because migrant workers working temporarily in Norway or Denmark may be less attentive to securing long-term benefits such as pensions and holiday pay. If such costs are not paid, this adds to the economic benefit employers gain from using foreign workers and thus puts pressure on domestic workers. The list of issues could be extended even further, but this will suffice to illustrate some of the similar challenges experienced in the two countries.

However, despite the general similarities between Norway and Denmark, there are some differences between the two countries that may be overlooked from the outside. First, there are some disparities regarding the level of organization and collective agreement coverage. While high unionization rates have long characterized both Nordic countries, these rates vary. Despite some decline over the past 15 years, trade unions still maintain a strong position in Denmark: 67 per cent of the workforce is unionized and 80 per cent is covered by collective agreements. Although still high compared to most European countries, Norway has a lower union density than Denmark: 'only' 52 per cent of employees in Norway are unionized and 'only' 72 per cent enjoy the protection of collective agreements. Furthermore, the Norwegian unions are more restricted than their Danish counterparts when it comes to industrial action. Danish unions are mostly faced with a fixed fine for action that is deemed unlawful, whereas Norwegian unions face a greater threat of having to compensate companies for losses caused by such action. In addition, although Norwegian unions can take industrial action without having members in the targeted firm, this very seldom takes place, unlike in Denmark (Stokke and Thornqvist, 2001). These dissimilarities have given the trade unions in the two countries quite different starting points in facing up to the challenges posed by post-enlargement labour migration.

At the same time, the two countries also differ with regard to their political situation. First, whereas Denmark is a member of the EU, Norway is not. However, it is important to recognize that Norway is a member of the EEA and adopts most of the legislation produced by the EU. Thus, the free movement of workers and services is just as valid in Norway as it is in Denmark. The main difference is that the EU/EEA is an issue that is more open for debate in Norway than in Denmark. In Denmark, a broad majority of political parties support the EU and are keen to mollify popular EU scepticism by toning down problems related to EU membership. Second, the two countries have differed with regard to the political colour of their governments. In the period from 2005 to 2013, Norway had a government led by social democrats, while Denmark had a government led by liberals until September 2011. This means that their respective trade unions have had quite different possibilities for influencing policy.

In Denmark and Norway, as in many other Western European countries, the mobility of labour and services in the wake of EU enlargement exceeded most expectations (Dølvik and Eldring, 2008). In the period from 2000 to 2011, more than 125,000 citizens from new EU member states moved to Norway, and about 75,000 to Denmark. In addition, numerous short-time migrants, posted workers and service providers entered the Danish and Norwegian labour markets. In both countries, these latter groups probably constitute around 40 per cent of the total employment from Central-Eastern Europe (Friberg *et al.*, 2014). It should be noted however that although both countries have experienced an increase in labour migration from European low-wage countries, the level is considerably higher in Norway. This can mainly be explained by the higher labour demand in the Norwegian labour market, which has persisted even throughout the financial crisis.

To sum up, the two countries are very similar in many ways, but there are dissimilarities with regard to their labour market models, their political constellations during the enlargement period and the number of migrants they have received. As we shall see, these dissimilarities have engendered quite different responses to the challenges raised by the new labour migrants, which in turn have affected the understanding of 'social dumping' in the two countries.

Defining social dumping through policy and discourse

Despite the differences described above, the two countries' initial responses to EU enlargement were fairly similar. Both Norway and Denmark established transitional schemes with regard to individual migration from new EU member states. In both countries, these schemes gave open access to the labour markets for workers from CEE countries, as long as the work was performed under employment conditions similar to those of domestic workers. In effect, these transition schemes could be regarded as a kind of temporary *erga omnes* system targeted specifically at the new labour migrants. In this sense, they could be seen as a break with the principles of voluntary collective negotiations that had dominated both countries theretofore. However, these schemes were supported by the trade unions in both Norway and Denmark, which had very similar slogans with regard to the new EU citizens: 'Everyone is welcome, but on equal terms' was the almost identical slogan of both the Norwegian and the Danish trade unions. Seen from this perspective, 'social dumping' would be any kind of unequal treatment, such as lower than normal wages, longer or shorter than normal working hours, and so forth. In this sense, the conditions of domestic workers were the reference point representing the social standards that social dumping practices would challenge.

However, proceeding from these initial similarities, both the policy responses and the discursive representations of the problems raised by the inflow of foreign workers began to diverge between the two countries. In both Norway and Denmark, there has been a constant interplay between the discursive representations made possible by the regulatory context and the regulatory responses made possible by the discursive representations of the issue. We will illustrate this for each country separately and then in the final discussion compare the tendencies we have identified.

Social dumping in Norway

The massive migration from the new EU member states has sparked off various debates in Norway on issues related to 'social dumping'. A simple media analysis clearly illustrates the increasing use of the term: while 'social dumping' was mentioned only 28 times in central news sources in 2003, the term occurred 253 times in 2004, and 446 times in 2006.[2] The debates on social dumping comprise a number of issues, including how the phenomenon should be conceptualized or defined. In Norway, the term acquired a kind of official status and recognition at a very early stage through the red-green government's active use of it and the launch and implementation of action plans to combat such practices. According to the government at the time, social dumping could be defined as follows:

> The government considers it to be social dumping when foreign workers are exposed to violations of health and safety regulations, including regulations on working time and housing standards, and when they are offered wages and other benefits that are unacceptably low compared to what Norwegian workers normally receive, or if the wages are not in compliance with legally extended collective agreements, if such are in place.
>
> (Ministry of Finance, 2006, p. 63)

This approach has served as the point of departure for most discussions on social dumping in Norway in recent years, although some actors claim that practices and standards that may be considered social dumping in the Norwegian context would be seen to be 'social jumping' for workers from societies and labour markets with lower standards, such as Poland (Fasting, 2012; also see Krings *et al.*, Chapter 1, this volume). Some also argue that substandard wage conditions and temporary employment can serve as a stepping stone into more ordinary jobs, and that a requirement of equal standards for all weakens the competitive advantage of migrant workers.

The most disputed issue has been where to draw the line between unacceptable and acceptable wages. While 'social dumping' was almost a non-debated issue a few years back, it is no exaggeration to say that currently this theme has a very prominent place in any debate or political discourse related to the development of the Norwegian labour market (and welfare state). In September 2013, the red-green coalition that had been in power since 2005 lost the parliamentary elections to a coalition headed by the Conservative Party. The red-green government had adopted the fight against social dumping as a kind of power brand, while the opposition voted against several of the implemented measures. The new government has signalled that it will renew policies in this area, but it remains to be seen in what form this will materialize. In the election campaign, both sides declared their willingness to secure a decent working life for all, albeit with some variations regarding the definition of acceptable standards and the ways to achieve them.

The red-green government launched its first action plan against social dumping in 2006. Core elements in the plan were the strengthening of the Labour Inspectorate, the requirement of identity cards for all workers at construction sites, a new register for temporary work agencies, chain liability in construction and certain revisions to the law relating to general application of wage agreements, while regulation of wages was still left to the labour market parties through collective bargaining. The plan was followed up with a new action plan in 2008 and a third action plan in May 2013.

Before 2004, the existing *erga omnes* mechanism in Norway making collective agreements generally binding had never been used. Facing increasing labour migration flows after the 2004 EU enlargement, the Norwegian policy-makers and social partners felt that if basic labour standards were to be upheld in the most exposed industries, the existing institutional framework would be insufficient (Alsos and Eldring, 2008). Largely based on legislation that had been introduced when Norway joined the EEA in 1994 but lain dormant until 2005, the policies for Norwegian labour market regulation have since then gradually changed from a system based on voluntary collective arrangements into one characterized by increasing state involvement in wage regulations. The first step was taken by the Norwegian Confederation of Trade Unions (LO), which, following internal debates, applied for the extension of the collective agreement in construction. This approach has progressed to also embrace industry-wide universal legal extensions of minimum provisions in collective agreements (so far in construction, shipyards, agriculture and cleaning), new legislation on chain liability, and increased control and enforcement by the state, as well as a number of other new statutory regulations regarding registration, liability and control (Eldring *et al.*, 2011). Overall, this shift represents a rather radical break with the traditional form of regulation, and has been promoted by reference to the struggle against 'social dumping'.

However, this break has helped the Norwegian trade unions tackle some of the dilemmas described above. In the sectors covered by *erga omnes*, it is no longer possible for companies to legally pay wages below the minimum wage level stipulated in the collective agreements. The collectively agreed minimum wages have in effect become legally binding, which allows the trade unions to engage directly in legal action against companies paying less than these minimum standards. In practice, however, this may have come at the cost of giving up collective bargaining in foreign companies or unorganized companies that rely on CEE workers. The minimum wage, then, has become the standard of reference for social dumping with regard to CEE workers, but it is a very effective reference in the sense that it does not need to be first imposed upon companies by making them enter into a collective agreement. Although the average wage for Norwegian workers in most sectors is above (and in some sectors far above) the central agreements' wage levels due to local bargaining, the unions at some point decided to accept the minimum rates as the benchmark for social dumping. The arguments were mixed but were mainly related to the idea that upholding a strong principle of equal pay would serve a protectionist purpose and could contribute to the exclusion of migrant workers who would thus lose the possibility of compensating skills, language and productivity differences by being willing to work for lower pay. Furthermore, it was also regarded as rather unrealistic that unions would be able to control the situation by establishing ordinary collective agreements. However, the use of extensions has influenced central collective bargaining in recent years, with higher demands on the unions' side when it comes to raising the agreed minimum rates.

Social dumping in Denmark

The term 'social dumping' has been used much less in Denmark than in Norway. A simple media analysis of the kind already described above shows that 'social dumping' was mentioned only 16 times in central news sources in 2003, and 105 times in 2005, before falling again to 15 times in 2007.[3] One explanation for this trend could be that the labour migration from new EU member states has been less intense compared to what was experienced in Norway. It took some time before Danish employers felt the need for and had the idea of recruiting from the new EU member states. However, this is not the full explanation. If we look at the media coverage, the new flow of migrants and the potential problems they could cause received quite a lot of attention in Denmark from the onset, but these problems were not subsumed under the heading of 'social dumping' as they were in Norway. Instead, there seem to be three different themes at play: first, a theme regarding criminal behaviour such as tax fraud, circumvention of the transitional regime, undocumented workers and conmen; second, a theme regarding working conditions, low wages, long working hours, and poor health and safety; finally, a third theme concerning the general ill treatment or exploitation of this new group of migrant workers, pointing to poor housing conditions, threats of violence and spontaneous dismissal. In a sense, all of these issues are part of the phenomenon of social dumping because they all contribute to the pressure on social standards and they are all themes found in the Norwegian debate on social dumping. However, in Denmark it was not until 2011 that all of these issues were summarized under the heading of 'social dumping'.

There are two explanations for this difference. First, unlike Norway, Denmark has sought to maintain the existing framework of voluntary collective bargaining, with the social partners opposing any moves towards increasing state regulation in response to international labour mobility (Andersen and Pedersen, 2010). Despite some internal debate, the Danish trade unions generally felt that the high level of collective agreement coverage, the high level of trade union affiliation and the relative ease with which unions could take industrial action together gave them sufficient strength to handle the challenges that the new migrant flow would present (Eldring *et al.*, 2012). It was assumed that the stronger Danish framework would be sufficient to resist the main problems associated with low-wage competition and worker exploitation in the face of increasing labour migration. Neither the trade unions nor the employers' organizations were willing to accept the problems raised by *erga omnes* procedures and the like. This has meant, however, that the regulatory issues posed by the new flow of labour migration have to be divided into two separate spheres that trade unionists, politicians and employers alike have struggled hard to keep distinct: on the one hand, issues regulated by law (tax fraud, undocumented workers, violation of health and safety rules, etc.) and, on the other, issues regulated by collective agreements (wages, working hours, overtime pay, pensions, etc.). For a long time, trade unionists made a virtue out of making this distinction clear and thus implicitly promoted a disaggregation of the problems that could otherwise have been summarized under the heading of 'social dumping'.

Second, the centre-right government in office from the enlargement in 2004 until 2011 never used the term 'social dumping' or any such terms that could highlight generalities of issues related to the new flow of workers. Instead, it treated incidences of tax fraud, low wages, or poor health and safety precisely as 'incidences' – singular events to be deplored and criticized, but not to be taken as representative of a broader social phenomenon calling for a regulatory response. Thus, the centre-right government not only disassociated itself from all issues regulated by collective agreements, but also gave little priority to a number of issues that fell within its regulatory competence (such as health and safety, tax inspection and the enforcement of the transitional regime in place until 2009). In addition, it made few efforts to improve the statistical material on the issue, and only reacted to difficulties if trade unions or the media provided clear evidence that there were systematic problems. This meant that the trade unions for a long time invested considerable day-to-day efforts in mobilizing the authorities to perform their duties in areas regulated by law and in documenting that these were general problems. The fundamental problem for the trade unions, so to speak, was the lack of a term like 'social dumping' that would transform any incidence of low pay, tax evasion or illegal activity into a manifestation of a more general social phenomenon.

This changed somewhat in 2011. Following the general election, a new centre-left government came into office and made 'social dumping' one of its prioritized policy areas. On the regulatory front, this has meant a number of legal initiatives, including a reform of the tax system that makes it very hard and costly to evade taxes, and a stronger emphasis on registration and statistics. More importantly, however, it has meant a significant increase in the resources, activities and competences of the labour inspectors, tax collectors and police in this area. They are now engaged in joint enforcement efforts, including multi-annual random checks of companies. At the discursive level, in 2012 the new government published an inter-ministerial report containing the first official definition of 'social dumping'. Along with the priority given to social dumping in the national budget negotiations of 2012 and 2013, this shows that the new government has really taken ownership of the concept. The 2012 inter-ministerial report defines social dumping in the following way:

> The concept of social dumping denotes relationships where foreign workers experience wages and working conditions below the usual Danish standards. This refers to conditions similar to relevant collective agreements in the sector. Social dumping also refers to situations in the labour market where foreign companies operate in Denmark without complying with Danish laws and regulations such as those regarding tax authorities, health, social security, and residence and work permits.
>
> (Danish Ministry of Employment, 2012, p. 12; authors' translation)

This definition clearly signals that the new government is well aware of the distinction between issues regulated by law and issues regulated by collective agreements. While the new government has increased efforts to tackle tax evasion, health and safety violations, and violations of the registration rules for foreign companies, it has left it up to trade unions and employers to resolve issues regarding low wages, long working hours without overtime payment, non-payment of pensions and other similar matters. However, the definition is not completely neutral in this respect. The former government's lack of engagement with the problems related to new labour migration had allowed the trade unions to define and articulate these issues almost single-handedly. Thus, the Danish trade unions were able to promote the ideal of equal treatment as the social standard against which social dumping should be measured. They therefore regarded wages below the average as an expression of social dumping even when they were within the bounds of the minimum wages stipulated by collective agreements. Employers, however, have increasingly tried to challenge this position by arguing that wages within the bounds of the collective agreements (even if they are far below the average wages within the same sector) should not be seen as social dumping. By equating social dumping with conditions below the standards of the relevant collective agreement in the sector, the new centre-left government seems to have lent some support to this employer argument, just as the emphasis on minimum standards seems to be in line with the European Court of Justice rulings in the *Laval* and *Rüffert* cases. All in all, this leaves the trade unions somewhat alone in their equal treatment perspective on social dumping.

Thus, the efforts of the Danish trade unions have come under pressure on several fronts. They are still faced with the dilemmas described above: that is, firms uncovered by collective agreements that can legally pay wages far below the minimum wage level; the lack of local negotiation, causing the minimum wage to become the normal wage for CEE workers; and the problems of obtaining the full benefits laid out in the collective agreements. As the main regulator of these issues, the trade unions have used considerable resources on industrial action against foreign companies. This has, however, been an uphill struggle and the problems seem to be persisting (Andersen and Arnholtz Hansen, 2008). As a result, the trade unions also tried to get new deals and tools through the collective bargaining rounds of 2007, 2010 and 2012. To some extent they have been successful, but on crucial issues, such as chain liability and large increases in the minimum wage, the employers have said no. Thus, the rhetoric of 'social dumping' may have helped to mobilize public opinion and political goodwill, but it has done little to improve negotiation positions vis-à-vis employers. In fact, the greater momentum gained in the political arena through the increasing use of the concept of social dumping has led to growing resistance by employer organizations to tackle the problems related to the issue. Instead, the employers have aimed at challenging the concept and using the low wages of CEE migrant and posted workers to attack Danish workers for being too picky about which jobs they want to accept.

Discussion

In both the Norwegian and the Danish contexts, we can identify company strategies similar to those described as 'social dumping' elsewhere in this volume. In fact, the analytical distinctions proposed by Lillie and Berntsen, as well as empirical material presented in other chapters, will surely be very useful for understanding some of the dynamics encountered in Norway and Denmark. However, we would argue that a focus on company strategies is not sufficient for understanding the phenomenon of social dumping. We need to also take account of the political struggles to define and delimit what social dumping is. To us, social dumping is not just a reality out there; it is also a category of perception that helps actors make sense of this reality.

We would therefore argue that scholars need to analyse not only the specific mechanisms and processes that put pressure on social standards, but also the political – both discursive and regulatory – struggles that determine whether such mechanisms and processes are understood as being acceptable and natural parts of an integrated European labour market *or* whether they are understood as an expression of abnormal and problematic tendencies. That is, to use Foucault's vocabulary, we need to study not just the abnormal and the efforts to normalize it; we need to also study the normation process that defines it as abnormal and thus in need of normalization.

However, we are very eager to make clear that we are not arguing that social dumping is 'just' a political catchphrase. We hope to have shown that it actually matters quite a lot whether such terms are used or not.

In the Norwegian context, the previous government's consequent and upfront use of the term 'social dumping' has unquestionably contributed to keeping issues related to increased low-wage competition and the substandard conditions of migrant and posted workers high on the public and the political agenda. Although neither the government's 'definition' of the term nor its action plans drew a crystal-clear line between acceptable and non-acceptable wage levels, it seems as though they served its purposes both on a rhetorical and practical level. First, to a certain degree it made it less relevant for unions to criticize the authorities for not adequately addressing the matters related to the harsh conditions of migrant workers and social dumping. Second, because so many policy measures were directly linked to the concept of social dumping, even those who initially strongly opposed the term eventually used it. In fact, even the Conservative Party's (Høyre) parliamentarian group at some point established an internal party committee labelled the 'social dumping group' that worked on developing policies to counteract the negative effects of labour migration. Third, it seems that the widespread use of the term exhausted (at least temporarily) the earlier debates between the political parties and the labour market actors on what social dumping really is, and moved them forward to more policy-oriented and practical discussions on how to do something about 'it'. However, it is very likely that the new government with its Minister of Labour coming from the right-wing Progress Party will challenge the relevance of the term and try to revive the debates on what social dumping is or is not.

In Denmark the situation has been the reverse. Without the term 'social dumping' to organize and give meaning to particular events, Danish trade unions struggled hard to illustrate the commonalities and thus the general tendency constituted by the pressures and issues raised by the new flow of labour migrants since EU eastern enlargement. After the term was adopted by the new Danish government in 2011, it has been employers (and recently also the Polish ambassador) who have had to dispute the relevancy of the term by arguing – often on a case-by-case basis – that some of the incidences claimed to be 'social dumping' are simply an expression of the market competition Denmark signed up for when it joined the EU. As such, the shift that has occurred in Denmark due to the change in government is a perfect illustration of the fact that a continuing struggle is going on – right now – about the very definition of social dumping, its limits and its substance. Both in Norway and Denmark, employers are pushing – through political rhetoric and legal arguments – to redefine the boundaries of the acceptable social standards, just as trade unions are trying to uphold these standards in part by articulating them as self-evident. In these struggles, both the lack of government recognition of the term social dumping and the way governments define the term may have implications for how actors can act and which practical steps they can take. As shown above, the centre-right Danish government's lack of engagement with the term made it difficult for the trade unions to establish the commonality between incidences, but also allowed them to maintain for far longer a perception that any kind of unequal treatment is by definition social dumping. By contrast, the adoption of the term as an official category by the new centre-left government has helped the trade unions make the case that a general problem is at stake and that public initiatives are needed, but at the same time it has put pressure on the unions to accept that only wages and working conditions below the minimum standards of the collective agreements are in fact social dumping.

Thus, rather than wanting to suggest that social dumping is 'just' a political catchphrase – a social or discursive construction without any importance for reality – we want to highlight that our analysis implies that there is a double challenge facing those wanting to maintain social standards. On the one hand, they have to engage in a number of practical efforts to prevent and challenge the systematic circumventions and violations of the norms that establish social standards. On the other hand, they also have to engage in a political struggle to define and defend the social standards at a discursive level, and to do so in a way that enables their practical struggles to prevent circumventions. To use the vocabulary of Foucault once again, the practical efforts to 'normalize' the wages and working conditions of migrant workers are heavily dependent on the 'normation' process that defines what is normal, but this 'normation' process is in itself heavily dependent on the practical problems encountered in the process of normalization.

It is in relation to this dual challenge that we can see the subtle difference between the Norwegian and the Danish approaches. Wanting to maintain their traditional institutional set-up, in part to insist on equal treatment as the standard for evaluating social dumping, the Danish trade unions are facing massive challenges in defining social dumping in a way that allows them to get practical support from the new centre-left government. In contrast, the willingness of the Norwegian trade unions to accept fundamental changes in the institutional set-up of the labour market has allowed them to acquire a number of effective tools for handling social dumping, but only at the cost of redefining social dumping in a way that makes less than equal treatment acceptable.

Finally, it is worth noting that actors are always located in a context that allows for different ways of handling challenges. If we were to put forward some of the factors that have caused the differences described between these two similar countries, we would emphasize factors that are related to the size of the inflow of labour migrants, to the strength of the trade unions, and to their institutional and political environment.

First, the severity of the challenge posed by migrant workers has influenced trade union strategies. Here, the – both numerically and institutionally – weaker Norwegian unions have been faced with far larger numbers of migrant workers than have their stronger Danish counterparts. This has given them greater reasons to follow a more pragmatic approach to setting a minimum threshold by way of *erga omnes*, chain liability and so forth. In contrast, the lower number of migrant workers in Denmark, and the greater possibility to impose collective agreements upon them, has given Danish trade unions leeway to take into account the consequences institutional change would potentially have for their purely domestic struggles. For them, preserving the principle of equal treatment has gone hand in hand with an insistence on the importance of local bargaining, which is crucial for maintaining trade union power at the local level. However, the economic downturn caused by the crisis has made the Danish unions more pragmatic; as the number of migrant workers continues to increase in sectors where the employment of Danish workers has declined significantly, the trade unions have called for help from politicians. National measures on chain liability and ILO 94 labour clauses in the public procurement tenders of municipalities are some of the measures trade unions are now calling for, even though they are slightly at odds with Danish tradition.

Second, the composition of the government has had an effect upon the trade unions' possibilities for building alliances. As already mentioned, an alliance to counter social dumping was made very early on between the unions and the government in Norway. It was in the context of this alliance that it was possible to introduce *erga omnes* and chain liability. While there was a broad coalition behind the Danish transitional regime, it is quite unlikely that the centre-right government would have agreed to introduce *erga omnes* and chain liability if the trade unions had so requested.

Conclusion

In this chapter we have attempted to show that the understanding of what constitutes social standards and accordingly social dumping can vary, even between very similar countries faced with very similar challenges. We have also argued that the understanding of social dumping is developing over time and that at this very moment a political struggle is taking place in both Norway and Denmark to define and redefine what social dumping is. Drawing upon Foucault, we have argued that it is important to pay attention to the abnormalities (understood as the strategies used by firms to undermine or circumvent social standards), to the normalization efforts (understood as the practical efforts of authorities and trade unions to counter this circumvention) and also to the normation process (understood as the process by which acceptable and unacceptable social standards are continuously defined). From this point of view, we want to argue that both the systematic violation of social standards and the redefinition of social standards may be seen as part of the phenomenon known as social dumping.

Notes

1 The analysis of the Norwegian data in this chapter has been carried out in part within the framework of a research programme on labour migration (funded by the Norwegian Ministry of Labour) and a research programme on collective bargaining (funded by the Norwegian Confederation of Trade Unions (LO)).

2 Source: Search via Retriever in *Aftenposten, Bergens Tidende, Dagens Næringsliv, Dagsavisen, Nordlys, NTB, Stavanger Aftenblad, VG.*

3 Source: Search via MediaInfo in *Jyllands-Posten, Politiken, Børsen, Berlinske Tidende og Weekendavisen.*

References

Alsos, K. and Eldring, L. (2008) 'Labour Mobility and Wage Dumping: The Case of Norway'. *European Journal of Industrial Relations*, 14(4): 441–459.

Andersen, S.K. and Arnholtz, J. (2013) 'Udfordringen fra øst – Fagforningsstrategier og den østeuropæiske arbejdskraft'. *Økonomi og Politik*, 86(1): 45–57.

Andersen, S.K. and Arnholtz Hansen, J. (2008) 'Strong Trade Unions Meet EEC Workers – Locating, Monitoring and Organizing EEC Workers in the Danish Construction Sector'. In Blanpain, R. and Dickens, L. (eds), *Challenges in European Employment Relations.* AH Alphen aan den Rijn: Kluwer Law International, pp. 101–116.

Andersen, S.K. and Pedersen, K. (2010) 'Social Dumping'. *FAOS forskningsnotat 110.* Copenhagen: FAOS.

Arnholtz, J. and Hansen, N.W. (2013) 'Labour Market Specific Institutions and the Working Conditions of Labour Migrants: The Case of Polish Migrant Labour in the Danish Labour Market'. *Economic and Industrial Democracy*, 34(3): 399–420.

Arnholtz Hansen, J. and Hansen, N.W. (2009) 'Polonia i København – et studie af polske arbejdsmigranters løn-, arbejds- og levevilkår i Storkøbenhavn'. *LO-Dokumentation*, No. 1. Copenhagen: LO, Danish Confederation of Trade Unions.

Barrett, A., McGuinness, S. and O'Brien, M. (2012) 'The Immigrant Earnings Disadvantage across the Earnings and Skills Distributions: The Case of Immigrants from the EU's New Member States'. *British Journal of Industrial Relations*, 50(3): 457–481.

Bengtsson, E. (2013) 'Swedish Trade Unions and European Union Migrant Workers'. *Journal of Industrial Relations*, 55(2): 174–189.

Cremers, J. (2011) *In Search of Cheap Labour in Europe – Working and Living Conditions of Posted Workers*, CLR Studies 6. Brussels: European Institute for Construction Labour Research.

Danish Ministry of Employment (2012) *Rapport fra udvalget om bekæmpelse af social dumping* [Report from the Committee on Countering Social Dumping]. Copenhagen: Beskæftigelsesministeriet.

Dølvik, J.E. (2011) 'State and Markets beyond the Crises: The Nordic Example'. In Cramme, O. (ed.), *Priorities for a New Political Economy: Memos to the Left.* London: Policy Network, pp. 39–45.

Dølvik, J.E. and Eldring, L. (2008) *Arbeidsmobilitet fra de nye EU-landene til Norden – Utviklingstrekk og konsekvenser.* Copenhagen: Nordic Council of Ministers.

Eldring, L. and Alsos, K. (2012) 'European Minimum Wage: A Nordic Outlook'. *Fafo-report*, No. 2012:16. Oslo: Fafo.

Eldring, L. and Arnholtz Hansen, J. (2009) 'Fagbevegelsen og arbeidsinnvandring: Strategier og resultater i Norge og Danmark'. *Søkelys på Arbeidslivet*, 1: 1–16.

Eldring, L., Fitzgerald, I. and Arnholtz, J. (2012) 'Post-accession Migration in Construction and Trade Union Responses in Denmark, Norway and the UK'. *European Journal of Industrial Relations*, 18(1): 21–36.

Eldring, L., Ødegård, A.M., Andersen, R.K., Bråten, M., Nergaard, K. and Alsos, K. (2011) 'Evaluering av tiltak mot sosial dumping'. *Fafo-report*, No. 2011:09. Oslo: Fafo.

Fasting, M. (2012) 'Social jumping'. *CIVITA.* Available at: www.civita.no/2012/07/06/social-jumping (accessed 1 September 2014).

Foucault, M. (2007) *Security, Territory, Population.* New York: Palgrave Macmillan.
Friberg, J.H. and Eldring, L. (2011) 'Polonia i Oslo 2010: Mobilitet, arbeid og levekår blant polakker i hovedstaden'. *Fafo-rapport*, no. 2011:27. Oslo: Fafo.
Friberg, J.H. and Eldring, L. (eds) (2013) *Labour Migrants from Central and Eastern Europe in the Nordic Countries – Patterns of Migration, Working Conditions and Recruitment Practices*. TemaNord Series, No. 570. Copenhagen: Nordic Council of Ministers.
Friberg, J.H. and Tyldum, G. (2007) 'Polonia i Oslo – En studie av arbeids- og levekår blant polakker i hovedstadsområdet'. *Fafo-report*, No. 2007:27. Oslo: Fafo.
Friberg, J.H., Arnholtz, J., Eldring, L., Hansen, N.W. and Thorarins, F. (2014) 'Nordic Labour Market Institutions and New Migrant Workers: Polish Migrants in Oslo, Copenhagen and Reykjavik'. *European Journal of Industrial Relations*, 20(1): 37–53.
Lillie, N. (2010) 'Bringing the Offshore Ashore: Transnational Production, Industrial Relations and the Reconfiguration of Sovereignty'. *International Studies Quarterly*, 54(3): 683–704.
Ministry of Finance (2006) *St. meld. nr.2 (2005–2006). Revidert nasjonalbudsjett 2006.* Oslo: Ministry of Finance.
Stokke, T.A. and Thornqvist, C. (2001) 'Strikes and Collective Bargaining in the Nordic Countries'. *European Journal of Industrial Relations*, 7(3): 245–267.
Stokke, T.A., Nergaard, K. and Evju, S. (2013) *Det kollektive arbeidslivet.* Oslo: Universitetsforlaget.
Traxler, F., Arrowsmith, J., Nergaard, K. and Molins, J. (2007) 'Organized Decentralization: The Backbone of Multi-level Bargaining? A Cross-national Comparison of Variable Pay in the Banking Sector'. In *European Conference of the International Industrial Relations Association*, Manchester, 3–6 September.
Wagner, I. (2014) 'Rule Enactment in a Pan-European Labour Market: Transnational Posted Work in the German Construction Sector'. *British Journal of Industrial Relations*. Published online at: DOI: 10.1111/bjir.12053. Abstract available at: http://onlinelibrary.wiley.com/doi/10.1111/bjir.12053/abstract (accessed 1 September 2014).
Woolfson, C. (2007) 'Labour Standards and Migration in the New Europe: Post-Communist Legacies and Perspectives'. *European Journal of Industrial Relations*, 13(2): 199–218.

5 Socioeconomic cleavages between workers from new member states and host-country labour forces in the EU during the Great Recession

Martin Guzi and Martin Kahanec

Introduction

The 2004 and 2007 EU enlargements led to the relocation, over the period 2004 to 2010, of about three million workers from the new EU member states to the old. The free mobility of workers in the enlarged EU provided a wider set of possibilities for its citizens and improved the allocative efficiency of EU labour markets (Kahanec and Zimmermann, 2010). The receiving countries gained additional 'hands and brains' without being generally affected in terms of natives' aggregate wages or employment (Kahanec, 2013); the sending countries, in turn, were relieved of labour slack and benefited from remittances. 'Brain drain' has been a potential risk for the sending countries, but the literature actually points to the possibility of 'brain gain', which may occur when migrants return to their home countries with additional skills acquired abroad or when the home population invests more in education in expectation of higher returns due to the possibility of using skills more freely abroad (see Zaiceva and Zimmerman, forthcoming). Similarly, although the down-skilling into jobs below a worker's qualifications that characterizes much of post-enlargement migration appears undesirable, it is unclear whether real inefficiencies vis-à-vis feasible counterfactual scenarios have materialized (Kahanec, 2013).[1]

Against this generally positive perspective, there are some fears that post-enlargement migration has created socioeconomic cleavages between workers from new EU member states and the labour force in the receiving countries in areas such as pay, access to employment and/or employment quality.[2] Such cleavages could – either directly or as a side effect – undermine economic and social standards in the receiving countries. The effects of immigration, then, may not immediately concern the wages or employment of natives, but rather materialize as persistent immigrant–native gaps in labour market outcomes, with potentially detrimental effects for the social fabric and cohesion of the receiving labour markets.

In this chapter, we use EU-wide micro-level datasets from Eurostat to empirically document labour market gaps between domestic labour forces and migrants from new EU member states. We distinguish between two origins of immigrant–native labour market gaps. First, we look at those parts of the observed raw gaps that can be explained by differences in the characteristics of immigrant and native populations. Such 'explained' gaps arise due to factors determined outside of the receiving labour market, including gaps in population characteristics between receiving and sending countries, the characteristics of migrants who decided to move from new EU member states, and immigrant–native differences in patterns of human capital acquisition in the receiving country.[3] These kinds of gaps could lead to immigrant–native inequalities and may call for policies that would mitigate problematic cleavages and provide for a cohesive and mutually beneficial coexistence between diverse populations. On their own, however, their existence does not indicate unequal treatment or differences in behaviour of otherwise equal immigrants and natives in the labour market.

Second, we measure gaps that are not explained by differences in characteristics between immigrant and native populations. Cleavages defined and measured in this way may result from differences in individual preferences, social or ethnic capital, discrimination, or other unobserved variables. The existence of unexplained gaps may be related to the segmentation of migrants into jobs of lower social or economic status. This may occur, for example, (1) as a temporary phenomenon related to adjustment to the demand for skills specific to the host country; (2) as a consequence of processes outside migrants' control such as discrimination; or (3) as an outcome of choices made by migrants as individuals or collectivities. As an example of choice-driven segmentation, some temporary migrants such as nurses may find it unprofitable – given the short time horizon over which the returns can be reaped – to invest in country-specific skills such as the language of the host country and may thus take up jobs below their formal qualification (e.g. domestic help or service activities), possibly with longer working hours (Kahanec and Shields, 2013).

Likewise, unexplained gaps in labour market outcomes between natives and immigrants may also signify strategic behaviour on the part of immigrant workers or the companies employing them aimed at reducing the costs of migrant labour as a consequence of any unobserved disadvantages or vulnerabilities migrant workers might face. In such circumstances, migrant workers may end up working for substandard remuneration or under substandard working conditions and, compared to observably similar natives, may not be integrated into the host country's social systems, work safety standards or collective bargaining agreements – a situation defined in this volume as social dumping. With regard to remuneration, for example, migrant workers may be willing to accept working for less than what is normally paid to observably similar natives (with similar qualifications, occupation and other characteristics) if it gives them a competitive advantage or, perhaps more accurately, compensates for some unobserved disadvantage (also see Krings *et al.*, Chapter 1, this volume). All in all, then, unexplained gaps signify different treatment or behaviour of observationally equal immigrant and native populations in the labour market and signal social cleavages arising as a consequence of the functioning of the labour market. A policy intervention aimed at the reduction of such cleavages would therefore need to change the way in which immigrants and natives interact in the host-country labour market.[4]

Although there is consensus in the literature that immigrants generally adjust in terms of their labour market status the more time they spend in the host country (Chiswick, 1978; Borjas, 1985; Kahanec and Zaiceva, 2009), the economic crisis that struck Europe shortly after the 2004 and 2007 EU enlargements, referred to in this chapter as the Great Recession, may have stalled or even reversed such adjustment processes. In addition, the significant increase in east–west mobility may have changed the nature of labour market competition in the receiving labour markets or have had consequences for the process of adjustment. East–west mobility within the EU may have interacted with inflows of non-EU migrants, resulting in heightened competition in the labour market (Biavaschi and Zimmermann, 2014; Marchetti *et al.*, 2014). These effects could vary across different aspects of the market, such as labour market participation, employment and its quality, or the incidence of self-employment.

This chapter provides a comprehensive perspective on labour market cleavages between migrants from new EU member states and natives in old EU member states for the period following the EU enlargements of 2004 and 2007 and during the Great Recession. It thus sheds light on how post-enlargement mobility, interacting with the consequences of the downturn, has affected the social fabric in the receiving countries. The chapter is structured as follows. In the first section, we discuss the main patterns and factors of immigrant integration in Europe. We then focus on post-enlargement migration and the integration of migrants from new EU member states in the old EU member states before and during the crisis. The methodology for measuring immigrant–native gaps and the data we use are outlined in the following sections. Finally, we measure immigrant–native labour market gaps, distinguishing between the part attributable to differences in the characteristics of the two groups and the cleavages resulting from unobservable factors. Brief conclusions follow.

Migrants and natives in European labour markets

The literature on migration and immigrant integration reports significant differences in the labour market outcomes of immigrants and natives, which may fade away, however, with immigrants' tenure in the host country (Kahanec and Zaiceva, 2009). Dustmann and Frattini (2011) investigate the labour market performance of EU and non-EU immigrants in Belgium, Germany, Finland, France and Italy. Using the 2009 wave of the EU Labour Force Survey (EU-LFS), the authors find that immigrant earnings are located at the bottom of the overall earnings distribution. They show that around 75 per cent of migrant households from new EU member states have earnings below the median income of native households. After controlling for demographic characteristics such as gender, age, education and occupation, the probability of being at the bottom of the earnings profile remains significantly higher for EU and non-EU migrants than for natives in Belgium, France and Italy.

Some of the theoretical explanations for the differences between immigrants and comparable natives include those based on the market value of the education acquired in different sending countries, the lack of country-specific skills such as language and/or knowledge of the receiving countries' labour market institutions, precarious employment, spatial segregation, institutional factors and various forms of discrimination (Huber *et al.*, 2010; De la Rica *et al.*, 2015). Language skills, for example, contribute positively to immigrants' human capital and increase their productivity in the labour market. In addition, the acquisition of language fosters social and economic integration. The relevance of language may be less significant for high-skilled workers, who are more likely to work in positions with English rather than the local language as the working language. It may also be the case, however, that immigrants, even those who are less skilled, work in ethnic enclaves and communicate in their own language at work. The link between language proficiency and productivity has been empirically substantiated by several studies. For Germany, Dustmann and Van Soest (2002) use a panel data analysis to show that a good command of the German language is associated with a 10 per cent wage premium among migrants. For Spain, Amuedo-Dorantes and De la Rica (2007) report that Latin American immigrants perform better in the labour market than immigrants from non-Spanish-speaking countries, thus supporting the idea that language is an important determinant of employment and earnings gaps. Entorf and Minoiu (2005) provide interesting evidence regarding the importance of language in European countries. The authors observe that students with foreign parents and the foreign language spoken at home underperform relative to their native counterparts in the PISA evaluation. The educational disadvantage of immigrant children may translate into a disadvantage on the labour market later in life.

Immigrants appear to be disadvantaged relative to natives also in terms of their employment probabilities and occupational distribution. Dustmann and Frattini (2011) investigate the labour market performance of immigrant workers from other EU countries using a pooled sample of EU-LFS surveys from 2007 to 2009. The authors show that even if immigrants and natives lived in the same areas and had identical demographic characteristics, immigrants would still have lower employment probabilities than natives in all countries except for Greece, where the conditional difference was found to be close to zero. The authors further measure the degree of segmentation of immigrants into particular occupations. Controlling for workers' age, gender, education and region of residence, they find that in most countries, EU immigrants work in less skilled occupations relative to their native counterparts. Only in Belgium, Finland, Ireland and the Netherlands does the occupational disadvantage between natives and EU immigrants disappear.

The labour market situation of migrants also depends on the level of their formal education. Huber *et al.* (2010) propose that high-skilled migrants are more vulnerable and face higher unemployment risks than low-skilled migrants when it comes to finding employment on arrival in a new country. Low-skilled migrants have lower chances that any job offered to them will be below their qualification, so ultimately more job offers are acceptable to them compared to highly skilled migrants. A conditional analysis based on EU-LFS data from

2006/2007 confirms the hypothesis that high-skilled migrant workers have lower probabilities of employment compared to less skilled migrants; this outcome holds generally for migrants across the origins distinguished in the survey. The authors further confirm that high- and medium-skilled migrants have a significantly higher probability of being over-qualified than natives, conditional on gender, age and sector of employment. Migrants from the EU-12 exhibit the highest probability of over-qualification in employment, while the probability of over-qualification is significantly lower for migrants born in the EU-15.[5]

Dustmann and Frattini (2011) show that the labour market performance of immigrants improves with time spent in the host country. Similarly, Huber *et al.* (2010) show that the probability of employment of the foreign born of all skill levels increases with the duration of their stay. These findings are corroborated by Kahanec and Zaiceva (2009), who compare the role of nativity and citizenship in old and new EU member states and show that it is foreign origin that is the key factor in Western Europe, whereas in Central-Eastern Europe (CEE), both foreign origin and citizenship result in substantial labour market gaps.

The higher incidence of precarious employment observed among immigrants may arise from a variety of factors, including labour market rigidities that tend to favour insiders over outsiders. Dustmann and Frattini (2011) point to the role of institutions, reporting that in countries with stricter employment protection legislation, the occupational distribution of immigrants is different to that of the natives, particularly for immigrants from outside the EU-15. The authors explain that in countries with higher employment protection, access to particular occupations is more difficult for immigrants, while the probability of employment is not associated with the protection legislation. D'Amuri and Peri (2010) confirm that immigrants push natives into occupations with higher skill contents in Europe, and that the reallocation is more intense in less protected markets. The authors conclude that a high degree of labour market protection reduces labour markets' ability to absorb immigrants through the occupational upgrading of natives.

The labour market status of immigrants is shown to be more sensitive to the business cycle than that of natives. Dustmann *et al.* (2010) find that the unemployment probabilities of immigrants in Germany and the UK are significantly more sensitive to the economic cycle than those of natives, even after conditioning for individual characteristics and the region of residence. De la Rica and Polonyankina (2013) explain how recently arrived immigrants displaced earlier immigrants during the recession years in Spain. They also demonstrate a negative impact of competition for jobs during the Great Recession. Specifically, for 2008 to 2012, the authors show that relative to natives, immigrants in Spain moved into jobs characterized by higher manual content, such as those requiring finger dexterity, body coordination and strength.

The evidence of discrimination against immigrants is based on their differential treatment in the labour market compared to natives with the same qualifications (e.g. lower call-back rates in response to submitted job applications). An edited volume by Kahanec and Zimmermann (2011) maps the social and labour market situation of ethnic minorities in Europe and demonstrates that immigrant and ethnic minority groups are often disadvantaged by unobservable factors such as gaps in social or ethnic capital, but also discrimination. Kahanec and Zaiceva (2009) report that while immigrants and non-citizens may possess sociodemographic characteristics that are superior to those possessed by native populations in the labour market, unobserved factors – such as discrimination – disadvantage them significantly. Kahanec *et al.* (2013) map the barriers to immigrant inclusion in the European labour markets and welfare systems: language barriers and human capital gaps, problematic recognition of foreign qualifications, unequal treatment, lack of transparency in the labour market and legal barriers.

Post-enlargement migration and the Great Recession

Following the EU enlargements of 2004 and 2007, the gradual extension of the right of free movement of workers enabled many citizens from new EU member states to seek employment in the old EU member states. As a consequence, the inflows of workers from CEE to Western European countries have risen significantly since 2004, although the trend declined sharply during the crisis (Kahanec, 2013). Zaiceva and Zimmermann (2008) evaluate the scale, diversity and determinants of labour migration in Europe and observe different patterns of migration into EU-15 countries. Cultural, linguistic and geographical distances between pairs of source and destination countries are found to be an important determinant of migration inflows. While Poland was the main sending country to most of the EU-15 countries, Estonians are dominant in Finland, and Romanians in Spain and Italy. Because these new migrants' decision to leave their own countries is for the most part driven by employment considerations, and because typical barriers to mobility such as visa or residence and work permits do not constrain their mobility within the EU (following the expiry of transitional arrangements wherever they were applied), these new migrant populations are quite fluid and able to respond to changing economic conditions (Pytliková, 2014; Kahanec *et al.*, forthcoming).

The Great Recession had a profound impact on the world economy, with significant consequences for European economies. It adversely affected labour markets, causing unemployment to increase rapidly across Europe. If immigrant workers encounter disadvantages in the labour market, these may remain latent in better times, but they become acute during economic downturns when jobs are destroyed and the competition for jobs intensifies. On the other hand, as immigrants from the EU-12 tend to be skilled and young (Kahanec, 2013), they may more easily move to alternative destinations within Europe; one could thus expect them to be relatively resilient to the crisis.

However, a recent OECD SOPEMI report (2013) shows that the recent downturn has had a substantial negative impact upon the labour force and especially on foreign-born individuals. The report uses individual EU-LFS data to descriptively compare the employment, unemployment and long-term unemployment trends of native and immigrant workers. The findings suggest that young and low-skilled migrants were among the most affected, while the performance of women and high-skilled migrants was less affected during the recession. Voicu and Vlase (2012) use three waves of the European Social Survey to confirm that high-skilled immigrants exhibited a greater ability to remain in paid employment during the recent crisis relative to medium- and low-skilled immigrants. However, the authors show as well that the high-skilled immigrants had lower odds of obtaining employment as compared to high-skilled natives, and that these differences were amplified during the economic downturn.

The OECD report further finds that a large share of the job losses was concentrated among those with temporary and fixed-term contracts and among those working in construction and manufacturing – in other words, in types of jobs and sectors with a high concentration of migrants. On the other hand, the services sector in Europe has recorded the greatest increases in migrant employment, given that many new jobs were created in 'residential care activities', 'activities of households as employers of domestic personnel' and 'human health services'. The balance of the effects of being a migrant in the enlarged EU during the Great Recession is thus an empirical question, which we will investigate in the next section.

Measuring migrant–native gaps

In the analysis of labour market gaps between natives and migrants from new EU member states, we employ the Blinder (1973) and Oaxaca (1973) counterfactual decomposition technique to study mean outcome differences between these groups. Non-linear regression models are applied to decompose the difference in an outcome variable between two groups – native and immigrant population – into a part that is attributed to differences in characteristics (interpreted as an explained component that does not imply any treatment or behavioural disparities in the labour market[6]) and an unexplained component that arises due to behavioural or treatment inequalities between observably equal workers in the labour market.

We adapt the framework to represent two groups, native (n) and migrant (m) individuals, characterized by two relationships:

$$Y_n = \alpha_n + X'_n \beta_n + \varepsilon_n \tag{1}$$

$$Y_m = \alpha_m + X'_m \beta_m + \varepsilon_m , \tag{2}$$

where Y is the outcome variable; X is the vector of individual characteristics; α and β are the intercept and the vector of coefficients, respectively; ε is an error term; and subscripts m and n denote migrants and natives, respectively. Each regression model also includes country dummies. In order to examine the sources of outcome differences between natives and migrants, a counterfactual equation is constructed where migrants are treated as natives. In other words, the intercept and coefficient in the migrants' equation are replaced by those of the natives' equation Y_m^*.

The average gap between natives and migrants can be decomposed into a characteristics effect (that is, differences between natives' outcome and counterfactual outcome), and a coefficients effect (that is, differences between counterfactual outcome and migrants' outcome).[7] The Blinder–Oaxaca decomposition equation is:

$$\bar{Y}_n - \bar{Y}_m = (\bar{X}_n - \bar{X}_m)'\hat{\beta}_n + \bar{X}'_m(\hat{\beta}_n - \hat{\beta}_m) \tag{3}$$

where $\bar{X}_n$ and $\bar{X}_m$ are vectors including the means of the variables for natives and migrants, respectively, and $\hat{\beta}_n$ and $\hat{\beta}_m$ are estimated coefficients from regressions (1) and (2). The first term of equation (3) on the right-hand side is the part of the gap due to different (average) characteristics of natives and migrants, while the second term is the part of the differential due to different coefficients that identifies differences in the treatment or behaviour of otherwise comparable migrant and native workers. It is this latter term that measures migrant–native cleavages that cannot be explained by observable differences between migrants and natives. The analysis may also be performed with a binary dependent variable following the adapted non-linear decomposition described in Yun (2004) for studying differentials in variables such as participation, employment or unemployment.

Data and sample characteristics

The European Union Labour Force Survey (EU-LFS) covering a representative sample of households in all EU member states is the main source of data for this study. The national statistical offices of each member country are responsible for data collection in accordance with a harmonized methodology. The EU-LFS collects information on respondents' personal circumstances (including nationality and country of birth) and their labour market status during a reference period of between one and four weeks immediately prior to the interview. Because the sampling structure of the EU-LFS focuses strongly on permanent residents, it is likely to omit short-term and seasonal migration. The survey collects several work characteristics of employed individuals that are useful for assessing the quality of employment over time. Unfortunately, the EU-LFS does not include information on the income status of households.

Owing to its large sample size, the EU-LFS provides reliable information on the share of immigrant population in a country and it is commonly used in research on immigration in the European context (see e.g. D'Amuri and Peri, 2010; Huber *et al.*, 2010; Dustmann and Frattini, 2011). In this study, the terms 'immigrant population' or 'immigrant individuals' are used in the broad context of immigration, and the origin of immigrants is based on country of birth. One exception is Germany, for which immigrant origin may be determined only by nationality. The EU-LFS allows us to concentrate on the situation of immigrants from the EU-12 countries and to contrast their performance with native workforces in the EU-15 countries. The final sample used in this study covers the period 2004 to 2011 and includes individuals of working age (15 to 65 years) in the EU-15, which amounts to more than 5.6 million individuals.

Worker mobility from EU-12 to EU-15 following the EU's eastern enlargements exhibits several noteworthy patterns. Figure 5.1 plots the stock of migrants from EU-12 and EU-15 origins in the working-age population separately for each of the 15 old EU member states. The data show that EU-12 migrants were relatively scarce prior to the 2004 enlargement. While the stock of EU-15 migrants remained stable at 2.4 per cent during the period studied, the stock of EU-12 migrants more than tripled, from 0.5 per cent in 2004 to 1.7 per cent in 2011. The steepest increase of EU-12 migrants is observed in the UK and Ireland, which fully opened their labour markets to EU-12 immigrants immediately after their countries' EU accession. The flow of EU-12 immigrants to Italy and Greece accelerated particularly after 2007 when Bulgaria and Romania joined the EU.

The outbreak of the crisis in the late 2000s had a visible negative effect on migration flows in countries greatly affected by the economic crisis, such as Ireland and Spain.[8] In other countries, the stock of EU-12 immigrants remained constant or continued to grow after 2008 despite the crisis. Interestingly, the Scandinavian countries became a destination for EU-12 immigrants only after

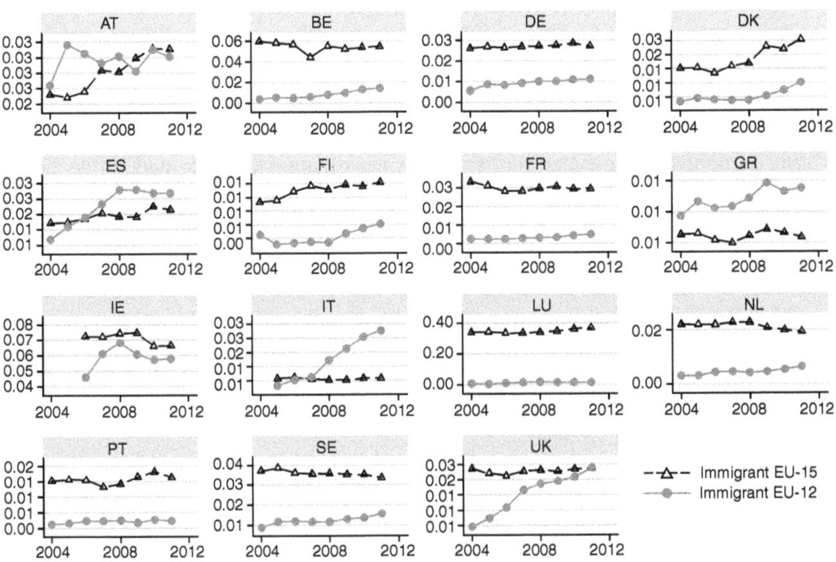

Figure 5.1 The share of immigrant population from EU-15 and EU-12 in the 15 old EU member states (as % of the population) (source: EU-LFS (2015)).

Note

The sample covers the period from 2004-2011. The origin of immigrants is determined by their country of birth, except for Germany, where immigrants are distinguished by their nationality. The sample is limited to individuals aged 15–65 and is weighted by personal weights.

2008, which may be explained by the relatively favourable economic conditions in these countries during the economic downturn. In 2011, immigrants from EU-12 countries made up about 13 per cent of the entire population of foreign residents in EU-15. Although mobility slowed down in Europe during the crisis, based on observed patterns it appears that not too many migrants returned home as a consequence of the economic crisis. This does not come as a surprise, given that the employment opportunities in the EU-15 countries also remained more favourable during the crisis than the alternatives in migrants' home countries.

Table 5.1 compares the characteristics of EU-12 migrants with the native population in EU-15 in the sample. The numbers show that, on average, the migrant group is younger and includes a higher percentage of women and comparatively fewer highly educated individuals than natives, and also that about half of the migrants are concentrated in densely populated urban areas. A comparison of education characteristics reveals that approximately 80 per cent of migrants attain at least upper-secondary education (compared to 74 per cent of natives), while 25 per cent attain at least tertiary education (compared to 29 per cent of natives).[9]

To study the labour market situation of EU-12 migrants in EU-15 countries, we construct a set of indicators regarding the labour market outcomes of migrant and native populations: (1) labour force participation, (2) unemployment, (3) self-employment; and three indicators for job quality measured in terms of (4) over-education, (5) low-skill employment, and (6) type of contract (see Table 5.2). The data show that while migrants exhibit a higher labour market participation rate than natives, they also suffer from a higher unemployment rate. The immigrant–native participation gap remained relatively stable during the period studied, while the unemployment gap increased substantially during the Great Recession. Migrants exhibit an almost three times higher incidence of low-skill jobs and a two times higher incidence of over-qualification compared to natives. In general, they are less likely to be self-employed and more likely be employed on temporary contracts.

Table 5.1 Descriptive characteristics of EU-12 migrants and EU-15 native populations (mean values)

Individual characteristics	*Migrants*	*Natives*	*Diff.*
Female	0.53	0.48	0.05
Age	35.6	40.1	−4.49
ISCED1 primary	0.05	0.06	−0.01
ISCED2 lower-secondary	0.16	0.20	−0.03
ISCED3 upper-secondary	0.47	0.41	0.06
ISCED4 post-secondary	0.06	0.04	0.02
ISCED5 university	0.25	0.29	−0.05
Urbanization: densely populated area	0.51	0.44	0.07
Urbanization: intermediate area	0.20	0.29	−0.09
Urbanization: thinly populated area	0.29	0.27	0.02

Source: EU-LFS (2015).

Table 5.2 Labour market indicators for EU-12 migrants and EU-15 natives over time

Outcome variables	*Migrants*				*Natives*			
	2006–2007	*2008–2009*	*2010–2011*	*Total*	*2006–2007*	*2008–2009*	*2010–2011*	*Total*
Participation rate	0.792	0.787	0.784	0.779	0.709	0.717	0.718	0.713
Unemployment rate	0.085	0.120	0.155	0.124	0.062	0.071	0.091	0.075
Self-employment	0.081	0.097	0.097	0.093	0.156	0.155	0.151	0.152
Over-education	0.360	0.369	0.368	0.359	0.161	0.169	0.171	0.162
Low-skilled job	0.275	0.271	0.299	0.280	0.099	0.095	0.092	0.096
Temporary contract	0.232	0.207	0.199	0.219	0.144	0.140	0.144	0.143

Source: EU-LFS (2015).

Migrant–native cleavages: empirical evidence

Do the raw gaps reported in the previous section reflect a disparate composition of migrant and native populations, or are they reflected in the labour market cleavages as an artefact of unequal treatment of otherwise equal individuals? We address these questions by decomposing immigrant–native raw gaps into the part that is due to differences in the characteristics of immigrant and native populations and the part that arises due to factors other than the observed differences. We look at migrant–native cleavages in the areas of labour force participation and in the incidence of unemployment, self-employment, over-education, low-skill employment and temporary contracts. The gaps in the outcome variables between immigrant and native populations are decomposed into a part explained by differences in observed characteristics (i.e. the explained part) and a part attributable to differences in the estimated coefficients or unobserved factors (i.e. the unexplained part). The compositional differences of the immigrant and native workforces are measured in terms of age, education, gender and the degree of regional urbanization.

Labour market participation

Given that the post-enlargement migration flows to the EU-15 from CEE countries were predominantly driven by better employment prospects (Kahanec and Zimmermann, 2010; Pytliková, 2014; Kahanec *et al.*, forthcoming), the participation of EU-12 immigrants in the labour market may be expected to be high. Following the International Labour Organization's definition, labour market participation rate refers to the number of people who are either employed or are actively looking for and can take a job, relative to the working-age population. Figure 5.2 depicts unconditional differences in the participation rates between EU-12 immigrants and natives across countries and over time. It shows that the participation rates of immigrants are visibly higher than those of the natives in the countries where the inflows are largest; that is, in Southern Europe, the UK and Ireland. In the continental European and Nordic countries, the participation rates of EU-12 migrants are broadly comparable and in several of them the rates are improving with respect to those of the natives. Figure 5.2 shows that the participation of the immigrant workforce also remained robust during the crisis period, thus confirming the strong attachment of migrant workforces to the labour market.

The decomposition analysis reported in Table 5.3 reveals that whereas the participation gap between EU-12 migrants and natives was small and insignificant in 2004, it steadily increased to as high as 7.7 percentage points in favour of migrants in 2007, levelling off at around 6 to 7 percentage points since then. About 3 to 5 percentage points of the gap are explained by differences in observable characteristics. Whereas unobserved factors disadvantaged migrants in 2004, the disadvantage disappeared in 2005 and turned into an advantage of around 2 to 4 percentage points in subsequent years. A possible interpretation is

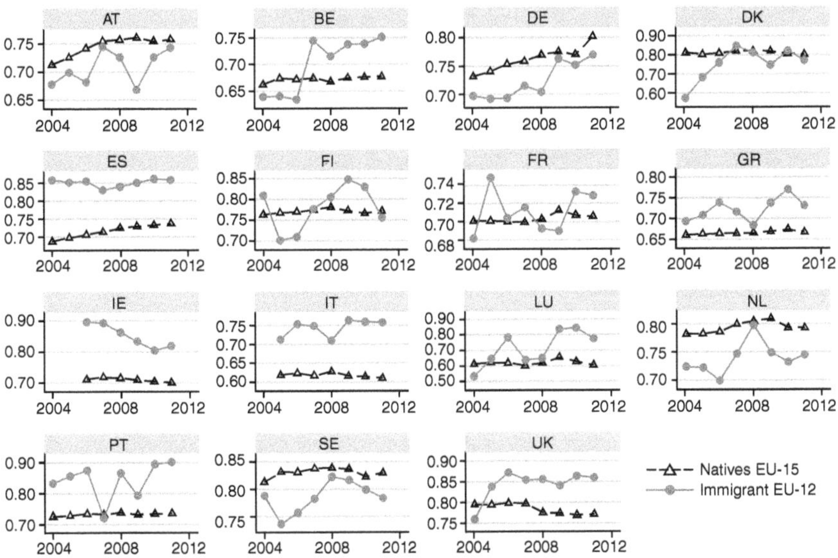

Figure 5.2 Labour market participation of EU-15 natives and EU-12 immigrants in the 15 old EU member states (source: EU-LFS (2015). Following the International Labour Organization's definition of unemployment, labour market participation rate refers to the number of people who are either employed or are actively looking for work).

Note
See note to Figure 5.1.

that pre-enlargement migrants (observed in 2004) were somewhat positively selected on observable characteristics, but that unobservable factors nullified this advantage. The observed pattern is consistent with the notion that the extension of the freedom of movement to citizens from the new EU member states allowed for a stronger positive selection in terms of observable and especially unobservable characteristics, yielding a positive participation premium overall. It may also be that following the 2004 and 2007 EU enlargements, the barriers to EU-12 citizens' participation diminished and that this enabled them to realize their potential in the receiving labour markets, as measured by the unexplained part of the participation differential.

Unemployment

During economic downturns, immigrant workers are often the first to lose their jobs, also because they are frequently employed in sectors that are particularly vulnerable to economic shocks (OECD, 2013). Figure 5.3 shows that migrants clearly run a higher risk of unemployment compared to natives in all countries except Greece, Portugal and the UK. Following the outbreak of the economic crisis in the late 2000s, the unemployment rates of migrants increased sharply compared to natives in several countries, while in other countries both groups

Table 5.3 Decomposition results: labour market participation rate

	2004 b/se	*2005 b/se*	*2006 b/se*	*2007 b/se*	*2008 b/se*	*2009 b/se*	*2010 b/se*	*2011 b/se*
Migrant	0.727*** (0.007)	0.728*** (0.007)	0.777*** (0.005)	0.796*** (0.004)	0.787*** (0.004)	0.787*** (0.004)	0.789*** (0.004)	0.786*** (0.004)
Native	0.724*** (0.001)	0.708*** (0.001)	0.713*** (0.001)	0.718*** (0.001)	0.721*** (0.001)	0.721*** (0.001)	0.719*** (0.001)	0.725*** (0.001)
Difference	0.003 (0.007)	0.021*** (0.007)	0.065*** (0.005)	0.077*** (0.005)	0.066*** (0.004)	0.065*** (0.004)	0.07*** (0.004)	0.061*** (0.004)
Explained	0.026*** (0.003)	0.031*** (0.003)	0.049*** (0.002)	0.048*** (0.002)	0.046*** (0.002)	0.039*** (0.002)	0.035*** (0.002)	0.03*** (0.002)
Unexplained	−0.023*** (0.007)	−0.01* (0.006)	0.015*** (0.005)	0.03*** (0.004)	0.02*** (0.004)	0.026*** (0.004)	0.035*** (0.004)	0.031*** (0.004)
Total	708,031	670,125	724,924	725,417	702,500	692,233	710,287	696,302
Migrant	3,749	4,308	6,285	7,699	8,502	8,878	10,035	10,976
Native	704,282	665,817	718,639	717,718	693,998	683,355	700,252	685,326

Source: EU-LFS (2015).

Note
***, ** and * denote 1 per cent, 5 per cent and 10 per cent confidence levels, respectively.

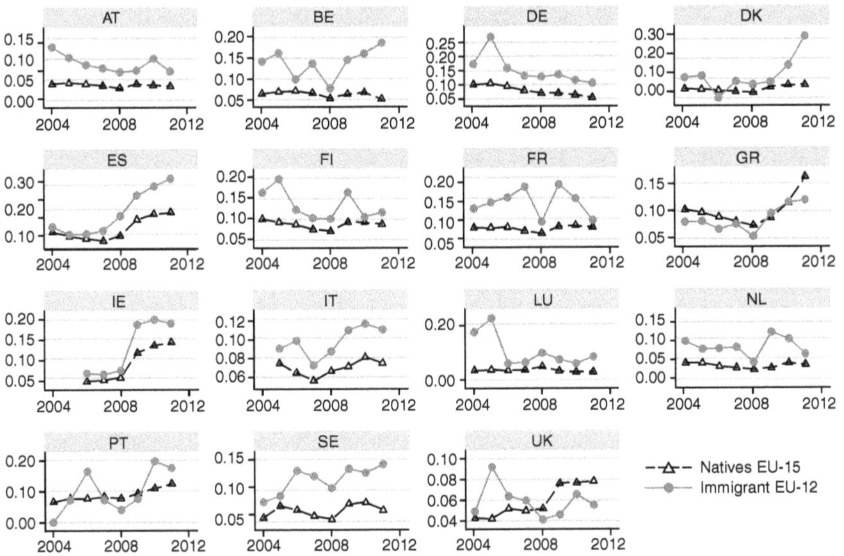

Figure 5.3 Unemployment rates of EU-15 natives and EU-12 immigrants in the 15 old EU member states (source: EU-LFS (2015).

Note
See note to Figure 5.1.

were equally affected (Greece), affected only a little (Luxembourg) or the migrant population was less affected (UK). This pattern is confirmed in the decomposition analysis (Table 5.4), which shows that during the period prior to the crisis, the immigrant–native unemployment differential decreased, but the increase in unemployment rates during the crisis was much more pronounced for immigrants. Whereas the pre-crisis gap and its decline are mainly due to unobserved factors, deteriorations in the observed characteristics as well as unobserved factors contributed to the increase in the gap during the crisis.

Self-employment

As shown above, the risk of unemployment increased during the Great Recession more for immigrants than for natives in many countries. The immigrant–native gap in the self-employment rate shows the inverse of the gap in unemployment rates. This counter-cyclical nature of the self-employment gap, although not very pronounced, is reflected in an increasing immigrant–native self-employment gap prior to the crisis and a diminishing gap since its outbreak. This indicates that during periods of job scarcity, self-employment may provide an alternative form of employment, especially for migrants. For example, if a scarcity of jobs leads to heightened discrimination of immigrants by employers, self-employment may be a way of avoiding such situations.[10] Alternatively, it

Table 5.4 Decomposition results: unemployment rate

	2004 b/se	*2005 b/se*	*2006 b/se*	*2007 b/se*	*2008 b/se*	*2009 b/se*	*2010 b/se*	*2011 b/se*
Migrant	0.125***	0.123***	0.090***	0.086***	0.093***	0.145***	0.155***	0.152***
	(0.006)	(0.006)	(0.004)	(0.004)	(0.004)	(0.004)	(0.004)	(0.004)
Native	0.079***	0.073***	0.065***	0.058***	0.059***	0.082***	0.091***	0.091***
	(0.000)	(0.000)	(0.000)	(0.000)	(0.000)	(0.000)	(0.000)	(0.000)
Difference	0.046***	0.050***	0.025***	0.028***	0.033***	0.064***	0.065***	0.061***
	(0.006)	(0.006)	(0.004)	(0.004)	(0.004)	(0.004)	(0.004)	(0.004)
Explained	0.006***	0.012***	0.005***	0.008***	0.015***	0.037***	0.033***	0.031***
	(0.001)	(0.001)	(0.001)	(0.001)	(0.001)	(0.001)	(0.001)	(0.001)
Unexplained	0.040***	0.037***	0.020***	0.020***	0.019***	0.026***	0.032***	0.030***
	(0.006)	(0.005)	(0.004)	(0.003)	(0.003)	(0.004)	(0.004)	(0.003)
Total	512,435	473,956	516,729	521,534	506,892	499,803	511,563	505,416
Migrant	2,700	3,139	4,859	6,122	6,684	6,979	7,918	8,620
Native	509,735	470,817	511,870	515,412	500,208	492,824	503,645	496,796

Source: EU-LFS (2015).

Note
***, ** and * denote 1 per cent, 5 per cent and 10 per cent confidence levels, respectively.

may be that during the downturn, companies employing migrants put additional pressure on their workers to adopt self-employed status in order to save on wage-related costs, which, according to the conceptualization developed by Bernaciak in the Introduction to this volume, would constitute social dumping. One should note as well that throughout the observed period, the rate of self-employment was lower among immigrants than within the native labour force. Between 20 and 48 per cent of the immigrant–native gap in self-employment rates is explained by differences in the observable characteristics included in the analysis (Table 5.5). Whereas the explained as well as the unexplained parts peak in 2006, the explained part fades away by 2011, but the role of the unexplained part increases in 2010 and dominates in 2011.

Quality of employment

During economic downturns, the probability of finding a job is reduced, so the incentives to take a lower quality job may be relatively higher. This may be especially true for migrants for several reasons. Unemployed migrants have limited access to the social safety net in the host (or home) country, and the earnings opportunities in low-skilled jobs may be acceptable with respect to the income standards in their home countries. In addition, immigrants have strong incentives to work in order to be able to support household members left in their home country. These factors could reduce migrants' reservation wages and channel them into lower quality employment vis-à-vis the natives. We restrict the sample to employed individuals and decompose the gap observed in working conditions such as the incidence of over-education, employment in low-skilled occupations and temporary contracts.

Over-education

The match between qualifications and jobs is an important measure for evaluating the performance of highly skilled workers in the labour market. In general, as argued by Huber *et al.* (2010), highly skilled migrants are more likely to occupy jobs beneath their level of education relative to the native workforce. The main reasons arise from differences between home- and host-country education systems, the lack of formal recognition of skills abroad or the lack of specific human capital (such as language skills or knowledge of labour market institutions), and various forms of discrimination. We construct a simple indicator of over-education to evaluate the skill matching of workers following the method of realized matches. Based on occupational codes (two-digit ISCO), in each occupational group we identify the level of education of the median worker, distinguishing between low, medium and high educational level. All workers in the same occupational group with a higher education than the median worker are then marked as over-educated. The identification of over-educated workers is conducted separately for each country to account for country-specific differences. The high incidence of qualification mismatch should be interpreted with caution because occupations are not a perfect proxy for job requirements.

Table 5.5 Decomposition results: self-employment rate

	2004 b/se	*2005 b/se*	*2006 b/se*	*2007 b/se*	*2008 b/se*	*2009 b/se*	*2010 b/se*	*2011 b/se*
Migrant	0.088***	0.107***	0.087***	0.089***	0.096***	0.106***	0.101***	0.098***
	(0.006)	(0.006)	(0.004)	(0.004)	(0.004)	(0.004)	(0.004)	(0.003)
Native	0.137***	0.157***	0.157***	0.155***	0.156***	0.154***	0.153***	0.150***
	(0.000)	(0.001)	(0.001)	(0.001)	(0.001)	(0.001)	(0.001)	(0.001)
Difference	−0.048***	−0.051***	−0.070***	−0.067***	−0.061***	−0.048***	−0.051***	−0.052***
	(0.006)	(0.006)	(0.005)	(0.004)	(0.004)	(0.004)	(0.004)	(0.004)
Explained	−0.013***	−0.021***	−0.027***	−0.027***	−0.025***	−0.021***	−0.015***	−0.009***
	(0.002)	(0.002)	(0.001)	(0.001)	(0.001)	(0.001)	(0.001)	(0.001)
Unexplained	−0.036***	−0.030***	−0.043***	−0.040***	−0.036***	−0.027***	−0.036***	−0.044***
	(0.006)	(0.007)	(0.005)	(0.005)	(0.004)	(0.005)	(0.004)	(0.004)
Total	471,667	439,205	483,140	490,779	476,396	458,332	464,534	458,818
Migrant	2,387	2,753	4,448	5,593	6,061	5,963	6,686	7,308
Native	469,280	436,452	478,692	485,186	470,335	452,369	457,848	451,510

Source: EU-LFS (2015).

Note
***, ** and * denote 1 per cent, 5 per cent and 10 per cent confidence levels, respectively.

Our findings suggest that highly skilled migrants face substantial difficulties in transferring skills across borders. Migrants exhibit an almost two times higher risk of over-education in their labour market position relative to natives. The results of the decomposition analysis reported in Table 5.6 reveal that the substantial part of the gap in over-education between immigrant and native workers is not explained by observable characteristics, which in fact work in favour of migrants. An important implication is that migrants accept jobs below their educational level mainly in relation to unobservable factors. A possible explanation is that over-education emerges due to the low language ability or more generally due to the low transferability of the unobserved skills of migrants. Our results further indicate that the incidence of over-education has increased especially among immigrants, and that most of the increase took place prior to the crisis, primarily as the result of a steep increase in the unexplained part of the differential. Given that those were the years of significantly increased east–west migration, this latter finding appears to underscore the importance of immigrant adjustment and imperfect skill transferability. Some qualification mismatch is likely to be explained by issues other than skills discrepancies, such as the skill heterogeneity among workers with the same qualifications.

Low-skilled jobs

Our results show that the high incidence of over-education among immigrant workers goes hand in hand with their concentration in the lowest-skill occupations. This outcome is confirmed by the share of migrant workers employed in the elementary occupations characterized by simple and routine tasks (ISCO group 9). Our findings reported in Table 5.7 show that immigrants are three times more likely to be employed in the elementary occupations compared to natives and that the gap cannot be explained by differences in observable characteristics. Since 2008, the incidence of taking a low-skilled job has increased for immigrants, while the opposite pattern is observed for native workers. A tentative explanation would be that immigrant workers who cannot access the welfare system are more likely to accept low-skilled jobs when the competition for jobs becomes tense, while the native workforce has more opportunities available to avoid lowest-skill employment, including drawing unemployment benefits, entering early retirement or inactivity, or relying on other sources of household income. The decomposition analysis confirms that employment in the low-skilled occupations is almost exclusively due to the unobserved characteristics of migrants.

Type of contract

We showed above that immigrants have higher incidences of over-qualification and low-skill employment and a higher risk of unemployment. In addition, a higher prevalence of temporary contracts is noticeable among immigrants, although the share of immigrants with temporary contracts exhibits a declining

Table 5.6 Decomposition results: incidence of over-education among workers

	2004 b/se	*2005 b/se*	*2006 b/se*	*2007 b/se*	*2008 b/se*	*2009 b/se*	*2010 b/se*	*2011 b/se*
Migrant	0.318*** (0.015)	0.377*** (0.011)	0.392*** (0.010)	0.419*** (0.009)	0.407*** (0.008)	0.427*** (0.009)	0.420*** (0.008)	0.453*** (0.008)
Native	0.178*** (0.001)	0.201*** (0.001)	0.201*** (0.001)	0.206*** (0.001)	0.209*** (0.001)	0.214*** (0.001)	0.218*** (0.001)	0.207*** (0.001)
Difference	0.140*** (0.015)	0.176*** (0.012)	0.190*** (0.010)	0.213*** (0.009)	0.197*** (0.008)	0.212*** (0.009)	0.202*** (0.008)	0.247*** (0.008)
Explained	−0.007 (0.010)	−0.010 (0.011)	−0.000 (0.009)	−0.002 (0.008)	−0.006 (0.007)	−0.004 (0.008)	−0.012* (0.007)	0.004 (0.007)
Unexplained	0.147*** (0.006)	0.186*** (0.007)	0.190*** (0.006)	0.215*** (0.005)	0.204*** (0.005)	0.217*** (0.005)	0.214*** (0.005)	0.243*** (0.005)
Total	386,467	346,981	381,210	389,089	380,201	367,775	376,220	371,187
Migrant	2,030	2,333	3,826	4,756	5,220	5,002	5,531	5,863
Native	384,437	344,648	377,384	384,333	374,981	362,773	370,689	365,324

Source: EU-LFS (2015).

Note
***, ** and * denote 1 per cent, 5 per cent and 10 per cent confidence levels, respectively.

Table 5.7 Decomposition results: incidence of elementary occupation

	2004 b/se	*2005 b/se*	*2006 b/se*	*2007 b/se*	*2008 b/se*	*2009 b/se*	*2010 b/se*	*2011 b/se*
Migrant	0.232*** (0.009)	0.249*** (0.008)	0.256*** (0.007)	0.266*** (0.006)	0.250*** (0.006)	0.262*** (0.006)	0.285*** (0.006)	0.282*** (0.005)
Native	0.085*** (0.000)	0.088*** (0.000)	0.088*** (0.000)	0.087*** (0.000)	0.085*** (0.000)	0.083*** (0.000)	0.083*** (0.000)	0.079*** (0.000)
Difference	0.147*** (0.009)	0.161*** (0.008)	0.168*** (0.007)	0.179*** (0.006)	0.164*** (0.006)	0.178*** (0.006)	0.201*** (0.006)	0.203*** (0.005)
Explained	−0.017*** (0.003)	−0.013*** (0.003)	−0.015*** (0.002)	−0.005** (0.002)	−0.009*** (0.002)	−0.005** (0.002)	0.006*** (0.002)	0.013*** (0.002)
Unexplained	0.164*** (0.009)	0.174*** (0.008)	0.183*** (0.007)	0.184*** (0.006)	0.173*** (0.006)	0.184*** (0.006)	0.195*** (0.005)	0.189*** (0.005)
Total	471,819	439,362	483,265	490,869	476,518	458,437	464,694	458,918
Migrant	2,389	2,754	4,449	5,567	6,065	5,930	6,688	7,309
Native	469,430	436,608	478,816	485,302	470,453	452,507	458,006	451,609

Source: EU-LFS (2015).

Note
***, ** and * denote 1 per cent, 5 per cent and 10 per cent confidence levels, respectively.

trend and the native–immigrant gap is closing. Our results in Table 5.8 illustrate that only a small part of the immigrant–native gap defining the quality of employment is explained by workers' characteristics, a larger part being due to cleavages that cannot be explained by observable differences, which may be related to immigrants' disconnectedness from social networks, differences in ethnic capital or discrimination arising, for example, from employers' inclination to employ migrants on temporary contracts (also see Berntsen and Lillie, Chapter 2, this volume).

Conclusions

This chapter has studied the labour market position of EU-12 immigrants in the old EU member states following the EU enlargements of 2004 and 2007 and during the Great Recession. Using EU-LFS data and the Oaxaca–Blinder–Yun type of decomposition techniques, we show that although immigrant–native gaps may be partly explained by group differences in individual characteristics, there still exist significant migrant–native cleavages in EU labour markets that cannot be explained by observable factors and that are therefore due to other factors, including differences in social or ethnic capital, language skills or discrimination.

Our results show a worrying trend of increased labour market gaps in most domains between EU-12 migrants and natives in old EU member states. The two exceptions among the outcome variables studied are self-employment, which exhibits steady gaps, and the incidence of temporary contracts, where the gaps declined during the period studied. Another imortant result is that these gaps can be only partly explained by observable characteristics such as age, gender or education. In most cases, a larger part of the gaps is due to unobserved factors. For labour market participation and unemployment, immigrant–native cleavages decreased following enlargement; however, the recent crisis slowed down these trends. Cleavages in self-employment (which perhaps served as a second-best option for those who were unable to find waged employment or which resulted from employees' or employers' efforts to minimize labour costs) exhibited patterns inverse to those we found for unemployment cleavages. As we expected, cleavages in the incidence of over-education and low-skilled employment grew in view of increased labour mobility in the early post-enlargement period but levelled off during the crisis. The unexplained gaps in temporary contracts decreased, especially prior to the Great Recession.

The observed differences concerning the incidence of self-employment, low-skilled employment and temporary contracts may be the result of strategic behaviour on the part of migrant workers or their employers aimed at reducing the costs of labour. However, on the basis of the available statistical data, it is not possible to directly measure the extent of social dumping incentives and/or practices as discussed by Bernaciak in the Introduction to this volume; nor is it possible to establish a causal link between social dumping practices and the persistence of the above-mentioned cleavages.

Table 5.8 Decomposition results: temporary contracts

	2004 b/se	*2005 b/se*	*2006 b/se*	*2007 b/se*	*2008 b/se*	*2009 b/se*	*2010 b/se*	*2011 b/se*
Migrant	0.287***	0.270***	0.236***	0.232***	0.216***	0.198***	0.193***	0.204***
	(0.009)	(0.009)	(0.006)	(0.006)	(0.005)	(0.005)	(0.005)	(0.005)
Native	0.144***	0.146***	0.144***	0.147***	0.143***	0.136***	0.143***	0.146***
	(0.001)	(0.001)	(0.001)	(0.001)	(0.001)	(0.001)	(0.001)	(0.001)
Difference	0.142***	0.125***	0.092***	0.085***	0.073***	0.062***	0.050***	0.058***
	(0.009)	(0.009)	(0.006)	(0.006)	(0.005)	(0.005)	(0.005)	(0.005)
Explained	0.019***	0.019***	0.005*	0.009***	0.004*	0.007***	0.002	0.003
	(0.004)	(0.004)	(0.003)	(0.002)	(0.002)	(0.002)	(0.002)	(0.002)
Unexplained	0.123***	0.106***	0.087***	0.076***	0.069***	0.055***	0.048***	0.055***
	(0.008)	(0.008)	(0.006)	(0.005)	(0.005)	(0.005)	(0.005)	(0.005)
Total	398,713	363,155	400,731	407,977	395,720	381,761	388,243	385,168
Migrant	2,153	2,429	4,026	5,052	5,428	5,289	5,954	6,549
Native	396,560	360,726	396,705	402,925	390,292	376,472	382,289	378,619

Source: EU-LFS (2015).

Note
***, ** and * denote 1 per cent, 5 per cent and 10 per cent confidence levels, respectively. This sample cover the period from 2004–2011.

The above limitation notwithstanding, the results of our study do suggest that Europe needs to do much more to facilitate and fully benefit from the free mobility of workers across its labour markets. In this respect, the unexplained gaps measured in this chapter are of particular concern because they signify linguistic, social or ethnicity-related barriers, skill mismatches in the labour market (also including discrimination of migrants) or possible vulnerabilities of migrant workers resulting in their exclusion from quality employment and working conditions. These cleavages may undermine the social fabric in the receiving countries and lead to a vicious circle of negative attitudes and ill-chosen migration and integration policies. They may also spark even greater fears of social dumping in the future because these cleavages essentially imply a lower quality of employment for otherwise equal migrants.

On the other hand, one needs to be careful when interpreting these cleavages. Mobility generally goes hand in hand with adjustment, which may be swift or sluggish, also depending on labour market institutions and policies. Migrants' choices matter, too. Temporary migrants may find it inefficient to invest in human capital specific to the receiving country if the costs of such investment are not compensated by higher earnings over a sufficiently long period of time. And yet, temporary and circular migrants may benefit from their migration experience, and mutual benefits in terms of better skill matching and economic efficiency from such migration may also result for the receiving and the sending countries. Finally, whenever the lack of adjustment results from institutional barriers to integration or unequal treatment of migrants, these and not migration as such are the primary sources of migrant–native cleavages. Against this background, we may conclude that whereas the free mobility of labour is by and large a success story, especially when it comes to the benefits for Europe's labour markets, equal treatment of migrants and the elimination of barriers to migrants' social and labour market integration remain among the key policy challenges for the enlarged EU.

Notes

1 To illustrate the logic, it may appear inefficient for a university-educated engineer to work as a receptionist, but this becomes less obvious if his or her only alternative in the home country would be unemployment or inactivity.

2 The term 'native' refers to the resident population in an old EU member state not originating from new EU member states. It does not imply nativity in the respective country.

3 It is, of course, possible that different labour markets attract different types of migrants, or affect the prospects of migrants and natives differently for acquiring human capital. Labour market attributes may thus play an indirect role in the human capital and other characteristics of the native and immigrant populations.

4 Certainly, explained gaps may result from unequal treatment outside of the labour market, and unexplained gaps may – through workers' expectations and subsequent decisions (e.g. to invest less in their own human capital in the case of a negative unexplained gap) – engender explained gaps.

5 EU-12 refers to the EU member states which joined the EU in 2004 and 2007. EU-15 refers to the pre-2004 EU member states.

6 However, sociodemographic differences of this type may result from inequalities arising outside of the labour market.
7 An important assumption in Oaxaca's approach is that labour supply and individual characteristics are fixed and would not respond to the changes in the outcome variable that would result from the elimination of discrimination.
8 In 2011, Spain reintroduced transitional arrangements that restricted Romanians' access to its labour market. These restrictions lasted until the end of 2013.
9 The variable 'highest qualification achieved' is coded in each country according to the International Standard Classification of Education (ISCED). The use of this classification may lead to difficulties in cross-country comparisons if ISCED does not adequately reflect the educational system of all countries. We consider this to be a minor problem, since our analysis includes migrants from European countries in which ISCED is commonly used.
10 It may also be that self-employment provided a way to circumvent transitional arrangements restricting the access of EU-12 workers to EU-15 labour markets. A gradual opening of labour markets would imply a decreasing self-employment rate over time for EU-12 workers in EU-15, and hence a diminishing self-employment gap. The outbreak of the crisis, however, slowed down the process and even inverted the trend.

References

Amuedo-Dorantes, C. and De la Rica, S. (2007) 'Labour Market Assimilation of Recent Immigrants in Spain'. *British Journal of Industrial Relations*, 45(2): 257–284.

Biavaschi, C. and Zimmermann, K. (2014) 'Eastern Partnership Migrants in Germany: Outcomes, Potentials and Challenges'. *IZA Journal of European Labor Studies*, 3: 7. Available at: www.izajoels.com/content/3/1/7 (accessed 3 September 2014).

Blinder, A.S. (1973) 'Wage Discrimination: Reduced Form and Structural Estimates'. *Journal of Human Resources*, 8(4): 436–455.

Borjas, G.J. (1985) 'Assimilation, Changes in Cohort Quality, and the Earnings of Immigrants'. *Journal of Labour Economics*, 3(4): 463–489.

Chiswick, B.R. (1978) 'The Effect of Americanization on the Earnings of Foreign-born Men'. *The Journal of Political Economy*, 86(5): 897–921.

D'Amuri, F. and Peri, G. (2010) 'Immigration and Occupations in Europe'. *CReAM Discussion Paper*, No. 26/10. London: Centre for Research and Analysis of Migration.

De la Rica, S. and Polonyankina, T. (2013) 'The Impact of Immigration on Occupational Specialisation among Natives in Spain: Does the Business Cycle Matter?' *Revista de Economía Aplicada*, 21(63): 51–74.

De la Rica, S., Glitz, A. and Ortega, F. (2015) 'Immigration in Europe: Trends, Policies and Empirical Evidence'. In Chiswick, B.R. and Miller, P.W. (eds), *Handbook of the Economics of International Migration*. Amsterdam: Elsevier, pp. 1303–1362.

Dustmann, C. and Frattini, T. (2011) 'Immigration: The European Experience'. *IZA Discussion Paper*, No. 6261. Bonn: Institute for the Study of Labor.

Dustmann, C. and Van Soest, A. (2002) 'Language and the Earnings of Immigrants'. *Industrial and Labour Relations Review*, 55(3): 473–492.

Dustmann, C., Glitz, A. and Vogel, T. (2010) 'Employment, Wages, and the Economic Cycle: Differences between Immigrants and Natives'. *European Economic Review*, 54(1): 1–17.

Entorf, H. and Minoiu, N. (2005) 'What a Difference Immigration Policy Makes: A Comparison of PISA Scores in Europe and Traditional Countries of Immigration'. *German Economic Review*, 6(3): 355–376.

EU-LFS (2015) 'European Union Labour Force Survey' database, various years. Available at: http://ec.europa.eu/eurostat/web/microdata/european-union-labour-force-survey (accessed 13 March 2015).

Huber, P., Landesmann, M., Robinson, C. and Stehrer, R. (2010) 'Migrants' Skills and Productivity: A European Perspective'. *National Institute Economic Review*, 213(1): R20–R34.

Kahanec, M. (2013) 'Labour Mobility in an Enlarged European Union'. In Constant, A.F. and Zimmermann, K.F. (eds), *International Handbook on the Economics of Migration*. Cheltenham: Edward Elgar, pp. 137–152.

Kahanec, M. and Shields, M. (2013) 'The Working Hours of Immigrants in Germany: Temporary versus Permanent'. *IZA Journal of Migration*, 2: 14. Available at: www.izajom.com/content/2/1/14 (accessed 3 September 2014).

Kahanec, M. and Zaiceva, A. (2009) 'Labour Market Outcomes of Immigrants and Non-citizens in the EU: An East–West Comparison'. *International Journal of Manpower*, 30(1/2): 97–115.

Kahanec, M. and Zimmermann, K.F. (eds) (2010) *EU Labor Markets after Post-enlargement Migration*. Berlin: Springer.

Kahanec, M. and Zimmermann, K.F. (eds) (2011) *Ethnic Diversity in European Labour Markets: Challenges and Solutions*. Cheltenham: Edward Elgar.

Kahanec, M., Kim, A.M. and Zimmermann, K.F. (2013) 'Pitfalls of Immigrant Inclusion into the European Welfare State'. *International Journal of Manpower*, 34(1): 97–98.

Kahanec, M., Pytliková, M. and Zimmermann, K.F. (forthcoming) 'The Free Movement of Workers in an Enlarged European Union: Institutional Underpinnings of Economic Adjustment'. In Kahanec, M. and Zimmermann, K.F. (eds), *Labor Migration, EU Enlargement, and the Great Recession*. Berlin: Springer.

Marchetti, S., Piazzalunga, D. and Venturini, A. (2014) 'Does Italy Represent an Opportunity for Temporary Migrants from the Eastern Partnership Countries?' *IZA Journal of European Labor Studies*, 3: 8. Available at: www.izajoels.com/content/3/1/8 (accessed 3 September 2014).

Oaxaca, R. (1973) 'Male–Female Wage Differentials in Urban Labour Markets'. *International Economic Review*, 14(3): 693–709.

OECD (2013) *International Migration Outlook: SOPEMI-2013*. Paris: Organisation for Economic Cooperation and Development.

Pytliková, M. (2014) 'The Effect of EU Enlargements and Labour Market Openings on Migration'. Mimeo.

Voicu, B. and Vlase, I. (2012) *High-skilled Immigrants and Social Integration in Times of Crisis. A Cross-European Analysis*. Mimeo. Bucharest: Romanian Academy of Science, Research Institute for Quality of Life.

Yun, M.-S. (2004) 'Decomposing Differences in the First Moment'. *Economics Letters*, 82(2): 275–280.

Zaiceva, A. and Zimmermann, K.F. (2008) 'Scale, Diversity, and Determinants of Labour Migration in Europe'. *Oxford Review of Economic Policy*, 24(3): 427–451.

Zaiceva, A. and Zimmermann, K.F. (forthcoming) 'Returning Home at Times of Trouble? Return Migration of EU Enlargement Migrants during the Crisis'. In Kahanec, M. and Zimmermann, K.F. (eds), *Migration and the Great Recession: Adjustments in the Labour Market of an Enlarged European Community*. Cheltenham: Edward Elgar.

Part II

Social dumping pressures in manufacturing sectors

6 Marketization and social dumping

Management whipsawing in Europe's automotive industry

Ian Greer and Marco Hauptmeier

Introduction

The social dumping debate in Europe is taking place parallel to broader debates on the changing relationship between society and the market. Varieties of capitalism theorists argue that little has changed in Europe's advanced industrialized economies since the 1980s, aside from the expansion of the 'peripheral' workforce relative to the 'core' (Emmenegger *et al.*, 2012). Most observers, however, see fundamental change, with detrimental implications for Europe's workforce – and not just labour market 'outsiders'. According to the liberalization argument, for example, the problem is not only that of the increasing size of a less well-regulated workforce; in addition, the function of industrial relations arrangements is changing for those workers who are still covered by welfare state provisions, democratic co-determination rights and encompassing sectoral collective agreements (Baccaro and Howell, 2011). This process is biased against social protections for workers and the poor in part as a result of the corrosive features of the market-making regulations emanating from the institutions of the European Union (Höpner and Schäfer, 2010; Lillie, 2010; Meardi, 2012; Bernaciak, Introduction to this volume), in part owing to the domestic restructuring of firms and industrial relations systems (Doellgast, 2012; Greer *et al.*, 2013) and in part because of generic features of capitalism (Dörre *et al.*, 2009; Vidal, 2013).

The focus of this chapter is one slow-burning change in the organization of capitalism in Europe, namely marketization (Hauptmeier, 2011; Greer and Doellgast, 2013). We argue that a specific form of marketization – management whipsawing – is causing social dumping in the automotive sector. By management whipsawing we mean large corporations' staging of economic competition between several production units in a way that extracts labour concessions by pitting local workers against each other in contests for investment and production. Numerous studies, whose findings we will discuss below, have examined whipsawing in the auto industry, mainly as a way of discussing the prospects for transnational industrial relations in Europe. Our contribution is to place this evidence in the context of marketization and social dumping debates.

Social dumping is defined in Bernaciak's Introduction to this book as 'the practice, undertaken by self-interested market participants, of undermining or evading existing social regulations with the aim of gaining a competitive advantage'. We argue that the large-scale imposition of market relations in Europe over the past few decades makes these types of practices both inevitable and pervasive. Social dumping is inevitable in the sense that the business community has a strong material incentive to use competition as a lever to extract concessions from labour and the state. Worker representatives, however sophisticated their countervailing strategies may be and however many years they have had to develop them (see Greer and Hauptmeier, 2012a), cannot really stop social dumping under the current institutional set-up of capitalism in Europe. Social dumping is pervasive in the sense that it takes so many different forms that it no longer requires a credible threat to relocate work from a high-wage country to a poor country. As research on service mobility and worker posting shows, for example, social dumping driven by European market making can also take place without the international relocation of production (Lillie, 2010; Wagner and Lillie, 2014), and the literature on the automotive sector also highlights cases of competition between high-wage locations (see e.g. Bernaciak, 2012).

This chapter follows this argument through in three steps. First, we introduce the concept of whipsawing and discuss certain similarities with other forms of marketization. We argue that in addition to intense competition, different kinds of marketization have in common several knock-on effects: the disorganization of non-market social protections through threats of exit, the development of private regulation by economic elites to extract profits, and the decline in workers' power, income and security. Second, we show how this dynamic has played out in the automotive sector since the 1990s, drawing upon the academic literature on problems faced by European Works Councils (EWCs). Our account also draws upon our own interviews with trade unionists and managers in the European automotive industry, mostly conducted between 2004 and 2013. We use empirical illustrations to show the diverse workings of the market mechanism within different firms as they whipsaw, the inadequacy of the industrial relations institutions in interrupting this process, and the difficulties faced by worker representatives in retaining jobs and bargaining with management. Third, we discuss the implications of whipsawing for the social dumping debate, including the role of governments and multinational firms and the need for new forms of transnational social regulation beyond the firm at the scale of the market.

Whipsawing as marketization

Through whipsawing, firms impose competition on their own workforces and within their own structures, with the consequence of social dumping. Whipsawing is a case of the broader phenomenon seen around Europe over the past 25 years of market change leading to a change in institutionalized worker protections. It is thus comparable with marketization phenomena as diverse as outsourcing, new public management techniques and active labour market policies.

These are all different examples in which price-based competition is imposed or intensified.

One similarity between whipsawing and other kinds of marketization is that it is not 'deregulation'. Marketization can lead to the multiplication of rules to stabilize the market and to compensate for any undesirable social consequence, and markets themselves require rules to emerge in the first place. Marketization is therefore institutionally thick with complex organizational dynamics and actors who possess discretion in deciding how competition works (MacKenzie and Martinez Lucio, 2005; Crouch, 2009; Brinkmann, 2011). The frequency of the transaction, the working of the price mechanism and the determination of who may compete are all features of market competition that – contrary to the neoliberal image of spontaneous markets determined by human nature – are usually imposed by some actor and regulated by some rules. Of course, markets change and vary widely on these dimensions.

A second similarity is that while whipsawing is powerful and has severe consequences in the workplace and beyond, it is determined outside the realm of democratic accountability. For other forms of marketization that hinge on regulation by the state – for instance, the regulation of privatized industries – this is also a problem. Most state regulation of markets is complex and technical, it does not attract the attention of the media and is not subject to public debate; consequently, policymakers are free to defer to the expertise of the business community (Culpepper, 2010). The features of production systems and investment allocation practices that enable whipsawing are similarly complex and bureaucratic; moreover, they are devised in the private sphere with no democratic accountability, even in principle. Managers in large publicly owned firms are, however, accountable to shareholders and therefore under pressure to make these decisions and design these rules in a way that maximizes profits or minimizes losses.

A third similarity is that whipsawing has corrosive effects upon collective bargaining and worker representation institutions, mainly in relation to the threat of exit (Hirschman, 1970). This increases employers' power over their workers by strengthening their discretion in how they 'enact' the rules of industrial relations in the workplace (Wagner, 2014). It also loosens the grip of national institutions on employers and reduces the power that these institutions provide to worker representatives in the determination of wages and working conditions. In extreme cases, marketization produces disorganization in which institutions lose their past functions and their constraining character.

Whipsawing in the European automotive industry is a good example of marketization in action. A transaction takes place between central management and local workforces in which worker concessions are exchanged for corporate investment. Rather than each plant having a fixed, dedicated and idiosyncratic production palate, the purpose of each plant is decided anew, based largely on labour and production costs. While this may be timed to correspond with the turnover of models and cycles of investments, if production is highly standardized, the relocation of production can also take place at short notice in the middle of a production cycle. In exchange for production allocation and investments, management asks labour representatives from different plants to pay a price in the form of concessions. The price mechanism is often obscure to worker representatives because it is unclear which concessions are sufficient to secure jobs, but it can be made more transparent to them with improved access to company information or with a formal procedure. There is therefore a wide variation in the way whipsawing proceeds within large corporations in terms of frequency of transaction, the number of competitors and the working of the price mechanism.

Whipsawing is powerful due to the exit threat. Because firms can move production away from a location, workers have reduced power in negotiations. The consequence is that the function of collective bargaining changes from one of ensuring worker voice, fair pay or macroeconomic stability due to strong worker demand to a focus by labour representatives on production allocation with the aim of securing jobs and maintaining previous labour gains. This is the case because key labour outcomes can only be defended if plants run at full capacity. Workers in underutilized plants face job losses or closure in the context of tight product markets. Along the way, multinational corporations (MNCs) import new practices into national institutional contexts where they had previously been resisted.

This process gives managers a tool to mitigate the profit squeeze caused by the saturation of the market – that is, by its highly competitive nature, overall excess production capacity and the absence of stable growth. The result is concession bargaining; in other words, unionized workers in industrial cores lose their ability to make gains. There are numerous examples of whipsawing leading to concessions targeted at particularly vulnerable groups of workers, such as young people and workers in easy-to-outsource support services. But this process presupposes a sense of insecurity across the workforce that includes 'core' workers and their representatives. While this insecurity has obvious negative implications for the power of trade unions and works councils, it can also lead them to become influential as co-managers if they focus their efforts on topics where they can agree with management on 'mutual gains'.

Our argument differs from the academic orthodoxies on the political economy of work that currently prevail in Europe. The image of insider–outsider conflicts, for example, has spread beyond the work of neoliberal think-tanks and neoclassical economists and into that of some writers otherwise sympathetic to non-market regulation. They argue that existing industrial relations institutions and welfare state entitlements exacerbate inequality by favouring a certain group of 'core' workers while excluding people with weak labour market attachment. It is the perverse consequences of non-market regulation that is the problem, not liberalization. Our argument here is that so-called insiders – skilled blue-collar workers employed in auto assembly plants – are equally under attack through marketization and social dumping. This enables us to examine not only the decline of worker protections but also the extension of market discipline across society, the rise of new regulatory arrangements and the resulting upward redistribution of resources in society.

Whipsawing and its effects in the automotive industry

Management whipsawing[1] emerged during the 1980s at the American firms General Motors (GM) and Ford (Katz, 1985; Turner, 1991), and spread during the 1990s and 2000s to European firms, including the Italian and German carmakers FIAT, Volkswagen (VW) and Daimler Benz (Meardi, 2000; Greer and Hauptmeier, 2008). This took place in a context of market liberalization and the creation of a single European auto market, which made it easier for companies to integrate production networks and shift production across borders. Whipsawing did not merely take place as a result of competition between high-wage and low-wage locations, although this did happen. Lower wage locations in Southern Europe were also threatened or closed, and often competition was staged between high-wage locations. While the best-known cases of whipsawing were competitions between locations in different countries, there were also instances of rivalry between locations in Germany.

The diversity of whipsawing

Over the past three decades, a number of different types of management whipsawing have emerged (Greer and Hauptmeier, 2012b). In the context of increasing market competition in Europe, management pursued two contradictory goals simultaneously. On the one hand, managers sought to extract concessions and reduce labour costs through whipsawing. On the other, they sought to establish labour–management partnership to ensure high-quality production, which managers also regarded as being essential for surviving in highly competitive markets. Companies struck this balance between forcing and fostering in different ways (Walton and McKersie, 1965) which shaped the emergence of various whipsawing practices.

An initial common pattern was *coercive whipsawing* (Mueller and Purcell, 1992; Katz, 1985): management pitched different plants against each other in competition over production and explicitly threatened the targeted plants with shifting production to other plants if the concessions were not high enough. Because this type of whipsawing regularly disrupted labour–management relations and led to conflict, management engaged in *informal whipsawing*. In these instances, local managers informally and casually mentioned that production decisions were coming up. This friendly tip by local managers often took place before collective bargaining rounds. Without explicitly threatening to shift production, the purpose of the hints was clear. Labour was supposed to agree to concessions or even to suggest them if they wanted to be considered for new production and investments by regional or world headquarters.

Another management strategy to balance collaboration and coercion in a different manner was the introduction of *rule-based whipsawing*. In these instances, managers sought to establish clear rules and expectations for the competitive assignment of production with the goal of increasing the legitimacy of the process. Management introduced a bidding process between competing plants, whereby the plants with the best bid (meaning, among other things, higher labour concessions) would receive the greatest share of production or the entire production volume. Here, management created a within-company market for the allocation of production (Hauptmeier, 2011). An accompanying rhetoric was often that management generally pointed to the efficiency and fairness of markets in societies, thus suggesting that the market mechanism is a fair allocation principle even if it may lead to concessions. Finally, managers developed what we refer to as *hegemonic whipsawing*. In this type of whipsawing, managers spent considerable time and resources on influencing labour representatives' ideas (Hauptmeier, 2012; Hauptmeier and Heery, 2014), seeking to convince them that whipsawing was necessary for survival in the highly competitive auto markets (Greer and Hauptmeier, 2012b). Management argued that the competitive assignment of production was necessary to stay 'fit' in competition with other firms. This discourse regularly connected with the sports-oriented and competitive mental frames of male labour representatives.

Coercive whipsawing was the dominant form at GM Europe between 1995 and 2003. It involved extracting concessions through explicit threats to move production. This was underpinned by the benchmarking of performance and practices, which allowed firms to compare locations for the purpose of making demands in collective bargaining. Coercive whipsawing was used in landmark concession bargaining in Germany, Belgium and the UK in 1995 and 1998, but it also helped discipline striking workers at VW's Spanish subsidiary SEAT, where management followed through on a threat to move work from Martortell (Barcelona) to Bratislava (Slovakia) in 2002. Another example is Ford Spain, where management threatened to move work from Almusaffes (Valencia) to Saarlouis (Germany) with the aim of squashing local labour protest.

However, firms often refrained from explicit threats. This may have been motivated by the need to preserve cooperative relations with unions, but could also have been due to a lack of excess production capacity (and the resulting difficulty of moving work). At Ford, for example, the more common pattern in Europe as well as in North America has been informal whipsawing. From the 1990s on, following the spread of rumours about new investment decisions within Ford Europe, German worker representatives would approach management with an offer of concessions in exchange for securing production. The background to this was a general awareness in the firm of potential overcapacities and the likelihood of eventual plant closures, as well as developing management benchmarking practices, but at the same time a desire on management's part to avoid disrupting partnership through raw coercion. It was this kind of whipsawing that led to concession bargaining in Germany in 1993 and 1997, which drove the convergence of previously higher company-level wages at Ford to that of the level of the sectoral collective agreement and provided legally enforceable guarantees of investment and production. These guarantees precipitated the end of Ford's 'blue oval' automotive production in the UK after more than 80 years. During the downturn of the European auto market at the end of the 1990s, Ford was forced to reduce production capacities. As the investments at the German production sites were protected, Ford decided to close the historic Dagenham plant.

Rule-based whipsawing was a further development of the phenomenon (Hauptmeier, 2011). Several establishments on a particular platform would be invited to bid to produce a particular model on the basis of costs and other criteria, and the plants whose bids did not succeed would be susceptible to closure. This approach was employed by GM in an attempt to increase the legitimacy and transparency of its drive for concessions following a Europe-wide work stoppage coordinated by the EWC. It was also used by VW after 1999 in its parts operations: plants would have to bid against external suppliers and adjust their labour costs accordingly.

Another sophisticated way for management to secure the consent of worker representatives is hegemonic whipsawing, which became the dominant pattern at VW during the 2000s. Unlike informal whipsawing, here there were explicit threats formulated by management, but these threats took place in a broader context in which worker representatives considered them a legitimate way to keep different workforces 'on their toes' with a focus on staying competitive. This was in part a result of management's efforts to influence the ideas of worker representatives, partly by entering into more thorough engagement with worker representatives than at the other firms, and partly by providing worker representatives with salaries equal to those of top managers as well as numerous perks. The latter involved management payments for prostitutes in the context of works council meetings, which were illegal, caused scandal and were later repudiated by the works council (Greer and Hauptmeier, 2008).

The organization of labour competition outlined above regularly coincides with the staging of two other forms of competition. First, MNCs set the geographical locales in which production locations are embedded in competition with each other in the following way. In the context of new investment and production decisions, management asks politicians for subsidies in the form of infrastructure, training, social benefits or provision of land in exchange for new investments (Drahokoupil, 2008). Since these requests involve jobs and economic growth that matter in elections – especially in the auto industry, which is highly symbolic of industrial success – politicians are as susceptible to whipsawing as labour representatives. This competition can be staged at different scales, and cities, regions/states and nations have variously been pitched against each other with the aim of extracting subsidies. The EU has sought to limit this type of competition and made various subsidies illegal. However, the new EU regulations have not been very effective, as could be seen during the financial crisis at the end of the 2000s, when different nation states subsidized automakers through scrappage bonuses and short-time working benefits.

Second, local managers from different plants are set in competition with each other in the context of investment decisions by the regional or world headquarters of multinationals. According to higher level managers in large auto companies, local managers are inclined to use the introduction of new car models to upgrade machinery and robots, which can be costly for MNCs. Because of these costs, local managers are also asked to submit a bid for new production, which is supposed to explain how much the roll-out of a new car model would cost at a given plant and how existing machinery may be used in an efficient manner. The bids of local managers and labour concessions by worker representatives are regularly submitted to the headquarters of the MNC at the same time. The staging of competition between different plants can have the effect that local managers and labour representatives explore shared interests and engage in local productivity coalitions (Windolf, 1989).

The institutional effects of whipsawing: concession bargaining

While market-making rules allowed whipsawing to emerge as a management strategy, industrial relations rules failed to break the dynamic. To the contrary, they altered the workings of industrial relations by changing the function, meaning and consequences of industrial relations institutions. The failure of the European Commission's EWC Directive to compensate is due not so much to its low take-up rate – though this is a real problem (Kerckhofs, 2006) – but to its failure to give workers a voice in shaping the broader product market to which MNC management was responding.

The differences in national institutions governing worker participation gave national workforces varying degrees of access to management, both locally and internationally. This gave rise to very different cultures and expectations in the workers' camp, which the EWC Directive did little to blunt. The restructuring of Rover by BMW was a notorious case of a failure to inform UK worker representatives of looming plant closures, despite the fact that German worker representatives had this information (Tuckman and Whittall, 2002). Aside from very basic problems with implementing the directive in firms and dealing with the language barrier, national differences between members of EWCs gave rise to low levels of trust (Timming, 2006). This led to certain creative efforts to promote social partnership practices well in excess of the statutory minima set out in the directive and the national laws that implemented it (Greer and Hauptmeier, 2008), including deliberate attempts to change ideas and promote a shared European identity (Whittall *et al.*, 2007; Greer and Hauptmeier, 2012a).

National employment relations practices were altered by whipsawing as firms used it to introduce forms of concession bargaining pioneered elsewhere. In Germany, for example, whipsawing was used to disrupt in various ways the former principle of encompassing and compressed pay scales and allowed firms to introduce multi-tier wage structures. Pioneered in the US, multi-tier wage structures allowed firms to save money while protecting incumbent workers by introducing reduced pay grades for selected and new groups of workers. In response to management threats to produce a new vehicle (the Touran) outside of Germany, for example, worker representatives agreed to a project known as 5000x5000, which created new jobs for unemployed people at a lower pay grade (Schumann *et al.*, 2006). At Daimler in 2004, a threat to move production from Stuttgart to Bremen led to an agreement to reduce the pay of workers in auxiliary services such as catering, cleaning, logistics and security, which was presented as an alternative to outsourcing. Pay structures within auto plants became extremely complex, with additional concessionary agreements differentiating workers by seniority and function, as well as employer, with different pay levels for agency temps, contractors and staff transferred because of joint ventures (Greer and Hauptmeier, 2008).

Another example of whipsawing-induced change to industrial relations practices and employment conditions is working time flexibilization. VW began to use working time flexibility as a means to reduce labour costs in the 1990s. VW's HR manager used the metaphor of the 'breathing company' in this context: workforces were supposed to adapt production levels to the demand in the markets, which meant, for example, longer weekly working hours during peak demand in the summer and shorter weekly working time during the winter months with weaker demand. VW introduced far-reaching working time flexibility across Europe in the 1990s; however, Spanish worker representatives at SEAT resisted these changes because they regarded a stable working week as a historic trade union gain, which they staunchly defended in several collective bargaining rounds during the 1990s. In 2002, VW asked once more for more working time flexibility and was again rebuked by the local labour representatives. Following the negotiations with labour, VW made good on its threats and moved 10 per cent of its production to the Bratislava plant in Slovakia within days. This came as a shock to the workforce and the allocation decision was only reversed once the labour representatives agreed to far-reaching working time flexibility in 2004 (Hauptmeier and Morgan, 2014).

Worker responses

These dynamics led to considerable innovation by workers' representatives. There was, for example, a proliferation of firm-level transnational agreements at Europe's MNCs with the explicit aim of curbing social dumping by introducing certain norms (see Da Costa and Rehfeldt, 2007; Fichter *et al*., 2011; Platzer and Rüb, 2014). Some of them – including the first agreement, which was at Ford's spun-off parts operation, Visteon – covered topics not usually found in collective agreements, such as norms for sourcing by Ford. Others, including Daimler's agreement, had various management mechanisms built in to enforce the rules. At these firms, transnational worker representation was augmented well beyond the minimal practices envisaged in the EWC Directive. At Daimler and VW, for example, there were several innovations aimed at improving transnational labour–management partnership, including the extension of the EWC to the global level as a World Works Council (Greer and Hauptmeier, 2008).

At GM, the EWC developed a sophisticated internationalization strategy combining a strong element of rank-and-file mobilization with demands for transnational collective agreements with management (see Fetzer, 2008; Bernaciak, 2010; Greer and Hauptmeier, 2012b). It intensified its work for some time in response to management whipsawing and its own failures in reacting, and consciously sought to compensate for the failures of national action by shifting its activities to the transnational level, which meant improving communications and relations between its members. They met frequently, learned a common language (English), created a blog in which debates continued between meetings, and organized numerous bilateral exchanges between plants in different countries. Much of this work consisted in convincing rank-and-file workers of the value of international work and in involving them via days of action. When management attempted to formalize the market for investment at the level of the 'platform', the EWC responded by creating a 'platform group' whose members agreed not to bargain individually with management.

These struggles, however, were limited in a number of ways. The story of labour transnationalism at GM Europe, for example, is one of a struggle against whipsawing and plant closures and not of the prevention of concessions. The solidaristic principle was to 'share the pain', not to reduce it. Furthermore, this principle was never fully realized in practice, since management did succeed over the years both in extracting local concessions and closing plants. Often this undermined trust between worker representatives because local agreements violated principles that had supposedly been agreed between worker representatives at the European level. There were therefore not only material conflicts of interest but also fierce rivalries and enmities. These not only divided workers by country but also within countries, as in the ongoing conflict between works councillors at Rüsselsheim and Bochum in Germany.

GM Europe was an unusually well-developed case of transnational worker representation. The more normal pattern for auto assemblers based in Germany, or whose European operations were centred on Germany, was for there to be far more labour–management cooperation. At VW, for instance, this usually implied an acceptance of between-plant competition as something healthy; at Ford, by contrast, it meant a more subtle dynamic of competition in which management did not normally have to issue clear threats. When it came to re-establishing solidarity, the problem was therefore not usually just ineffectiveness or lack of power; more often, worker representatives were not able to overcome conflicting interests.

The economic crisis that started in the late 2000s brought renewed state intervention, which not only stoked conflict between members of GM's EWC but also increased the broader political stakes at the national level (see Fetzer, 2012; Klikauer, 2012; Bernaciak, 2013). In a dramatic turn of events in 2009, GM initiated a bankruptcy process in the US, solicited takeover bids for its European operations, and then reversed its decision and announced its own restructuring plans. This round of restructuring exacerbated tensions between worker representatives at GM and sidelined the EWC as an institution. This was not only because this round of restructuring was, even more than usual, certain to lead to plant closures – with winners and losers. It was also because members of the EWC were working publicly – and in close cooperation with national governments – to influence the outcome. German trade unionists openly favoured a takeover bid from a Canadian–Russian consortium with strong loan guarantees from the German state in exchange for guarantees of jobs and production in Germany. Trade unionists in Spain and the

UK feared they would be sidelined in an independent European firm and were relieved by the eventual outcome. Spanish unions went on strike against the threatened move of production to Germany, and Tony Woodley, leader of the British union UNITE, called on the European Commission to block the deal. In the end, plants were closed in Antwerp and Bochum, and the European headquarters were moved from Zürich to Rüsselsheim.

The European automotive industry provides telling examples of what happens when market relations are imposed with little in the way of new countervailing social protections. What is remarkable is not that there are particular and conflicting interests in the labour camp that prevent a solidaristic settlement. Such conflicts of material interest are well-known and well-understood features of international trade. It is also not surprising that the institutions aimed at promoting social dialogue are inadequate in enabling workers to stand against wage-based competition and social dumping. Just as national-level collective bargaining and co-determination rules proved to be inadequate for coping with an internationalized economy, so EWCs at the scale of the firm were never going to be very useful for coping with the consequences of fierce competition at the scale of the product market. More interesting is that whipsawing, an important example of social dumping with obvious and severe corrosive effects upon formerly egalitarian industrial relations institutions, could repeat itself for so long in a continent supposedly renowned for strong worker rights and social protections. Also remarkable are the long-lasting attempts by trade unionists to fight whipsawing and build solidarity within an institutional framework so conducive to corporate divide-and-rule strategies.

Implications for the social dumping debate

What does our analysis of whipsawing as marketization have to do with the policy debate in Europe over social dumping? In our view, it has implications for understanding the actors and the processes involved. While the term 'social dumping' has been used in many ways, a common way to discuss it is to point to low-wage countries passing unfair regulations that attract jobs from high-wage countries. In the Introduction to this volume, Bernaciak provides a conceptual critique of this position; the task here is to provide contrasting empirical evidence, propose a marketization-focused alternative and suggest political implications.

Our analysis highlights differences between the crude version of the social dumping argument and the reality of the European automotive sector. First, the key actors driving the phenomenon of whipsawing are central management in multinationals and, to a lesser extent, firm- and plant-level worker representatives and local managers, and not national government in poor countries. The latter only rarely play a central role in whipsawing. States do matter, but it is more often the institutions – the sedimented results of past legislation – that shape these dynamics. They tend to do so in unintended ways; for example, when works councils use their right to democratic participation in the workplace to outcompete their counterparts elsewhere.

The examples given above show that competition is not merely between high-wage and low-wage countries but is happening right across the production system and product market. The decisions of management may be swayed by reductions in labour costs brought about by concessions, but there are other considerations as well, such as proximity to markets and labour productivity. Sometimes competition is within a country or between high-wage countries, and sometimes high-wage countries succeed in attracting jobs from low-wage countries. In addition, the high-wage/low-wage division is in flux. Sometimes, as in the case of Spain, a low-wage country becomes a high-wage country; and at other times, as in the case of Poland and its neighbours to the east, a low-wage country finds itself in competition with even lower wage countries.

In addition, the moral dimension of whipsawing is more complex than the crude social dumping argument would have it. Whipsawing may be unfair in that it is used to extract concessions from workers and distribute resources to shareholders; but often managers try to make it legitimate in the minds of worker representatives by taking seriously information and consultation mechanisms at the transnational level or by creating a consistent framework of rules. Sometimes they succeed. The ethics of bargaining under a threat of plant closure are also far from clear-cut. While the problems created for workers by footloose capital are clear, the workers involved in any given case have to make a difficult decision over a trade-off between conceding past accomplishments of the labour movement and protecting regional jobs and manufacturing.

Marketization – in this case, transnational whipsawing by management – is closely related to social dumping. While whipsawing is enabled by the liberalization of markets for goods and capital across Europe, it is fundamentally driven by management. The decisions that shape worker outcomes are made by managers and not by politicians who are accountable to voters, bureaucrats who are accountable to politicians or trade unionists who are accountable to members. The function of industrial relations becomes the upward redistribution of resources in the name of securing jobs, and an institutionally thick arrangement emerges within the corporation to stage market competition to ensure that this happens. The threat of exit has central importance in this kind of social dumping, and this process is governed by the internal structures, rules and practices of the firm in question with an eye to increasing profitability or mitigating losses.

One implication of this analysis is that any policy initiative to stop social dumping (and the resulting trend towards inequality in Europe) needs to deal with other market-making institutional changes. It may be that changes in taxation, industrial relations, welfare or other areas of policy can compensate to a limited degree. But there is little evidence that they have reversed the overall trend, in part because states also make concessions in these areas to appease markets or (more specifically) the powerful actors in markets such as managers in large corporations. In the automotive industry, firms extract concessions from the state in the form of subsidies such as scrappage schemes, loan guarantees, infrastructure investment and wage supports, all on the eve of a pan-European drive for public sector austerity. The policies that allow firms to extract these concessions by threatening exit in various ways are market-making policies creating a global automotive sector.

A second implication is that social regulation is needed at the level of the market. It is, after all, the firms that are organizing transactions such as an exchange of concessions for investment. The extension of worker participation rights to the transnational scale does strengthen worker voice in this context, but the experience of German automakers shows that this kind of social regulation is insufficient. To the extent that workers are integrated into the management of firms that are competing in saturated product markets, their representatives also internalize the demands of the market as co-managers and engage in concession bargaining. While markets are made to a large extent by states, the stories of production allocation outlined above show that the day-to-day working of competition is organized by private actors who are not subject to any sort of democratic accountability.

It may seem naïve to propose bringing the marketizing face of European integration to a halt; but while marketization continues, it would be naïve to believe that reforms in other areas might produce a 'social' Europe or prevent social dumping. Market change is a root cause and should be dealt with accordingly.

Note

1 Whipsawing strategies similar to those described in our chapter are used by the management in other industries as well (see e.g. Trappmann's account of interplant benchmarking in the European steel industry in Chapter 7, this volume).

References

Baccaro, L. and Howell, C. (2011) 'A Common Neoliberal Trajectory. The Transformation of Industrial Relations in Advanced Capitalism'. *Politics and Society*, 39(4): 521–563.

Bernaciak, M. (2010) 'Cross-border Competition and Trade Union Responses in the Enlarged EU: Evidence from the Automotive Industry in Germany and Poland'. *European Journal of Industrial Relations*, 16(2): 119–135.

Bernaciak, M. (2012) 'Social Dumping: Political Catchphrase or Threat to Labour Standards?' *ETUI Working Paper*, No. 2012.06. Brussels: European Trade Union Institute.

Bernaciak, M. (2013) 'Labour Solidarity in Crisis? Lessons from General Motors Europe'. *Industrial Relations Journal*, 44(2): 139–153.

Brinkmann, U. (2011) *Die unsichtbare Faust des Marktes: Betriebliche Kontrolle und Koordination im Finanzmarktkapitalismus*. Berlin: Sigma.

Crouch, C. (2009) 'Marketisation'. In Flinders, M. *et al.* (eds), *The Oxford Handbook of British Politics*. Oxford: Oxford University Press, pp. 879–898.

Culpepper, P. (2010) *Quiet Politics and Business Power: Corporate Control in Europe and Japan*. Cambridge: Cambridge University Press.

Da Costa, I. and Rehfeldt, U. (2007) 'European Works Councils and Transnational Bargaining about Restructuring in the Auto Industry'. *Transfer*, 13(2): 313–316.

Doellgast, V. (2012) *Disintegrating Democracy at Work: Labor Unions and the Future of Good Jobs in the Service Economy*. Ithaca, NY: Cornell University Press.

Dörre, K., Lessenich, S. and Rosa, H. (2009) *Soziologie, Kapitalismus, Kritik. Eine Debatte*. Frankfurt am Main: Suhrkamp.

Drahokoupil, J. (2008) *Globalization and the State in Central and Eastern Europe: The Politics of Foreign Direct Investment*. London: Routledge.

Emmenegger, P., Häusermann, S., Palier, B. and Seeleib-Kaiser, M. (eds) (2012) *The Age of Dualization: The Changing Face of Inequality in Deindustrializing Societies*. Oxford: Oxford University Press.

Fetzer, T. (2008) 'European Works Councils as Risk Communities: The Case of General Motors'. *European Journal of Industrial Relations*, 14(3): 289–308.

Fetzer, T. (2012) 'From Nationalism to European Patriotism? Trade Unions and the European Works Council at General Motors'. *Journal of European Public Policy*, 19(3): 342–357.

Fichter, M., Helfen, M. and Sydow, J. (2011) 'Employment Relations in Global Production Networks: Initiating Transfer of Practices via Union Involvement'. *Human Relations*, 64(4): 599–622.

Greer, I. and Doellgast, V. (2013) 'Marketization, Inequality, and Institutional Change'. *Working Paper*, No. WERU5. London: University of Greenwich.

Greer, I. and Hauptmeier, M. (2008) 'Political Entrepreneurs and Co-managers: Labour Transnationalism at Four Multinational Auto Companies'. *British Journal of Industrial Relations*, 46(1): 76–97.

Greer, I. and Hauptmeier, M. (2012a) 'Identity Work: Sustaining Transnational Collective Action at General Motors Europe'. *Industrial Relations*, 51(2): 275–299.

Greer, I. and Hauptmeier, M. (2012b) 'Whipsawing: Organizing Labor Competition in Multinational Auto Companies'. In *ILERA Conference*, Philadelphia, PA, 2–5 July.

Greer, I., Böhlke, N. and Schulten, T. (2013) 'How does Market Making Affect Industrial Relations? Evidence from Eight German Hospitals'. *British Journal of Industrial Relations*, 51(2): 215–239.

Hauptmeier, M. (2011) 'Reassessing Markets and Employment Relations'. In Blyton, P., Heery, E. and Turnbull, P. (eds), *Reassessing the Employment Relationship*. Basingstoke: Palgrave Macmillan, pp. 171–194.

Hauptmeier, M. (2012) 'Institutions Are What Actors Make of Them – The Changing Construction of Firm-level Employment Relations in Spain'. *British Journal of Industrial Relations*, 50(4): 737–759.

Hauptmeier, M. and Heery, E. (2014) 'Ideas at Work'. *International Journal of Human Resource Management*. Published online at: DOI: 10.1080/09585192.2014.936235. Abstract available at: www.tandfonline.com/doi/ref/10.1080/09585192.2014.936235#preview (accessed 5 September 2014).

Hauptmeier, M. and Morgan, G. (2014) 'Ideas and Institutions – The Evolution of Employment Relations in the Spanish and German Auto Industry'. In Hauptmeier, M. and Vidal, M. (eds), *Comparative Political Economy of Work*. London: Palgrave Macmillan, pp. 162–185.

Hirschman, A.O. (1970) *Exit, Voice, and Loyalty; Responses to Decline in Firms, Organizations, and States*. Cambridge, MA: Harvard University Press.

Höpner, M. and Schäfer, A. (2010) 'A New Phase of European Integration: Organised Capitalisms in Post-Ricardian Europe'. *West European Politics*, 33(2): 344–368.

Katz, H.C. (1985) *Shifting Gears: Changing Labor Relations in the U.S. Automobile Industry*. Cambridge, MA: MIT Press.

Kerckhofs, P. (2006) *European Works Councils: Facts and Figures 2006*. Brussels: ETUI-REHS.

Klikauer, T. (2012) 'A General Motors Works Council's Response to the Capitalist Global Financial Crisis: A Case Study from Germany'. *Capital and Class*, 36(2): 303–322.

Lillie, N. (2010) 'Bringing the Offshore Ashore: Transnational Production, Industrial Relations and the Reconfiguration of Sovereignty'. *International Studies Quarterly*, 54(3): 683–704.

MacKenzie, R. and Martinez Lucio, M. (2005) 'The Realities of Regulatory Change Beyond the Fetish of Deregulation'. *Sociology*, 39(3): 499–517.

Meardi, G. (2000) *Trade Union Activists, East and West: Comparisons in Multinational Companies.* Aldershot: Ashgate.

Meardi, G. (2012) *Social Failures of EU Enlargement: A Case of Workers Voting with Their Feet.* London: Routledge.

Mueller, F. and Purcell, J. (1992) 'The Europeanization of Manufacturing and the Decentralization of Bargaining: Multinational Management Strategies in the European Automobile Industry'. *International Journal of Human Resource Management*, 3(1): 15–34.

Platzer, H.W. and Rüb, S. (2014) 'It Takes Two to Tango. Management and European Company Agreements'. *Transfer*, 20(2): 255–270.

Schumann, M., Kuhlmann, M., Sanders, F. and Sperling, H.J. (2006) *Auto 5000: Ein neues Produktionskonzept. Die deutsche Antwort auf den Toyota-Weg*? Hamburg: VSA.

Timming, A.R. (2006) 'The Problem of Identity and Trust in European Works Councils'. *Employee Relations*, 28(1): 9–25.

Tuckman, A. and Whittall, M. (2002) 'Affirmation, Games, and Insecurity: Cultivating Consent within a New Workplace Regime'. *Capital and Class*, 26(1): 65–93.

Turner, L. (1991) *Democracy at Work: Changing World Markets and the Future of Labor Unions*. Ithaca, NY: Cornell University Press.

Vidal, M. (2013) 'Postfordism as a Dysfunctional Accumulation Regime: A Comparative Analysis of the USA, the UK and Germany'. *Work, Employment and Society*, 27(3): 451–471.

Wagner, I. (2014) 'Rule Enactment in a Pan-European Labour Market: Transnational Posted Work in the German Construction Sector'. *British Journal of Industrial Relations*. Published online at: DOI: 10.1111/bjir.12053. Abstract available at: http://onlinelibrary.wiley.com/doi/10.1111/bjir.12053/abstract (accessed 24 August 2014).

Wagner, I. and Lillie, N. (2014) 'European Integration and the Disembedding of Labour Market Regulation: Transnational Labour Relations at the European Central Bank Construction Site'. *Journal of Common Market Studies*, 52(2): 403–419.

Walton, R. and McKersie, R. (1965) *A Behavioral Theory of Labor Negotiations*. New York: McGraw Hill.

Whittall, M., Knudsen, H. and Huijgen, F. (eds) (2007) *Towards a European Labour Identity: The Case of the European Works Council*. London: Routledge.

Windolf, P. (1989) 'Productivity Coalitions and the Future of European Corporatism'. *Industrial Relations*, 28(1): 1–20.

7 Social dumping with no divide

Evidence from multinational companies in Europe

Vera Trappmann

Introduction

Multinational companies (MNCs) are important economic actors in developed countries and even more so in developing markets, where they provide the capital and technologies necessary for modernizing old assets and contribute to the development of particular sectors or types of economic activity. They also have a destructive potential however, especially with regard to employment and working conditions. First, within the value chain of a large corporation, production and service work are no longer bound to a single locality; rather they can easily be shifted between sites. Consequently, production relocations carry the threat of inducing job losses at traditional industrial locations. Second, interplant rivalry often leads to the lowering of employment standards; this may be a result of unilateral management decisions, but it can also be a consequence of concession bargaining, whereby workers accept longer working hours, an unsafe working environment or lower pay in order to make their site competitive and attract new production.

All in all, in the face of intensifying competition, MNCs seek to lower labour costs by taking recourse to practices that – according to the conceptualization developed in this book – may be considered to be social dumping. Current scholarly knowledge on MNC-driven social dumping is based on evidence coming from a limited number of industries. This chapter's contribution rests in extending the analysis to steel and IT; in other words, to two sectors in which at face value one would not expect social dumping to occur. The steel industry is a traditional manufacturing sector characterized by high levels of social protection; for decades, trade unions have actively defended the interests of its (mainly male) production workers in all the examined countries. The segment of the IT industry studied here comprises only high-skilled services. Almost all its employees have academic degrees, are used to an individualized labour market and could, in principle, make use of individual exit options because their competences are in high demand (see also Boes and Kämpf, 2009). Both case studies are based on fieldwork conducted by the author in 2010 to 2013 (involving semi-structured, confidential expert interviews with HR managers, union and works council representatives, and national trade union officials) and on document analysis.[1]

Despite the seemingly low likelihood of social dumping in these two sectors, this chapter documents a plethora of employer-driven strategies that ultimately lead to the lowering of wages and social entitlements, redundancies, relocations via so-called 'best shoring' and site closures. The driving mechanisms of these changes are interplant 'beauty contests' based on benchmarking, outsourcing, employment flexibilization and concession bargaining. The chapter argues that these social dumping practices, initiated and supervised by the companies' headquarters, have become particularly widespread since the outbreak of the economic crisis in the late 2000s. It also shows that given the limited power of local managers, the only source of resistance to social dumping pressures is the resourcefulness of local worker representatives.

The chapter is divided into five parts. The following section reviews the scholarly debate on social dumping at MNCs. Two empirical sections then present the evidence from steel and IT companies. The subsequent section discusses labour reactions to social dumping, outlining the possibilities and limits of their local and transnational strategies. The final section discusses the role of central managements in furthering the social dumping agenda and concludes the chapter with some brief remarks.

Social dumping at multinational companies

In the political economic literature, the relationship between MNC practices and social dumping is contested. Whereas some authors claim that MNCs initiate a 'race to the bottom' in the spheres of employment conditions and worker participation (Marginson, 2006; Meardi *et al.*, 2013), others are more optimistic and point out that, under certain circumstances, foreign direct investment can have a positive impact in these areas. Mosley (2011), for instance, argues that the effect of MNCs depends on how they organize their overseas production. On the basis of the evidence from developing countries, the author claims that direct ownership of production sites may boost employee rights, inducing a 'climb to the top' (Mosley, 2011, p. 12) because MNCs have material incentives to uphold a certain level of labour standards given the international surveillance of their corporate practices and the increased importance of Corporate Social Responsibility. Subcontracting arm's-length production, by contrast, may have a negative effect upon labour rights because transactions take place within the market and thus beyond the firm's scope of control. An alternative view is presented by Lakhani *et al.* (2013), who argue that, depending on value chain configurations, MNCs may seek to improve labour standards even in supplier firms (also see Telljohann, Chapter 8, this volume). As for the impact of organized labour, Mosley is optimistic in her assessment of the role it can play in improving working conditions at MNCs. Her position is contested by Silver (2003), however, who shows that bolder demands voiced by workers and growing union density tend to be followed by production relocations to cheaper and unorganized locations.

Many scholars have focused on the so-called country-of-origin effect of MNCs, assuming that companies will transfer the labour standards and traditions of social dialogue of their home country to foreign locations (Ferner, 1997; Bluhm, 2007; Meardi *et al.*, 2009). In line with this assertion, an MNC headquartered in a coordinated market economy would be expected to 'export' an employment model based on social dialogue, long-term employment relations, and investments in training and qualification, which, from the perspective of host-country locations, would often imply an upward adaptation instead of 'a race to the bottom' (Bluhm, 2007). More recent accounts, however, challenge the existence of the home-country effect. Meardi *et al.* (2013) study of MNCs headquartered in different countries shows that the companies do not apply home-country standards at their foreign sites but instead seek to take full advantage of local market possibilities at host locations. Even German automotive companies, portrayed as best-practice cases in terms of transferring employment standards (Jürgens and Krzywdzinski, 2009; Krzywdzinski, 2014), have often been hostile to attempts to establish worker participation structures at their Central and Eastern European (CEE) subsidiaries.

In terms of social dumping practices pursued by MNCs, the literature has focused on cost-driven relocations, measures aimed at increasing employment flexibility and interplant 'beauty contests', also referred to as 'whipsawing' (Greer and Hauptmeier, Chapter 6, this volume). Unlike market-seeking investments, cost-driven relocations often have a 'substitution effect on domestic [i.e. home-county] … employment' (Galgóczi *et al.*, 2006, p. 503). A mere threat of relocation has a disciplining effect on the workers, discouraging them from the formation of employee representation (Bronfenbrenner, 1996) or leading them to moderate their pay demands (Ahlers *et al.*, 2007). According to Atkinson (1984), employment flexibility can take four different forms: numerical, involving fluctuations in worker headcount; internal, based on changes in working time organization; external, calculated as the ratio of permanent and 'atypical' workers; and functional, involving the transfer of workers to different activities and tasks within the firm. Companies can make use of one or several forms of flexibility at the same time. Whipsawing was first experienced at General Motors as early as the 1980s, when the company management urged each US location to place a competitive bid for new products, threatening the workforce with plant closures in order to win concessions from local unions (Katz, 1985; Kochan *et al.*, 1986). This strategy engendered rivalry between individual production sites, even those located within a single country. Most of the available scholarly accounts of whipsawing focus on the automotive sector (see e.g. Pulignano, 2006; Greer and Hauptmeier, 2008) and the household appliances industry (Telljohann, 2008).

The diversity of MNC-driven social dumping practices paints a dark picture of employment relations in Europe. Given the high share of workforce employed by MNCs, MNC-driven social dumping affects large portions of Europe's working population (Edwards *et al.*, 2013). At the same time, MNCs have a substantial impact upon the direction of change in national systems of employment relations insofar as local companies tend to copy MNCs' practices in their quest for competitive advantage (Batt *et al.*, 2009). MNCs are also involved in lobbying activities, and many of the changes to national labour legislation implemented in EU member states in the context of the recent crisis may be seen as a result of MNCs' pressures. In Spain, for instance, MNCs pressured the government to deregulate the labour market, threatening to move out of the country if their demands were not met (see Meardi, 2014). In Poland, labour law amendments that entered into force in 2013 abolished the regulation on an eight-hour working day, flexibilizing working time to such an extent that workers had to remain on standby for seven days a week and work for 12 hours if so requested as a result of extended working time reference periods. The reforms echoed the demands for higher internal flexibility voiced by large foreign investors such as German automotive companies (Meardi and Trappmann, 2013). As a by-product of the changes, workers were entitled to no overtime bonuses and no resting time compensation, with the ultimate result that increased working time flexibility came hand in hand with the reduction of employee remuneration (Trappmann, 2014).

In addition to their lobbying activities at the EU and national levels, MNCs pursue a multitude of social dumping strategies at their own locations. The following two sections examine the scope and character of such practices at multinational firms in the steel and IT industries.

The steel industry: from organized price competition to social dumping

The steel sector used to be a national and even publicly owned industry, but since the mid-1990s it has seen a major process of concentration. All the sites examined here – whether located in Western Europe or in the former socialist countries – once belonged to the state in question but are currently owned by MNCs. They have also all experienced several takeovers and mergers, and have undergone substantial restructuring in order to remain competitive on the global market.

With the creation of the European Coal and Steel Community (ECSC) in 1952, the steel industry became the first sector subject to a supranational industrial policy. For several decades, this policy was exemplary in its respect for the principles of the 'European Social Model' as governments and the ECSC tried to shelter the industry from direct market pressures via state aid and subsidies. The so-called Davignon Plan, adopted in 1977 by the then EEC Commission, sought to coordinate the aid across ECSC member states. The aim was to distribute the hardships of shrinking demand and the costs of market exit among all European steel plants. The plan introduced Community-level price-formation mechanisms and competition rules involving production quotas and anti-dumping taxes for steel imports; violations of the joint rules were sanctioned with financial penalties (Buntrock, 2004). With the expiry of the ECSC Treaty in 2002 however, this regulatory approach was abandoned, which opened the door to the marketization of the industry. At present, the only – albeit important – legacy of state and EU industrial policy are governments' attempts to influence the competitiveness of the European steel sector by subsidizing energy costs for selected heavy industries.

The corporation examined in this chapter (SCOR) is one of the major global steel producers, with production sites on all continents except Australia. Although it is not a European firm, its headquarters are based in Luxembourg and the UK. The study focuses on SCOR's largest production sites in Germany, Poland and Romania, all of which are integrated steelworks producing flat steel used mainly in the automotive industry and construction. In Germany, two large plants were analysed – one located in the east (SEG) and one in the north of the country (SNG). Whereas SEG is closer to the Eastern European market, SNG has the strategic advantage of being close to the sea. Both plants employ about 3,000 workers of a similar age structure. The sites in Poland and Romania (referred to, respectively, as SPL and SRO) are former state enterprises located in mono-industrial towns. Since their privatization in the early 2000s, both plants have undergone major restructuring involving substantial layoffs that were engineered mainly through early retirement and severance payments. SPL's sale to the current owner was contested by the local trade unions; in the end, the latter managed to negotiate a social package stipulating that the new owner would refrain from forced redundancies up until 2009 (Trappmann, 2013). In Romania, employment guarantees lasted until 2006 thanks to government involvement (Sznajder-Lee and Trappmann, 2010). The current employment levels – almost 10,000 at each site – are much higher than those at SEG and SNG, whereas productivity is lower. In the eyes of the central management, the two CEE plants are still substantially overstaffed.

The steel industry is one of few industries to display similar industrial relations in old and new EU member states. All examined SCOR sites have works councils, and the company's European Works Council has existed since 1996. Both in the west and in the east, union density is relatively high, even though trade union fragmentation at SPL and SRO makes efficient social dialogue at the two sites difficult. Sectoral collective agreements have been in place, at least until recently.

Production at SCOR is planned globally and managed via benchmarks. The individual sites must document every element of the production process: use of raw material, energy consumption, maintenance costs, number of workplace accidents and personnel costs.[2] As a result of the benchmarking process, SCOR's locations have become comparable in terms of their cost structures, and they compete with each other over production quotas and investments. The rivalry divides the plants into winners and losers: only the five top-performing units (due to their good reputations as cost-saving plants) receive new investments. Under these circumstances, even profitable locations are threatened with closure.

This interplant 'beauty contest' acquired a new characteristic when the recent economic crisis broke out in the late 2000s. Following a major slump in demand for steel, SCOR's central management decided that it needed more flexibility in order to be able to push down labour costs during downturns. It accordingly sought to decrease the headcount to 80 per cent of capacity utilization per site, demanding that this should be implemented by increasing external flexibility; in other words, by reducing the core workforce by 20 per cent and replacing it with agency workers or zero-hours contract workers. The individual sites tried to meet the new requirement in a variety of ways. In Romania, the original strategy of reducing the workforce through voluntary retirement schemes was continued. The number of workers was eventually reduced to 80 per cent of capacity utilization, so that there was no need to rely on agency workers due to the decrease in production volumes and the productivity growth achieved thanks to earlier investments. In Poland, the social package was in place until the end of 2009 and thus no forced redundancies occurred. Since 2010 however, workers have been dismissed, especially from units that were not generating much profit, and they have received only the minimum level of severance pay stipulated by law. Half of the dismissed workers were rehired as agency workers with a guarantee that their salary would not be reduced for the following two years. According to the local management, this served as an incentive for the employees to join the temporary work agency.

At the two German plants by contrast, neither redundancies nor transformation of employment contracts took place. It was difficult for the management to push for external flexibility measures not only because of the traditional social partnership culture and the power of organized labour at the two sites, but also because workplaces in the German steel industry are not very Taylorized: most positions are multifunctional, and agency workers would thus not be experienced enough to fulfil the different tasks assigned to them. As a consequence, in Germany the cost-saving goal was achieved through what I refer to as 'organizational flexibilization'. In line with this approach, some permanent workers were transferred to newly created internal subsidiaries providing services to different divisions of SNG and SEG. Formally separate from the company, their transfer helped reduce the head-count at the sites and thus satisfy the central management's demands. To ensure that a sufficient amount of work was assigned to the new subsidiaries, SNG and SEG insourced services – such as loading and packaging – that had previously been provided by external companies. In contrast to external flexibility through traditional outsourcing and agency work, organizational flexibilization allowed the workers to maintain their employment contracts with SNG and SEG and preserve their social rights and entitlements. While the workforce has remained exactly the same, from the point of view of corporate statistics, the number of production workers has been lowered and the productivity rate, counted as manpower per tonne, has improved.

To summarize, social dumping at SCOR has taken two distinct forms: whipsawing (or interplant 'beauty contests' based on benchmarking) and external employment flexibility measures. Whipsawing has resulted in closures of SRO plants (though not those examined in this chapter), whereas the reliance on external flexibility has led to redundancies at SPL and SRO. Only at SNG and SEG has a more worker-friendly approach based on organizational flexibility been adopted.

The IT sector: 'best shoring' or violating labour law?

The IT sector encompasses hardware and computer technology, telecommunications, software and IT services (Boes and Baukrowitz, 2002). In the early period of development, it was characterized by an unprecedented growth dynamic and relied on high-skilled creative work and new models of work organization. The dot-com crisis of 2001 prompted intense internationalization and Taylorization of work, as well as the commodification of IT labour (Boes and Kämpf, 2008).

The company examined here (ITCOR) is a global player in the IT sector with its headquarters in the US. Since the mid-2000s, the company has undergone several restructuring rounds and a large number of mergers and acquisitions. ITCOR produces technological devices and provides services to customers worldwide. The sites located in Western Europe are relatively large, with 18,000 workers employed in the UK (ITUK), 12,000 in Germany (ITGER) and 8,000 in Spain (ITE). In these three countries, the average age of software engineers employed by the corporation is quite high, which entails higher personnel costs compared to locations that employ younger workers.[3] ITCOR's sites in the new EU member states – all greenfield investments – are located in Poland, Romania and Bulgaria (ITPL, ITRO and ITB, respectively). At all three locations, employment levels have been steadily growing, and in 2013, 4,000 workers were employed in each country. Their average age is 26 to 29 years and their qualifications are very diverse, but all have academic degrees.

In Europe, collective interest representation in the IT sector is poor. Not all the examined ITCOR sites have organized labour representation; at ITPL, ITRO and ITB, for instance, a union-hostile management has until recently been successful in preventing the creation of trade unions and works councils.[4] In most countries, there are no sectoral collective agreements regulating wages. The only existing sectoral agreement in Spain was terminated in July 2013, and the employer is reluctant to negotiate a new one. Plant-level collective agreements exist only at ITE and ITUK, whereas at other sites wages are negotiated on an individual basis between HR and employees. As a consequence, workers complain that no pay rise has occurred. Only at ITUK, where union density stands at 25 per cent, have workers benefited from negotiated pay increases. The share of agency workers varies, from 15 per cent at ITB to 50 per cent at ITE.

Social dumping practices at ITCOR have been encouraged by considerable wage discrepancies within individual sites resulting from mergers and acquisitions. Even at ITE, where unions are relatively influential and collective bargaining takes place, almost no agreements have been negotiated for a site as a whole. Instead, there exist numerous agreements for specific units, which exerts a downward pressure on unions' bargaining demands. ITGER, where wages and social benefits negotiated by the local works council in the context of its merger with ITCOR had been higher than those at other company sites, was kept under scrutiny and eventually closed.

The company's search for cost efficiency has intensified since the late 2000s. The number of ITCOR employees in the new EU member states doubled, while at ITGER and ITUK, 20 per cent of the personnel was dismissed in conjunction with the relocation of certain tasks and divisions. The establishment of additional capacities in Romania, for instance, has been linked to the creation of a shared service centre and the insourcing of certain divisions and services, such as call-centre operations and salary administration, that were previously performed in other countries. While these practices are not a novelty in the IT sector (see e.g. Boes and Kämpf, 2009), relocations and offshoring from old to new EU member states has clearly become more frequent since the outbreak of the crisis. The company has also begun relocating further east (to India and China), and in some cases has even shifted production from CEE to Asia. The management tends to call offshoring 'best shoring' and claims that relocation is the best solution because it enables the firm to offer its services at low prices.

As an alternative to further relocations, the company demanded that the Western European sites lower their labour costs. This was most evident in ITE, where the management asked employees to renounce their annual pay indexation rights and accept the extension of daily and annual working time without a salary increase. Furthermore, the management sought to declare all wage-related provisions of the collective agreements void, which was contrary to Spanish labour law. Most of the demands have been scrapped due to fears of possible resistance and counteractions from the side of the Spanish unions (see the following section). At the same time however, amendments introduced to Spanish labour law in 2013 gave ITCOR enough room to lower labour standards. The new regulations have made dismissals easier, and at ITE the majority of employees were soon replaced by new workers who received only a small percentage of the salaries of the former personnel. According to unions' estimations, 70 per cent of employees have been downgraded and earn less than €1,000 a month, whereas formerly the wages stood at €4,000 to €5,000 a month. At the same time, the share of agency workers at ITE has considerably increased. There has also been a tendency to dismiss workers who are older than 40 years and who worked in strongly unionized units, which has considerably weakened collective worker representation at the plant. A similar strategy was pursued at ITGER, where the entire site was closed down because it was relatively highly unionized and cost intensive. A substantial part of the customer services previously provided by the German site were shifted directly to ITB. At the new location, the company planned to set up teams that would be fluent in German in order to satisfy the needs of the German customers, even though the labour market was very tight in Bulgaria for German-speaking software engineers. ITGER's closure was therefore not driven purely by business considerations, or workload or client needs; rather it also served to fight union opposition and please the financial markets. At the same time, it has created considerable organizational problems both at ITGER and ITB.

To summarize, social dumping at ITCOR has taken many different forms, ranging from increased reliance on external flexibility measures, rehiring under inferior working conditions and the dismissal of older and/or unionized workers, to site closures, offshoring and relocations. In this regard, one could argue that, in most cases, 'best shoring' has undermined labour law and social norms; it has thus been 'best' only for the employer, while the ultimate savings have been made at the cost of lower wages and less favourable working conditions.

Labour reactions to employer-driven social dumping

Labour reactions to employer-driven social dumping are conditioned by the existence and the form of organized labour representation. While all sites at SCOR were unionized, not all sites at ITCOR had a works council or a local trade union committee. Where labour representation exists, two channels – local and transnational – have been used by workers to resist employer-driven social dumping pressures.

Local strategies at the steel plants

Path-dependent passivity

At SPL, local trade union committees felt powerless in the face of the announced redundancies and did not directly oppose the process. To an extent, it seems that they recognized the need to increase the site's productivity and accepted that, in addition to investment, this goal could be achieved through personnel reduction. Their main concerns were, on the one hand, to attract new production and, on the other, to secure high severance payments for the dismissed workers. This attitude is linked to their role as co-managers during the privatization process and their failure to reinvent themselves as effective worker representatives following the systemic transition from socialism to capitalism (also see Trappmann, 2011).

At SRO, social dialogue virtually did not exist, with unions perceiving the management as obstructionist and uncooperative, while the management claimed that the unions lacked 'any strategy for workers' representation'. The local trade unions did not cooperate with each other, spending more time on their internal battles than on the negotiations with the management. It seems that, similar to their Polish counterparts, the Romanian unions still suffer from legacies of the past and have not managed to develop effective strategies that could counterbalance social dumping at the workplace. The local situation is further aggravated by the significant loss of unions' institutional power resulting from the recent reforms of Romanian labour law and the country's collective bargaining system.

Concession bargaining

At both SEG and SNG, labour representatives became involved in concession bargaining. At the latter site, the talks resulted in the cancellation of Christmas bonuses and a reduction of working time to 33.66 hours; that is, below the provisions of the collective agreement. The working time reduction was applied to all workers receiving payment above the standard salary and also to management. At SEG, the concession agreement stipulated a step-by-step reduction of working time to 32 hours; the scheme was to last until the end of 2011 and, according to the management, would safeguard 200 jobs. After the expiry of the agreement, workers could choose whether they wanted to work 32 or 35 hours. In addition, SEG workers renounced a 2 per cent pay rise and bonuses so that, all in all, they earned about 9 per cent less of their pre-crisis gross income. This constituted a substantial sacrifice, given that the workload actually increased during the crisis, especially for intermediate management and the administration.

German worker representatives were quite satisfied with the agreements, arguing that they helped keep the two sites open. From the analytical point of view however, concession bargaining may also be viewed as a form of social dumping. Even if workers save their locations, they do it at the cost of social entitlements, and the concessions are made in order to improve a given site's competitive position vis-à-vis other plants. In this regard, it is symptomatic that instruments which previously served to further workers' rights – such as collective bargaining and co-determination – are currently used to push through social dumping measures.

Employment flexibilization

At SPL, worker representatives were opposed to employment flexibility, in particular to functional flexibility. They resisted the introduction of multifunctional working places and increased worker mobility across the Polish sites, arguing that this would lead to a higher incidence of workplace accidents. On the other hand, when the management pushed for external flexibility measures, the unions at SPL and SRO yielded and accepted the layoffs. At present, approximately a quarter of the workers at both sites are agency workers. They have fewer entitlements and weaker job protection than permanent employees, and the management can thus put them under pressure more easily, forcing them to intensify work and accept inferior working conditions. Moreover, temporary work agencies are generally hostile to unions and most agency workers are therefore not unionized. Another problem is the limited job experience of agency workers hired in the steel industry. According to the Polish unions, the increase in the number of accidents at the country's steel-producing sites, including fatal accidents, is linked to the introduction of agency work.

At SEG and SNG, flexible working time arrangements were widespread and helped avoid dismissals during the recent downturn. The introduction of organizational flexibility – i.e. the establishment of service divisions consisting of reserve employees who could be shifted between different units, combined with the insourcing of services that had previously been provided by external companies – has also had a positive, employment-safeguarding effect at both German sites. Encouraged by these experiences, the works councils are currently trying to replace zero-hour contracts with contracts assigned to the internal service division.

All in all, the steel sector shows substantial cross-country differences in terms of the strategies and power resources used by organized labour. In Germany, where works councils enjoyed strong co-determination rights and where internal flexibility was an accepted instrument, works councils actively defended the interests of their local constituencies. In CEE, where organized labour suffered from post-transformation legacies, the unions were unable to prevent social dumping.

Local solutions at the IT sites

At ITCOR, organized labour was in a much weaker position than at SCOR. The only instance of an effective resistance to the company's social dumping practices was an indefinite strike staged at ITE. This historic protest, which lasted for a week and drew together nearly 90 per cent of the workforce, compelled the company to abandon its initial plans involving working time extension and the renunciation of annual pay indexation rights, and thus prevented labour law breaches. The strike was successful also because ITE's management feared potential conflict with the central management resulting from negative press and thus sought to stop the strike action as quickly as possible. At ITGER, labour also staged protest actions against the site's impending closure and tried to attract media attention, but the plant was nevertheless shut down.

In the new EU member states, employment at ITCOR was continuously growing while wages remained lower than in Western Europe. Consequently, the company's strategy in this region did not focus on direct wage cuts, but rather on undermining employee rights as laid down in the labour code. At ITRO and ITPL, no resistance to this form of social dumping has so far taken place, especially given that neither site is organized. At ITB by contrast, a newly founded trade union committee launched a number of initiatives aiming to improve labour conditions at the site. It accused ITCOR of labour law breaches and brought the firm to court – a move that exposed it, however, to intensified attacks from the side of the management.

Transnational solutions

In view of the cross-border character of MNCs' operations, the establishment of employee representation at transnational level as well as direct union initiatives based on solidarity may be used to counteract employer-driven social dumping. In both sectors examined here, these forms of labour cooperation exist, but their effectiveness has so far been rather limited.

European Works Council

The European Works Council at SCOR seems powerless in the face of the management's cost-cutting drive. It is not well informed about company developments; during the crisis, for instance, EWC members learned only from the press that the company's steel mills were to be temporarily closed down. Moreover, the composition of the body does not always reflect the actual structure of the workforce. This stems from the fact that EWC elections are organized every four years, while the redundancies that take place in the meantime significantly change employment levels at individual sites. Currently, the majority of EWC delegates come from CEE, and they are perceived by their Western counterparts as being rather passive: according to a German EWC member, CEE representatives seldom complain about the management's practices or report irregularities at their sites. From the point of view of CEE members however, the body has had some positive effects. As observed by union representatives at SPL, cooperation among unions at SPL has intensified because of EWC pressures for such coordination. Moreover, participation in EWC meetings helps worker representatives clarify their own views and strengthens their bargaining position vis-à-vis the local management. It also gives them access to information that they would not obtain from the local management, which renders them better informed about the future plans for their sites and enables them to adjust their own strategies accordingly.

At ITCOR, there was virtually no cooperation between the EWC and local worker representatives at CEE sites. At ITB, the members of a newly founded trade union never met with EWC members representing their site. This suggests that some EWC members from the new EU member states represented the local management rather than the workers, and are thus perceived by the latter not as a partner but as an enemy. The body was eventually dissolved in 2013 following major violations of rights granted by the EWC Directive. Specifically, the central management did not inform the EWC about its restructuring plans and prohibited the participation of union experts in EWC meetings with the management.

Transnational union solidarity

In the steel sector, national trade unions have difficulty organizing themselves on a cross-border scale despite the existence of an active union federation at the EU level: IndustriAll (formerly the European Metalworkers' Federation). Apart from organizational reasons related to the low numbers of staff and the limited financial resources of the unions' international departments, the main problem remains the low degree of international solidarity. As shown by the SCOR example, individual production sites compete with one another and unions tend to defend their own constituencies, the national workforces. As the head of the works council at SEG admitted: 'Each blast furnace closed somewhere else makes my location more secure.' The works council member at SPL held a similar view: 'Pay rise is not a priority at our cheaper locations as it would destroy the competitive advantage.'

Transnational solidarity actions have been more effective at ITCOR. Once the tension between the EWC and the central management became more pronounced, employees created the so-called Workers Alliance – an institution parallel to the EWC that could be joined only by unionized worker representatives. The Alliance holds regular meetings and is used for information exchange and strategic planning. Since the dissolution of the EWC, the Alliance has become the only platform that can be used by employees to prepare a new EWC application. Worker solidarity within the Alliance was manifested through the support it lent to the newly founded union at ITB, whose leaders have several times been denied pay rises and annual bonuses and have even been threatened with dismissal. An international workshop was held at ITB together with the local trade union committee and the Workers Alliance, demonstrating that violations against the right to form a union would not be tolerated by ITCOR employees. The Alliance also tried to encourage workers from other CEE locations to get organized.

Discussion and conclusion

In the steel and IT companies analysed here, employer-driven social dumping has taken various forms: interplant ‘beauty contests’ based on the benchmarking process, concession bargaining and measures to increase employment flexibility; there have also been attempts on the side of the employers to breach national labour law. In order to improve their balance sheets, the two firms have outsourced business divisions, relocated production and closed entire sites. A particularly damaging practice has been the rehiring of workers under inferior conditions and the dismissal of certain segments of the workforce such as older or unionized workers.

At first sight, there seems to be no difference between the two companies in regard to their central managements’ social dumping orientation. In both cases, cost-cutting measures were pursued irrespective of national economic systems and of the negative implications they have had for labour. This may be because both MNCs originate from Anglo-Saxon countries: ITCOR is headquartered in the US and SCOR in the UK. US MNCs are notorious for their hostile attitude towards unions and often launch centrally coordinated anti-union policies (see e.g. Ferner *et al*., 2005). The massive resistance against the foundation of the workplace union at ITB illustrates clearly how resourceful management can be in this respect.

While it is difficult to draw generalizable conclusions on the basis of the two cases, it may nevertheless be useful to look at the observed similarities and differences between the case studies. Employment flexibilization measures were introduced in both sectors and in all countries. Redundancies and plant closures (though not yet of the divisions analysed in this chapter) occurred in both the steel and the IT sectors; in the former they were linked to interplant ‘beauty contests’, whereas in the latter they were part of a general plan by central management and did not involve a benchmarking process. ‘Best shoring’ and relocations took place only in the IT sector, which indicates that co-determination at Western European steel sites may have helped local workforces to safeguard their locations. Nonetheless, negotiations at SNG and SEG had a defensive character and were oriented towards the protection of individual sites. In this respect, forging labour solidarity not only across borders but even beyond particular locations remains a daunting challenge.

Workers’ reactions to social dumping were partly conditioned by differences in national industrial relations systems and sectoral characteristics (see Bechter *et al*., 2012). Rather than macro-level variables however, it seems that the most important factors accounting for the variation in the effectiveness of labour responses were the resourcefulness and the agency of local actors. This finding is consistent with arguments put forward by Kahancová (2007) and Doellgast (2010), who claim that employment relations are to a large degree determined by micro-political negotiations at the workplace. As a result, in similar institutional settings, only the interactions between unions and local management in each plant determine different outcomes in terms of labour standards. This argument has to be further qualified however. In the cases analysed in this chapter, MNCs' strategies were formulated primarily at the central level, and thus local managers had a very limited impact upon the choice of policies pursued at their sites. Consequently, it is primarily the agency of local works councils or unions that explains the varying extents of social dumping at individual company sites. At SNG and SEG, for instance, where union density was high and the decades-old co-determination tradition had helped build a self-awareness among steelworkers as a kind of 'labour elite' and co-managers of their own plants, local worker representatives considered it their duty to resist cost-cutting pressures and to become more resourceful in preventing social dumping. Their efforts to introduce organizational flexibility measures in order to prevent layoffs are a good example of this proactive attitude. Local representatives have reflected on their commitment, writing in a book by local works councils that '[h]ere in German steel, works councils still have the heart to do something. Even if this is a daily fight' (Breidbach *et al.*, 2013, p. 34, author's translation). In contrast, where labour representation was weak or in decline, as in the case of ITGER, local worker representatives were unable to counter the central management's cost-cutting pressures.

In many European countries, labour law reforms implemented during the recent crisis have further facilitated social dumping. Governments have given in to the pressure of MNCs to make labour law more employer friendly, and, as a result, a new employment regime has been created at the expense of the well-being of workers. The reforms have often arrived under the cloak of the need to fight the economic and financial crisis (Clauwaert and Schömann, 2012). It seems, then, that in the eyes of the policymakers, social dumping per se becomes an answer to the crisis. On the other hand, in many cases (including the case studies presented in this chapter), the crisis argument has been used by management to legitimize social dumping strategies that had already been launched before the downturn. Under these circumstances, the lack of transnational solidarity among workers makes it easier for employers to play off individual workforces against each other. In light of the limited effectiveness of localized approaches, a new supranational policy and regulation is needed to contain the spread of social dumping.

Notes

1 The fieldwork was made possible through a grant from the Deutsche Forschungsgemeinschaft (DFG) within the framework of Collaborative Research Centre 580, Project A2, and was subsidized by a project on the transnationalization of labour representation financed by the German metalworking trade union IG Metall. The author would also like to thank Alexandra Seehaus and Tina Rosner for providing excellent research assistance.

2 In most MNCs, the international architecture of HR enables international monitoring of employment levels, labour costs, labour productivity, turnover and employee attitudes (Edwards *et al.*, 2013).
3 This factor has recently placed the German location under threat of closure.
4 In most CEE countries, if labour representation exists at all, it is strongest at the company level, where trade union committees are established. In Bulgaria, three employees are needed to form a trade union committee, compared to ten employees in Poland and 15 in Romania. Works councils are often perceived as competitors to unions. For the different effect of labour organization by works councils or union committees, see Trappmann *et al.* (2014). In the new EU member states, there often exist only so-called employee forums – toothless bodies consisting of elected employee representatives that formally serve as mediators between the management and the staff. The elections to employee forums are organized by the management.

References

Ahlers, E., Oez, F. and Ziegler, A. (2007) 'Company Relocation: The Consequences for Employees – An Analysis of the WSI Works Council Survey'. *WSI Discussion Paper*, No. 151. Düsseldorf: Institute of Economic and Social Research.

Atkinson, J. (1984) 'Manpower Strategies for Flexible Organizations'. *Personnel Management*, 15(8): 28–31.

Batt, R., Holman, D. and Holtgreve, U. (2009) 'The Globalization of Service Work: Comparative Institutional Perspectives on Call Centers. Introduction to a Special Issue of ILRR'. *Industrial and Labour Relations Review*, 62(4): 453–488.

Bechter, B., Brandl, B. and Meardi, G. (2012) 'Sectors or Countries? Typologies and Levels of Analysis in Comparative Industrial Relations'. *European Journal of Industrial Relations*, 18(3): 185–202.

Bluhm, K. (2007) *Experimentierfeld Ostmitteleuropa? Deutsche Unternehmen in Polen und der Tschechischen Republik.* Wiesbaden: VS Verlag für Sozialwissenschaften.

Boes, A. and Baukrowitz, A. (2002) *Arbeitsbeziehungen in der IT-Industrie – Erosion oder Innovation der Mitbestimmung.* Berlin: Edition sigma.

Boes, A. and Kämpf, T. (2008) 'Hochqualifizierte in einer globalisierten Arbeitswelt: von der Erosion der "Beitragsorientierung" zu neuen Arbeitnehmeridentitäten'. *Arbeits- und Industriesoziologische Studien*, 1(2): 44–67.

Boes, A. and Kämpf, T. (2009) 'Offshoring und die neuen Unsicherheiten einer globalisierten Arbeitswelt'. In ver.di (ed.), *Hochseilakt – Leben und Arbeiten in der IT-Branche. Ein Reader.* Berlin: ver.di, pp. 23–41.

Breidbach, M., Hering, K. and Kruse, W. (2013) *Globale Unternehmen und locale Interessenvertretung. Stahl-Betriebsräte 'vor Ort': machtvoll & ohnmächtig? Bremen als Beispiel.* Hamburg: VSA Verlag.

Bronfenbrenner, K. (1996) 'Final Report: The Effects of Plant Closing or Threat of Plant Closing on the Right of Workers to Organize'. *Cornell University ILR School.* Available at: http://digitalcommons.ilr.cornell.edu/cgi/viewcontent.cgi?article=1000&context=intl (accessed 22 October 2014).

Buntrock, O. (2004) *Problemlösung im europäischen Mehrebenensystem. Das Beispiel der Stahlpolitik der europäischen Gemeinschaft für Kohle und Stahl (EGKS).* Wiesbaden: Deutscher Universitätsverlag.

Clauwaert, S. and Schömann, I. (2012) 'The Crisis and National Labour Law Reforms. A Mapping Exercise'. *ETUI Working Paper*, No. 2012.04. Brussels: European Trade Union Institute.

Doellgast, V. (2010) 'Collective Voice under Decentralized Bargaining: A Comparative Study of Work Reorganization in US and German Call Centres'. *British Journal of Industrial Relations*, 48(2): 375–399.

Edwards, T., Marginson, P. and Ferner, A. (2013) 'Multinational Companies in Cross-national Context. Integration, Differentiation and the Interactions between MNCs and Nation States'. *Industrial and Labor Relations Review*, 66(3): 547–587.

Ferner, A. (1997) 'Country of Origin Effects and HRM in Multinational Companies'. *Human Resource Management Journal*, 7(1): 19–37.

Ferner, A., Almond, P., Colling, T. and Edwards, T. (2005) 'Policies on Union Representation in US Multinationals in the UK: Between Micro-politics and Macro-institutions'. *British Journal of Industrial Relations*, 43(4): 703–728.

Galgóczi, B., Keune, M. and Watt, A. (2006) 'Relocation: Concepts, Facts and Policy Challenges'. *Transfer*, 12(4): 499–520.

Greer, I. and Hauptmeier, M. (2008), 'Political Entrepreneurs and Co-managers: Labour Transnationalism at Four Multinational Auto Companies'. *British Journal of Industrial Relations*, 46(1): 76–97.

Jürgens, U. and Krzywdzinski, M. (2009) 'Work Models in the Central Eastern European Car Industry: Towards the High Road?' *Industrial Relations Journal*, 40(6): 493–512.

Kahancová, M. (2007) 'One Company, Four Factories: Coordinating Employment Flexibility Practices with Local Trade Unions'. *European Journal of Industrial Relations*, 13(1): 67–88.

Katz, H.C. (1985) *Shifting Gears*. Cambridge, MA: MIT Press.

Kochan, T.A., Katz, H.C. and McKersie, R.B. (1986) *The Transformation of American Industrial Relations*. New York: Basic Books.

Krzywdzinski, M. (2014) 'How the EU's Eastern Enlargement Changed the German Productive Model. The Case of the Automotive Industry'. *Revue de la régulation*, 15(1). Available at: http://regulation.revues.org/10663 (accessed 30 October 2014).

Lakhani, T., Kuruvilla, S. and Avgar, A. (2013) 'From the Firm to the Network: Global Value Chains and Employment Relations Theory'. *British Journal of Industrial Relations*, 51(3): 440–472.

Marginson, P. (2006) 'Between Europeanisation and Regime Competition: Labour Market Regulation Following EU Enlargement'. *Warwick Papers of Industrial Relations*, No. 79. Coventry: University of Warwick.

Meardi, G. (2014) 'Employment Relations under External Pressure: Italian and Spanish Reforms during the Great Recession'. In Hauptmeier, M. and Vidal, M. (eds), *Comparative Political Economy of Work*. London: Palgrave, pp. 332–350.

Meardi, G. and Trappmann, V. (2013) 'Social Dialogue in Crisis. Evidence from Poland'. *Transfer*, 19(2): 195–204.

Meardi, G., Strohmer, S. and Traxler, F. (2013) 'The Race to the East, Race to the Bottom? Multi-nationals and Industrial Relations in Two Sectors in the Czech Republic'. *Work, Employment and Society*, 27(1): 39–55.

Meardi, G., Marginson, P., Fichter, M., Frybes, M., Stanojević, M. and Tóth, A. (2009) 'The Complexities of Relocation and the Diversity of Union Responses: Efficiency-oriented FDI in Central Europe'. *European Journal of Industrial Relations*, 15(1): 27–47.

Mosley, L. (2011) *Labor Rights and Multinational Production*. New York: Cambridge University Press.

Pulignano, V. (2006) 'Still "Regime Competition"? Trade Unions and Multinational Restructuring in Europe'. *Industrial Relations*, 61(4): 615–638.

Silver, B.J. (2003) *Forces of Labour. Workers' Movements and Globalization since 1870*. Cambridge: Cambridge University Press.

Sznajder-Lee, A. and Trappmann, V. (2010) 'Von der Avantgarde zu den Verlierern des Postkommunismus: Gewerkschaften im Prozess der Restrukturierung der Stahlindustrie in Mittel- und Osteuropa'. *Industrielle Beziehungen*, 17(2): 192–231.

Telljohann, V. (2008) 'Relocation Processes in the European Household Appliances Industry and Forms of Social Regulation'. In Galgóczi, B., Keune, M. and Watt, A. (eds), *Jobs on the Move. An Analytical Approach to 'Relocation' and its Impact on Employment*. Brussels: PIE Peter Lang, pp. 199–234.

Trappmann, V. (2011) 'Labour as Entrepreneurs: The Ambivalent Role of Labour in Restructuring in the Polish Steel Industry'. *Warsaw Forum of Economic Sociology*, 2(4): 7–28.

Trappmann, V. (2013) *Fallen Heroes in Global Capitalism. Workers and the Restructuring of the Polish Steel Industry*. Basingstoke: Palgrave Macmillan.

Trappmann, V. (2014) *Die Gewerkschaften in Polen: Neue Bündnisse, mehr Schlagkraft?* Berlin: Friedrich-Ebert-Stiftung.

Trappmann, V., Jasiecki, K. and Przybysz, D. (2014) 'Institutions or Attitudes? The Role of Formal Worker Representation in Labour Relations'. In Bluhm, K., Martens, B. and Trappmann, V. (eds), *Business Leaders and New Varieties of Capitalism in Post-communist Europe*. Abingdon: Routledge, pp. 176–204.

Trif, A. (2013) 'Romania: Collective Bargaining Institutions under Attack'. *Transfer*, 19(2): 227–237.

8 Coordinated interest representation along the automotive value chain as a response to social dumping practices

Volker Telljohann

Introduction

Since the early 1990s, corporate restructuring has increasingly been characterized by a concentration on 'core' activities at original company locations and the outsourcing of a range of business functions to external companies. These processes have resulted in the decomposition of sectors, companies, workplaces and jobs, with far-reaching consequences for employment levels, job security, job quality and work organization; they have also contributed to labour market segmentation (Marchington *et al.*, 2005). Over time, governance and power relations within value chains have grown increasingly complex (Huws, 2006). Although most subcontractors and suppliers are small and medium-sized companies in a dependent position vis-à-vis the main contractors, large-scale, global service providers and suppliers who are able to negotiate the terms of their contracts with client companies have also emerged (Flecker *et al.*, 2007).

The automotive industry has been one of the pioneers of outsourcing. A rapid decline in profitability, alongside cost considerations related to the expansion of automotive production in developing countries and the competition posed by these new locations, has induced carmakers to delegate a range of activities to external companies (Calabrese and Erbetta, 2005). This has led to a substantial reorganization of the automotive production process, which has become more hierarchical and segmented and, in most cases, internationalized (Bardi and Garibaldo, 2005). At the same time, wages and working conditions along the automotive chain have become increasingly differentiated. While 'core' companies tend to comply with sectoral or plant-level collective agreements, their suppliers at lower levels – put under considerable pressure to minimize costs – often rely on low-paid, precarious labour. They are also more likely than the main contractors to prohibit the establishment of employee representation structures at their premises.

This chapter describes social dumping practices related to the fragmentation of the automotive value chain and examines unions' efforts to minimize the negative effects of outsourcing on employment conditions and workers' interest representation. Examining the relationships between an automotive company headquartered in Germany and its Italian subsidiaries, and with logistics companies located in both Italy and Germany, it documents the impact of outsourcing on wages, working conditions and industrial relations. The second part of the chapter documents union strategies aimed at reconstructing industrial relations along the value chain and at minimizing the social dumping threats associated with outsourcing. In the setting examined here, such approaches have mainly involved unions' organizing campaigns and efforts to coordinate employee interest representation beyond firm and sectoral boundaries. These local strategies have been supported by transnational tools, in particular by Transnational Company Agreements (TCAs), whose application has helped improve standards regarding employee rights and working conditions not only in 'core' firms but also at the level of subcontractors.

The empirical material presented in this chapter was gathered between September 2012 and November 2013 within the framework of the research project 'Information and Consultation along the Automotive Value Chain' (InCAValC), financed by the European Commission. The project's goal was to analyse the effects of restructuring processes upon pay and working conditions at 'core' companies, also referred to as original equipment manufacturers (OEMs), and along their supply chains. In addition, the project examined structures of employee interest representation and collective bargaining patterns along automotive value chains. It adopted a comparative perspective and focused on six European regions: Emilia-Romagna (Italy), Wielkopolska (Poland), Aquitaine (France), Pais Valencia (Spain), Hesse (Germany) and Bavaria (Germany).

The chapter is structured as follows. It first outlines social dumping practices related to the disintegration of the automotive value chain and discusses the impact of outsourcing upon employee interest representation. It then documents local-level employee efforts aimed at minimizing social dumping threats and restoring union representation in the sector. Finally, it examines the regulatory potential of TCAs in the context of automotive value chains. Using evidence from the Hesse and Emilia-Romagna regions, it shows that TCAs can be effectively used by employee representatives to secure better working conditions at logistics and supply companies. The chapter ends with conclusions and brief policy recommendations.

Wage dumping and precarious work within automotive value chains

Outsourcing can be motivated by considerations linked to product quality, management capacities and human resource management (Flecker *et al.*, 2007), but most often it is used by employers as a cost-cutting instrument in the face of intensifying competitive pressures. The evidence from the InCAValC project largely confirms the cost-cutting motivation behind outsourcing practices. In all six regions examined in the project, there is a systematic disparity between the

OEMs and their supply and subcontracting companies in terms of the extent of employee rights and the standard of employment conditions. A progressive deterioration of wages and working conditions may be observed along the subcontracting chain, as well as a proliferation of discriminatory practices related to gender, age and nationality.

The delegation of certain tasks to external companies has often entailed the displacement of unionized workers on open-ended contracts by low-paid and unorganized labour. Atypical employment contracts and precarious work are being used increasingly by supplier companies, and the share of atypical jobs in these companies is markedly higher than in 'core' companies.[1] In supplier firms, about 30 per cent of the total workforce may be considered precarious, whereas the share of such workers at 'core' company locations is nearly three times lower. Wage dumping is a common practice under these conditions. In Italy, for example, automotive suppliers using temporary workers hired them from specialized cooperatives whose workers performed exactly the same task as the supplier's own employees on open-ended contracts, except that their wages were on average 25 to 30 per cent lower.

Automotive suppliers belong not only to the metalworking industry but also to other sectors such as rubber, plastic and logistics. The share of precarious employment varies across these different sectors and is particularly high in manufacturing (27.6%), administration (20%) and warehouse activities (18%). In addition, there is a significant proportion of migrants (42%) and women (23.56%) among the atypical workers. The latter figure suggests that the increase in precarious employment in the automotive industry has an important gender dimension. The share of female workforce is particularly high in supplier companies, where the bulk of low-paid, insecure jobs are concentrated. This finding is symptomatic for structural problems related to the status of women in the labour market, in particular the close link between gender and job insecurity also observed in many other manufacturing sectors and services.

The proliferation of precarious working conditions in supplier companies is encouraged by the procurement mechanism used by the OEMs to select their business partners. It is based on the lowest-bid award system, which forces the suppliers to adopt cost-reduction strategies that negatively affect the working conditions and wages of their employees. By shifting social costs and business risks on to supply companies, major automotive groups contribute to the spread of social dumping practices at the subcontractor level. Wage dumping used by service cooperatives in Italy, the proliferation of mini-jobs in Germany and the increasing reliance upon temporary agency workers in Poland may all be viewed as a consequence of OEMs' approach to selecting their suppliers. The carmakers' practice in this regard is similar to that of large French building firms described by Kahmann (Chapter 3, this volume), which outsource many construction tasks at price levels that cannot be met without violations of pay and employment regulations at lower levels of the supply chain.

Outsourcing as a challenge for industrial relations

Outsourcing processes threaten employee interest representation insofar as they entail the vertical disintegration of companies and the disorganization of plant and sector-level collective bargaining. As observed by Doellgast and Greer (2007, p. 55),

> suppliers and subcontractors at the lower levels of the supply chain hierarchy, subsidiaries, and temporary agencies often have no collective bargaining institutions, weaker firm-level agreements, or are covered by different sectoral agreements. As core employers move jobs to these firms, they introduce new organisational boundaries across the production chain and disrupt traditional structures of interest representation.

This fragmentation of employees' interest representation structures has a negative impact upon the processes of information, consultation and worker participation, as well as upon company-level collective bargaining, especially in companies positioned at the lower levels of the supply chain.

The evidence from the InCAValC project exposes the weakness of employee representation structures at supply companies and the difficulties involved in organizing these companies' – mostly precarious – employees. Automotive supplier companies are characterized by a much weaker presence of trade unions and a lower use of collective bargaining than 'core' company sites. Even when employees succeed in creating their own representation at the plant level, they are often not fully aware of their information and consultation rights, and this often goes hand in hand with a lack of experience in the bargaining process on the side of their company's management. By the same token, trade unions and works councils have only limited knowledge concerning the pay and working conditions of female and temporary workers, which precludes the effective representation of the interests of these most vulnerable employee groups. In the context of the InCAValC project, more than one-third of the interviewed employee representatives were not able to specify differences in pay and working conditions between male and female workers, or to specify the concrete disadvantages suffered by precarious workers with regard to pay and working conditions. More than half of the respondents did not answer questions regarding the share of the female workforce employed at their sites on precarious contracts.

These problems are further aggravated by the fact that, despite functional interdependence, there is often no coordination between structures of interest representation located at different levels of the supply chain. Trade unions rarely organize information exchanges or coordination activities between employee representatives in 'core' companies, on the one hand, and those active in supply firms, on the other. In many cases, there is no contact whatsoever between the respective trade union structures or works councils. The lack of coordination can have different causes. First, in many cases, employee interest representation at supply companies is either absent or too weak to become involved in effective coordination processes. Second, companies along the supply chain are often organized by different sectoral trade unions, and it has proved difficult for worker representatives to cooperate on a cross-sectoral basis. Third, in countries characterized by trade union pluralism, such as Poland and Italy, an additional problem stems from the lack of communication, or sometimes even open rivalry, between the different trade union organizations that are active at the workplace level. Last but not least, in certain cases there seems to be no interest on the part of the OEM's employee representatives in cooperating with employee representatives at supply companies. Such representatives are more oriented towards developing alliances with the local management in order to defend the structural advantages of their own locations and the 'core' company as a whole.

The weakness of employee interest representation structures makes it easier for companies to pursue unilateral cost-cutting schemes and social dumping practices. It is therefore essential for unions to (re-)build union membership and works councils along the value chain. In recent years, new strategies in this regard have been developed in sectors characterized by a high intensity of outsourcing practices. Even though they still represent isolated 'best-practice' cases, they do point to the growing importance of coordinated approaches that respond to structural changes in the industry, and go beyond company, sectoral and national boundaries. The following two sections present some innovative initiatives identified in the context of the InCAValC project.

Overcoming the fragmentation of employee interest representation: the local dimension

Union efforts to strengthen employee interest representation along the automotive value chain have included both local initiatives and transnational strategies. Locally, unions have mainly tried to improve the coordination of employee interest representation, both at the level of supply parks working for car manufacturers and at the regional level. This strategy has been used in the so-called 'motor district' of Emilia-Romagna and also at supply parks located in Germany and Spain.

The most successful coordination initiatives so far have taken place within a German-based supply park. This park is situated next to an OEM subsidiary employing 35,000 workers. At the time of this study, the park consisted of 13 sites used by 25 suppliers that altogether employed 4,000 people. One-third of the companies were industrial firms, while two-thirds were service companies, including a large number of logistics enterprises. The occupational structure of the suppliers was characterized by a high share of low-skilled workers of migrant origin. The unionization rate among these workers was low, and working conditions at several companies were particularly poor.

In order to improve the working environment and address the challenge of organizing the employees working in the supply companies, the German metalworkers' union IG Metall, which also organized the OEM's employees, launched a new strategy. In an effort to reintegrate various phases of the production cycle that had become disintegrated as a result of the outsourcing processes, the union decided to treat the entire supply park as a single company. In order to ensure an effective coordination of employee interest representation at the level of the supply park, the union sought to organize all companies irrespective of the sector to which they belonged. This approach was chosen in view of the fact that other relevant sectoral trade unions, in particular the services trade union ver.di and the chemical industry trade union IG BCE, were not yet operating at the park.

Following the first positive results of the organizing strategy, IG Metall established a network at the level of the supply park that included trade union officers, members of the works councils, union workplace representatives and representatives of young trade union members. Apart from the supply companies' representatives, representatives of the works council of the OEM's subsidiary also participated in the coordination meetings. The network's members met regularly in order to organize an exchange of experiences and to discuss and coordinate the successive steps with regard to the above-mentioned objectives. The union also published a newsletter and distributed it among the supply companies' employees in order to guarantee that information exchange also took place in the interim between the coordination meetings.

In order that the union's project would meet with success, it was crucial to invest the necessary resources and to clearly divide responsibilities with regard to the planned activities. IG Metall followed a gradual, clearly structured approach in building up employee interest representation at the supply park. The first step always involved organizing the employees of the respective company; only after having reached a certain level of unionization did the union try to establish a works council. Given that, in certain cases, the management tried to impede the creation of a works council, the union drew on the OEM's Social Charter, which provided for the right to set up company-level structures of interest representation at the OEM's first-tier business partners (see the following section for details). Following the establishment of a works council, the third step involved a struggle for the application of the regional collective agreement for the metalworking industry. In addition to the creation of union and works council structures, actions at the local level were aimed at limiting the share of precarious employment and at turning such relationships into permanent contracts. This type of negotiation was the result of the works councils' decision to deal with the temporary workers' problems, even if these were not formally employed by the companies but by temporary work agencies.

In 2013, following a 12-month campaign, the metalworkers' union had succeeded in gaining 280 new members, which secured it a relatively strong trade union presence at five supplier companies. On this basis, the union moved on to the next step and focused on setting up company-level works councils. IG Metall was also able to attract new members in other companies, but the level of unionization was not yet considered sufficient to take the next step of forming a works council. Despite these drawbacks, the achievements of the project were nevertheless significant: IG Metall succeeded in increasing the trade union presence within the supply park and contributed to a more systematic application of information and consultation rights as laid down in Directive 2002/14/EC, which was particularly important for workers employed by firms located at the lower end of the automotive value chain.

Beyond the German-based supplier park, it has generally proved difficult for works councils and trade unions to foster coordination between employee representation structures operating at different levels of the automotive value chain. In the Emilia-Romagna region however, there have also been a number of positive examples of coordinated bargaining and cooperation between the union representatives of different companies. These efforts have led to the improvement of working conditions and wages for workers at supplier companies characterized by a high share of precarious employment. Considerable progress in this regard has been achieved in the case of a sports car manufacturer located in Bologna and its logistics service provider, as well as at another logistics company and its controlled cooperative (see the following section for details).

Reform of public procurement procedures is another instrument that could potentially limit the spread of precarious work and wage dumping practices at lower levels of the subcontracting chain. According to trade unions, two strategies can be particularly useful in this regard: the enactment of regulations governing the social and environmental responsibility of supplier companies, and the introduction of minimum binding requirements for supplier companies in the domain of wages and working conditions. Local institutions and regional authorities should also be involved in the promotion and design of standards for new industrial sites and in their subsequent enforcement. So far, however, no specific anti-social dumping approach to public procurement has been identified in the examined regions.

Combating social dumping with Transnational Company Agreements

In the highly internationalized automotive sector, Transnational Company Agreements (TCAs) represent an important instrument for guaranteeing minimum social standards as well as information and consultation rights (Telljohann *et al.*, 2009; Stevis, 2010; Papadakis, 2011; Leonardi, 2012). They may also facilitate the coordination and integration of interest representation and help unions overcome their limited capacity for action, which so far is mainly confined to national borders (Telljohann, 2012; Pulignano *et al.*, 2013). A number of large car manufacturers, such as Volkswagen, General Motors Europe, DaimlerChrysler, Renault, PSA Peugeot Citroen and Ford, have already signed TCAs; such agreements have also been concluded by global supply companies such as Bosch and Freudenberg. In some cases, TCA provisions apply not only to 'core' companies but also to their suppliers and subcontractors. These agreements are of particular importance because they promote the application of core standards along the automotive value chain. In order to illustrate how local and transnational strategies can be combined to ensure better working conditions and more consolidated employee interest representation, the remainder of this section will present experiences regarding the implementation of TCAs signed by a German-based OEM in the regions of Hesse (Germany) and Emilia-Romagna (Italy).

The German OEM and its approach to social responsibility

The German OEM examined here adheres to the principles of sustainability and social responsibility. The company defines sustainability as efforts to reconcile high levels of health and safety standards at the workplace with economic efficiency, and pledges to pursue this goal at all levels of its value chain. This approach has been followed since 2010, when the company introduced a Code of Conduct to ensure its own compliance with international conventions, laws and internal rules regarding employment conditions, including the International Labour Organization's conventions and recommendations. In particular, the OEM recognizes the basic right of all workers to be organized in a trade union and to be represented by company-level bodies of employee interest representation; it also rejects child labour as well as forced and bonded labour. The company has set up a specialized network of internal managers in order to promote the application of these rules at its subsidiaries.

In the years that followed, the company concluded a number of TCAs which tackled social as well as health and safety issues. In 2002, for instance, the management, the World Works Council of the OEM and the International Metalworkers' Federation signed a Declaration on Social Rights and Industrial Relations, also referred to as the Social Charter. The Charter is applicable for production sites located in all countries and regions represented in the OEM's World Works Council, but the firm has also invited its subcontractors and business partners to join the agreement. In 2006, the Charter was followed by a document entitled 'Requirements Regarding Sustainability in its Relationships with Business Partners'. These requirements are applicable to carmakers' first-tier suppliers, who are obliged to comply with the environmental and social standards laid down in the OEM's internal guidelines and specifications, with the Social Charter and with the external international standards followed by the OEM. With regard to employee compensation and benefits, the document states that wages at the OEM's partner companies have to correspond at the very least to legally valid and guaranteed minima. In cases where legal regulations on wage levels or collective agreements do not exist, compensation and benefits should be based on typical industry-specific wages paid in the respective region. If business partners do not comply with these requirements, the OEM reserves the right to end the relationship by terminating the business contract. The company also expects its first-tier suppliers to urge their subcontractors to comply with the above requirements.

In 2012, the OEM signed a Global Agreement on the Issue of Temporary Work with the aim of providing uniform rules regarding the use of temporary employment across all its production sites. Temporary workers still account for about 7 to 8 per cent of the OEM's workforce worldwide, but the agreement sets a ceiling of 5 per cent on the use of a temporary workforce. In order to enforce the new rule, employee representatives at the various levels have the right to be informed by management about the share of temporary personnel active on individual sites. The document also sets a 36-month limit on the length of temporary assignments and provides for the equal treatment of the company's permanent and temporary workers. Equal treatment regards, in particular, wage levels, working hours, access to corporate information, health and safety measures, and social standards.[2] The Global Agreement also states that the OEM will cooperate exclusively with temporary work agencies that comply with its 2006 'Requirements Regarding Sustainability in its Relationships with Business Partners'.

All in all, between 2002 and 2012, the OEM signed five TCAs. It may therefore be concluded that transnational agreements have become an established regulatory tool of this company. As shown by the two case studies presented below, workers at the OEM's supplier firms and business partners have often referred to these documents to assert their right to organize and improve employment conditions at their locations.

Raising pay at logistics companies in the Hesse region

When the logistics activities were outsourced from the OEM's plant located in the Hesse region at the end of the 1990s, the subcontracted companies neither had company-level employee interest representation structures nor did they apply collective agreements. Even though works council structures were eventually created, pay levels in the logistics companies remained very low, amounting to only €5.38 per hour in 2011. In order to raise the wage levels, the trade union confederation DGB North Hesse set up a working group consisting of works councillors from the OEM and the logistics companies, as well as representatives from IG Metall and the services union ver.di. The establishment of the working group was an important organizational innovation insofar as it provided a new platform for information exchange and cooperation between trade union officers and works councils representing different companies, sectors and regional union structures.

Referring to the OEM's Social Charter, according to which compensation and benefits at supplier companies should correspond 'at least to the respective national legal minimum requirements or those of the respective economic sectors', the works councils and trade unions demanded that the logisitcs companies cooperating with the OEM comply with the minimum pay level laid down in the regional sectoral collective agreement for the transport sector. This strategy was initially not successful however, because, in Germany, legal minimum requirements concerning remuneration are calculated on the basis of the definition of 'decent pay'. According to the jurisprudence of the country's Federal Labour Court, wages can be considered immoral when there is an obvious disparity between performance and reward; that is to say, when the salary does not amount to at least two-thirds of the wage usually applied in that sector and region. In this particular case, the usual pay in the region was defined by the minimum pay laid down in the regional collective agreement for the transport sector. As a consequence, pay at one of the logistics companies was initially increased from €5.38 to €6.82, and then to €7.00 at the beginning of 2012.

In view of the substantial difference between the calculation of the 'decent' wage and the collectively agreed minimum wage, the employee representatives at the logistics companies continued to insist on the application of the collective agreement. This required not only closer cooperation between the members of the working group, but also greater trade union density at the logisitcs companies in order to ensure sufficient mobilization capacity. Consequently, IG Metall and the logistics companies works councils intensified their efforts to recruit new union members from among the logistics workers. This was a new approach, given that in the past the employees of the logistics companies and their works councils had tended to rely on the strength and influence of the OEM's works council. Only after long discussions between the works councils of the logistics companies and the OEM did the two sides realize that reciprocal support was necessary. Although the logistics companies' employees and works councils still depended on the OEM's strong works council, which was able to exert pressure on the OEM's management, it was nevertheless important that the OEM works council's actions were complemented by strong employee representation in the logistics firms, which could mobilize workers and demonstrate strength vis-à-vis the logistics companies management. In 2013, when union density in the logistics companies reached 50 to 60 per cent, ver.di succeeded in carrying out negotiations with three companies providing logistics services for the OEM. At the same time, the OEM's works council struck a deal with the central management, guaranteeing that in the course of future procurement rounds the companies would not be disadvantaged by the fact that they had complied with the sectoral collective agreement for the transport sector. As a consequence, the collective agreement was applied at all logistics companies contracted by the OEM, which meant that over the course of just two years the wages of logistics workers rose from €5.38 to €11.25.

In this case, the Social Charter proved an effective tool to ensure the payment of legally defined decent wages, but it failed to guarantee the application of the collective agreement. This illustrates the limits of TCAs, which are often too generic in content. In Hesse, employee representatives ultimately succeeded in applying the sectoral collective agreement thanks to an innovative strategy of cross-sectoral union cooperation backed by high unionization levels at the logistics companies.

Improving working conditions and regulating temporary work in Emilia-Romagna

In 2012, an Italian sports car manufacturer belonging to the German OEM signed a company-level agreement regulating the use of temporary agency workers. According to this deal, temporary agency workers can only be used under clearly defined conditions – such as the launch of a new model – and for a maximum period of 18 months. At the moment of recruitment, the company is obliged to hire workers from a pool of current or past temporary workers, and the selection must take place in accordance with a clearly defined ranking order based on qualification, seniority and professional development. In addition, the pay and working conditions of temporary workers should be equal to those of the firm's permanent employees.

The temporary workers were represented in the negotiations by the sports car manufacturer's employee representatives. This proved to be more efficient than employee interest representation in the temporary work agencies, given that the interest representation structures of the sports car manufacturer were closer to the temporary workers and their daily problems. Moreover, the temporary workers' rights and employment conditions had been negotiated by the sports car manufacturer's employee representatives; it was thus a logical choice for the latter to continue to represent their interests. From the temporary workers' point of view, this approach was also advantageous given that worker representation in the sports car manufacturer was much more influential and more assertive vis-à-vis the management than agency-based structures. In the sports car manufacturer, there was a so-called 'bilateral technical commission' responsible for dealing with the implementation of the provisions in the field of temporary agency work. This commission monitored the application of the rules laid down in the company-level collective agreement and developed concrete solutions to problems linked to the use of temporary workers. For instance, the body was instrumental in introducing specific training measures for temporary workers that were necessary to guarantee product quality standards. Thanks to local employee representatives' pressure, it was also possible to transform 100 temporary jobs at the manufacturing plant in question into open-ended employee contracts.

Beyond the issue of temporary employment representation, the Italian metalworking union Fiom-Cgil used the German OEM's Global Agreement on the Issue of Temporary Work to improve pay and working conditions at a logistics company providing services to the sports car manufacturer and located on the premises of the latter. The strong position of unions in the 'core' enterprise made it easier to organize the logistics firm; the same trade union officer was subsequently put in charge of collective bargaining at both the sports car manufacturer and the logistics company. The union managed to secure the application of the sectoral collective agreement for metalworking instead of the sectoral agreements for transport or commerce that are usually applied to logistics companies. From the employees' point of view, this was an important victory because the agreement for the metalworking sector provides for higher standards in the field of pay and working conditions.

Recently, workers' representatives have also made use of TCAs signed by the OEM in order to ensure reasonable working conditions in the logistics company examined here, which had tried to save costs by turning off the heating at the firm's premises. The employee representatives at the logistics company appealed to the OEM management, arguing that their employer's failure to guarantee decent working conditions represented a breach of the Social Charter and the

'Requirements Regarding Sustainability in its Relationships with Business Partners', which stipulates that the OEM's business partners have to ensure certain standards in the field of social rights and working conditions.[3] At the same time, the logistics company's employee representatives managed to gain the support of their counterparts at the sports car manufacturer as well as the territorial trade union organization, which assisted it in organizing a protest against the unacceptable working conditions. All the employee representatives of the sports car producer participated in the strike, demonstrating their solidarity with the logistics company workers and encouraging the latter to join the protest. The strike at the business partner had a negative impact upon production levels of the sports car manufacturer, inducing its management to intervene and tackle the problems regarding the critical working conditions in the supplier firm. In the end, the conflict was successfully resolved and working conditions were improved. Moreover, the German-based central management of the logistics company decided to change the local management of its Italian subsidiary, which brought about a shift from conflict-oriented to more cooperative industrial relations in the plant.

Given the vicinity to the sports car manufacturer, the metalworking union of the logistics company also strove to ensure that the standards related to the employment of atypical workers were similar to those negotiated at the former site. With regard to temporary agency work, for instance, a company-level agreement signed at the logistics company provided for equal treatment of temporary workers, set out clear criteria concerning the share in overall employment and specified the maximum duration of their engagement. In addition, it stated that the logistics company was not allowed to use any other form of atypical employment than temporary work. In 2014, the logistics company employed 40 workers with open-ended employment contracts, 26 temporary agency workers and six workers with fixed-term contracts. This meant that the company was exceeding the approved share of temporary workers and thus had to transform some of the contracts into open-ended ones. As a result, the employment contracts of the six workers with fixed-term contracts and of two temporary agency workers were transformed into open-ended employment contracts.

In line with TCAs signed by the OEM, its business partners are encouraged to make sure that their own suppliers adhere to basic social and environmental standards. Trade unions in Italy have already started to use this provision to push for better employment conditions at the level of second-tier suppliers. In 2014, for instance, the management of the logistics company examined here tried to subcontract elements of the production process to cooperatives bound by the collective agreement that guaranteed lower levels of pay and working conditions than those applicable in the logistics company. The union opposed the management strategy, arguing that it would imply risks with regard to service quality; it also refused to accept that workers active at the same plant and doing exactly the same work should be treated unequally. In this case, it was again possible to persuade the management of the sports car producer to intervene with the management of the logistics company. Since the latter was keen to uphold high-quality standards, the company eventually refrained from subcontracting production to the cooperatives.

Conclusion

The decomposition of sectors and companies through outsourcing and subcontracting has exerted downward pressure on wage levels and working conditions along the automotive value chain, and it has also weakened employee interest representation. The innovative union approaches analysed in this chapter have sought to minimize social dumping risks related to outsourcing and to prevent the disintegration of industrial relations in the sector by combining local actions with transnational tools. TCAs have played a particularly important role in this regard, insofar as they have ensured the application of core labour standards in supplier companies and promoted new forms of employee cooperation reaching beyond company, sectoral and national boundaries.

On the other hand, the evidence presented in this chapter points to limits with regard to the scope and the effectiveness of TCAs. First, as mentioned in the previous section, TCAs are often underspecified and it is thus difficult for unions to claim concrete rights on the basis of their provisions. Second, the cut-throat competition that characterizes the automotive supplier markets results in a collective action problem: if a single company complies with TCA provisions, it risks losing upcoming tenders to cheaper competitors who are not bound by the TCA and/or sectoral collective agreements. This may discourage firms from improving employment conditions and recognizing employee representation at their locations. Finally, it must be remembered that the TCAs analysed here were applied almost exclusively to OEM plants and their first-tier business partners. To uphold their profit margins, these companies cooperate with subcontractors in Central-Eastern Europe who offer far worse pay and working conditions. To an extent, then, it may be argued that the costs of the OEM and the first-tier suppliers' compliance with TCA provisions are shifted to lower levels of the supply chain that do not fall within the scope of the agreements. Hence, there is a danger that subcontracting may cement the existing social and economic imbalances within the EU and foster 'a race to the bottom' in the area of pay and working conditions at lower levels of the automotive supply chain.

In order to avoid putting the compliant firms at a disadvantage and shifting the costs of TCAs' provisions to lower tier suppliers, the application of the company agreements should be extended to all subcontractors and business partners. An alternative solution would involve the introduction of the general contractor's liability for the whole supply chain. In the latter case however, ensuring that purchasing practices along the entire value chain comply with the sustainability requirements may have a negative impact upon the OEM's profit margin and put it at a competitive disadvantage. Rather than at the level of individual companies, then, the liability rules for subcontracting should be introduced in the form of generally binding sectoral agreements. In the context of the highly internationalized automotive industry, it would be worthwhile introducing such regulation at the level of the EU market as a whole.

Notes

1 Within the framework of the InCAValC project, all forms of fixed-term and/or non-standard employment are considered to be precarious work. This definition includes part-time work, fixed-term employment, ad interim jobs, bogus self-employment, illegal work, jobs on call, so-called zero-hours contracts, seasonal work and work at home.
2 The Agreement does not specify to which social standards it refers.
3 Moreover, the requirements for sustainable supplier relationships specify that environmental and social problems should be identified and avoided, which implies the early detection of risks.

References

Bardi, A. and Garibaldo, F. (eds) (2005) *Company Strategies and Organisational Evolution in the Automotive Sector: A Worldwide Perspective*. Frankfurt: Peter Lang.

Calabrese, G. and Erbetta, F. (2005) 'Outsourcing and Firm Performance: Evidence from Italian Automotive Suppliers'. *International Journal of Automotive Technology and Management*, 5(4): 461–479.

Doellgast, V. and Greer, I. (2007) 'Vertical Disintegration and the Disorganisation of German Industrial Relations'. *British Journal of Industrial Relations*, 45(1): 55–76.

Flecker, J., Holtgrewe, U., Schönauer, A., Dunkel, W. and Meil, P. (eds) (2007) *Restructuring across Value Chains and Changes in Work and Employment*. Synthesis report on the Work Organisation and Restructuring in the Knowledge Society (WORKS) project. Available at: www.forba.at/data/downloads/file/362-Case_Study_Report_D10.1.pdf (accessed 10 November 2014).

Huws, U. (2006) 'The Restructuring of Global Value Chains and the Creation of a Cybertariat'. In May, C. (ed.), *Global Corporate Power: (Re)integrating Companies into the International Political Economy*. Boulder, CO: Lynne Rienner, pp. 65–82.

Leonardi, S. (ed.) (2012) *Transnational Company Agreements. A Stepping Stone towards a Real Internationalisation of Industrial Relations?* Rome: Ediesse.

Marchington M., Vincent, S. and Cooke, F.-L. (2005) 'The Role of Boundary-spanning Agents in Inter-organizational Contracting'. In Marchington, M. *et al.* (eds), *Fragmenting Work. Blurring Organizational Boundaries and Disordering Hierarchies*. Oxford: Oxford University Press, pp. 135–156.

Papadakis, K. (ed.) (2011) *Practices and Outcomes of an Emerging Global Industrial Relations Framework*. Geneva: International Labour Organization/Palgrave Macmillan.

Pulignano, V., da Costa, I., Rehfeldt, U. and Telljohann, V. (2013) 'Local Actors and Transnational Structures: Explaining Trends in Multinational Company-level Negotiations in Europe'. In Fairbrother, P., Lévesque, C. and Hennebert, M.A. (eds), *Transnational Trade Unionism: Building Union Power*. London: Routledge, pp. 141–160.

Stevis, D. (2010) 'International Framework Agreements and Global Social Dialogue: Parameters and Prospects'. *Employment Working Paper*, No. 47. Geneva: International Labour Office.

Telljohann, V. (2012) 'The Implementation of the Global Labour Relations Charter at Volkswagen'. In Leonardi, S. (ed.), *Transnational Company Agreements. A Stepping Stone towards a Real Internationalisation of Industrial Relations?* Rome: Ediesse, pp. 105–121.

Telljohann, V., Da Costa, I., Müller, T., Rehfeldt, U. and Zimmer, R. (2009) *European and International Framework Agreements – Practical Experiences and Strategic Approaches*. Luxembourg: Office for Official Publications of the European Communities.

Part III

The deregulation agenda at the EU and national levels

9 EU economic freedoms and social dumping

Jan Cremers

Introduction

The White Paper, 'Growth, Competitiveness, Employment: The Challenges and Ways Forward into the 21st Century', issued by the European Commission in 1993, was aimed at laying the foundations for the sustainable development of European economies. It was written as the Commission's answer to economic difficulties faced by EU member states soon after the creation of the Internal Market. The Commission presented it as a blueprint for a medium-term strategy for growth, competitiveness and employment:

> All Member States are suffering serious short-term unemployment problems. The scale of these problems should not divert the Community from the longer-term tasks, however. An end to recession will not bring an end to employment difficulties. Short-term concerns should be balanced against the longer-term imperatives of expanding employment opportunities and of ensuring that economic and social progress march in step.
>
> (European Commission, 1993, p. 115)

This document may be seen as a stock-taking exercise regarding the initial experiences with the growing mobility of capital and technology following the launch of the Internal Market project. The Commission admitted that, as a result of the economic freedoms, the interdependence of markets together with new technology had become an inescapable fact of life for all economic and financial operators. However, it also argued that joint flanking policies launched to ensure economic and social cohesion had helped restore the balance in the development of the European market. It further defended the 'European Social Model' and stressed that, with national industrial relations systems and regulatory frameworks being so different, any proposals for joint social policies had to be presented with sensitivity and caution. Combined with the Action Programme linked to the Community Charter of Fundamental Rights of Workers, the White Paper offered the institutional environment a new package of EU legislation in the fields of labour mobility, workplace health and safety, and worker participation.

The social legislation put in place in the following decade was often formulated with the best of intentions but was subsequently watered down by poor implementation, lack of enforcement and the primacy of economic freedoms pushed through by the EU institutions. This primacy has resulted in a general policy of deregulation and so-called 'competitive legal pluralism' in the field of company law and the free establishment of companies (Cremers, 2013a). Dominated by competitive thinking, it has directly and indirectly interfered in the social systems of the EU member states.

This chapter looks at the side-effects of policies pursued by EU institutions that can pose a threat to national working conditions and labour standards. It first presents selected parts of the *acquis* that are relevant for the free movement of workers, in particular rules concerning social security coordination and the pay and working conditions of posted workers. It then examines key issues related to the free establishment of firms. Two empirical sections illustrate the problematic relationship between economic freedoms and workers' rights in the areas of road transport and employee posting. The final section addresses problems regarding the derivation and the enforcement of rights in a cross-border context.

Social security and the free movement of citizens and workers

From the outset, the idea of European integration has rested on the notion that citizens should gain from the common market. The 1957 Rome Treaty establishing the European Economic Community (EEC) contained several provisions aimed at ensuring social improvements for citizens. One of the key provisions was the free movement of citizens and workers (Treaty of Rome, 1957, Articles 48–51). After the Treaty of Rome was signed, European citizens obtained the right to go to another EEC member state to seek employment and to work in all EEC member states. The Treaty underpinned the extension of residence, labour and equal treatment rights. The guiding principle for free movement was that it would take place in line with the so-called *lex loci laboris* principle, which means that the regulations of the new country of residence would apply. Workers obtained the right to settle with their families in their new host country and to be treated equally as national workers in that host country.

As the plans for creating the Internal Market were drawn up, the mobility of workers and citizens' free movement, in general, came to occupy an even more central position on the EU institutions' socioeconomic agenda. Although the Commission reported on a number of occasions that the expectations of the 1980s about mobility in Europe had not been realized, at the same time it acknowledged that the opening up of the EU member states' markets had brought about some unexpected 'side-effects' (European Commission, 2008a). The recruitment of foreign workforces involved the risk of social dumping, while the freedom of establishment, production relocations and competition in the spheres of taxation and social security had created the possibility of regime shopping and of the emergence of a beggar-thy-neighbour climate among EU countries.

The coordination of national social security schemes became one of the first regulated fields of EU-level cooperation related to the right to free movement following the creation of the EEC (European Council, 1958). The subsequent Regulation 1408/71 governed social security coordination in Europe for more than 25 years. The coordination was – and still is – based on the principle that persons moving within the EU are subject to the social security scheme of only one EU member state. Although the form and the contents of social security provisions belong to the competences of the individual EU member states, the coordination of different systems in cross-border situations has been subject to a dynamic process of legislation and modification. As Regulation 1408/71 bulged in size as a result of numerous amendments and additions, the European legislator completely revised the rules. In the new Regulation 883/2004 and its Implementation Regulation 987/2009, applicable from 1 May 2010, the principle of the country where the work is pursued remains the basic premise of the coordination principle. Workers who move to another EU member state have the right to be treated as if they were citizens of that host state (see Table 9.1). An exception to this principle was the so-called posting of workers, where workers stayed temporarily in another EU member state in order to provide services but remained under the subordination of the posting company in their home country. Posted workers were brought under the application of the coordination principles for social security in the sense that they stayed in the home- instead of the host-country regime; here again, only one country's legislation applied.

The European legislator also explicitly intended to bring international road transport under the general scheme of the social security coordination regulations. In order to avoid the circumvention of the principle of one-country legislation, given that the institutions of more than one country were involved, it was necessary to anticipate possible abuses that could lead to regime shopping. It had to be determined whose legislation applied and who was liable for the payment of certain benefits.

Table 9.1 Social policy fields relevant for the free movement of workers

Issue / *Category*	*Social security (Reg. 883/2004 and Reg. 987/2009)*	*Working conditions and pay*
1 EU citizens	As nationals	As nationals (national legal and bargaining frame)
2 Self-employed EU citizens	As nationals	As nationals (not regulated)
3 Posted workers	Home country	Directive 96/71

Source: author's compilation.

Note

The table is simplified in that several other groups, such as third-country workers, cross-border commuters, seasonal workers and cross-border temporary agency workers, are not included.

Regulation 883/2004 still offered two options: either the person stayed in the social security scheme of his or her country of residence, or the activity in the country of residence was so minor that the decision could be taken to transfer the person to the country of the registered office or place of business of the undertaking, or the employer employing him or her. The rules had to determine which institution had the competence to start the process of figuring out the applicable national regime. For international road transport, the solution as to which social security legislation applied was found in the mechanism of handing over the competence to initiate the process of decision-making regarding the applicable social security regime to the country where the worker lives. The necessary verification of the validity of documents or supporting evidence for the accuracy of the facts should take place on the basis of a relationship of trust with the competent authorities in other involved countries. The competent institution in the country of residence thus has the task of providing a provisional determination if the decision has not already been taken by common agreement.

One of the elements involved in the final determination in cases of cross-border outsourcing of transport activities and the use of intermediaries is whether these go-betweens are genuine undertakings. The question remains whether the social security institution in one country has the capacity and the competence to judge the bona fide standing of a company that has a registered office or place of business in another country. EU rules in the field of social security coordination give some guidance and refer to an undertaking that ordinarily performs 'substantial activities, other than purely internal management activities, in the territory of the Member State in which it is established, taking account of all criteria characterizing the activities carried out by the undertaking in question' (Article 14.2, Regulation 987/2009). This was further elaborated in a practical guide issued by the European Commission (2011). For instance, the expression 'which normally carries out its activities there' refers to an undertaking that ordinarily carries out substantial activities in the territory of the EU member state in which it is established. If the undertaking's activities are confined to internal management, the undertaking will not be regarded as normally carrying out its activities in that EU member state. In determining whether an undertaking carries out substantial activities, account must be taken of several other criteria characterizing the activities carried out by the undertaking in question. For the transport sector, this was specified by the Commission:

> In assessing the 'substantial part of the activity' for this group of workers it is considered that working time is the most appropriate criterion on which to base a decision. However, it is also recognised that dividing activity between two or more Member States may not always be as straightforward for a transport worker as for those in 'standard' employment. Accordingly, a closer examination of the working arrangements may be needed in order to determine the applicable legislation in such cases when the working hours in the Member State of residence are difficult to estimate.

A regulation for the transport sector concluded in 2009 (Regulation 1071/2009) provides similar control mechanisms that give EU member states an opportunity to assess the 'genuine' character of an undertaking. Next to criteria related to the company, formulated in Article 3 ('to have an effective and stable establishment; to be of good repute; to have appropriate financial standing; and have the requisite professional competence'), Article 5a of the Transport Regulation is an important reference. In order to become active in a state, an undertaking will:

> have an establishment situated in that Member State with premises in which it keeps its core business documents, in particular its accounting documents, personnel management documents, documents containing data relating to driving time and rest, and any other document to which the competent authority must have access in order to verify compliance with the conditions laid down in this Regulation. Member States may require that establishments on their territory also have other documents available at their premises at any time.

These notions, elaborated by the Commission's social and transport departments, do not, however, seem to have had any serious impact upon the policy related to the freedom of establishment developed by other Commission services, where the fight against 'red tape' has become the guiding principle. The Directorates-General for the Internal Market and for Competition are firm promoters of the free establishment principle with limited possibilities for other countries than the country of establishment to control the genuine character of undertakings. The dominant policy of the Commission is to ease the provisions governing the establishment of service providers at home or abroad. Different treatment of foreign undertakings can only be accepted on grounds of public policy, public security and public health. In general, all other restrictions on the freedom of establishment have to be objectively justified in accordance with the case law of the European Court of Justice (ECJ). The consequences of this approach are clear. Countries are hindered and discouraged from controlling foreign undertakings and there is no strict guidance on how to deal with violations. At the same time, the Commission is very active with infringement procedures every time a country creates 'barriers to the free provision of services'.

The modification of the rules for the coordination of national social security systems and the application of mandatory national rules on working conditions within the framework of free movement of persons have led to a series of debates about the application of home- versus host-country legislation, especially regarding the treatment of persons moving within the EU who temporarily pursue activities in (several) other EU member states than the country of origin. The first indications of the practice of bypassing the applicable rules through the establishment of letter-box companies led to question marks related to the role of cross-border labour recruitment in an open labour market and to the possibility of keeping the *lex loci laboris* principle upright in the field of labour law and pay.

Pay and working conditions in a cross-border context

For pay and conditions of employment in the case of migration for work, the country-of-employment principle applies; discrimination on grounds of nationality is prohibited. In principle, this means that workers who come on their own initiative to work in a country other than their country of origin have the same rights as the host-country citizens. They have the same possibility to claim these rights, whether through union membership or another type of collective representation, individual action or the path to justice. Over time, however, different forms of cross-border recruitment and temporary work abroad have been introduced. In some areas, EU legislation has been recently renewed, notably with regard to seasonal and third-country workers. The pay and other working conditions of seasonal workers were often formulated in the underlying bilateral agreements between countries. For workers involved in daily cross-border commuting, a mixture of case law and legislation established a certain *acquis*.

The introduction of free movement principles in the 1980s created an attractive open market for businesses. However, given that workers posted in the context of temporary services provision abroad were not supposed to seek permanent access to the host country's labour market, their position with regard to the applicable wages was ambiguous. Some countries had a regulatory frame that made their minimum-wage legislation and collective agreements generally binding for all workers on their territory. In Belgium, for instance, national laws (or, to be precise, a combination of generally binding laws and collective agreements that had to be observed by foreign employers with respect to the working conditions of their posted workers) existed in this area, whereas other countries excluded temporarily posted foreign workers from the application of the *lex loci laboris*.

The legal machinery for making the country-of-employment principle apply across Europe was lacking until the mid-1990s and the enactment of the Posted Workers Directive (Directive 96/71, hereafter PWD). At the time when this contested piece of EU legislation was issued, the starting point was respect for national social policy frames. There was a hard core of minimum prescriptions; in addition, EU member states could decide on general mandatory rules or public policy provisions applicable within their territory – as long as these rules did not lead to discrimination or protection of their market. In the first drafts of the PWD, it was stated very clearly that Community law:

> does not preclude Member States from applying their legislation or collective labour agreements entered into by the social partners, relating to wages, working time and other matters, to any person who is employed, even temporarily, within their territory, even though the employer is established in another State.
>
> (European Commission, 1991, p. 11)

Two court cases in the 1990s underpinned this idea. The ECJ ruled almost identically in the *Rush Portuguesa* case (ECJ C-113/89, 1990):

> Community law does not preclude Member States from extending their legislation, or collective labour agreements entered into by both sides of industry, to any person who is employed, even temporarily, within their territory, no matter in which country the employer is established; nor does Community law prohibit Member States from enforcing those rules by appropriate means.

The *Arblade* case (ECJ C-369/96, 1999) confirmed that provisions classified as public order legislation are crucial for the protection of the political, social and economic order. Both rulings were seen as the confirmation of EU member states' competence to define the regulatory framework for the protection of all workers who pursue their activities on the country's territory. The PWD seemed to provide a possibility to apply, in a non-discriminatory manner, employment conditions that may be seen as public policy provisions.

But quite soon problems emerged as the relationship was underscored between the working conditions of workers involved in temporary cross-border activities and the free provision of services. According to the ECJ and the Commission, it was not up to EU member states to define unilaterally the notion of public policy or to impose all mandatory provisions of their employment law on suppliers of services established in another country. Referring to Council Declaration No. 10 on Directive 96/71/EC, the ECJ stated that rules and requirements that are not specified in the exhaustive list of the PWD have to be judged within the limits of the legislator's definition of mandatory rules (Cremers, 2010, 2013b). According to the ECJ interpretation, EU member states no longer have the unilateral right to decide on the mandatory rules applicable within their territory, even if these mandatory rules would guarantee better provisions for the workers concerned. The Declaration as applied by the ECJ, with the backing of the Commission, restricts the mandatory rules in such a way that the guiding principles of the PWD are no longer effective. The ECJ thus creates a situation whereby foreign service providers do not have to comply with mandatory rules that are imperative provisions of national law and that therefore have to be respected by domestic service providers. Elsewhere I have already questioned who – if not the EU member states – is to decide which provisions in the social field are to be respected:

> Europe then is no longer a unity of Member States with open markets combined with well-defined national social policy systems (a unity in diversity), but a unified economic bloc with a clear hierarchy: the radical ECJ interpretation of article 49 of the Treaty (now article 56 of the Lisbon Treaty) makes every national host-country mandatory provision in principle a restriction to the free provision of services.
>
> (Cremers, 2011)

The Internal Market thus no longer functions merely as a market of cross-border activities; rather it is interfering directly with national regulatory frames.

Following the launch of the Internal Market project, the Commission and the ECJ, unhindered by the EU member states, have worked out an unrivalled deregulation agenda that puts the free provision of services first and shrugs off the starting point of the posting rules. As a result, the *lex loci laboris* principle has come under social dumping pressures.

The holy grails of competition and free establishment

Since the late 1990s, the objective of strengthening the protection of shareholders' rights has gone hand in hand with the notion that company law 'should provide for a flexible framework for competitive business' (High Level Group of Company Law Experts, 2002). The deregulation policy characterizing current national and EU company law reform leads to a situation of an emerging transnational legal pluralism that in the long run may stimulate regime shopping within the EU. The starting point nowadays seems to be the competition between systems of private law, or at least of company law (Cremers, 2013a). On the basis of EU legislation and ECJ jurisprudence, the freedom of establishment makes it possible for firms to be founded in accordance with the law of one EU member state and to have their registered office, central administration or principal place of business in another EU member state. Such an establishment is defined as the actual pursuit of an economic activity through a fixed establishment in another EU member state for an indefinite period. One may think that EU rights and obligations are, first of all, for companies with a real economic link to Europe, not for letter-box companies created through artificial arrangements in order to circumvent national law. However, the relevant legislation in this area does not provide direct effective instruments to enforce such provisions and to facilitate the fight against abusive practices. As a result, there is hardly any effective control as to whether an established subsidiary is pursuing activities or is involved in no real activity. Companies can install a considerable part of their legal frameworks in other EU member states without pursuing any activities there. This may be seen as a by-product of legislative interest in allowing companies the benefit of freedom of establishment by way of Article 49 of the Treaty.

The EU Treaty and ECJ case law allow certain restrictions to free establishment if they are justified and proportionate under European law. In the *Societé de Gestion Industrielle* (ECJ C-311/08, 2010) judgment, the ECJ argued that European law did not affect the possibility of national legislation/measures to prohibit companies from invoking EU law when, in reality, these 'wholly artificial arrangements' were designed to circumvent national legislation (abuse of the freedom of establishment by foreign companies through artificial arrangements in order to escape mandatory rules). Focusing on tax evasion, the ECJ stated that national legislation was acceptable as long as it pursued legitimate objectives that were compatible with the Treaty and constituted overriding reasons in the public interest such as the prevention of abuse or fraudulent conduct, or the protection of the interests of, for instance, creditors, minority shareholders, employees or the tax authorities. A proportionality test of the national measure was added to the criteria to ascertain whether the provision at issue goes beyond what is necessary to attain the objectives pursued.

However, there are crucial limits to the restrictions that could affect the application of social policy provisions. A national measure that is considered a restriction incompatible with EU law can only be justified on limited grounds. In addition, although the starting point was that social policy is up to national legislators to decide upon, the ECJ has brought certain elements of social policy under supranational competence. The Commission and the ECJ have clearly abandoned the principle that EU member states can decide on general mandatory rules or public policy provisions applicable within their territory as long as these rules do not lead to discrimination or protection of their market.

While the correction of breaches must be established on a case-by-case basis, how can a worker who is confronted with a letter-box company derive rights from this common law? And what about companies that conduct no business in their country of establishment but instead operate exclusively through subsidiaries (or even through the provision of services) in other countries? The fact that a company was formed in a particular EU member state for the sole purpose of enjoying the benefit of more favourable legislation, such as flexible company law, taxation advantages or easy registration rules, does not constitute an abuse – even if that company conducts its activities entirely or mainly in another state – as long as the protection of third parties' interests is not at stake. The existing ECJ judgments in this area concern companies whose only presence in their state of incorporation and establishment was at best a letter box. The next section illustrates this clash between the EU's economic freedoms and the social dimension on the basis of examples from the international road transport sector.

Social dumping in international road transport

In 2011, several transport companies in the Benelux countries received the offer to transfer their workforces to intermediate companies located in Cyprus, Liechtenstein or Hungary, and to hire the staff through these intermediate service suppliers. These intermediate suppliers have glossy websites in several European languages and act through companies distributed all over Europe.[1] Their offers were simple and straightforward. With reference to the changes in the coordination of social security as a result of the new scheme based on Regulations 883/2004 and 987/2009, the intermediate suppliers offered to act as employers for the workforce. The original employer of the truck drivers would become the 'client' and only receive an invoice for supplying services, while the truck drivers would continue to work for the original employer. The intermediate suppliers presented themselves as groups of companies with extensive experience in contracting, payrolling and other services in the maritime, hotel and catering sectors, and international road transport. By opening an office abroad – for instance, in Cyprus – the intermediate suppliers claimed that is was justifiable to offer a Cypriot employment contract to the truckers, even though they did not live there and never visited the island. The use of such go-betweens constitutes a clear instance of social dumping: it is an ideal way to save money because it enables the reduction of social security costs and avoidance of taxes. It also implies no employer costs for the original employer, no health and safety services, no wage indexation, the denial of a labour relation between the client and the driver, and no trade union involvement.

The user undertakings received offers with alternative options. One was the total transfer of the workforce, while the other was the reflagging of the trucks. In both cases, the authorities of the intermediate supplier's official place of registration had to be persuaded that the intermediate was a viable licensed company. In the case of reflagging, the trucks had to be inspected, but that could be done anywhere in Europe. In order to facilitate formal recognition in the place of registration, the intermediate supplier had in one case already 'organized' a licence through the Dutch Ministry of Transport and had received the assignment to act as an institution that was licensed 'to temporarily make personnel in the haulage sector available'. A similar licence was procured from the German Federal Employment Agency. The general trend to deregulate has led to a marginal assessment before licences are provided (see Ministerie van Sociale Zaken en Werkgelegenheid, 2013). Hence, free establishment made it possible to open a company in another country with no staff, an office that is no more than a letter box, and with no activities in the country of registration. These companies are subsidiaries of existing transport companies or are owned by economic opportunists in pursuit of easy money.

An industrial action and subsequent investigation conducted by the Dutch transport unions revealed various similar practices. In a 2012 court case, the union accused a transport company of letter-box practices in Hungary. In this case, the drivers, mainly Hungarians, were directly engaged by the Dutch headquarters. However, they were on the payroll of a Hungarian subsidiary based in one of the premises of PricewaterhouseCoopers in Budapest that had one half-time administrative worker on parental leave. All formalities were handled by PricewaterhouseCoopers. There were no trucks stationed in Hungary, but the truckers were constantly put under pressure because the 'Hungarian way' was cheaper.

In yet another case, the German–Latvian agency Dinotrans recruited workers from the Philippines. The latter are third-country workers who do not have the right to enter the EU. However, they are recruited to Latvia with the argument that there is 'a shortage of skilled labour for international trucking' in the country, which is one of the reasons for which permission to enter the EU may be given. As soon as they have entered Latvia, the drivers are hired out to other undertakings in Europe.[2] The company's own financial statements make it clear that the haulage contractor is paying the drivers approximately €2.36 per hour, which can only be defined as a slave wage. It is clear that the company owners do not care who gets the cargo to the customer or how, as long as it is the cheapest way.

These and other practices may be regarded as social dumping, although some business advisers will maintain that they are perfectly legal. Apart from tax evasion, which would require a separate explanation, the abuses discussed here are related to the denial of an employment contract and the circumvention of social security payments. The recruitment of 'cheap' labour has become a 'business case', and the creation of a labyrinth of companies all over Europe is one of the best ways to circumvent national standards and regulations (see also Berntsen and Lillie, Chapter 2, this volume). One such intermediate, an Austrian–Liechtenstein broker, was characterized during a court case in the following way: 'through a maze of subsidiaries and foundations, [the company owners] have orchestrated the formal and technical transposition of the suspected crimes' (Schneider, 2011). The right to free establishment and the deregulation of company law, in particular easy registration and the lowering of other statutory obligations, have opened doors for such fraudulent intermediaries. The employment contract is based on the 'official' address in the registered office of the intermediate (in other words, with a fictitious firm in an obscure office in a country with neither activity nor turnover); at the same time, the risk of inspection is almost zero. In some cases, drivers found themselves on the payroll in a foreign country without having been informed; others came under pressure from their former employer and had to choose between the 'intermediate track' or serious pay cuts.

In the examined instances, the fact that the employment relationship with the original employer remains legal is often very evident. This does not mean, however, that it is easy for a worker to exercise his employment rights based on the *lex loci laboris* principle. In one case, a truck driver was fired by his original employer (referred to as the 'client'), and a week later he received confirmation from the Cyprus intermediate supplier that he was no longer needed. The confirmation letter was typed on the writing paper of another letter-box company based in Luxembourg, posted with a Dutch stamp and accompanied by an official Belgian form for the dismissal. How should a worker proceed through this labyrinth of clashing constituencies?

In the transport sector, circumventing the payment of social security contributions often takes place through the provision of A1 (previously E101) forms in the intermediate's country of registration. However, the new regime for the coordination of the social security rules locates the competence to answer the question as to which social security system applies with the authorities in the country where the worker lives. In the case of intermediate suppliers using letter boxes in a foreign constituency, it can never be that foreign constituency. As a consequence, workers travel around with irregular forms – a situation that was not the aim of the EU coordination rules. Moreover, payslips that were collected during the campaign by the Dutch transport unions illustrate that the payment of social security contributions in the country where the intermediate supplier is registered is limited to the basic (minimum) wage and does not include other wage components. In effect, even the country of establishment is defrauded.

In one case brought up by the Dutch transport unions, it took 16 months (and a change of government) to persuade the social security authorities to enforce Dutch social security and working conditions. The case was clear from the beginning and was transmitted to the Dutch authorities in March 2012, but, partly owing to the fear that the authorities of the workers' country of residence would be accused of 'creating barriers to the free provision of services', the competent social security institution – Sociale Verzekeringsbank (SVB) – was reluctant to act immediately. The final statement issued by SVB in October 2013 was clear, however: based on Regulations 883/2004 and 987/2009, truck drivers living in the Netherlands and on the payroll of one of the intermediate suppliers had to stay in the social security system of their country of residence – the Netherlands. The case had other far-reaching consequences. The SVB stated that the employment relationship was still intact with the client (the original employer), 'as the activities were still pursued under the subordination and authority of the client'. The SVB concluded that the intermediate firm could not prove that it was a real undertaking with activities in the country of registered office. All in all, the link between the driver and the intermediate supplier was qualified as artificial and having been created with the sole aim of circumventing social security obligations in the country of residence. These arguments were already formulated by the transport union in March 2012; as a result of the delay, the drivers involved were confronted with the obligatory payment of overdue social security contributions.

The abuse of posting regulations

Posting of workers as part of a provision of services is not a new phenomenon. A decision to subcontract other undertakings can be motivated by the search for expertise and know-how not belonging to the firm's own core activity, labour shortages and/or efficiency considerations. It may also represent a traditionally evolved division of labour, with partners' cooperation based on mutual trust, routine or historical reasons. In 2003, one of the first assessments dedicated to the implementation of the PWD evaluated both the legal context and the practical functioning of posting in the framework of the free provision of services (Cremers and Donders, 2004). The research focused on key characteristics of posting: the existence of a direct labour contract in the home country and the maintenance of the employment relation; the genuine character of the posting company that temporarily performs services abroad on the basis of a commercial contract; and the subordination of the posted worker to the posting company while temporarily performing work related to the commercial contract between the posting company and the user undertaking. The conclusion was that the national measures to ensure compliance with the posting rules were not well developed. Not all EU member states had implemented the notion of 'maintenance of an employment relation' directly into national law, and the grey area of economically dependent workers also existed. The fact that under the social security coordination rules, the decisive authority as to whether a person is self-employed or employed is the sending state, whereas under the PWD it is the receiving state, provoked misunderstandings and a lack of clarity for the institutions responsible for the enforcement of the rules. The verification of whether labour regulations were really applied was an arduous task. Checking whether the undertaking in the home country was a genuine undertaking pursuing economic operations on a stable basis turned out to be very difficult. Host countries had to rely entirely on information from the home country, and the crucially necessary cooperation and mutual exchange were absent. In practice, most EU member states applied the posting periods stipulated in the social security coordination regulations. However, it was not easy to control in the host country whether the posting was just workforce supply or in fact a service contract.

In another study conducted in 2010 (Cremers, 2011), a team of experts reinvestigated the functioning of the posting rules in 12 country cases. The focus was on social and economic disparities between the formal legislative or conventional rights and the real wages, working time, paid leave, living conditions, and health and safety of posted workers. Compared to the results of the 2003 study, even greater divergence in transposition and actual application was found. This was largely because the PWD was issued in the early 1990s and thus could not account for the consequences of the EU accession of Central-Eastern European states characterized by weak collective bargaining systems. The second trend has been the extension and the intensification of cross-border agency work, subcontracting and outsourcing in numerous labour market segments. Both developments had a serious impact on how posting was actually organized. The use of the posting mechanism ranged from normal and decent long-established partnerships between contracting partners, to completely fake letter-box practices of labour-only recruitment. In the 2011 report, four applications of posting-related cross-border recruitment were distinguished. The authors identified so-called *normal posting*, with specialized subcontractors providing temporary services in another EU member state and well-paid skilled workers or qualified staff both belonging to the posting companies' core workforce. They also documented *legal posting* in the form of labour-only subcontracting where the calculation was made between engaging the domestic workforce or bringing in workers from abroad under the free provision of services' banner: a supplier providing workers from a country with low social security costs was cheaper than a domestic supplier. In several countries, *questionable practices accompanying legal posting* were identified, where the legally posted recruited workers were confronted with deductions for administrative costs, for lodging and transport, tax deductions and the obligatory refunding of (minimum) wage payments after returning home. Finally, different forms of *fake posting* were found: for instance, the copying and distribution of a mass of falsified E101/A1 forms; the recruitment of posted workers already present in the host country; workers turned into bogus self-employed; and recruitment via letter-box companies and unverifiable invoices for service provision.

Moreover, the study found that the use of posting in labour-intensive segments of the labour market involved new recruitment practices. The problem appeared as soon as cross-border labour-only subcontracting was presented as provision of services.[3] For the recruitment of 'cheap' labour, companies relied on small subcontractors and the use of agencies, gangmasters and other intermediaries. Groups of workers were recruited via letter-box companies, advertising and informal networking. Posting has thus become one of the channels for the cross-border recruitment of 'cheap' labour without reference to the rights that may be derived from the EU law related to genuine labour migration. The concentration of posted workers in the lower echelons of the labour markets and in specific regions, segments and sectors implies serious risks, such as the distortion of competition, the erosion of workers' rights and the evasion of mandatory rules. Employment conditions, in particular the wages offered to posted workers, if not subject to proper monitoring and enforcement, may undercut the minimum conditions established by the host country's law or negotiated under generally applicable collective agreements. Next to the abuse of posting rules, cross-border agency work and the provision of services by bogus self-employed can also function as a means of circumventing rights-based labour migration. Even the European Commission (2008a) has conceded that if such practices take place on a large scale, they may undermine the organization and functioning of local labour markets.

Monitoring and enforcement problems

Adequate implementation and enforcement are key elements guaranteeing the effectiveness of the applicable EU rules (European Commission, 2007, 2008b). However, the Commission has thus far neglected the problems related to the question as to whether the recruiter is a genuine undertaking, as well as the control of the existence of an employment contract and of compliance with the corresponding working conditions, whereas the ECJ rulings have restricted the necessary control and enforcing competences to the country of origin. In the ECJ's *Laval* (ECJ C-341/05, 2007) and *Luxembourg* (ECJ C-319/06, 2008) rulings, the application and control of the host-country labour standards were seen as restrictions to the free provision of services; additional administrative domestic rules should not hinder this free provision. This fight against the 'administrative burden' makes systematic and effective control in the host country an illusion. At the same time, the identification of the country where the work is carried out depends on the cooperation of the home country. The reply to requests for information can take time and by then the employer and the workers have often disappeared.

The existence of enforcement problems was underscored by a recent transnational project, 'Posting of workers: Improving collaboration between social partners and public authorities in Europe', conducted in 2012/2013 by the French umbrella organization of labour inspectors INTEFP.[4] The project confirmed that fraudulent posting is used to circumvent the national regulatory frames of pay, labour, working conditions and social security in the host state. In particular, the following irregularities were identified:

- cross-border recruitment via (temporary) agencies;
- bogus self-employment in cases where the distinctions between a commercial contract for the provision of services and an employment contract are blurred;

- fake posting because control is inadequate or easily bypassed;
- shifting to other industries where wages are lower and/or working conditions less favourable to workers (regime shopping);
- manipulation of free establishment (fictitious companies and arrangements) and of country of residence;
- abuse of entitlements that are guaranteed by the posting rules (working time, minimum wage, pay scaling not in line with skill level, absurd deductions).

The control of the regularity of posting and the collection of evidence and supporting documents are hindered by poor registration and the lack of necessary competence in the host country. Once irregularities are detected, the accumulation of breaches is the rule rather than the exception. These irregularities, of course, raise not only the question of how to find justice. Even more relevant is the question as to where the competence lies for the overall control of compliance. As long as registration and notification in the host country are seen as an administrative burden and not as an essential tool to control compliance, an effective solution is unlikely to be found.

Conclusion

This chapter has argued that the European legislator sought to install a legislative frame for genuine labour mobility. However, monitoring cross-border labour posting and recruitment through foreign service providers has proven difficult. Non-compliance, a lack of cross-border cooperation, the difficulty of tracing circumvention in cross-border situations and the weakness of the existing sanctioning mechanism have led to frustration on the side of rule-enforcing institutions and other stakeholders.

Poor implementation makes legislation a paper tiger, and legislation that is powerless is worse than no legislation at all. In order to avoid social dumping and the distortion of competition for domestic service providers and to establish a level playing field for these service providers, a policy of prevention of fraud and anticipation of abusive practices is needed. However, such policy is still in its infancy, and thus the cross-border provision of services is increasingly an alternative way to recruit 'cheap' labour. By the same token, the freedom of establishment has created a new industry of incubators that can deliver ready-made companies with no other purpose than to circumvent national regulations, labour standards and social security obligations. In theory, the EU has started to tackle this problem. However, workers in a foreign constituency who have been exploited live and work far away from this theoretical dispute. They have no real way to derive rights from these highly abstract judicial deliberations. Therefore, prevention and anticipation have to come from instruments that are labour-market oriented and shaped with and borne by the institutions and bodies that have created the conventional and legislative frame for industrial relations.

Based on the findings of Cremers and Donders' 2004 research project on employee posting, the European Construction Industry Federation (FIEC) and the European Federation of Building and Woodworkers (EFBWW) – social partners representing a sector that has been highly affected by fraudulent practices discussed in this chapter – formulated a joint statement, pinpointing several fundamental problems and proposing solutions. They noted that the grey zone of economically dependent work remained a growing problem in the sector. A precise definition of 'employees' and 'self-employed' could avoid problems with the application of the existing legislation. Furthermore, it was important to be able to verify, legally and in practice, if a worker was correctly posted and fell under the scope of the PWD, and to decide about liability in cases of fake self-employment and/or fake posting. FIEC and EFBWW also recommended implementing a provision defining who was deemed to be the real and genuine employer and who could be held liable in cases of fake posting by letter-box companies or bogus self-employment. Finally, they advocated a more effective execution of sanctions in cross-border situations and closer cooperation among national social and labour inspectors. These recommendations provide enough items for an ambitious EU social agenda. However, the correlation with the economic freedoms, notably the freedom of establishment and the free provision of services, has so far obstructed fundamental political proposals in this respect.

Notes

1 See, for instance, www.mebo.lu, www.christaintershipping.lu, www.sealux.ch, and the related www.afmb.eu and www.seoc.com.cy in Cyprus.

2 There are several Dinotrans companies and related subsidiaries across Europe. The Latvian Sia Dinotrans is the leading company. Dinotrans' Dutch address is in a simple dwelling. The Swedish Dinotrans has the largest turnover, although it employs only one person, and the German Dinotrans is small but responsible for 23 per cent of the turnover. See: www.transport-online.nl/site/40529/dino-trans-zoekt-opnieuw-filipijnse-vrachtwagen chauffeurs/ (accessed 10 September 2014); www.stoppafusket.se/2013/08/20/drivers-working-for-slave-wages-at-sia-dinotrans/ (accessed 10 September 2014).

3 This term originates in the Anglo-Saxon tradition and denotes a type of employment system whereby a contractor hires, on a labour-only basis, a subcontractor who is often an individual worker or a collection of individuals.

4 See www.eurodetachement-travail.eu/synthese/the_project.html (accessed 10 September 2014).

References

Cremers, J. (2010) 'Rules on Working Conditions in Europe: Subordinated to Freedom of Services'. *European Journal of Industrial Relations*, 16(3): 293–306.

Cremers, J. (2011) *In Search of Cheap Labour in Europe. Working and Living Conditions of Posted Workers*. CLR-Studies 6. Utrecht: International Books.

Cremers, J. (2013a) 'From Harmonisation to Regulatory Competition'. In Vitols, S. and Heuschmid, J. (eds), *European Company Law and the Sustainable Company: A Stakeholder Approach*, Vol. 2. Brussels: European Trade Union Institute, pp. 89–114.

Cremers, J. (2013b) 'Free Provision of Services and Cross-border Labour Recruitment'. *Policy Studies*, 34(2): 201–220.

Cremers, J. and Donders, P. (eds) (2004) *The Free Movement of Workers in the European Union. Directive 96/71/EC on the Posting of Workers within the Framework of the Provision of Services: Its Implementation, Practical Application and Operation*. CLR-Studies 4. Brussels: European Institute for Construction Labour Research/Reed Business Information.

European Commission (1991) 'Proposal for a Council Directive Concerning the Posting of Workers in the Framework of the Provision of Services'. COM(91) 230 final – SYN 346. Brussels.

European Commission (1993) 'Growth, Competitiveness, Employment – The Challenges and Ways Forward into the 21st Century'. White Paper, COM(93) 700. Luxembourg: Office for Official Publications of the European Communities.

European Commission (2007) 'Posting of Workers in the Framework of the Provision of Services: Maximising its Benefits and Potential while Guaranteeing the Protection of Workers'. Communication from the Commission to the Council, the European Parliament, the European Economic and Social Committee and the Committee of the Regions, COM(2007) 304 final. Brussels.

European Commission (2008a) *Employment in Europe 2008*. Luxembourg: Office for Official Publications of the European Communities.

European Commission (2008b) 'Recommendation of 31 March 2008 on Enhanced Administrative Cooperation in the Context of the Posting of Workers in the Framework of the Provision of Services'. OJ No. C85/01, 4 April. Luxembourg: Office for Official Publications of the European Communities.

European Commission (2011) *Practical Guide: The Legislation that Applies to Workers in the European Union (EU), the European Economic Area (EEA) and in Switzerland*. Brussels.

European Council (1958) Council Regulations 3/58/EEC of 25 September and 4/58/EEC of 15 December on social security for migrant workers. OJ Nos 561 and 597. Luxembourg: Office for Official Publications of the European Communities.

High Level Group of Company Law Experts (2002) *A Modern Regulatory Framework for Company Law in Europe: A Consultative Document of the High Level Group of Company Law Experts*. Brussels. Available at: http://ec.europa.eu/internal_market/company/docs/modern/report_en.pdf (accessed 9 September 2014).

Ministerie van Sociale Zaken en Werkgelegenheid (2013) *Beantwoording kamervragen over 'premieshoppen op Cyprus'*. Available at: www.rijksoverheid.nl/documenten-en-publicaties/kamerstukken/2013/03/05/beantwoording-kamervragen-over-premie shoppen-op-cyprus.html (accessed 9 September 2014).

Schneider, R. (2011) 'Wer ist wer im Hypo-Sumpf?' *Die Zeit*, 30 December 2010. Available at: www.zeit.de/2011/01/A-Hypo (accessed 10 May 2014).

10 Have your competitiveness and eat it too

The pull and limits of cost competition in Hungary and Slovakia

Vera Šćepanović

Introduction

The role of the state in international economic competition has changed over recent decades. Trade liberalization, privatization and the shift towards supranational regulation have deprived governments of many tools they once used to control economic activity in their own jurisdictions, and have allowed capital to move freely across borders. Unable to influence the behaviour of firms directly, states have had to concentrate their efforts on manipulating other socioeconomic factors so as to best capture the interest of increasingly footloose capital. They have thus become more self-conscious participants in the economic race, vying with one another for investments from mobile private actors. At the same time, these changes have also meant that from the standpoint of public policy, 'competitiveness' has ceased to be the exclusive concern of individual companies and has become instead a feature of society as a whole, spanning a variety of policy domains, from taxation and labour market regulation to education, welfare and land management (Stopford and Strange, 1991; Fougner, 2006). Viewed from this perspective, interstate rivalry for capital may be seen as a special case of social dumping, in which governments are at the same time regulators and participants in the competitive process. This makes it possible to extend the definition of social dumping developed in the Introduction to this volume so as to encompass state attempts to tailor social and labour policies to the needs of foreign investors.

In the EU, this gloomy vision of globalization as interstate rivalry emerged with special urgency during the accession of ten Central-Eastern Europe countries (CEECs) that appeared to be even more vulnerable to the pressures of international competition than the old EU members. The collapse of socialism had plunged these economies into recession, wiping out almost one-third of industrial output in only a few years (Kolodko, 2001). In the absence of local capital and know-how, foreign direct investment (FDI) was seen as the only force that could revive their industries and halt spiralling unemployment, and the hunt for investors soon became the cornerstone of the region's industrial policies (Drahokoupil, 2008). In a desperate race to attract foreign capital, CEECs cut taxes and relaxed labour regulation, competing ferociously for every new investment coming to the region. Taking advantage of this situation, investors often played the potential host states against each other so as to maximize their own gains, adding to the fears of an all-out 'race to the bottom' (Kolesár, 2006; Bohle, 2008; Drahokoupil, 2008). As the date of accession approached, the CEECs' eagerness to please investors, together with their low wages and weak labour unions, began to elicit accusations of 'unfair' competition from the EU's older members. It did not help that multinational corporations (MNCs) were indeed beginning to use the option of eastern relocations more explicitly to extract concessions from governments and workers elsewhere in Europe. In one of the more politically charged disputes, Spain threatened to block Slovakia's accession to the EU after Volkswagen moved some of its Spanish production there (Lönnborg *et al.*, 2004).

This chapter examines the evidence for the claim that CEE states engage in systematic social dumping as a strategy for attracting investment. It argues that while the weakness of CEE states vis-à-vis mobile foreign capital may indeed be a threat to the standards of social protection in both the East and the West, there are equally powerful forces that limit the scope for state-led dumping practices in the CEE region. The transitional recession and high unemployment may have devastated union organizations and depressed wages in the East, but as soon as the economic situation began to improve, the demands for better pay and working conditions returned (Meardi, 2007; Mrozowicki *et al.*, 2010). EU membership, tied from the outset to hopes of better, 'European' living standards, also created political expectations that made further competitive deregulation politically costly for the region's governments. Moreover, it soon became apparent that lower wages and meagre social protection would not get these countries very far in the long run. With the emergence of even cheaper locations further east, CEE governments had to find alternative sources of competitiveness and attract more skill- and technology-intensive investments. Indeed, as wages in the region increased, even investors began to demand not only more flexible regulation but also more investment in infrastructure and a better supply of skilled workforce.

Does this mean that the threat of social dumping was nothing more than a temporary scare? Yes and no. The findings of this chapter indicate that the strategy of reducing costs in order to attract mobile international capital tends to be quickly exhausted. The more successful it is in bringing economic growth, the more likely it is to generate powerful opposition forces in the shape of rising social demands and thus push governments from a simple focus on lower cost to a more complex approach to competitiveness that stresses the provision of high-quality services. At the same time however, the pressure of competition does create an environment in which it is almost impossible for states to convince the owners of capital to share the burden of providing these services. Faced with the triple demand of improving social standards, providing better business services *and* still keeping business costs low, most governments in the region responded with a mix of two strategies: running deficits to finance the competing requirements and/or rearranging the structure of spending and taxation to make the costs less visible. However, if the financial burden became too large, the threat of collapsing budgets also helped silence public opposition, allowing states to revert to dumping-like means of restoring competitiveness.

Consequently, instead of a 'race to the bottom', what we observe in CEE is a series of policy oscillations as these states find themselves caught between the political pressure to move away from low-cost competition and the lack of funds to meet all the conflicting demands this shift would require. Moreover, while alternative factors of competitiveness may gain in importance during the periods of growth, social dumping and competitive deregulation remain the default options for boosting competitiveness in times of crisis. While this confirms the temporary character of dumping methods, in the long run such oscillations are likely to undermine the continuity of investments in skills and services that are necessary to escape the trap of cost-based competition.

This chapter proceeds as follows. It first discusses in more detail the problem of competitiveness in CEE and the difficulties of accommodating the demands for better social standards while preserving and upgrading the investment flows that are essential to the region's economic growth. The following section analyses the ways in which the CEE governments sought to balance these competing demands, using the examples of two new EU member states: Hungary and Slovakia. Brief conclusions follow.

Seeking competitiveness high and low

We have seen above that 'competitiveness', in the sense of attractiveness to mobile transnational capital, has become a central concern of state economic policy. Nevertheless, competitiveness remains a notoriously elusive notion (Van Apeldoorn, 2003; Fougner, 2006). In the argument linking interstate competition for capital to social dumping, competitiveness is usually understood to be strongly related to costs. This is, indeed, the most basic definition: everything else being equal, the more competitive entity on the free market is the one that provides the same goods or services at a lower price (Hay, 2011). Things are, however, rarely equal, and much of the discussion about competitiveness in recent years has focused on highlighting other factors, such as the quality of institutions, infrastructure or workforce skills, which may outweigh a firm's concerns with costs. The ability of some countries to remain attractive despite high wages has led many observers to conclude that even in the face of fierce international competition, there is still a way for states to avoid the trap of 'low-road' competition by means of ever lower taxes, cheaper labour and meagre social protection, and to embrace the 'high road' of quality services, skills and innovation (Milberg and Houston, 2005). Vukov (2013), who provides the most extensive operationalization of the high/low state competitiveness strategies to date, also shows that a number of European states, including some of the CEECs, have been able to move away from the low-cost path.

Unsurprisingly, the idea that 'high-road' competitiveness is a viable, even superior alternative to the social dumping practices associated with cost-based competition is especially popular among policymakers from high-wage countries. If good public services, including certain elements of social policy, may be shown to be essential for the maintenance of a country's competitiveness, then competition need not undermine the existing standards of social regulation. The same hopeful view has been championed by the EU competitiveness programme: its Lisbon Strategy for Growth and Jobs, for example, enthusiastically lists everything from infrastructure to environment and social cohesion as features capable of fostering competitiveness (European Council, 2000). The problem, however, is that the neat division between the 'high' and the 'low' roads assumes all too easily that investors also understand that better services come at a higher cost and are willing to pay for them. In reality, although the ability to provide excellent skills or infrastructure may indeed shield some countries from the worst pitfalls of cost-driven competition, most governments are faced with simultaneous demands for lower taxes and more employment flexibility, as well as better education and an 'improved business environment'. Reconciling these demands is difficult enough even for those countries that are already well equipped for the pursuit of a 'high road'. They are all the more daunting for those that have little claim to being high-tech innovation powerhouses and must therefore convince investors to accept higher costs now in order to obtain better services in the future.

Yet this is precisely the challenge that confronted the new EU member states as their economies began to recover from the difficulties of transition. In the early stages of integration into the European economic space, the region had found itself on the 'low road' almost by default. With obsolete industries and crumbling internal markets, the only asset they had to attract the essential external capital was a cheap labour force. This does not mean, however, that they happily accepted the prospect of forever remaining a source of low-wage labour for foreign multinationals. On the contrary, the narrative embraced by both the governments and their voters was that this was a temporary setback that would lead to a more prosperous future. In other words, accepting lower wages and weaker social protection was necessary in the short term in order to attract new investment and jobs that could alone guarantee workers' welfare in the long run. The labour unions appeared to concur with this view: even in the most successful subsidiaries of foreign MNCs where the unions were strong and the productivity gains high enough to justify faster wage growth, the workers often agreed to temporary wage restraint in order to secure further investments in their plants (Bernaciak, 2011).

While this roundabout logic of forgoing welfare today in order to have it tomorrow did help to placate the resistance against unpopular reforms, it also created expectations of a 'payback' once the economic situation improved. The approach of EU membership only strengthened these expectations – in the imagination of Eastern European citizens, the 'return to Europe' had always been tied to the hope of convergence with the living standards of the affluent West. By that time, the labour markets in most CEECs were also recovering, and the unions became much bolder in their demands for better wages and working conditions (Meardi, 2007). The increase in the workers' bargaining power began to push wages upward: between 2000 and 2007, the average pay in the CEE manufacturing sector practically doubled, rising from barely 15 per cent to about 25 per cent of the EU-15 average. The employers in the region, however, were far from thrilled. Although the wage increases still remained broadly in line with productivity, investor surveys indicated growing dissatisfaction with the cost and quality of the available workforce (AHK, 2008). What was once the main competitive asset of the region – its cheap and plentiful labour force – was now becoming a major source of concern. Press reports from the countries that until very recently had feared an exodus of jobs to the East began to suggest, a little gleefully, that the region was already on the way to losing its competitive edge (Spiegel Online, 2007; Vetter and Steuer, 2007). International organizations such as the OECD voiced similar concerns, urging more wage and employment flexibility in order to prevent 'overheating' (OECD, 2009).

However, even if it were possible to reverse the rapid wage growth through public intervention, few governments were willing to take the political risk of doing so. The fiscal austerity and deregulation that had accompanied the transition may have met with little outright protest, but they were certainly far from popular: in the 15 years between the fall of socialism and the EU accession, very few governments in CEE managed two consecutive terms in office (Bohle and Greskovits, 2012). Unable or unwilling to restore the original low-cost equilibrium, the new EU member states began instead to experiment with a different approach: nudging investors away from the cost-sensitive sectors and activities into those that could accommodate the rising labour costs.

This task was made somewhat easier by the nature of the CEECs' industrial structure. Despite the technological gap with Western Europe, some of the new EU member states, in particular the so-called Visegrád countries (Poland, Slovakia, Hungary and the Czech Republic) have inherited a solid basis in the more complex manufacturing sectors such as transport equipment and machinery, and these were precisely the industries that attracted the most attention from transnational firms (Bohle and Greskovits, 2012). For such investors, costs were never the only motivating factor. The investment agreements signed with the flagship automotive companies, for instance, did feature cost-related provisions such as tax deductions, but also included government guarantees of workforce training and complementary infrastructural investments (Kolesár, 2006; Drahokoupil, 2008). Even when wages began to grow more rapidly, the most common complaint among the leading industrial firms was not so much the cost, but rather the lack of a qualified workforce and the dubious quality of skills they were getting at this new, higher price (Šćepanović, 2013).

The CEECs thus did have some leeway to shift towards the 'high-road' competition strategy, and previous research by Vukov (2013) has demonstrated that some of them did indeed take that path. As the remainder of this chapter shows, however, it was a very narrow one. Although investors welcomed government efforts to provide better services and workforce skills, they were adamantly unwilling to pay for them. In Slovakia, the 2008 vocational training reform had been tailor-made to satisfy the demands of the automotive industry, whose representative association was the main force behind the new policy. However, its members flatly rejected the government proposal for a small mandatory training levy to finance the reform.[1] Attempts to raise additional revenue for less specific purposes met with even fiercer opposition. When the Hungarian government introduced a temporary 4 per cent tax surcharge on corporate income in 2006 in order to prop up the country's failing public finances, its largest exporter, Audi, threatened to cancel all future investments in the country unless it received an exemption (Drahokoupil, 2008). New duties were not the only measures to come under fire. The pressure of competition for skilled workers may have forced investors to concede generous wage increases, but it had the exact opposite effect on their attitude towards taxes. In order to contain the losses, the investor associations tried to cut down the non-wage portions of labour costs, demanding lower income taxes and social contributions (Šćepanović, 2013).

If the most productive elements of the economy could not be mobilized to finance the shift to the 'high road', CEE governments had to find more creative ways to rearrange their finances so as to maintain social peace while keeping investors happy. One popular strategy was to pass the costs on to society at large, but in a manner that was less obvious and thus less likely to provoke popular dissatisfaction. The prime example is the shift towards indirect taxation, which saw VAT and other consumption taxes gradually make up a larger share of government revenue as direct income taxes declined (Vukov, 2013). Another way was to target the reductions at the less vocal but also more vulnerable segments of the population, such as the unemployed. This was made even easier by the fact that such cuts could be framed as an attempt to free the unemployed and the inactive from the 'welfare trap' and help them back into the labour market. However, while unemployment benefits declined, spending on active labour market policies remained extremely modest by European standards. Social assistance benefits and early retirement programmes suffered a similar fate: in some cases, persons who had already been retired early for reasons of disability were asked to undergo a reassessment of work ability under more stringent rules (Duman and Scharle, 2011).

More often than not however, these forms of covert austerity were not enough to cover the expenses of pleasing both investors and voters. The most common response of the CEE governments was therefore simply to run budget deficits, hoping that their efforts to increase competitiveness would result in enough growth to boost revenues and decrease future demand for welfare, eventually allowing them to rebalance the budgets. During the years of rapid catch-up growth, this expectation was not unreasonable, but it nevertheless implied a substantial risk. As we have seen in the recent crisis, in the event of an economic downturn, a demonstrated inability to maintain a sound fiscal balance could quickly damage a country's standing in the eyes of foreign investors, who see it as a sign of irresponsible governance. When the imbalance is so large as to require external assistance – by the EU or the IMF – the reputational pressures are likely to be compounded by direct demands to undertake difficult reforms in order to restore fiscal stability. Almost as a rule, these come in the form of spending cuts rather than tax increases, pushing the country back on to the low road.

This section has thus far provided a general outline of the mechanism that keeps the new EU member states suspended between the two paths to competitiveness: the political pressures against the 'low road' and the inability to muster the financial commitments necessary for the pursuit of the 'high road' without risking the anger of investors. Nevertheless, the exact policy response to these pressures will depend on each country's internal conditions, its prior experiences, and the political skill and beliefs of its leaders. In the following section, these dynamics are examined in greater detail using the examples of two CEE countries: Hungary and Slovakia.

The dilemmas of competitiveness

Hungary and Slovakia offer a very good starting point for the study of the contradictory forces that shape a country's approach to international competition. At the time of their accession to the EU, these two countries appeared to be heading in very different directions. While Hungary seemed ready to abandon the low-cost approach, raising wages and expanding investment in alternative factors of competitiveness, Slovakia clung to its cost advantage, pursuing a hardline policy of economic liberalization. Both policies, however, turned out to be unsustainable, and by the time the global financial crisis struck, the two countries had almost reversed their original trajectories. The differences, as well as similarities, between the two help illuminate the range of policy options available to states in circumstances of dependence on mobile external capital, the tension between these options, and the conditions under which states are most likely to resort to dumping-like strategies in order to restore competitiveness.

Hungary: the costly dreams of convergence

From the outset of post-socialist transition, Hungary enjoyed the reputation of a 'star reformer' and a favourite destination for foreign capital in CEE. While most of their neighbours started off with experiments in some form of national capitalism, the Hungarians chose foreign investment as the quickest way to revitalize the economy (Stark and Bruszt, 1998). Foreign firms were allowed full access to the privatization process, and, as early as 1992 the incoming investors could count on a generous system of incentives that included up to ten years of tax holidays, as well as trade benefits for firms settling in the special economic zones (Antalóczy and Sass, 2001). In 1995, when the corporate income tax (CIT) rate still stood at above 30 per cent in every other European country, Hungary cut its own CIT rate to only 16 per cent. As a result of these efforts, throughout the1990s Hungary single-handedly accounted for over one-third of all FDI in the CEE region.

This readiness to pamper investors did not, however, extend to other areas of socioeconomic policy. Hungary had initially tried to deal with the costs of economic restructuring by offering generous benefits and early retirement options to those who could not cope with the demands of the new economy (Vanhuysse, 2006). But with the recovery taking longer than expected, these measures soon turned into an unbearable financial burden. To prevent a rapid increase in debt, in 1995 the government led by the Hungarian Socialist Party (MSZP) unleashed one of the most radical austerity programmes in the country's history. A combination of wage and employment cuts in the public sector, currency devaluation, and reduced social benefits and education subsidies lowered the Hungarians' real incomes by more than 10 per cent in a single year (Andor, 2000). The ousting of the socialists from power in 1998 changed little at first: the new centre-right government led by the Alliance of Young Democrats (Fidesz) continued the restrictive fiscal policy. To block the rising resentment among Hungarian workers, the Fidesz government disbanded the tripartite National Interest Reconciliation Council, denying the unions institutional access to the policymaking process (Héthy, 2001).

It was not until the recovery was fully underway that the government's fiscal position began to soften. The major shift came with the elections of 2002, which were coloured by expectations of Hungary's accession to the EU. The economy was already well out of recession and growing at a steady rate of about 4 per cent per year. The investment boom had also cut the unemployment rate from over 10 per cent in 1995 to about 6 per cent by 2002. Meanwhile, wages increased far more slowly, especially in the public sector, where the government had maintained a wage freeze for several years. Now, the demands to 'close the wage gap' (*bérfelzárkóztatás*) with the EU-15 began to feature much more prominently in the unions' discourse and eventually spilled over into the parties' electoral slogans. In the heat of the election campaign, Fidesz doubled the minimum wage, bringing it up to 40 per cent of average earnings. The party still lost the elections, but the new government led by the socialists hurriedly topped Fidesz's show of generosity with a 50 per cent pay rise for public sector employees. Pension benefits were also increased with the addition of a thirteenth monthly payment, which brought spending on pensions up to 10.2 per cent of GDP. In a gesture towards the unions, the incoming MSZP-led government also pledged to reinstate the tripartite body and reform labour regulations in a way that would 'restore the balance between employees and employers' (Kiss, 2002).

Nevertheless, the new government took every precaution to ensure that its moves did not upset investors. To compensate the employers for the rise in minimum wages, all income up to that amount was exempted from income tax, and social security contributions were reduced by 4 per cent. Similarly, the labour law reform passed in 2002 turned out to be symbolic in that it brought no major changes in the level of employment protection. Its main achievement was to give more rights to the unions: obliging employers to consult them in cases of major reorganization, providing more time off for union representatives and repealing the provision that had previously allowed works councils to conclude collective agreements, thus weakening the unions on the shop-floor (Neumann and Tóth, 2002). Given the low unionization rates in the country, these provisions caused little concern among employers, who were far more riled by the introduction of a small pay premium for Sunday work. The same cautious approach was evident in the transposition of the EU directive on temporary employment. The total duration of fixed-term contracts was capped to prevent abuse, but at five years it was still far above that permitted by any of the old EU members. To appease the disappointed trade unions, the government asked the social partners to continue negotiations on further reform in the reconstituted tripartite council, but the talks remained inconclusive (Neumann, 2004).

Despite these balancing acts, Hungary was slowly losing its place as the darling of foreign investors in CEE. The competition was becoming stiffer as other countries proffered even more generous incentive packages (Kolesár, 2006; Šćepanović, 2013). In 2003, Hungary's bid for a large greenfield investment by the South Korean car manufacturer Kia was rejected in favour of neighbouring Slovakia, which offered both lower labour costs and higher subsidies. In the same year, just as its ten-year tax holiday expired, the US electronics giant IBM closed its disc-making unit in northern Hungary and moved production to China, leaving 3,000 workers without jobs. These events made it clear that the country could no longer hold its own in low-road competition and had to find a way to replace these firms with less cost-conscious investors. The system of investment incentives was subsequently revamped to support higher value-added activities. Special programmes were created for companies willing to establish research and development centres, and R&D expenses were made fully deductible from the tax base. The system of vocational training was reformed in order to provide employers with more up-to-date skills, and the private sector was urged to join in the design of vocational curricula. At 4 per cent and 5.5 per cent respectively, government spending on infrastructure and education also remained among the highest in the region, and indeed higher than in many EU-15 states.

The combination of increased social spending, investments in skills and infrastructure, and attempts to hold investors' interest with further cost concessions took a high toll on Hungary's fiscal balance. Between 2001 and 2002, the budget deficit jumped from −2 per cent to −6 per cent of GDP, reaching −9 per cent by 2006. Almost as soon as it joined the EU, Hungary found itself subject to the European Commission's excessive deficit procedure, which required it to implement urgent fiscal adjustments. However, despite repeated warnings from the Council of the EU, Hungary's trouble with public finances was not yet seen as a major risk to its competitiveness. The euphoria over EU accession had also spread to investors, and, despite occasional hiccups, the annual FDI inflows still averaged close to 6 per cent of GDP. The Hungarian public was also in no mood for more austerity: an early proposal in 2004 to reduce the deficit through employment cuts in the public sector met with fierce union opposition and was quickly shelved (Neumann and Tóth, 2004).

It was not until 2006, when the MSZP-led coalition succeeded in winning another term in power, that it finally turned to the task of consolidating public finances. Even then, however, the government remained too fearful of a public backlash – or perhaps too confident that the country was still on the right track – to completely change the policy course. Rather, it tried to patch the holes with a quick revenue boost, imposing a temporary 4 per cent 'solidarity surcharge' upon corporations and individual high-income earners. The protesting employers were solemnly promised that these ad-hoc measures would be replaced by a flat 20 per cent income tax as soon as the stabilization programme expired (Neumann and Tóth, 2006). But the confidence was short lived. In September 2006, the Hungarian media broadcasted a leaked speech from the MSZP party congress in which the new prime minister, Ferenc Gyurcsány, confessed that the socialists had won re-election by lying about the actual state of the economy and that the country was on the brink of bankruptcy. What followed was a political uproar that undermined Hungary's image as a stable investment location even more than had the admission of government dishonesty.

To restore the country's reputation, the Hungarian authorities now reached for more radical measures to end fiscal profligacy, including an increase in the minimum pension age, the introduction of mandatory co-payments for medical services, a reduction in the number of publicly funded places in higher education, and increases in VAT and energy prices. Such a package would have been difficult to pass at the best of times, but now the public mood was positively explosive. Protests erupted around the country, often led by the largest opposition party Fidesz, which even collected signatures for a plebiscite against the healthcare reform. The result was a resounding defeat for the government, contributing to the early resignation of the prime minister in 2009.

By then, the combination of political instability and a weakening economy had already plunged the country's investment ratings into the junk zone, and the arrival of the global economic crisis added the final straw. In November 2008, Hungary was forced to plead for assistance from the IMF and the EU, promising in turn to proceed with the austerity package in order to regain fiscal balance. Although they managed to reverse the debt spiral and halt speculative attacks on the Hungarian currency, these measures only deepened opposition against the socialist government. In the spring of 2010 Fidesz won a landslide victory, which translated into a two-thirds majority in the Hungarian Parliament – enough to give it a free hand in redesigning the country's socioeconomic system.

Banking on the popular resentment against austerity, Fidesz promised to deliver the nation from the clutches of foreign creditors and revive economic growth and competitiveness. To do so however, it first had to fulfil the demands set by Hungary's international partners. Thus, while making a show of restoring national autonomy in policymaking, the Fidesz government largely followed the standard procedure of spending cuts and used its parliamentary dominance to muscle in many of the measures it had rejected while in opposition – the foremost example being the unpopular education reform of 2011, which cut the number of publicly funded places at universities by one-third. Interestingly enough, one issue on which Fidesz went firmly against the EU recommendations was its determination to lower taxes in order to reignite competitiveness, despite fears that the loss of revenue would further destabilize the budget. In 2011, the previously progressive personal income tax (PIT) was replaced by a flat 16 per cent rate, and CIT was reduced from 19 per cent to 10 per cent on incomes up to 500 million HUF.

While these measures reduced production costs and increased the competitiveness of export-oriented firms, the missing revenue had to be made up by increasing the burden on those who remained bound to the domestic market. This included above all consumers – the VAT rose to 25 per cent (the highest in Europe) – but also the banking and retail sectors, which were saddled with a new 'crisis tax'. Other sources of savings were found through changes in social policy, which mainly involved cutting support to certain categories of welfare recipients and moving them back into the labour market. The duration of unemployment benefits, for instance, was cut from six to only three months and made strictly dependent on the commitment to job search. The government also ended the early retirement programme and announced its plans to return some 100,000 to 150,000 disability pensioners to work (Komiljovics, 2011). At the same time, apart from some expansion of public works, benefit cuts remained the only method of 'reactivation'. The government also slashed spending on active labour market policies, which were now to be financed mostly from the European Structural Funds (Government of Hungary, 2011). Even the services that had earlier been considered essential for a shift towards high-road competitiveness were affected: spending on education fell from an average of 5.5 per cent of GDP in 2004 to 2006 to 4.7 per cent in 2011, while infrastructure spending fell from 4 per cent to 3.1 per cent during the same period.

What had begun as an effort at budget consolidation thus turned into a fully fledged slide back into low-road competition. The change in orientation was confirmed by the announced comprehensive reform of the labour code, which the Fidesz government promised would be 'one of the most flexible in Europe' (Government of Hungary, 2011). Although it was advertised as a move to improve competitiveness, the reform was not necessarily motivated by the desire to please foreign investors. In the aftermath of the crisis, Fidesz had discovered that appealing to nationalist sentiments against the *multik* (MNCs) was as useful for securing popularity as winning major investment deals, and it maintained a careful balance between the two (Dobszay, 2013). The reform shows that the neoliberal dictum of 'austerity today for prosperity tomorrow' had become a reflex policy response in the region that resurfaced time and again in times of crisis and could be seamlessly merged with the conservative ideologies of national revival and self-help. Either way, the consequences for the standards of labour protection were severe. In anticipation of the 'most flexible law', the national tripartite council was once again disbanded, and the social partners were given only two weeks to submit their comments on the draft. The result was a bill that radically abrogated trade union rights and shifted employment relations towards individual contractual law. This meant, among other things, allowing collective agreements and even works council agreements to set employment terms that were worse than those prescribed by the law, and also increasing workers' financial liability for damages to employers. The law additionally restricted employees' right to compensation in cases of damage or work interruption, lowered the base for the calculation of redundancy payments and reduced protection against unlawful dismissal (Tóth, 2012).

Slovakia: tired of the low road?

Unlike in Hungary, the approach of EU accession in Slovakia was no occasion to rest on the laurels of hard-won competitiveness. Under the semi-authoritarian rule of independent Slovakia's first prime minister Vladimir Mečiar, it had remained closed to foreign investment well into the 1990s, and his attempt at a 'national capitalism' proved to be costly in both political and economic terms. At the close of the decade Slovakia was still grappling with delayed privatization, uncompetitive exports and rising unemployment, and as late as 1997 the country was declared unfit to proceed towards EU membership (European Commission, 1997). The dread of being left behind finally pushed the Slovak opposition forces into a common front and, in November 1998, Mečiar was ousted from power.

The new coalition government under liberal-minded Prime Minister Mikuláš Dzurinda immediately set out to liberalize the economy and draw in FDI that would revitalize the dormant export sector. A generous new incentive programme offered long-term tax holidays for large investments, as well as cash subsidies for new jobs (Sedmihradsky and Klazar, 2002). Mimicking the trends in other CEECs, corporate tax was slashed from 40 per cent in 1998 to 25 per cent in 2002, and the PIT rates were reduced by 5 per cent in both income brackets. Investment instantly began to trickle in, but it was not enough to contain the negative effects of belated restructuring on employment. In the first two years of the new government, the unemployment rate nearly doubled, reaching 20 per cent by 2000. Some of the coalition parties took this as a sign that the reform process should be slowed down, but Dzurinda insisted that only more radical measures would bring about a complete recovery. The opportunity arrived with the 2002 elections, in which his newly assembled Slovak Democratic and Christian Party (SDKÚ-DS) won the largest share of the vote and was able to forge a more cohesive government. Its master plan for the revival of the Slovak economy included a sweeping restructuring of public spending, partial privatization of the pension system and the replacement of the complex tax code by a single 19 per cent tax.

The programme sought to lower the costs of economic activity in the country and to make the labour force as cheap and as flexible as possible. The tax reform that had cut the top PIT rate in half also reduced the costs at the bottom of the pay scale by raising the amount of tax-free income to 50 per cent of the average wage (Saavedra, 2007). Changes in the taxation policy were followed by a similarly radical reform of labour regulation in 2004. As in Hungary several years later, the new labour code was touted as 'one of the most liberal in Europe' (HNonline, 2004). The new legislation significantly weakened shop-floor unions, denying them the right to monitor employers' compliance with labour regulations, abolishing wage compensation for the time spent on union duties and curtailing protection against dismissals of employee representatives. The overall costs of dismissal were also halved, given that employees could now receive either their due notice period or their due severance pay, but not both. Employees on fixed-term contracts fared even worse. Although the duration of such contracts was formally limited to three years, they could be extended indefinitely and cancelled on a mere 15-day notice without justification.

The Slovak reform of 2003/2004 is probably the clearest example of a dumping-like competitiveness strategy in the region, with the government purposely lowering social standards in order to attract investors. Not only was this the most commonly invoked rationale for the reform, but the associations of foreign investors, most notably the American Chamber of Commerce, actively participated in its design (Drahokoupil, 2008). On the other hand, very little was done to shift the competitive advantage away from costs. Between 2003 and 2006, combined spending on infrastructure and education averaged 6.4 per cent of GDP per year, compared to about 9.5 per cent in Hungary. Unlike Hungary, however, the Slovak government also managed to avoid a rise in the budget deficit, offsetting the loss of revenue from the tax reform with increases in indirect taxation and welfare cuts. The discount VAT rate on basic food products was abolished and replaced by the uniform 19 per cent tax; the healthcare reform sharply raised the amount of private co-payments for hospital visits and medication; and unemployment benefits were cut in both amount and duration (Vukov, 2013).

In terms of investment attractiveness however, the reform was a success. From 2004 to 2005, Slovakia shot up ten places in the World Economic Forum's Global Competitiveness index and was called the world's 'leading reformer' by the World Bank (World Bank, 2005). On the back of strong FDI flows, the economy began to expand at an unprecedented rate, hitting 10 per cent growth rate in 2007. Unemployment decreased more slowly, but by 2007 it had fallen below 10 per cent, the lowest point since the beginning of the transition. But the growing economy also awakened the population's sense of entitlement and demands for a faster improvement in living standards. Falling unemployment emboldened the unions to push for better wages and working conditions, and their first target was the controversial labour code. Ahead of the 2006 parliamentary elections, the largest trade union – the Confederation of Trade Unions of Slovakia – signed a cooperation agreement with the populist left-leaning party Smer, in which it promised union support at the elections in exchange for labour reform (Cziria, 2006).

Smer's campaign was squarely built on opposition to the recent welfare reforms. The party argued that Slovakia relied too much on cheap labour and that it ought to invest more in improving the quality of jobs and social services. Mocking the Christian Democrats' pride in the 'most liberal' labour law, its leader, Robert Fico, pointed out that Slovakia was 'not in Latin America, but in the middle of Europe' and that its legal framework should be more socially oriented (SME.sk, 2007). These sentiments clearly resonated with the Slovak public, and, despite its remarkable success in restoring the Slovak economy to growth, SDKÚ-DS was voted out of office in the summer of 2006. It was replaced by a new coalition led by Smer, which duly fulfilled its promise to the unions. The new labour code passed by Parliament in 2007 reinstated privileges for union representatives, made redundancies more difficult and increased protection for workers on temporary contracts. A year later, another amendment to the law on collective bargaining also gave the government the right to extend multi-employer collective agreements to entire sectors without the employers' consent. The healthcare reform was halted, and a discount VAT rate was reintroduced on books and medical supplies.

Despite these concessions, the new government made only very cautious departures from its predecessor's cost-conscious policies (Vukov, 2013). It preserved the flat tax, which had by now become the trademark of Slovakia's competitiveness, and convinced public sector unions to accept wage moderation to ensure Slovakia's entry into the eurozone in 2009. Compared to the pompous electoral promises of moving the country away from low-wage jobs and into the 'knowledge economy', very little was actually done to boost investments in skills and research. The most significant change was the 2008/2009 vocational training reform, which was launched in response to employers' demands for a greater supply of medium-level engineering skills. Apart from that, even the efforts to stimulate research and innovation-related activities sought to keep costs as low as possible – for instance, by transferring resources from basic to applied research (Guellec and Wunsch-Vincent, 2009).

Ironically enough, it was the global economic crisis that truly spurred the new Slovak government to step up investments. This was partly due to the way in which the crisis had affected the country. Unlike Hungary, where the crisis was seen as a catalyst that revealed the deeper failures of the economy, Slovakia remained insulated from the worldwide financial downturn through its impeccable fiscal balance, stellar growth record and low levels of private and public debt. When the crisis finally arrived, it was through the falling demand for Slovak exports in the suffering European markets. If it revealed any fundamental problems with the economy, they did not concern its competitiveness – and certainly not its cost competitiveness. Rather, they were related to Slovakia's overexposure to a limited number of external markets, its low domestic demand and the economy's dependence on a small set of highly cyclical industries such as car manufacturing and electronics. Accordingly, the government response focused on providing assistance to firms in distress and expanding investments to support internal expansion and upgrading. The social partners were invited to contribute to the design of anti-crisis measures, first in the tripartite Economic and Social Council and later in the newly founded Economic Crisis Council. The result was an important amendment to the labour law that introduced for the first time the option of work time accounts. This enabled a more flexible reallocation of work to protect employment, but gave unions co-determination rights over its deployment (Kahancova, 2013). Other protective measures included subsidies for short-time work and training, increased spending on investment support, and increases in social spending to accommodate the growing number of unemployed. The government also launched an extensive programme of infrastructural investment that included building a new nuclear power station, expanding the central airport in Bratislava and completing the network of motorways across the country (Buček, 2012).

This bout of public spending helped Slovakia weather the most difficult year of the crisis, and the economy returned to growth as early as 2010. However, unemployment still remained relatively high, and the combination of high spending and falling economic activity pushed the budget deficit from a low 2 per cent in 2008 to as high as 8 per cent in 2009. This gave plenty of ammunition to the opposition to denounce the government's 'irresponsible' policies and mount a campaign to restore the health of the public finances and improve competitiveness. At the 2010 elections, Smer still won the largest number of votes but failed to build a coalition, and the Christian Democrats returned to office. Although much had changed since their first term in power, the programme unveiled by the new SDKÚ-DS government offered the same mixture of austerity and liberalization that had served the country so well half a decade previously. Investments in the expensive motorway project were halted and the subsidies to the private sector were discontinued (Buček, 2012). Further savings were to be made through employment cuts in the public sector, which was to reduce the wage bill by some 10 per cent over the next few years. In what had by now become a defiance contest between the two leading parties, the new government once again undid the changes to the labour code implemented by its predecessor, reinstating the earlier liberal version. Hoping to repeat the 'branding' success of the flat tax, the new Minister of Economy even tried to eliminate the mandatory minimum wage (Pravda.sk, 2011).

This time however, the Slovak public was far less patient. The minimum wage was preserved following a wave of angry protests by trade unions, but the sporadic conflicts with public sector employees continued into 2012. The biggest quarrel, however, erupted within the governing coalition itself, when austerity-bent Slovakia was asked to approve the new European Stabilisation Fund – the facility designed to provide financial assistance to highly indebted members of the eurozone. SDKÚ-DS was ready to support the fund, but the irony of the situation was not lost on other members of the coalition, who threatened to call a no-confidence vote. The Stabilisation Fund was eventually approved with the help of Smer, but not before the government agreed to hold a snap election. In the spring of 2012 Smer returned to power, ending the short-lived experiment in austerity. While it is still uncertain whether the second Smer government will have a more coherent programme of moving Slovakia towards the high-road competition path, it is clear that the low road is no longer the preferred policy option. As one of the first moves upon its return to office, Smer again reversed the liberal amendments to the labour code and raised the minimum wage. In

2013, the one-time symbol of Slovakia's commitment to the low-cost path – its flat tax – was also abolished. Personal income taxes returned to a progressive scale and Slovakia became the first country in CEE in 25 years to officially raise the CIT rate.

Conclusion

This chapter has examined the evidence for state-led social dumping as an integral part of competitiveness strategies in Central and Eastern Europe. Its findings suggest that even under conditions of fierce competition for capital, purposeful attempts to lower social and employment standards in order to attract investment remain relatively rare. The need to please investors is counterbalanced, on the one hand, by the political pressure of popular demands for better living standards and, on the other, by the widespread concern among policy-makers that the region cannot hold on to its cost advantage for ever and must find alternative ways to bolster competitiveness. In good times, this combination of factors has led to improvements in social and labour regulation, as well as to attempts to increase spending on infrastructure and education in order to attract less cost-conscious firms.

Nevertheless, this chapter also reveals important constraints that competition imposes upon the states' ability to move away from low-cost policies. Even when they try to increase the quality of services, the CEECs are usually unable to share the costs of such measures with investors. Indeed, they have even sought to compensate them for market-driven increases in labour costs by continuously reducing the tax burden, which has meant that all additional spending has had to be financed by debt or by increases in indirect taxation, or both.

Most importantly however, despite the powerful counter-pressures, dumping-like policies are still considered the most effective way to quickly restore competitiveness in times of crisis. All strategies to channel investment flows towards one's jurisdiction are, after all, exercises in national marketing, and the experience of CEECs over the past two decades suggests that radical moves such as flat taxes, 'lowest corporate tax' or 'the most liberal labour code' are far better at attracting attention than respectable increases in education spending. Moreover, to the extent that such episodes are closely connected to crises of public finances, as in Hungary in 2008 and in Slovakia in 2010, the threat of imminent national bankruptcy is also likely to weaken opposition to 'dumping' – both at home and abroad. There is probably no better illustration of this than the experience of the recent crisis, when the same EU leaders who a few years earlier had denounced the unfairness of lower wages in the East now earnestly advised Southern Europeans to cut their labour costs.

All of this suggests that the trend of policy oscillations is likely to continue. This is bad news for the CEE states, as it makes it hard to sustain the kinds of investments that may eventually help them overcome dependence on low costs. Recent decisions by both Hungary and Slovakia to increase capital taxes and thus force investors to share some of the burden of recovery are encouraging, although they come at a price of growing populism in both countries and, in Hungary at least, of openly anti-European rhetoric. Both countries have also voiced their unease with the Franco-German proposal to include corporate tax harmonization in the new European Fiscal Compact (BBC, 2011; SME.sk, 2013). The fact that the final version of the Compact leaves tax policy to the member states, but stipulates stringent limits on government spending, indicates that social policy will probably remain an important part of competitiveness strategies in the future – either as a tool or as a victim.

Note

1 Interview with Juraj Vantuch, Slovak State Institute of Vocational Education and Training (ŠIOV), 29 March 2011.

References

AHK (2008) 'Konjunkturbericht Mittel- und Osteuropa 2008. Konjunkturerwartungen und Investitionsklima. Ergebnisse einer Umfrage der deutschen Auslandshandelskammern in 14 Ländern Mittel-und Osteuropas'. Available at: www.ahk-balt.org/fileadmin/ahk_baltikum/Publikationen/Konjunkturbericht_MOE_2008_01.pdf (accessed 11 September 2014).

Andor, L. (2000) *Hungary on the Road to the European Union: Transition in Blue*. Westport, CT: Praeger.

Antalóczy, K. and Sass, M. (2001) 'Greenfield Investments in Hungary: Are They Different from Privatization FDI?' *Transnational Corporations*, 10(3): 39–60.

BBC (2011) 'Hungary, Czechs Wary of EU Tax Harmonisation Plan'. *BBC News Europe*. Available at: www.bbc.com/news/world-europe-16206783 (accessed 11 September 2014).

Bernaciak, M. (2011) *Trade Union Responses to Cross-border Competition in the Enlarged EU: Evidence from the Automotive and Construction Sectors*. PhD Dissertation. Budapest: Central European University.

Bohle, D. (2008) 'Race to the Bottom? Transnational Companies and Reinforced Competition in the Enlarged European Union'. In Van Apeldoorn, B., Drahokoupil, J. and Horn, L. (eds), *Neoliberal European Governance and Beyond: The Contradictions and Limits of a Political Project*. Basingstoke: Palgrave Macmillan, pp. 163–186.

Bohle, D. and Greskovits, B. (2012) *Capitalist Diversity on Europe's Periphery*. Ithaca, NY: Cornell University Press.

Buček, J. (2012) 'Crisis in Slovakia 2009–2010: From Saving the Economy to Saving Public Finance'. In Gorzelak, G., Goh, C.C. and Fazekas, K. (eds), *Adaptability and Change: The Regional Dimensions in Central and Eastern Europe*. Warsaw: Wydawnictwo Naukowe Scholar, pp. 334–359.

Cziria, L. (2006) 'New Government Programme Includes Union Demands'. *European Industrial Relations Observatory On-line*. Available at: www.eurofound.europa.eu/eiro/2006/09/articles/sk0609019i.htm (accessed 11 September 2014).

Dobszay, J. (2013) 'A kormány a multik ellen'. *HVG*. Available at: http://hvg.hu/hvgfriss/2013.41/201341_kormany_kontra_multik_kuruclabancok (accessed 11 September 2014).

Drahokoupil, J. (2008) *Globalization and the State in Central and Eastern Europe: The Politics of Foreign Direct Investment*. London: Routledge.

Duman, A. and Scharle, Á. (2011) 'Hungary: Fiscal Pressures and a Rising Resentment against the (Idle) Poor'. In Clasen, J. and Clegg, D. (eds), *Regulating the Risk of Unemployment: National Adaptations to Post-industrial Labour Markets in Europe*. Oxford: Oxford University Press, pp. 232–254.

European Commission (1997) 'Agenda 2000: Commission Opinion on Slovakia's Application for Membership of the European Union'. DOC/97/20, 19 July. Brussels: European Commission.

European Council (2000) 'Presidency Conclusions: Lisbon European Council, 23 and 24 March'. Available at: www.consilium.europa.eu/uedocs/cms_data/docs/pressdata/en/ec/00100-r1.en0.htm (accessed 11 September 2014).

Fougner, T. (2006) 'The State, International Competitiveness and Neoliberal Globalisation: Is There a Future Beyond "the Competition State"?' *Review of International Studies*, 32(1): 165–185.

Government of Hungary (2011) 'Report on the Measures Taken in Response to Council Recommendation of 7 July 2009 under Article 126(7) of the Treaty'. Available at: http://2010-2014.kormany.hu/download/1/6e/60000/edp%20progress%20report_EN.PDF (accessed 11 September 2014).

Guellec, D. and Wunsch-Vincent, S. (2009) *Policy Responses to the Economic Crisis*. Paris: OECD Publishing.

Hay, C. (2011) 'The "Dangerous Obsession" with Cost Competitiveness ... and the Not So Dangerous Obsession with Competitiveness'. *Cambridge Journal of Economics*, 36(2): 463–479.

Héthy, L. (2001) 'Social Dialogue in Hungary: Its Rise and Decline'. *South-East Europe Review for Labour and Social Affairs*, 4: 55–70.

HNonline (2004) 'Ľudovít Kaník: Dôchodková reforma je súčasťou celej sociálnej reformy'. *Hospodárske noviny*. Available at: http://hn.hnonline.sk/hnclub-178/ludovit-kanik-dochodkova-reforma-je-sucastou-celej-socialnej-reformy-116223 (accessed 11 September 2014).

Kahancova, M. (2013) 'The Demise of Social Partnership or a Balanced Recovery? The Crisis and Collective Bargaining in Slovakia'. *Transfer*, 19(2): 171–183.

Kiss, P. (2002) 'Felszólalás adatai'. Comment on the Draft Labour Law in the Hungarian Parliament by the Minister of Labour and Employment Policy, 11 June 2002. Available at: www.parlament.hu/internet/plsql/ogy_naplo.naplo_fadat_aktus?p_ckl=37&p_uln=7&p_felsz=189&p_felszig=286&p_aktus=37 (accessed 11 September 2014).

Kolesár, P. (2006) *Race to the Bottom? The Role of Investment Incentives in Attracting Strategic Automotive Foreign Direct Investment in Central Europe*. MA Thesis. Budapest: Central European University.

Kolodko, G.W. (2001) 'Globalization and Catching-up: From Recession to Growth in Transition Economies'. *Communist and Post-Communist Studies*, 34(3): 279–322.

Komiljovics, M. (2011) 'Reform of Pension System Stirs Controversy'. *European Industrial Relations Observatory On-line*. Available at: www.eurofound.europa.eu/ewco/2011/06/HU1106031I.htm (accessed 11 September 2014).

Lönnborg, M., Olsson, M. and Rafferty, M. (2004) 'The Race for Inward FDI in the Baltic States and Central and Eastern Europe'. In Oxelheim, L. and Ghauri, P.N. (eds), *European Union and the Race for Foreign Direct Investment in Europe*. Oxford: Elsevier, pp. 323–353.

Meardi, G. (2007) 'More Voice after More Exit? Unstable Industrial Relations in Central Eastern Europe'. *Industrial Relations Journal*, 38(6): 503–523.

Milberg, W. and Houston, E. (2005) 'The High Road and the Low Road to International Competitiveness: Extending the Neo-Schumpeterian Trade Model beyond Technology'. *International Review of Applied Economics*, 19(2): 137–162.

Mrozowicki, A., Pulignano, V. and van Hootegem, G. (2010) 'Worker Agency and Trade Union Renewal: The Case of Poland'. *Work, Employment and Society*, 24(2): 221–240.

Neumann, L. (2004) 'Labour Lawyers Propose Overhaul of Labour Code'. *European Industrial Relations Observatory On-line*. Available at: www.eurofound.europa.eu/eiro/2004/11/feature/hu0411102f.htm (accessed 11 September 2014).

Neumann, L. and Tóth, A. (2002) 'Major Amendment of Labour Code Comes into Effect'. *European Industrial Relations Observatory On-line*. Available at: www.eurofound.europa.eu/eiro/2002/10/feature/hu0210101f.htm (accessed 11 September 2014).

Neumann, L. and Tóth, A. (2004) 'Renewed Tensions between Public Sector Unions and Government'. *European Industrial Relations Observatory On-line*. Available at: www.eurofound.europa.eu/eiro/2004/09/feature/hu0409101f.htm (accessed 11 September 2014).

Neumann, L. and Tóth, A. (2006) 'Employer Organisations Critical of Tax Increases'. *European Industrial Relations Observatory On-line*. Available at: www.eurofound.europa.eu/eiro/2006/07/articles/hu0607049i.htm (accessed 11 September 2014).

OECD (2009) *OECD Economic Surveys: Slovak Republic 2009*. Paris: OECD Publishing.

Pravda.sk (2011) 'Vláda Zákonník práce odklepla, minimálne mzdové nároky vypadli'. *Pravda.sk*. Available at: http://profesia.pravda.sk/zamestnanie/clanok/18470-vlada-zakonnik-prace-odklepla-minimalne-mzdove-naroky-vypadli/ (accessed 11 September 2014).

Saavedra, P. (2007) 'Flat Income Tax Reforms'. In Gray, C., Lane, T. and Varoudakis, A. (eds), *Fiscal Policy and Economic Growth: Lessons for Eastern Europe and Central Asia*. Washington, DC: The World Bank, pp. 253–280.

Šćepanović, V. (2013) *FDI as a Solution to the Challenges of Late Development: Catch-up without Convergence?* PhD Dissertation. Budapest: Central European University.

Sedmihradsky, M. and Klazar, S. (2002) 'Tax Competition for FDI in Central European Countries'. *CESifo Working Paper*, No. 647(I). Munich: Center for Economic Studies and Ifo Institute for Economic Research.

SME.sk (2007) 'Fico: Kľúčovým zákonom roka 2007 bude Zákonník práce'. *SME.sk*. Available at: www.sme.sk/c/3078398/fico-klucovym-zakonom-roka-2007-bude-zakonnik-prace.html (accessed 11 September 2014).

SME.sk (2013) 'Fico: Pri harmonizácií daní by som hľadal dohodu s opozíciou'. *SME.sk*. Available at: http://ekonomika.sme.sk/c/6808285/fico-pri-harmonizacii-dani-by-som-hladal-dohodu-s-opoziciou.html?utm_source=link&utm_medium=rss&utm_campaign=rss (accessed 11 September 2014).

Spiegel Online (2007) 'Skoda Workers Want VW Wages: Eastern Europe Pricing Itself Out of Cheap Labor Market?' Available at: www.spiegel.de/international/business/skoda-workers-want-vw-wages-eastern-europe-pricing-itself-out-of-cheap-labor-market-a-478052.html (accessed 11 September 2014).

Stark, D. and Bruszt, L. (1998) *Postsocialist Pathways: Transforming Politics and Property in East Central Europe*. Cambridge: Cambridge University Press.

Stopford, J.M. and Strange, S. (1991) *Rival States, Rival Firms: Competition for World Market Shares*. Cambridge: Cambridge University Press.

Tóth, A. (2012) *The New Hungarian Labour Code – Background, Conflicts, Compromises*. Budapest: Friedrich Ebert Foundation.

Van Apeldoorn, B. (2003) 'European Unemployment and Transnational Capitalist Class Strategy: The Rise of the Neo-liberal Competitiveness Discourse'. In Overbeek, H. (ed.),

The Political Economy of European Employment: European Integration and the Transnationalization of the (Un)Employment Question. London: Routledge, pp. 113–134.

Vanhuysse, P. (2006) *Divide and Pacify: Strategic Social Policies and Political Protests in Post-Communist Democracies.* Budapest: Central European University Press.

Vetter, R. and Steuer, H. (2007) 'Das Kreuz mit den Kosten'. *Handelsblatt.* Available at: www.handelsblatt.com/politik/international/loehne-in-osteuropa-das-kreuz-mit-den-kosten/2803038.html (accessed 11 September 2014).

Vukov, V. (2013) *Competition States on Europe's Periphery: Race to the Bottom and to the Top.* PhD Dissertation. Florence: European University Institute.

World Bank (2005) *Doing Business in 2005: Removing Obstacles to Growth.* Washington, DC: The World Bank.

11 Tracing the competitiveness discourse in Spain

Social dumping in disguise?

Mònica Clua-Losada

Introduction

On 12 June 1985, following six years of intense negotiation, Spain signed the Accession Treaty to join the European Economic Community (EEC). The event took place just a few months before the tenth anniversary of Francisco Franco's death and was an important turning point in Spain's contemporary political history. It served as proof of the international recognition of Spain's new democratic political regime and signalled that the country was ready to leave the tumultuous twentieth century behind as a legitimate and internationally acknowledged liberal democracy. It also represented an opportunity to consolidate the electoral success of the Spanish Socialist Party (PSOE), or what has been termed by Holman (1996) as the hegemonic project of the Spanish socialists. The Spanish democratic transition, which has been held up as exemplary by many, cannot be understood without bearing in mind the stability provided by 14 consecutive years of government by the PSOE (1982–1996).

The period following Spain's EEC/EU entry was characterized by a contradiction between 'societal corporatism at the national level and economic liberalism at the European level [which] was resolved to the benefit of the neo-liberals in government' (Holman, 1996, p. 77). This contradiction manifested itself in a specific concern with 'competitiveness', which continued throughout the period considered in this chapter and beyond. Specifically, this chapter argues that during the period of Spain's political and economic integration with the EU, the term 'competitiveness' was used by successive Spanish governments to justify profound changes in the spheres of welfare and labour market policy; it was also one of the main drivers of social dumping practices undertaken by both local and foreign businesses. This does not mean that all policy changes carried out under the 'competitiveness-enhancing' label entailed the lowering of social standards or encouraged rule-bending practices. It has to be remembered, however, that the expansion of the European market to the Southern European countries coincided with the launch of the EU Internal Market agenda, which was dominated by a thrust towards deregulation and liberalization. The subsequent emphasis placed by the EEC/EU and national-level actors on the removal of regulatory 'constraints' gave the green light to business interests to pursue social dumping. At the same time, with the removal of barriers to capital flows in Europe, competition between the peripheral EU countries intensified, leading them to launch 'competitiveness-boosting' social dumping policies in order to attract foreign investors (also see Šćepanović, Chapter 10, this volume).

In order to substantiate the above argument, this chapter shows how competitive pressures that were inherent to Spain's European integration process were translated into a narrative of competitiveness, and it examines how this narrative was used by state actors to rationalize their attacks on the existing social norms. Focusing on the first 22 years of the country's EEC/EU membership – i.e. the period from 1986 to 2008 – it observes the use of the competitiveness rhetoric by the country's successive prime ministers, and confronts the discursive use of the term with the social and labour market reforms implemented during their respective terms of office. The chapter identifies a double-track policy approach, showing how social policies were sometimes used strategically to pacify society and to obtain its consent for regressive labour market reforms by compensating the 'losers' of labour market deregulation. For instance, the maintenance of unemployment insurance schemes based on previous contributions preserved the material well-being of certain groups of unemployed workers, but it did so at the expense of labour market activation policies. This resulted in a conflicting development of welfare and labour policies in modern Spain: the preservation of certain social protections was accompanied by retrenchment in many other policy areas. On closer examination, the developments in Spain seem to reflect policy contradictions at the EU level, where efforts to incorporate a 'social dimension' into wider EU integration projects clash with the need to boost the 'competitiveness' of the European economy or with the goal of macroeconomic convergence (Bailey, 2008).

The chapter is structured as follows. It first offers a brief discussion of the concept of social dumping in line with this volume's theoretical concerns, highlighting the difficulties of applying it to the Southern European context. It then traces the development of competitiveness discourses in Spain and matches them with the welfare and labour market reforms implemented during the period between the country's EU accession in 1986 and the outbreak of the economic crisis in 2008. The final section discusses the empirical evidence and links it to the theoretical discussion developed in the first part of the chapter.

Problematizing the concept of social dumping in the Southern European context

From a critical political economy perspective, it may be argued that 'social dumping' is a concept engaging with the idea of power asymmetry between labour and capital that has become prominent in political and academic discourses of recent decades. It is based on the assumption of a declining political agency on the part of the working class. During the initial decades following World War Two, capital and labour had managed to achieve a balancing act, and a more 'human' form of capitalism was able to cohabit with a pacified labour. The growing importance of neoliberal ideas, however, created an overwhelming conviction on the side of capital that for economic growth to occur it was no longer necessary to forge compromises with workers. This inevitably led to a series of losses by labour, notably in the spheres of workers' and welfare rights (Tilly, 1995). The perception of the growing power imbalance between capital and labour was also related to the fact that whereas the former can be easily shifted around the globe, the latter has remained largely immobile, constrained within national boundaries. As Anderson (1992, p. 366) puts it, there is a 'massive asymmetry between the international mobility and organization of capital, and the dispersal and segmentation of labour, that has no historical precedence'. Increased capital mobility creates a sense within much of the political imaginary that political institutions no longer have the power to regulate capital flows; that the state is in a process of retreat because it is no longer able to 'tame' capital (Strange, 1996). According to Epstein (1996), the sense of hyper-mobility of capital has further strengthened the process of state retreat: the idea that capital can fly from a national territory at the touch of a button has acted as a public policy restraint for state policymakers. In other words, the *perception* of capital's hyper-mobility may actually be stronger than the actual scope of the phenomenon. In Spain, for instance, the process of regional integration at the European level was often presented by the PSOE as a possible way to counteract this apparent loss of power by political institutions. It was believed that by combining and coordinating states' efforts to control capital flows, capital may once again be brought under the control of political institutions, even if the latter are established above the level of individual national states. In practice however, the opposite mechanism was at work: as argued in the Introduction to this volume, the EU integration process was largely synonymous with top-down marketization and deregulation, and it deprived the EU member states of the ability to control and regulate capital at the national level.

This chapter aims to contribute to this volume, and to wider academic and policy debates, by problematizing the notion of social dumping in terms of a direct relation to increased capital mobility and the loss of state power. Key to this understanding of social dumping is the question of what terms are used in reference to rule-evading practices – and by whom. It is noteworthy that, in the EU context, the term 'social dumping' has featured primarily in Northern and Western European discourses, which have generally focused on how the EU enlargement to the south, and later to the east, has impacted upon wages and working conditions in the high-wage EU member states (Bernaciak, 2012; see also Arnholtz and Eldring, Chapter 4, this volume). By contrast, social dumping has hardly ever been discussed in the Southern European and CEE member states. For instance, although Spanish workers in some manufacturing sectors (in particular in the automotive industry) expressed anxiety on the eve of the EU's eastern enlargement, their concerns were rarely framed within a social dumping discourse. There have even been quantitative attempts to demonstrate that the notion does not apply to the Southern European context, as exemplified by Guillén and Matsaganis' (2000) analysis of the Spanish and Greek welfare states.

The low salience of social dumping in the public discourses among peripheral EU countries would suggest that social dumping affects only highly developed national economies and that it is not an issue in states characterized by lower wages and inferior working conditions. Instead of denying the relevance of the concept for the latter context, this chapter argues that in the Spanish discourse and policymaking process, deregulation policies and market actors' efforts to evade existing regulatory constraints have simply been 'packaged' in a different way – using the frames of 'competitiveness' and 'competitiveness-enhancing measures'. The chapter will therefore focus not so much on the analysis of concrete instances of social dumping in Spain as on the use of the 'competitiveness' discourse to justify the deregulatory policies and the attacks on labour market norms that have been implemented by successive Spanish governments (social democratic and conservative alike) in the course of the country's EU integration process and its accession to the eurozone.

The analysis shows that competitiveness – or the lack thereof – has been a powerful buzzword accompanying measures aimed at increasing economic efficiency at the cost of social welfare and labour rights. It is immediately striking that whereas the term 'social dumping' had clearly negative connotations in Spain, 'competitiveness' had the opposite effect. As a result, deregulation and social dumping became something to aim for rather than something one must defend against, as was the case in Northern and Western Europe. For this reason, the title of this chapter refers to competitiveness, which is actually meant to signify social dumping in disguise.

Moreover, the chapter argues that the pursuit of 'competitiveness', voiced by all Spanish prime ministers who were in office during the examined period, had a negative effect upon Spain's labour market regulations. It demonstrates how the process of European integration, especially in the post-Maastricht period, brought increased pressure for internal devaluation as the only possible means of economic adjustment for countries joining the European Monetary Union (EMU). In Spain, this found direct expression in labour market reforms designed to increase labour market flexibility. At the same time, both in the case of Spain and other Southern European countries,[1] welfare policies appear to have followed a path that challenges the social dumping hypothesis, even though the reforms undertaken in the latter area were also based on the competitiveness discourse. This finding suggests that the competitiveness framework permits the coexistence of two seemingly contradictory dynamics: the systematic erosion of labour rights coupled with a differentiated trajectory of welfare reforms, with upward convergence in some cases, and the near dismantling or the lack of development of social protection in other social policy areas.

Beyond the Spanish case, this chapter argues that the increase of competitiveness, defined as the 'deepening and expansion of the market-mediated and competition-driven profit venture far beyond the corporate sphere' (Wigger and Buch-Hansen, 2013, p. 605), has become the main goal of EU macroeconomic policy. As argued in the introductory section, the concept of competitiveness is linked to social dumping, but it is broader insofar as it encompasses not only measures aimed at the lowering of welfare and labour standards, but also those designed to encourage economic growth, such as investing in skills, developing adequate infrastructure and enhancing administrative capacity. At the same time however, at the micro level, the intensification of competitive pressure that accompanies the adoption of the competitiveness framework forces market actors to look for ways to evade regulatory constraints in order to improve their position vis-à-vis their rivals. In this regard, 'competitiveness-enhancing' measures implemented at the level of the EU and the individual EU member states inevitably open the door to bottom-up social dumping practices.

Spanish welfare and labour policy in 1986 to 2008: periodization in relation to EU developments

This section examines Spain's political discourses between 1986 and 2008, paying particular attention to the use of the 'competitiveness' argument to justify policy changes in the fields of labour and welfare policy. The time frame encompasses the period from Spain's EU entry until the outbreak of the global financial and economic crisis. The reason for choosing this extended period is to ensure that the observed policy changes and attitudes regarding welfare and labour policies were not only due to austerity measures related to the recent economic crisis and implemented under the supervision of the Troika (i.e. the European Commission, the International Monetary Fund and the European Central Bank).

This section applies Vanhuysse's (2006) concept of strategic social policies to show how the policies implemented by successive Spanish governments – often acting as part of a tripartite corporatist structure – led to uneven developments in the sphere of welfare and labour policy. Strategic social policies, by favouring certain social groups or workers while removing social and labour protection from others, have the effect of preventing political disruption and social contention. These policy packages providing compensation for certain parts of society '[a]re likely to enhance governments' success in implementing economic reforms' (Vanhuysse, 2006, p. 133). The concept of strategic social policies was originally applied to the CEE countries' transition from socialism to capitalism,[2] but it may also be used, with caution, for the analysis of the Southern European context of the 1980s. In Spain, this was a period of transition to democracy that was threatened from all angles, for example, by the attempted military *coup d'état* in 1981 which, according to some scholars, made the EEC aware of the necessity to speed up the process of Spain's accession (see e.g. Crespo MacLennan, 2000). Stability as a precursor to democratic consolidation became paramount and, as such, it was understood to be achievable through the incorporation of key political and social actors into the political system and through economic growth that would ensure progressive convergence with the 'old' EEC/EU member states. The EU was seen not just as a wealthy neighbour and the country club that one wished to join, but also as the only possible guardian of Spain's young and fragile democracy. In the Spanish context however, the subsequent reliance on strategic social policies resulted in an imbalance between, on the one hand, welfare protections that were kept in place for certain groups (such as unemployed workers from previously protected industries), and, on the other hand, the flexibilized labour market.

In order to trace the interplay between the EU integration process and the strategic social policies used in the Spanish context, the analysis focuses on policy priorities outlined by incoming prime ministers in their investiture speeches. The periodization is related to EU developments and their impact upon Spain's political economy. The first period, from 1986 to 1991, was the initial phase of Spain's EU integration, often referred to as the 'catching-up' phase. During these first five years, the EU was seen as an external force that provided successive Spanish governments with an expansive policy paradigm; in other words, it helped them justify policies designed to bring the levels of public and social expenditure in line with the 'old' EU member states' standards. The second period, from 1992 to 2000, was the time between the signature of the Maastricht Treaty and the adoption of the Lisbon Agenda. It was characterized by a very different type of convergence – a macroeconomic one – which was often carried out at the expense of the previous goal of catching up with the rest of the EU in the sphere of welfare. It was also the period when some of Spain's difficulties in the domain of the labour market (specifically the country's particularly high levels of unemployment) became accepted as structural features (Harrison and Corkill, 2004). The final period, between 2002 and 2008, coincides with the implementation of the Lisbon Agenda and the adoption of the euro as the common European currency.

1986 to 1991: the 'honeymoon period' of Spain's EU integration

Coinciding with Spain's entry into the EU, the PSOE won another general election. In his investiture speech, the returning prime minister, Felipe González, highlighted the need to invest in the country's infrastructure in order to stimulate socioeconomic development. He also viewed an increase in social expenditure, the development of essential services and the enhancement of public sector capacity as indispensable elements of an EU member state's policy (González, 1986). All in all, this initial 'honeymoon period' was characterized by efforts to improve living conditions in the country and to set up the necessary infrastructural and public sector prerequisites for a modern economy. At the same time, between 1986 and 1989, the share of unemployed people receiving benefits grew by nearly a quarter, while expenditure on unemployment benefits went up by nearly 40 per cent (Bermeo, 1994). This suggests that the PSOE government maintained unemployment benefits as a way to compensate the negative effects that the restructuring of the Spanish economy had on Spanish society.

By 1989, employment creation was seen as a crucial step in boosting the country's competitiveness. In line with the prime minister's investiture speech delivered that year, competitiveness was to be best achieved by reducing domestic demand because inflation was reaching very high levels (González, 1989). Spain was increasingly being seen as uncompetitive by both the architects of the EMU and the PSOE, who therefore believed the country had to increase its efforts to become a more export-oriented economy (Crespo MacLennan, 2000; Farrell, 2001). The successive Spanish governments of that time saw export-oriented strategies as a means to build a more versatile, open economy that was able to move away from agriculture and services towards more capital-intensive activities such as manufacturing (Holman, 1996). Such an economy would provide the opportunities for employment creation.

During this period, the reduction of Spain's historical social deficit was a priority, albeit a costly one.[3] By the early 1990s, the goal of increasing social expenditure to the spending levels of the old EU member states came under growing pressure from the economic recession that hit Spain and called for austerity; in other words, for a reduction in public expenditure. Unfortunately, this happened before Spain was able to catch up with the rest of Europe in relation to social expenditure. For example, in both health and family policy, Spain has had consistently lower expenditure per capita than the rest of the EU (Clua-Losada, 2012a, 2012b). As Farrell (2001, p. 95) points out:

> for Spain, from the end of the 1970s through to the signing of the Maastricht Treaty in 1992, convergence in the public sector meant expanding towards a level comparable with the EU average. It is somewhat ironic that, having made such strenuous efforts to converge with the EU average, European integration would then force a reversal of Spanish authorities' expansionary phase through the limitations imposed on public sector deficits and government debt under the convergence criteria set out in the Maastricht Treaty.

The next section highlights the nature of the period between 1992 and 2001, or what one could call the country's bumpy road towards the fulfilment of the requirements for entry into the EMU.

While it is important to highlight that, up until 1992, there was a short but important period of welfare state expansion driven partly by the initial process of catching up with the rest of the EU, this expansion was not driven by consensus. For example, Threlfall (1997, pp. 8 and 9) points out that even though the PSOE policymakers viewed the push from the EU towards minimum standards of worker protection as positive and desirable, they nonetheless understood it 'in relation to employment conditions, rather than in the wider sense of social protection from all the major risks to which citizens are subject'. The European push towards the development of a Spanish welfare state was therefore interpreted in a very particular way: the goal was not to increase citizenship rights, but rather to enhance the competitiveness of companies and workers.

1992 to 2001: the Maastricht Treaty and the reality check

The period between the conclusion of the Maastricht Treaty and the launch of the Lisbon Agenda was one of contradiction between tight economic policy and the needs of the developing Spanish welfare state. The Maastricht Treaty set forth strict macroeconomic convergence criteria that EU member states had to meet in order to join the EMU. It also created a framework in which inflation and high deficits were monitored so that they remained within predefined limits. This microeconomic strait-jacket proved particularly restrictive for Spain – a catching-up economy that was in the middle of the process of building a welfare state. The needs of social policy were increasingly subsumed under a particular view of competitiveness, understood as a combination of increased productivity by private companies with enhanced capacity on the part of the public sector. As such, social policy became closely linked to efficiency, understood as institutional capacity, in relation to both the public and the private sectors. By this point, the Spanish government's and the EU's understanding of the relationship between social policy and competitiveness had started to become aligned. Following the conclusion of the Maastricht Treaty, they both sought to subject social and labour policy to broader macroeconomic concerns rather than to social justice considerations (Bailey, 2008). The competitiveness narrative acquired a level of coercion as it became apparent that the state had to reduce its expenditure if it was going to comply with the Maastricht criteria. As a result, the emphasis put on reducing the public deficit had a detrimental effect upon Spain's expansionary needs during its attempts to develop a welfare state.

Soon after the path towards the EMU was set in 1992, Spain held another general election that was once again won by the PSOE, which subsequently designated Felipe González as prime minister. In his 1993 investiture speech, the narrative of competitiveness was at centre stage:

> Competitiveness does not just depend on the productivity of the private sector in the economic sphere, but also on the quality and the good functioning of public administrations. This means we must modernize the administration in three ways: achieving efficiency in order to improve the relationship between costs and benefits, improving the quality of services being offered to citizens, and flexibilizing rigidities, increasing transparency, becoming more accessible.... In short, fellow Members of Parliament, we want to achieve reduced and efficient administrative structures focused on societal demands. This is why this government will continue with a policy of freezing public sector employment.
>
> (González, 1993, author's translation)

Many buzzwords were used during this period by the Spanish government, as the above quote shows. One of them was the need for a more 'flexible' society, which in practice meant the streamlining of public sector employment and the overall reduction of employment protection. Hence, it is not a coincidence that the reform of Spanish labour legislation enacted during the same year as the investiture speech allowed for a wide use of temporary employment contracts. The labour law reform was designed to reinforce the 1984 labour market reform, which opened the door to a two-tier labour market (Polavieja and Richards, 2001) through the introduction of part-time and service contracts – short-term contracts that were highly regulated and used under specific circumstances, such as Christmas campaigns in shops. The new set of regulations revolutionized the Spanish labour market, as may be seen in the evolution of temporary employment in Figure 11.1, which shows that the reform opened a Pandora's box for Spanish workers. Employers used it to hire workers with little protection; and hiring and firing costs were likewise reduced. The rise of temporary employment provided both employers and the state with a means to withstand economic shocks without taking responsibility for the social consequences. The state also benefited from the change because, given the rigid unemployment insurance system, most of these temporary workers did not qualify for receiving unemployment support when they were fired. In addition, temporary employees served (and still serve) as a handy buffer within the Spanish economy: in the event of an economic downturn, restructuring becomes much easier with a large group of workers that can be hired and fired without notice.

These competitive pressures did not apply only to the labour market. Social policy provisions such as old age pensions and the organization of the public sector were directly framed around the narrative of competitiveness. Importantly,

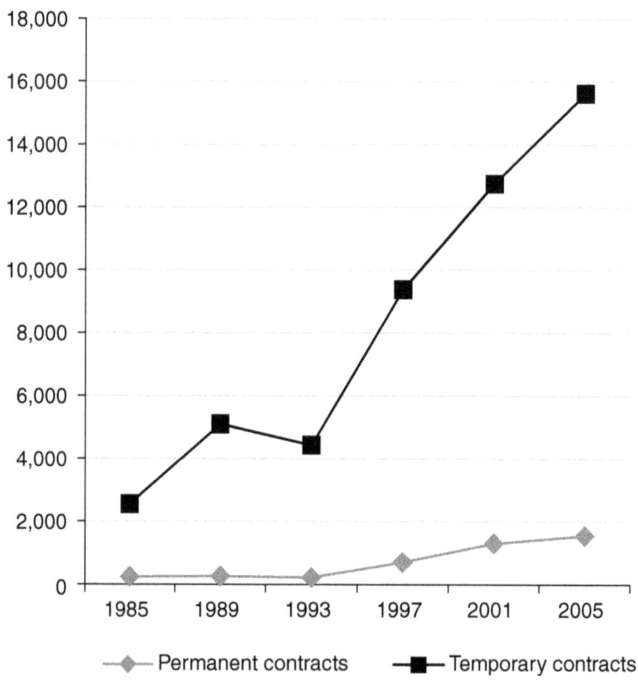

Figure 11.1 New employment contracts in Spain, 1985 to 2005 (in '000s) (source: 'Annual Labour Statistics', Spanish Ministry of Labour and Social Affairs, as presented in Gómez *et al.* (2008)).

Note
See note to Figure 5.1.

by then it was becoming evident that the focus on a limited expansion of social policy was being superseded by economic concerns. The fiscal discipline imposed by the EMU was translated in Spain into a reining in of social expenditure. In this regard, the European Industrial Relations Observatory noted in its 1997 Annual Review that 'in ... Spain, the changes required to prepare for EMU, particularly in terms of public spending, have played a large role in shaping collective bargaining and social dialogue' (EIRO, 1997). Social dialogue during this period found its expression in the '*Pacto de Toledo*' tripartite agreement on public pensions of 1995, which was designed to ensure the sustainability of the system. In this case, once more, sustainability was understood in economic rather than social terms. The agreed restructuring of pensions would only affect future generations, leaving those of a pensionable (and voting) age with similar levels of protection to those they had been led to expect during their working and contributing years. In this sense, one could argue that while the process of European integration may have led to the improvement of certain labour market conditions such as working time and gender equality in the workplace, policies that had redistributive effects, such as changes in taxation or universal welfare benefits, were more often than not neglected in favour of macroeconomic adjustment.

Over time, the expansive elements of social policy were being reduced, not just in Spain but also in other EU member states. In Spain, some key areas were protected, such as contributory insurance designed to mitigate the effects of industrial restructuring upon traditional workers. It became clear that 'the convergence criteria established under the Maastricht Treaty impose[d] strong constraints on Member States' fiscal and monetary policies and indirectly promote[d] privatization as a resource for budgetary revenues' (Bohle, 2009, p. 168). These strict benchmarks not only promoted the privatization of public assets, but also constrained the policy choices of national governments in relation to welfare policy (Ferrera, 2006, p. 117). As monetary policy gained in importance, countries were going to be left with just one type of macroeconomic policy option: internal devaluation of their labour markets and of their social policy provision. As Scharpf (2002, pp. 665f.) explains:

> In the process of European integration, however, the relationship has become asymmetric as economic policies have been progressively Europeanized, while social-protection policies remained at the national level. As a consequence, national welfare states are constitutionally constrained by the 'supremacy' of all European rules of economic integration, liberalization and competition law. At the same time they must operate under fiscal rules of monetary union while their revenue base is eroding as a consequence of tax competition and the need to reduce non-wage labour costs.

This asymmetrical relationship between economic and social and labour market policy had its own dynamics in Spain. In 1996, the Partido Popular (PP) with its leader José María Aznar won the general election that ended the 14-year period of PSOE rule. Aznar was convinced, along with many of his European counterparts, that public enterprises, particularly utilities, needed to be privatized so that Spain's competitiveness vis-à-vis other EU member states could be improved. Moreover, it was clear in his investiture speech that EU integration was no longer interpreted as a tool for the expansion of welfare state policies, such as labour and social policy; on the contrary, the latter two areas were given secondary importance after issues such as deregulation and privatization (Aznar, 1996). In 2000, the PP won yet another general election, which allowed Aznar to continue with this agenda. Overall, the development in social and labour market policy during this period should not be characterized as divergent but as contradictory. This was primarily because contributory social policy instruments were maintained, but at the same time, temporary workers had limited or no access to such rights. Both policy areas came under deregulatory pressures in line with 'competitiveness' discourses that were focused on the achievement of macroeconomic convergence.

2002 to 2008: competitiveness with a human face?

Following the introduction of the euro as the common European currency in 2002, the economic and social pressures on the EU member states became more overt, particularly in the case of the peripheral EU states. It was also during this period that interstate rivalry over foreign direct investments (FDI) intensified, which became particularly apparent in three policy areas with direct effects on labour and social policy (Bohle, 2009). First, competition pushed governments to reform their tax regimes in the direction of 'business-friendly' taxation systems. Second, European governments launched investment incentives that involved a variety of policy measures, including the reduction of social security contributions. Finally, the deregulation of the labour market brought the weakening of employment protection and the growing flexibilization of the employment relationship.

In Spain, this was an era of economic growth driven by speculative financial capital and construction (Charnock *et al.*, 2014). The government policies implemented during this period were aimed at supporting this developmental model. Tax breaks were introduced to encourage foreign companies to transfer their production to Spain, targeting in particular – but not only – the automotive industry. At the same time, previously national utility companies received significant government assistance in order to expand across Latin America, as part of the effort to encourage export-led growth. The two successive PP governments that were in power between 1997 and 2004 emphasized the need for economic growth, even at the expense of employment protection and social welfare. The asymmetry between these two policy areas was increased during this period and was accompanied by numerous breaches of tripartite agreements and the reduction of the scope of collective bargaining agreements.

The way the PP handled the tragic events related to the Atocha train station terrorist attack by Al-Qaeda led to a change in the elections of 2004, which were won by the PSOE with Zapatero as its leader. The new government focused on enhancing civil and political freedoms and rights while maintaining social and labour policies in line with the Lisbon Agenda, which meant defining '"the social" mainly in terms of adaptability of the labour force to the exigencies of competitiveness in a globalized world economy' (Van Apeldoorn, 2009, p. 29). For instance, education and research were presented as being crucial to the development of the knowledge-based economy envisaged by the Lisbon Agenda. This did not fall on deaf ears in Spain, and Zapatero's premiership highlighted the importance of education and research for Spain's competitiveness, with government expenditure in R&D rising with a view to achieving a knowledge society. Improving the country's infrastructure was still seen as a competitiveness-boosting measure, but it also contributed to a model of economic growth founded on construction and financial speculation. The high levels of growth maintained throughout the 2000s were based on a construction bubble fuelled by public investment and business-friendly policies. The construction of airports in many Spanish cities as well as the development of a high-speed rail network are cases in point. It is noteworthy that, during this final period, the government committed itself to maintaining and strengthening social corporatist structures, precisely as a means to enhance and secure economic growth. This commitment, however, was merely of discursive significance and was not translated into concrete tripartite agreements.

Zapatero's investiture speech in 2008 was characterized by a marked European undertone. Europe received far more mentions in 2008 than in any previous speech made by incoming Spanish prime ministers. This, however, was not due to the crisis that was starting to loom large; the 2008 investiture speech appeared largely blind to what was to come. Instead, most references to Europe had to do with Spain's impending European presidency in 2010, which was seen as an opportunity to broadcast the country's political, social and economic advancement to its European neighbours. In a sense, this final period illustrates the blindness of Spain's political class to what was about to happen. In 2008, Zapatero claimed that:

> [i]n the last four years we have grown more and we have created more employment than any other country nearby. We have been loyal to budgetary stability, we have been able to save and reduce public debt, and because of all that, in 2008 Spain has a stronger economy than in 2004.
>
> (Zapatero, 2008, author's translation)

During this period, Spain developed many of its social and labour market policies through the use of business-friendly policy instruments that increased its competitiveness compared to other member states. For example, as mentioned earlier, Spain introduced numerous tax allowances and subsidies to encourage automobile production in the country. In terms of labour market policy, its active labour market programmes were largely limited to tax breaks for employers who hired workers from particular groups, such as young people, women and the long-term unemployed. Overall, the period following the launch of the Lisbon Agenda was characterized by increased competitive pressures also within the EU, resulting in interstate rivalry based around two core pillars: the ability to attract FDI and the extent of export-oriented activities within a national economy.

In Spain, FDI was seen in terms of both industrial capacity and the large-scale service economy. This reinforced Spain's model of development based around a large tourist sector. At the same time, certain companies (primarily previously nationalized utilities), as well as some banks (the paradigmatic case being the financial services giant Banco Santander), were encouraged, and aided financially, to expand across the globe, particularly into the Latin American market. The deregulatory efforts and policies of subsidization pursued by the Spanish government during this period provided incentives for investors. At the same time however, they testify to an active role of states in the competitive race for FDI, in the course of which governments themselves become social dumping actors (also see Šćepanović, Chapter 10, this volume).

Discussion and conclusion

This chapter has argued that it may be wrong to assume that social dumping has not been an issue in the peripheral EU member states, despite the absence of the notion in popular debates and academic discourses. It has explored the relationship between social dumping and competitiveness narratives and concluded that, in the case of Spain, deregulatory policies and social dumping practices were presented as competitiveness-enhancing measures that were justified – and often even openly encouraged – by state actors. If we briefly return to the initial discussion about the relationship between global capital and national states, the Spanish example considered in this chapter shows that the state has the capacity to act – and does so – even in the context of regional economic integration. However, the policies pursued by the government do not respond to social needs; rather, they are put in place at the service of capital. For example, the introduction of temporary work contracts, which flexibilized the Spanish labour market, was carried out in order to attract investors. At the same time, certain groups within the labour market continued to enjoy high levels of protection, which led to the emergence of a two-tier labour market marked by a sharp division between those with secure employment contracts and access to future unemployment insurance, and those who lacked material security both in the present and for their future.

The analysis of social and labour market reforms undertaken by successive Spanish governments in the period 1986 to 2008 has shown that Spain's process of EU integration may be viewed as an apparent contradiction. In the time frame examined here, the reduction of labour market protection went hand in hand with relatively stable social expenditure. Referring to Vanhuysse's (2006) concept of strategic social policies, this chapter has argued that Spanish governments used certain social provisions to buy societal consent for deregulatory measures and to compensate the 'losers' in the labour market deregulation process.

The development of the two-tier labour market and the use of strategic social policies (primarily contributory rights that are often only accessible to permanent workers) represent the heavy social costs of such macroeconomic management. In the period under scrutiny, employment policy was the most frequently changed policy area in Spain: between 1981 and 1996, there were 45 instances of reform in this field (Glatzer, 1999). What is even more significant is the narrative behind the changes. Discourses about responsibility towards trade unions and left-wing parties, together with a positive narrative of EU integration and the related narrative of competitiveness, allowed for an uneven strategy of expansion and erosion in the spheres of social and labour rights.

The analysis ends with the outbreak of the current financial crisis, but it can nevertheless help in understanding the current wave of austerity linked to the conditionality of the Troika. In Spain, austerity does not represent a new development but, rather, the historical continuation of the deregulation process affecting social and labour market rights that was put in place during the first few years of the country's democratic transition. In this respect, competitiveness-enhancing measures provided a perfect backdrop to state and market actors' efforts to undermine Spain's fragile system of social and labour market regulation.

Notes

1 See Guillén and Matsaganis (2000) for a comparison between Greece and Spain, and Sotiropoulos (2004) for a case study of Greece.

2 For example, '[g]overnments in Hungary and Poland increased replacement rates and spending levels for pensioners but reduced them for the unemployed or young families, in ways that suggested political motives above and beyond changing demographic and social needs' (Vanhuysse, 2006, p. 91).

3 The concept of 'social deficit' has been used by Spanish scholars to highlight the relative underdevelopment of the Spanish welfare state. This view has sought to underline the contradiction in policymakers' concern with focusing on fiscal deficits. For an overview of the concept's development in relation to the Spanish case, see Navarro (2006, 2009).

References

Anderson, P. (1992) *A Zone of Engagement*. London: Verso.

Aznar, J.M. (1996) 'Discurso de investidura'. Congreso de los Diputados, 3 May 1996. Available at: www.lamoncloa.gob.es/presidente/presidentes/paginas/InvestiduraAznar 1996.aspx (accessed 25 November 2014).

Bailey, D. (2008) 'Explaining the Underdevelopment of "Social Europe": A Critical Realization'. *Journal of European Social Policy*, 18(3): 232–245.

Bermeo, N. (1994) 'Sacrifice, Sequence, and Strength in Successful Dual Transitions: Lessons from Spain'. *Journal of Politics*, 56(3): 601–627.

Bernaciak, M. (2012) 'Social Dumping: Political Catchphrase or Threat to Labour Standards?' *ETUI Working Paper*, No. 2012.06. Brussels: European Trade Union Institute.

Bohle, D. (2009) 'Race to the Bottom? Transnational Companies and Reinforced Competition in the Enlarged European Union'. In Van Apeldoorn, B., Drahokoupil, J. and Horn, L. (eds), *Contradictions and Limits of Neoliberal European Governance. From Lisbon to Lisbon.* Basingstoke: Palgrave Macmillan, pp. 163–186.

Charnock, G., Purcell, T. and Ribera-Fumaz, R. (2014) *The Limits to Capital in Spain: Crisis and Revolt in the European South.* Basingstoke: Palgrave.

Clua-Losada, M. (2012a) 'L'estat del benestar avui: Catalunya i Espanya'. *Societat Catalana 2012*. Barcelona: Institut d'Estudis Catalans, pp. 53–70.

Clua-Losada, M. (2012b) '30 anys de polítiques socials a Catalunya (1980–2010): inversión pública, estat del benestar, canvis de model i reptes polítics'. Barcelona: Unicef-Catalunya.

Crespo MacLennan, J. (2000) *Spain and the Process of European Integration, 1957–85*. Basingstoke: Palgrave.

EIRO (1997) *EIRO 1997 Annual Review*. Available at: www.eurofound.europa.eu/eiro/annualreports_1997.htm (accessed 19 November 2014).

Epstein, G. (1996) 'International Capital Mobility and the Scope for National Economic Management'. In Boyer, R. and Drache, D. (eds), *States Against Markets. The Limits of Globalization*. London: Routledge, pp. 211–226.

Farrell, M. (2001) *Spain in the EU. The Road to Economic Convergence*. Basingstoke: Palgrave.

Ferrera, M. (2006) *The Boundaries of Welfare. European Integration and the New Spatial Politics of Social Protection*. Oxford: Oxford University Press.

Glatzer, M. (1999) 'Rigidity and Flexibility: Patterns of Labour Market Policy Change in Portugal and Spain, 1981–96'. *South European Society and Politics*, 4(3): 90–110.

Gómez, S., Contreras, I. and Gracia, M.D. (2008) *Las reformas laborales en España y su impacto real en el mercado de trabajo en el período 1985–2008. IESE Business School working paper*. Navarra: Universidad de Navarra.

González, F. (1986) 'Discurso de investidura'. Congreso de los Diputados, 22 July 1986. Available at: www.lamoncloa.gob.es/presidente/presidentes/paginas/InvestiduraGonzalez1986.aspx (accessed 25 November 2014).

González, F. (1989) 'Discurso de investidura'. Congreso de los Diputados, 4 December 1989. Available at: www.lamoncloa.gob.es/presidente/presidentes/paginas/Investiduragonzalez1989.aspx (accessed 25 November 2014).

González, F. (1993) 'Discurso de investidura'. Congreso de los Diputados, 8 July 1993. Available at: www.lamoncloa.gob.es/presidente/presidentes/paginas/InvestiduraGonzalez1993.aspx (accessed 25 November 2014).

Guillén, A.M. and Matsaganis, M. (2000) 'Testing the "Social Dumping" Hypothesis in Southern Europe: Welfare Policies in Greece and Spain during the Last 20 Years'. *Journal of European Social Policy*, 10(2): 120–145.

Harrison, J. and Corkill, D. (2004) *Spain: A Modern European Economy*. Aldershot: Ashgate.

Holman, O. (1996) *Integrating Southern Europe. EC Expansion and the Transnationalization of Spain*. London: Routledge.

Navarro, V. (2006) *El subdesarrollo social de España. Causas y consecuencias*. Barcelona: Editorial Anagrama.

Navarro, V. (2009) *Bienestar insuficiente, democracia incompleta: Sobre lo que no se habla en nuestro país*. Barcelona: Editorial Anagrama.

Polavieja, J.G. and Richards, A. (2001) 'Trade Unions, Unemployment and Working-class Fragmentation in Spain'. In Bermeo, N. (ed.), *Unemployment in the New Europe*. Cambridge: Cambridge University Press, pp. 203–244.

Scharpf, F. (2002) 'The European Social Model: Coping with the Challenges of Diversity'. *Journal of Common Market Studies*, 40(4): 645–670.

Sotiropoulos, D.A. (2004) 'The EU's Impact on the Greek Welfare State: Europeanization on Paper?' *Journal of European Social Policy*, 14(3): 267–284.

Strange, S. (1996) *The Retreat of the State: The Diffusion of Power in the World Economy*. Cambridge: Cambridge University Press.

Threlfall, M. (1997) 'Spain in Social Europe: A Laggard or Compliant Member State?' *South European Society and Politics*, 2(2): 1–33.

Tilly, C. (1995) 'Globalization Threatens Labor's Rights'. *International Labor and Working-class History*, 47: 1–23.

Van Apeldoorn, B. (2009) 'The Contradictions of "Embedded Neoliberalism" and Europe's Multi-level Legitimacy Crisis: The European Project and its Limits'. In Van Apeldoorn, B., Drahokoupil, J. and Horn, L. (eds), *Contradictions and Limits of Neoliberal European Governance. From Lisbon to Lisbon.* Basingstoke: Palgrave Macmillan, pp. 21–43.

Vanhuysse, P. (2006) *Divide and Pacify. Strategic Social Policies and Political Protests in Post-communist Democracies.* Budapest: Central European University Press.

Wigger, A. and Buch-Hansen, H. (2013) 'Competition, the Global Crisis, and Alternatives to Neoliberal Capitalism: A Critical Engagement with Anarchism'. *New Political Science*, 35(4): 604–626.

Zapatero, J.L.R. (2008) 'Discurso de investidura'. Congreso de los Diputados, 8 April 2008. Available at: www.lamoncloa.gob.es/presidente/presidentes/paginas/investidura-zapatero2008.aspx/ (accessed 25 November 2014).

Conclusion

Magdalena Bernaciak

In the political-economic literature, the recent phase of market expansion is usually viewed as a top-down process – the result of liberalization and deregulation policies pursued at the supranational and national levels. In this volume we have argued, however, that marketization is not exclusively the domain of policymakers. Forced to act according to a short-term market logic, self-interested market participants have an incentive to circumvent or 'bend' existing social regulations, viewing them as barriers to profit maximization. In so doing, they set in motion a bottom-up marketization process and expand the sphere governed exclusively by market forces. It is this practice of undermining or evading social norms and regulations, undertaken with the aim of gaining a competitive advantage, that we have conceptualized as social dumping.

At the same time, we have claimed that social dumping and top-down marketization initiatives do not take place in isolation and that actors' efforts to undercut social regulations have been encouraged by policy initiatives to expand markets. Focusing on the European context, we have shown how two major EU integration projects – the launch of the EU Internal Market, and EU enlargement to the south and to the east – have led to the intensification of price-based competition, providing market participants with new incentives and strategic opportunities to undermine and avoid social norms. To substantiate this claim, in the empirical chapters we have presented EU and national policies that pose a threat to labour standards; we have examined specific social dumping practices developed in the context of intra-EU employee posting, migration and cross-border organization of production; and we have traced the process of the formation of social norms at the level of individual member states.

This concluding chapter reviews the findings of the book's empirical contributions through the prism of the conceptualization of social dumping outlined above. It first presents a broad perspective on social norms and accounts for the varying perceptions of social dumping in different political-economic settings. It then revisits popular misconceptions regarding the concept, presents different typologies of social dumping practices, and reflects upon the influence of the recent economic crisis on actors' propensity to engage in rule-evading practices.

Finally, it outlines the consequences of social dumping in terms of both its short-term impact on wages and working conditions, and its implications for the stability of social and economic systems. It ends with suggestions for future research and some policy recommendations.

Varieties of norm systems, varieties of social dumping

Throughout this volume, the social norms that structure relations between market participants and protect society, from excessive exposure to 'bare' market forces, are defined very broadly. They encompass supranational and national-level laws in the fields of labour market and social policy, and workplace health and safety. They also refer to 'negotiated regulations' established in the course of social dialogue or collective bargaining and laid out in national, sectoral or plant-level agreements. Finally, they include unwritten, informal rules and codes of conduct that are specific for a given political-economic setting. To give an example: the practice of paying workers above the minimum rates specified in collective agreements may be considered a consensual norm (see Chapter 2 by Berntsen and Lillie and Chapter 4 by Arnholtz and Eldring). The same may be said about what is defined in the German-speaking literature as a 'normal employment relationship' (Keller and Seifert, 2011); that is, the practice of employing workers on full-time, long-term contracts. While still dominant in Europe, this type of employment relationship is gradually being replaced in some sectors and occupations by more flexible – and often precarious – forms of employment, such as temporary or agency work.

Irrespective of the origin of norms, the exact contents of regulations and the limits of permissible behaviour – and, as a corollary, the assessment as to which practices constitute social dumping – are specified in concrete settings by political and social actors. As argued by Arnholtz and Eldring (Chapter 4), this so-called normation process (i.e. the process whereby norms are defined) reflects specific vulnerabilities of regulatory systems and the power balance between major socioeconomic groups within a given political economy. It thus takes different shapes in different contexts and results in context-specific, 'localized' definitions of social dumping. This fact to a large extent explains the long absence of a universally accepted definition of the concept: by focusing on country- or sector-specific norms and norm-bending strategies, both participants in the public discourse and scholars have been able to identify instances of social dumping that are characteristic for a given regulatory setting, but they have found it difficult to compare them across different regulatory systems. In order to avoid this trap, in the Introduction to this volume we define social dumping in terms of the *mechanisms* that it involves. We are therefore concerned with actors' actions geared towards undermining or evading the existing social norms, irrespective of their exact content. In line with this logic, the mechanism behind social dumping practices remains constant across the different political-economic settings depicted in our case studies, whereas the normative systems are inevitably context specific.

Dispelling misconceptions about social dumping

The empirical evidence presented in our volume challenges four common presumptions about social dumping found in the European public discourse and in recent academic studies on the topic. First, it shows that social dumping is not limited to cross-border labour mobility and employee posting. Following EU enlargement to the south and to the east, the term has indeed been used mainly in relation to pressure on wages and working conditions that is made possible, or facilitated, by intra-EU labour migration and service provision. As demonstrated by Telljohann (Chapter 8), Trappmann (Chapter 7), and Greer and Hauptmeier (Chapter 6), however, the practice of undercutting or circumventing social regulations, guided by the desire to gain a short-term competitive advantage, has been equally widespread in manufacturing sectors. This finding confirms our earlier claim that in order to determine whether a certain type of behaviour constitutes social dumping, one should first pay attention to the logic behind actors' actions. The focus on the mechanism behind social dumping – rather than on its most easily identifiable manifestations – makes it possible to bring seemingly unrelated phenomena under a common analytical umbrella. It also enables a more precise assessment of the spread of social dumping practices within a given political-economic setting.

Second, social dumping is not the exclusive domain of actors coming from new EU member states or, more generally, from low-wage countries. While cross-border differences in wage rates and levels of social protection give market participants an incentive to evade stricter regulations, the popular view of low-wage country actors as those 'dumping' on their richer counterparts does not paint the full picture. Chapter 6 by Greer and Hauptmeier shows that multinational companies originating from and/or headquartered in high-wage countries actively search for ways to avoid regulatory constraints – in high- and low-wage settings alike. High-wage country actors may also indirectly force other market participants into social dumping practices. Large construction companies, for instance, induce social dumping at lower levels of the production chain (often 'populated' by low-wage-country firms and migrant workers) by setting exceptionally low prices for their subcontractors. This strategy allows them to keep their own costs down and at the same time avoid responsibility for rule avoidance (see Kahmann, Chapter 3).

Third, social dumping should not be viewed solely as a company strategy. In particular, the role of workers in furthering social dumping, albeit controversial and often indirect, should also be taken into account. It is true that, in the majority of cases, companies' efforts to undermine or evade the existing social regulations result in employee abuse. On the other hand, workers often participate in the 'race to the bottom': in the case of concession bargaining, for instance, they accept the rules of the game set by the employer and seek to obtain a competitive advantage by compromising on wages and working conditions (Trappmann, Chapter 7). In the absence of systematic micro-level evidence, it is difficult to draw a definitive line between workers' exploitation and practices that are in breach of the existing norms but are nevertheless viewed by workers as 'permissible'. Krings *et al.* (Chapter 1) present the case of Polish migrant workers in Ireland who were aware of being paid below the legal minima, but who – at least initially – did not object to the gap because their dumping wages in Ireland were in any case higher than those in their country of origin. Furthermore, it is important to acknowledge the role of states and EU institutions in providing strategic 'windows of opportunity' for social dumping practices. By easing regulatory constraints and introducing market mechanisms to areas previously sheltered from market pressures, these two groups of actors have been instrumental in fostering the current wave of regulatory evasion. At times, national governments have acted simultaneously as legislators and as participants in the competitive game, for example, when they have sought to attract foreign investors (see Chapters 10 and 11 by Šćepanović and by Clua-Losada).

Last but not least, social dumping does not have to be a transnational phenomenon. Rule evasion and the undercutting of social standards are arguably more widespread in a cross-border context, where the differences between social standards and, as a corollary, possible gains from rule evasion are higher than in the single-country setting. But while the transnational character of business activity is related to the most often evoked and easily detectible manifestations of social dumping, it is neither the necessary nor the sufficient condition for the practice to occur. Company-induced whipsawing and the resulting concession bargaining may involve plants located in one and the same country. By the same token, the external flexibilization of workforces (i.e. the practice of replacing a permanent workforce with cheaper and more vulnerable temporary and agency workers), portrayed in Trappmann's and Telljohann's contributions (Chapters 7 and 8), may well take place within one country or even within a single establishment.

Social dumping typologies

The national- and sector-level studies presented in this volume depict a wide array of social dumping practices. In order to better grasp this empirical variety, different methods of classifying social dumping may be applied. With regard to the broad *fields of activity*, for instance, it is possible to identify social dumping practices developed in the context of migration, cross-border service provision, employee posting, investment distribution, subcontracting and intra-organizational division of work. As argued above, it is the logic behind actors' actions – the desire to gain a short-term market advantage by undermining or evading the existing social and industrial relations regulations – that provides a common denominator for activities pursued in these different areas. An alternative, *'norm-based' catalogue* of social dumping practices places the emphasis on the types of norms under attack. In line with this classification, social dumping may involve the breach or circumvention of wage norms, but also of non-wage regulations regarding working time, non-wage benefits, social entitlements, employment security, and health and safety. Another method of categorizing social dumping activities, which could be referred to as a *'process-based' typology*, is developed in Berntsen and Lillie's contribution (Chapter 2). By looking at ways in which market participants interact with EU and national regulatory systems, the authors identify three patterns of social dumping behaviour: regulatory evasion, or outright violation of the existing rules; regulatory arbitrage, which involves strategizing between different regulatory systems and choosing to comply with specific provisions in order to achieve cost savings or to maximize profits; and regulatory conformance, referring to situations where an individual or a company formally follows the applicable norms but manipulates them for cost-saving reasons in ways that create pressure on social standards and working conditions. Finally, from a strictly legalistic point of view, it is possible to make a distinction between *illegal and legal social dumping*. The former involves the breach of formal, written rules, whereas the latter category refers to practices that remain in line with the law but ignore informal social norms. This second type of behaviour is not subject to legal prosecution, even though it may represent a threat to the existing social order and undermine the established levels of social protection. The European context provides examples of such – perfectly legal – social dumping practices. For instance, posting companies create downward pressures on wages in host-country economies by disregarding informal wage norms and paying posted workers according to minimum, not average rates. Similarly, the practice of replacing permanent employees with temporary and agency workers may in principle comply with the letter of the law, but in the majority of cases it increases employment insecurity and income inequality, and is motivated by cost considerations.

The above account does not provide a complete catalogue of social dumping activities; nor should it be considered to be an exhaustive list of social dumping classifications. Rather, the goal of this typology-building exercise is to demonstrate that the notion of social dumping is multidimensional, and that it can be analysed from a variety of perspectives. Future research should look more deeply into these and other manifestations of social dumping in order to better understand their causes, the interactions between the actors engaging in them, and their short- and long-term effects.

Social dumping in hard times

Available research indicates that Europe has been badly hit by the recent crisis and the subsequent recession; since the late 2000s, the majority of EU member states have recorded a significant drop in wages, employment rates and investment levels (ETUI, 2014). At the same time however, relatively little is known about how crises, or changing economic conditions in general, shape the process of market competition. In particular, are market participants more likely to pursue social dumping practices in bad times than in good times?

The individual chapters in this volume approach this question in different ways. Some contributions focus upon the mechanism behind actors' social dumping actions and thus do not directly tackle the variable of economic conditions. Berntsen and Lille (Chapter 2) for instance, reconstruct the logic behind the social dumping practices used by firms operating in the Dutch and Finnish construction and distribution sectors, which should in principle be valid at any time under the current regulatory setting, irrespective of the business climate. This approach is in a way consistent with the conceptualization of social dumping developed in the Introduction, according to which incentives to contest or sidestep regulatory constraints are part and parcel of the capitalist mode of competition, making social dumping pertinent in both good and bad times.

The evidence presented in other chapters suggests, however, that during a downturn, pressure on wages and working conditions and the incidence of social dumping may increase. Trappmann's study on multinational companies operating in the steel and IT industries (Chapter 7) demonstrates that interplant 'beauty contests' and employment flexibilization measures, which had already been introduced by the management during the good times, became even more widespread during the recent crisis. Similarly, Krings *et al.* (Chapter 1) show that once the Irish 'boom' turned into a 'bust' in the late 2000s, attacks on labour law and collectively agreed provisions became more frequent – both in union-free, deregulated areas of the labour market, such as hospitality, and in traditional union strongholds like construction. On the other hand, it seems that the term 'crisis' does not necessarily refer to a macroeconomic phenomenon. The worsening of the economic climate in a given sector, or even a slowdown experienced by a group of companies, may be sufficient to induce a change in the behaviour of market actors, leading them to intensify their quest for cost savings by undermining or evading the existing social standards. Greer and Hauptmeier (Chapter 6) illustrate this logic, showing that the use of whipsawing in the European automotive industry largely coincided with the falling demand and growing competitive pressures that had beset the sector long before the Great Recession of the late 2000s.

While recourse to social dumping seems common during downturns, as a business strategy it may actually be counterproductive. This is because during periods of economic contraction, when the 'market pie' shrinks due to falling demand, companies are unlikely to increase their market share by cutting wages and reducing social expenditure and employment protection. Moreover, Frank's (2011) account of capitalist competition suggests that if all companies operating in a given market economized on the social dimension, their relative position would not change; the only consequence of the cost-cutting drive would be an across-the-board reduction of the level of social protection in a given setting and the elimination of the beneficial social effects of market exchanges. In the context of the recent downturn, it seems that a similar logic applies to recommendations formulated in relation to crisis-ridden EU member states by the European Commission, the International Monetary Fund and the European Central Bank, which focused on 'competitiveness-building' measures largely limited to wage-cutting, the dismantling of collective bargaining systems and other deregulatory reforms. If all countries implemented the suggested measures and the interstate regulatory 'race to the bottom' intensified, the result would be an overall decline in the level of social protection in Europe, without any change in states' relative positions in the 'competitiveness' ranking.

An alternative argument that could be made to account for the relative stability of countries' positions in 'competitiveness' classifications is that in the eye of the investors, the attractiveness of a given economy does not depend only on labour costs, but also on other factors such as its institutional capacity, its potential to innovate, the availability of a skilled workforce, or the quality of services and infrastructure. As demonstrated by Šćepanović (Chapter 10) however, an exclusive focus on cost competitiveness may prevent EU member states, in particular the less developed ones, from abandoning social dumping policies and embarking on a 'high road' developmental path that benefits broader societal groups. It would also be likely to give rise to new strategies of rule-bending and regulatory evasion.

Consequences of social dumping

In the short term, the negative consequences of social dumping practices are discernible primarily in the social sphere. The intensification of efforts to undercut or circumvent social standards and regulations is likely to exert downward pressure on wages and working conditions. With regard to pay, for instance, employers may seek to offer minimum rates rather than apply more advantageous provisions laid down in collective agreements. As shown by Berntsen and Lilie (Chapter 2) and by Cremers (Chapter 9), in settings where no legal or collective agreed minima exist, or where it is difficult to monitor and enforce the existing provisions, there is practically no bottom line for wage dumping. Non-wage benefits, working time and social security payments often fall victim to social dumping practices; other elements of broadly defined job quality, such as employment security, can also be negatively affected. Notably, the spread of rule-bending is likely to induce a change in the behaviour of previously rule-abiding market participants: when adherence to social and labour standards turns into a competitive disadvantage, such participants will have no choice but to follow suit and compromise on their own compliance.

Over a longer period of time, if social dumping practices become rampant or even legally sanctioned, the consequences of regulatory evasion may be even more profound. Social dumping practices create new social divisions or reinforce the divisions that already exist. The spread of non-standard and precarious work, for instance, may widen the gap between workers remaining on permanent, open-ended contracts and those in non-standard employment. In a similar vein, the fragmentation of value chains, in particular the outsourcing of production and service activities depicted by Trappmann and Telljohann (Chapter 7 and 8) creates disparities in terms of wages, working conditions and employee representation mechanisms between core company sites and units that are external to the company. Finally, social dumping could also be one of the factors accounting for differences in terms of types and quality of employment between host-country populations and migrant workers. As rightly noted by Guzi and Kahanec (Chapter 5) persisting inequalities of this kind pose a serious threat to social cohesion in the receiving states and become a major policy challenge.

The dismantling of social regulations will also do away with the beneficial economic effects that such 'constraints' have upon company performance (Streeck, 1997). For instance, the deterioration of working conditions and the growing use of whipsawing practices such as those depicted by Greer and Hauptmeier (Chapter 6) may undermine workers' trust, negatively affecting their motivation and preventing productivity improvements. Short-term profit orientation and an unconditional quest for labour-cost savings may also discourage companies from attracting high-skilled personnel and investing in the development of high value-added products that bring a return only in a long-term perspective. Worse still, if market regulations are dismantled or become a 'paper tiger' as a result of pervasive rule evasion and/or the lack of efficient enforcement mechanisms, competition may result in market failure. In line with Frank's (2011) argument presented in the Introduction to this volume, this is because in the absence of adequate regulation, market participants tend to focus primarily on boosting their relative performance and investing in positional goods such as their place in the market ranking. Such races could significantly reduce, or even impede, market actors' ability to engage in beneficial market exchanges. Paradoxically, then, the spread of social dumping practices – actions aimed at extending the domain regulated by market forces – may actually lead to the disintegration of the market order.

Closing remarks and outlook

This book has demonstrated that social dumping is a multidimensional phenomenon. Defined as the practice of undercutting and evading social regulations it can take a variety of forms, depending on the specific configurations of norms in a given political-economic setting. Our volume may be viewed as the first attempt to offer a broader perspective on social dumping and to provide a common conceptual framework for phenomena that have so far been analysed in isolation, often within different academic disciplines. Future research is needed to better understand specific social dumping strategies. Moreover, it would be worthwhile to explore in more detail the link between specific deregulation and liberalization initiatives undertaken by governments and supranational institutions, and specific forms of bottom-up social dumping practices. Finally, we need more detailed knowledge regarding the consequences of social dumping, both in terms of its effects in the social sphere and its impact upon economic performance. Admittedly, the considerable variety of social norms makes it difficult to measure the extent of social dumping and compare it across polities. Such assessments are further hindered by the fact that market actors often become involved in multiple rule-bending activities, simultaneously undermining or evading a number of different social rules and regulations.

As shown in our book, trade unions have attempted to combat social dumping through national- and transnational-level initiatives, but their ability to prevent rule circumvention and the abuse of employee rights has been limited. For this reason, long- and short-term threats posed by social dumping call for a resolute policy response. There is a need to curb deregulation and to provide adequate monitoring and enforcement of existing norms. In certain policy areas where social dumping is most prevalent, such as cross-border employee posting or freedom of establishment, re-regulation and the strengthening of controlling measures is necessary to prevent further abuse, to sustain wage levels, employment conditions and worker participation mechanisms, and to ensure the undisrupted functioning of markets. As argued by Clua-Losada (Chapter 11), economic regionalization and the intervention of supranational governance structures such as the EU could compensate for the loss of state power. By enacting appropriate regulations at the supranational level, they could limit market participants' rule-bending endeavours. In view of the current political climate in Europe however, it seems that the prospects for a re-regulation of areas prone to social dumping are rather meagre. As shown by the recent debate over the PWD Enforcement Directive and the subsequent legislative compromise, even appropriate enforcement of the existing rules is seen by policymakers and business lobbyists as an undesirable restriction upon the EU's economic freedoms. However, as long as the neoliberal policy frame guides the direction of EU and national policies, and the emphasis is put on deregulatory measures that openly encourage cost-based rivalry, social dumping may actually remain on the rise. Only the (re)introduction of effective regulation can prevent, or at least limit, the spread of social dumping practices in Europe.

References

ETUI (2014) *Benchmarking Working Europe 2014*. Brussels: European Trade Union Institute.

Frank, R.H. (2011) *The Darwin Economy. Liberty, Competition and the Common Good.* Princeton, NJ: Princeton University Press.

Keller, B. and Seifert, H. (2011) 'Atypische Beschäftigungsverhältnisse. Stand und Lücken der aktuellen Diskussion'. *WSI-MItteilungen*, No. 3/2011. Düsseldorf: Hans-Böckler-Stiftung, pp. 138–145.

Streeck, W. (1997) 'Beneficial Constraints. On the Economic Limits of Rational Voluntarism'. In Boyer, R. and Hollingsworth, J.R. (eds), *Contemporary Capitalism. The Embeddedness of Institutions.* Cambridge: Cambridge University Press, pp. 197–221.

Index

Page numbers in *italics* denote tables, those in **bold** denote figures.

ABC 63, 69–77n5
active labour market policies 10, 27, 126, 195, 200, 221
agency work *see* temporary work
ALMPs *see* active labour market policies
Arblade case 179
Atlanco Rimec 51–3, 58n4

bogus craftsmen 67
bogus self-employment 15, 170n1, 185–6, 188

capitalism 125–6, 148, 196, 201, 211–12, 214
capitalist markets 5, 8–9
casual work 32, 34, 38–9
casualization of work 25, 34, 36, 38–9
Celtic Tiger 25–6
cleavages: migrant–native 17, 97–121
collective agreements: application only to core workforce 68; application to migrant workers 84, 88, 94, 98, 178; application to posted workers 48–9, 54, 178, 186; application to subcontractors and supplier companies 157, 160, 162, 164–6, 168–9; application to temporary workers 167, 179; in automotive industry 157, 162, 164–6; breach of 16, 25, 32, 34, 52, 55–6, 62, 232; circumvention of (*see* collective agreements: breach of); in Denmark 83–4, 89–91; dilution to core elements of 71–2, 91; in Finland 48, 54; in French construction industry 69–71; in Hungary 197–8, 200–1; in Irish construction industry 29, 31–2, 34; in IT sector 146–7; in the Netherlands 48–9, 55–7; in Norway 83–4, 87–8; and social dumping 25, 31, 46, 86–8, 90–1, 93, 98, 125, 133; in steel industry 144, 148; transnational 133; violation of (*see* collective agreements: breach of); *see also* collective bargaining; Transnational Company Agreements
collective bargaining: in automotive industry 158, 167; in Central-Eastern Europe 185; circumvention of 38; impact of outsourcing on 160; and informal norms 7, 227; in Ireland 34, 39; in Romania 148; in Slovakia 203; and social dumping 38, 45, 88, 135, 149; in Spain 209, 220; effect of whipsawing on 18, 127–30; *see also* collective agreements; concession bargaining
competition: between company plants 18, 129–32, 134, 137n1, 140–2, 144–5, 149, 152, 231 (*see also* whipsawing); cost-based 19, 45, 192–3, 234; 'high-road' strategy 192, 194, 200, 204; for jobs 10, 101–2, 115; labour-cost 43–4; 'low-road' strategy 192, 198, 200; positional 6–7, 10, 19n3; 'unfair' 3, 5, 81, 191; wage 15, 44, 89, 92, 135
competitiveness: discourse in Spain 19, 210–11, 213–23; strategies in Central-Eastern Europe 190–3, 195–6; strategies of Hungarian and Slovakian governments 196–206, 231–2; and social dumping 1, 4–5, 190, 192–3, 196, 202, 205
competitive pressure(s) 3, 11, 13–14, 47, 81, 158, 221, 231; in Spain 211, 214, 218

concession bargaining 18, 128; as effect of whipsawing 130, 132; and social dumping 18, 126; *see also* collective bargaining; whipsawing
concessions: extraction under threat 15, 130, 136–7; extraction via whipsawing 18, 125, 127–31, 134, 136; *see also* whipsawing
country-of-employment principle 178; *see also* Posted Workers Directive
country-of-origin effect 141–2
country-of-origin principle 15–16; *see also* Services Directive
crisis 1970s oil 12, 66–7; economic *see* economic crisis; financial 85, 131, 153, 196, 214, 223
Cyprus: location of agencies and companies in 52–3, 56, 181, 183, 188n1

Daimler Benz/Chrysler 129, 132–3, 163
deregulation: in Central-Eastern Europe 18–19, 191–2, 194; of Irish labour markets 34, 39, 231; and marketization 9–10, 18, 127, 212, 226; policy of EU institutions and member states 174, 180, 182–3, 210, 226, 231, 233–4; and social dumping 11, 180, 192, 210–11, 213, 222, 233–4; of Spanish labour market 19, 143, 211, 213, 220, 222–3
Directive 96/71/EC *see* Posted Workers Directive
discrimination of migrant workers 17, 98, 100–2, 111, 113, 118, 120, 121n7, 178
displacement: of native workforces 27–8, 34, 101; of producers 4; of unionized workers 159

eastern enlargement *see* EU enlargement
ECJ *see* European Court of Justice
economic boom (Ireland) 25–7, 29, 32–5, 38–9, 231
economic crisis: in Denmark 94; in France 67; in Hungary 199–200, 203; impact on immigrant workforces 99, 102–3, 108–9, 111, 113, 115; impact on immigrant-native cleavages 118, 121n10; impact on industry 130, 144, 149; impact on labour migration 102–3, 105–6; in Ireland 29, 32–3, 37, 39–40n4, n5; in Slovakia 203–5; and social dumping 141–4, 147, 149, 153, 192, 205, 226, 230–1; in Spain 211, 214, 221; *see also* recession
economic downturn *see* economic crisis; recession
economic freedoms *see* EU economic freedoms
economic growth: contribution of migration to 25, 38; and social dumping 2, 7, 19, 25, 27, 191–2
economic integration *see* EU integration
education *see* over-education of migrant workers
EEA *see* European Economic Area
EEC *see* European Economic Community
employee posting: fake 185–8; via letter-box companies 53, 56, 185, 188; via posting firms 57, 184; regulation of 15, 44, 47–9, 57, 178–80, 184–5; and social dumping 15–16, 18, 46–7, 49, 53, 55, 126, 180, 226, 228–9, 234; strategic 53–5, *55*; via subcontractors 47, 49, 57, 185; via temporary work agencies 47, 49–50, 57, 185; *see also* posted workers; Posted Workers Directive
employment conditions *see* working conditions
employment standards *see* labour standards
EMU *see* European Monetary Union
equal treatment: of migrant workers in Denmark 17, 81, 86, 90–1, 93–4; of migrant workers in France 77n2; of migrant workers in Norway 86–8; of temporary workers 48, 165, 167–8, 174
EU economic freedom(s): clash with social dimension 181; ECJ rulings on 13, 45; primacy of 13, 16, 18, 45, 174; restrictions on 14, 234; and social dumping 173; and workers' rights 174
EU enlargement: impact on labour markets 4, 26; impact on non-EU workers 61; impact on wages 61, 212; impact on working conditions 212; as opportunity for rule evasion 15, 226; and regime competition 16; responses of old member states to 15, 85, 87; and resulting socioeconomic cleavages 97–121; and social dumping 2, 4, 16, 31, 80–1, 89, 212, 228; *see also* labour migration post-enlargement
EU integration: of labour markets 91; as marketization 212; rationale for 12, 174; reduction to liberalization 14; of service markets 13; and social dimension 211–12, 215, 219–10, 223; and social dumping 1–2, 5, 11, 82, 137, 226; and

whipsawing 129; *see also* EU Internal Market
EU Internal Market: creation of 2, 9, 12, 173–4, 210; and interference with national regulations and standards 15, 18, 61, 179–80; and liberalization 13–14, 210; and social dumping 3, 15, 16, 174, 226; *see also* EU integration
EU Labour Force Survey **27**, 99–102, 104–5, **105**, *106–7*, **109**, *110*, **111**, *112*, *114*, *116–17*, 118, *119*
EU-LFS *see* EU Labour Force Survey
EU Services Directive *see* Services Directive
Eurofound *see* European Foundation for the Improvement of Living and Working Conditions
European Construction Industry Federation 1, 51, 187–8
European Court of Justice 13–16, 44–6, 48, 58n3, 91, 177–81, 186
European Economic Area 40n6, 85, 87
European Economic Community 11–16, 143, 174–5, 210–11, 214
European Foundation for the Improvement of Living and Working Conditions 3, 5, 19n1
European Monetary Union 213, 216–17, 219
European Works Council 126, 131–5, 144, 150–1
EWC *see* European Works Council
EWC Directive 132–3, 151
exploitation of migrant workers 37, 63, 75, 88–9, 187, 228

FIEC *see* European Construction Industry Federation
financial crisis 85, 131, 153, 196, 214, 223
fiscal policy *see* taxation policy
flexibility: employment 37–9, 141–2, 144–5, 147, 149, 152, 193–4, 220, 227, 231; external 144–5, 147, 149, 229; internal 143, 149; labour market 4, 19, 28, 33, 55, 68, 213, 215, 222; organizational 145, 149, 153; and outsourcing 29, 141; of production 66, 142, 144; and social dumping 38, 141–2, 147, 229, 231; of working conditions 4, 26; of working time 133, 143, 149
Ford 129–31, 133–4, 163
Fordism 66
free movement of labour 12–13, 97, 102, 109, 120, 178; application to Norway 85; removal of barriers to 44; regulation of 47, 174; restrictions on 46; and social dumping 45, 174; and social security 174, 175, *175*, 177; and working conditions *175*, 177
free movement of services 12–13, 178; application to Norway 85; clash with social dimension 188; ECJ rulings on 186; and employee posting 184–5; regulation of 47; (removal of) barriers to 44, 177, 184; restrictions on 46, 179, 186; and social dumping 45, 180; and social security 184; and working conditions 179
free provision of services *see* free movement of services
freedom of establishment 174, 180; abuse of 18, 180, 182–5, 187; clash with social dimension 181, 188; restrictions on 177, 180; and social dumping 234

General Motors 129–31, 133–4, 142, 163
Global Agreement on the Issue of Temporary Work 164–5, 167
GM *see* General Motors

health and safety at the workplace: EU legislation on 173; of irregular migrant workers 64, 71–2, 74; of posted workers 185; and social dumping 86, 88–90, 140, 182, 229; under Transnational Company Agreements 164–5

IG Metall 153n1, 161–2, 165–6
ILO *see* International Labour Organization
IMF *see* International Monetary Fund
Implementation Regulation 987/2009 *175*, 175–6, 181, 184
inequality: immigrant–native 98, 103, 121n6; income 230; insider–outsider 128; and social dumping 136, 232
informal wage norms 72, 230
informal work culture 25, 31
informality: in construction industry 25, 32, 34, 40n3; in hospitality sector 25, 34, 36
informalization of employment 34, 39, 40n5
International Labour Organization 94, 108, **109**, 164
International Monetary Fund 195, 199, 214, 231
International Standard Classification of Education *106*, 121n9

Irish Ferries dispute 28, 36
irregular migration 17, 61–2; exploitation of 62–4, 71–3, 75; policy responses to 62–3, 65; and social dumping 61–4, 73–6
ISCED *see* International Standard Classification of Education
ITCOR 146–8, 150–2

JLCs *see* Joint Labour Committees
Joint Labour Committees 34, 38

labour inspection: and employee posting 49, 54, 186–8; in French construction industry 63, 65, 71, 73; in international transport sector 182–3; strengthening of in Denmark and Norway 87, 90
labour law 8, 11, 227; attacks on 231; breaches of (*see* labour law: violations of); and cross-border labour recruitment 177; and European jurisdiction 13, 57, 61, 173, 175, 180–1; in Finland and the Netherlands 48–9; and Posted Workers Directive 48, 178–80, 184; reform in Central-Eastern Europe 197–8, 202–3; reform under MNC pressure 142–3, 148, 153; reform in Spain 217–18; violations of 51–2, 56, 145–7, 150, 152
labour legislation *see* labour law
labour (market) conditions *see* working conditions
labour market dislocations 28, 34
labour migration post-enlargement: development of 81, 85, 102, 105; impact on labour standards 16, 25, 28; and integration of migrants 39, 75, 98–100, 120; pressures and challenges raised by 80, 85, 92; regulatory reforms since 81; *see also* EU enlargement
labour standards: circumvention of 187; as competitive disadvantage 232; competitive pressure on 38, 46–7, 80; and employee posting 44, 48, 50, 53; enforcement of 18, 39, 49, 51; impact of migration on 16–17, 25, 28, 87; lowering of to attract investment 205; lowering of through interplant rivalry 140; lowering of in Spain 19; in multinational companies 141, 153; non-compliance with 30, 36; regulation of 25, 48; as restrictions to free movement 186; and social dumping 1, 3, 5, 45–6, 84, 86–8, 214; at supplier companies 141–2, 169; threat to from EU institutions 18, 174, 226; *see also* working conditions
labour unions *see* trade unions
Latin America 203, 220, 222
Laval case 16, 45–6, 58n3, 91, 186
Laval quartet 45, 48–9, 58n3
letter-box companies 18, 53, 56, 177, 180–3, 185, 188
lex loci laboris principle 174–5, 177–8, 180, 183; *see also* country-of-employment principle; country-of-origin principle; Posted Workers Directive; Services Directive
liberalization: EU economic 2, 12–14, 45, 47, 125, 129, 136, 210, 219, 226; in Slovakia 196, 201, 204; and social dumping 233; trade 2, 14, 190
Lisbon Agenda *see* Lisbon Strategy for Growth and Jobs
Lisbon Strategy for Growth and Jobs 27, 193, 215–16, 220–1
LO *see* Norwegian Confederation of Trade Unions
lobbying: by business 13, 234; by multinational companies 142–3
Luxembourg case 58n3, 186

Maastricht Treaty 213, 215–17, 219
marketization: 'bottom-up' 226; and deregulation 9–10, 18, 127, 212, 226; and social dumping 5, 10–11, 125, 128, 135–7, 226; 'top-down' 11, 16, 18, 212, 226; and whipsawing 125–7, 135–6
migrant workers: employment rights of 26, 28, 31–2, 39–40n6, 63, 65, 75, 84
minimum wage: in Denmark 83–4, 90–1, 93; ECJ ruling on 46, 48; in Finland 48, 54; in Germany 46; in Hungary 197; in Ireland 31; in the Netherlands 48; in Norway 83–4, 88; and posted workers 48–9, 53, 58n1, 185, 187, 230; regulation of 9, 83, 163, 178; in Slovakia 204; and social dumping 46, 82, 88, 90–1, 93; *see also* National Minimum Wage
MNCs *see* multinational companies
multinational companies: country-of-origin effect of 141–2; and employee posting 47; extraction of concessions by 130, 136–7, 148, 193; labour cooperation at 150–2; lobbying by 142–3; monitoring of 154n2; production relocations by 18, 140–2, 146–7, 152, 191; and social dumping 4, 135, 140–7, 126, 150,

152–3, 228, 231; social responsibility at 141, 163–4, 168, 170n3; subcontracting by 141; transnational agreements at 133; whipsawing in 128, 131–2, 135; working conditions in 4, 140–1, 147, 149–50

National Employment Rights Authority 29, 36, 39
National Interest Reconciliation Council 197, 200
National Minimum Wage: in France 62, 71, 74; in Ireland 37, 39
neoclassical economics 5, 128
neoliberal ideology 9, 12, 16, 127, 200, 212, 234
NERA *see* National Employment Rights Authority
Norwegian Confederation of Trade Unions 87, 94n1

OECD *see* Organisation for Economic Cooperation and Development
OEM *see* original equipment manufacturers
Organisation for Economic Cooperation and Development 25, 70, 102–3, 109, 194
original equipment manufacturers 158–69
outsourcing: in automotive industry 18, 157–9; and employee interest representation 158, 160–2, 165–9, 232; impact on wages of 18, 158–9, 232; impact on working conditions of 157–9, 232; increased use in construction industry 17, 29, 68, 71, 159; in multinational companies 18, 145, 152; in road transport sector 176; and social dumping 18, 141, 158; and whipsawing 126, 128, 133–4
over-education of migrant workers 35, 97–8, 100–1, 106, *107*, 108, 113, 115, *116*, 118
over-qualification *see* over-education

posted workers: in Belgium 178; in Denmark 85, 91; in Finland 17–18, 45, 48–52, 54; in the Netherlands 17–18, 45, 47–8, 52–4, 57; in Norway 85, 92; recruitment of 48, 185–7; rights of 53, 57, 174, 185–6; social security of 47, 53–4, *55*, 56, 174–5, *175*, 184–6; wages of 15, 46, 48–9, 53–4, *55*, 56, 58n1, 77n6, 91, 174, 178, 185–7, 230; working conditions of 46, 48–50, 92, 174, 178, 185–7; *see also* employee posting; Posted Workers Directive
Posted Workers Directive 13, 15, 48, 53–4, 58n1, *175*, 178–9, 184–5, 188
precarious employment 15, 33–4, 63, 73, 100, 227, 232; actions against 162–3; irregular migrants in 64, 101; at supplier companies 157–60, 170n1
production relocation: to Central-Eastern Europe 191; by multinational companies 18, 140–2, 146–7, 152; and social dumping 4, 82, 126, 141, 147, 152, 174; and whipsawing 127, 142
PSOE *see* Spanish Socialist Party
PWD *see* Posted Workers Directive
PWD Enforcement Directive 16, 234

Quarterly National Household Survey **30**, **35**

REAs *see* Registered Employment Agreements
recession in Central-Eastern Europe 190–1, 197
recession, Great: competition for jobs during 101–2; impact on migrant workers 99, 102; and migrant-native cleavages 108–18; and social dumping 231
recession in Ireland: and collapse of social partnership 39; impact on hospitality sector 34, 37; impact on labour market 26, 39; impact on wages 33; as pretext for organizational change 37; and social dumping practices 39; strength of unions during 33, 39
recruitment: agencies 30, 33; of 'cheap' labour 183, 185–7; of foreign workers 29, 45, 88, 174, 177–8, 185, 187; via letter-box companies 185; of posted workers 48, 185, 187; by temporary work agencies 47–8, 53–4, 57, 73, 182, 186; of temporary workers 167
'regime shopping' 14, 174–5, 180, 187
Registered Employment Agreements 29, 30–4
Regulation 883/2004 175–6, *175*, 181, 184
Regulation 987/2009 175–6, *175*, 181, 184
Regulation 1071/2009 177
Regulation 1408/71 175
regulatory arbitrage 17, 44, 50, 53–4, 57, 230
regulatory conformance 17, 44, 50, 55–7, 230

regulatory evasion 17, 44, 50–3, 57, 229–30, 232
relocation *see* production relocation
rights: co-determination 125, 149, 204; to collective action 43, 46; collective agreement 84, 203; consultation 160, 163, 197; economic 16, 180; employee 32, 141, 150, 158–9, 201, 233; employment 26, 29, 31–2, 39–40n6, 57, 82, 84, 183; enforcement of 174, 187; to equal treatment 28, 174–5; to exploit competitive advantages 45; to free establishment 183; to free movement 102, 175–5; to industrial relations 45; information 160, 163, 165; labour 31, 63, 75, 141, 213, 223; of migrant workers 28, 31–2, 39–40n6, 63, 65, 75, 84, 174–5, 178; negotiation 68; pay indexation 147, 150; pension 52; of posted workers 53, 57, 174, 185–6; shareholder 180; social 13, 17, 47, 145, 164, 168, 223; social security 52–3, 71, 168, 220, 222; of temporary workers 167, 220; of trade unions 46, 200, 202; to unionization 152, 164–5; welfare 212–3; worker 47, 82, 135, 141, 149, 173–4, 181, 186, 212, 223; to workplace participation 135, 137; to workplace representation 43, 68, 162, 164
Rome Treaty 12–13, 174
Rüffert case 58n3, 91
rule-bending 16, 44, 210, 226, 232–4
Rush Portuguesa case 15, 178

SCOR 144–5, 148–53
seasonal work 34, 63, 170n1, 178
segmentation: of labour market 39, 55, 66, 157, 212; of migrant workforce 28, 98, 100
self-employment: incidence of among migrants 99, 106, *107*, 108, 113, 118; increase in among migrants 111, *114*, 121n10; *see also* bogus self-employment
Services Directive 13, 15–16
Services, Industrial, Professional and Technical Union 28, 31
shell companies 50–2, 57
SIPTU *see* Services, Industrial, Professional and Technical Union
social regulation(s): erosion of 3, 47, 223, 233; EU coordination of 13, 174–7, 181, 183–5; and EU enlargement 15; evasion of 15–16, 47, 82, 126, 226, 228–9, 233; as market element 8, 137; and market expansion 14; need for transnational approach to 126, 137; and social dumping 10–11, 82; undermining of 193, 226, 228
social responsibility 56, 141, 163–4, 168, 170n3
social security contributions: circumvention of regulations on 2, 18, 183–4, 186–7; cross-border enforcement of regulations on 49; employer savings on 15, 54, *55*, 56; and free movement of workers 47, 174; in international road transport 176–7, 181–3; location of payments of 52–4, 56, 183–4; lowering of to attract investment 195, 197, 220; of posted workers 47, 53–4, *55*, 56, 174–5, *175*, 184–6; prevention of acquisition in home or host country 52; and regime shopping 14, 174–5; and secretive deductions 52–3; and social dumping 2, 46, 90, 181, 232; of temporary workers 15, 18, 47, 49, 52–6, 64, 71, 174, *175*, 185–6, 220; under-declarations to 71; *see also* Regulation 883/2004; Regulation 987/2009
social standards: circumvention of 94, 231–2; efforts to uphold 38, 82, 92–3; and employee posting 15; formation of 2, 83, 94; improvement of in Central-Eastern Europe 191–2; lowering of to attract investment 202, 205, 210; pressure on 43, 47, 89, 91, 97, 230–1; and social dumping 2, 81, 82, 86, 89, 94, 229; guarantee of through transnational agreements 163–5, 168, 170n2
Spanish Socialist Party 210, 212, 215–17, 219–20
strategic posting *see under* employee posting
subcontracting: in automotive industry 157–69; in construction industry 29–34, 62–3, 67–8, 70, 72, 74, 228; and employee posting 47–9, 54, 57, 184–5, 188n3; impact on labour rights and standards 141, 158–9, 169; increase in 30, 34, 62, 67–8, 72, 76, 185; and non-compliance with collective agreements or labour standards 25, 30, 32, 34, 50, 74, 165; and social dumping 159, 163, 229; and transnational company agreements 163–9

TAWD *see* Temporary Agency Work Directive

taxation policy 136, 197, 201, 203, 206, 219–20
TCAs *see* Transnational Company Agreements
Temporary Agency Work Directive 48, 198
temporary contracts: exploitation related to 55–6, 70–1, 73–4; Hungarian legislation on 198, 202–3; increased use of in Spain 217–18, *218*, 222; migrant employment on 103, 106, *107*, 108, 113, 115, 118, *119*; use of by automotive suppliers 159–60, 162, 167–8; *see also* temporary work agencies; temporary workers
temporary employment *see* temporary work
temporary employment agencies *see* temporary work agencies
temporary work: increase in 30, 33–4, 48, 68, *69*, 147, 159, 185, 218, *218*, 227
temporary work agencies: abuse and evasion by 17, 49, 51–7, 70–4, 184–7; and employee posting 47–50, 54, 57, 185; in Finland 49, 54; in France 17, 63–8, 70–6; location of 47, 53–4, 57; in the Netherlands 48–9, 53–6; recruitment by 47–8, 53–4, 57, 73, 182, 185–6; regulation of 48, 198; and social dumping 49, 73, 230; *see also* temporary contracts; temporary workers
temporary workers: in automotive industry 133, 159–68; in construction industry 29–30, 33–4, 51–7, 63–8, *69*, 69–76; equal treatment of 48, 165, 167–8, 174; in France 63–8, *69*, 69–76; health and safety of 72, 149; interest representation of 68–70, 160, 162, 164–8, 178; in Ireland 29–30, 33–4; in IT sector 144–5, 147; permanent employment of 72–3; replacement of permanent workforces by 18, 144–5, 229–30; rights of 167; social security of 15, 18, 47, 49, 52–6, 64, 71, 174, *175*, 185–6, 220; unionization of 31, 149; wages of 66, 71, 178; working conditions of 48–9, 149, 160, 166–8, *175*, 178; *see also* temporary contracts; temporary work; temporary work agencies
trade liberalization *see* liberalization
trade union(s): in Central-Eastern Europe 191–3, 197–8, 200, 202–4; cross-sectoral cooperation between 158, 161–2, 166; ECJ rulings regarding 45–6, 48; intervention on behalf of migrant workers by 26, 28, 31, 39, 70, 81, 86; intervention on behalf of posted workers by 53, 182–4; intervention on behalf of temporary workers by 52, 56, 159, 163, 166–8; in multinational companies 142, 144, 146–53, 193; resistance to whipsawing by 133–5; responses to social dumping practices by 2, 28, 81–2, 87–94, 158, 233; transnational strategies of 150–2, 161, 163–5, 169, 233
Transnational Company Agreements 18, 133, 158, 163–9
transnational employee interest representation 18, 125, 133–4, 136–7, 148, 150–3, 153n1, 158, 161–9, 233
transnational regulations 2, 48, 57, 126, 186
transnational strategies against social dumping 141, 148, 150–3, 158, 163–9; *see also* European Works Council; Transnational Company Agreements
Treaty of Rome *see* Rome Treaty
Troika 214, 223
TWAs *see* temporary work agencies

unequal treatment: of migrant populations in Europe 98, 102, 108, 120, 120n1; and social dumping 86, 93; of workers 168

ver.di 162, 165–6
Viking case 16, 46, 58n3
Volkswagen 129–31, 133–4, 163, 191
VW *see* Volkswagen

whipsawing: in automotive industry 125–37, 142, 231; coercive 129–30; hegemonic 130–1; impact on collective bargaining 18, 127–8, 130, 132–4; impact on employee interest representation 127–8, 130–1, 133–6; impact on employment conditions 133, 233; impact on industrial relations 18, 126, 129, 133, 136; informal 129–31; management 125, 129, 133, 136, 137n1; and marketization 125–7, 135–6; and outsourcing 126, 128, 133–4; rule-based 129, 131; and social dumping 126, 135–6, 229; in steel industry 145
working conditions: acceptable and unacceptable 83, 168; in Central-Eastern Europe 191, 193–4, 202; of cross-border workers 178–9, 183, 186–7; flexibilization of 4, 133; impact of

working conditions *continued*
competition on 6–7, 10; impact of EU policies on 174–80; impact of migration on 25, 28; impact of outsourcing on 18, 157–8, 169, 232; improvement through Transnational Company Agreements 158, 163, 165–9; of irregular migrants 17, 65, 74; of migrants in Denmark and Norway 81–3, 84–5, 88, 90–3; of migrants in Europe 2, 85, 98, 113, 120; of migrants in Finland and the Netherlands 44–5, 48–9; of migrants in Ireland 17, 26, 31–9; in multinational companies 4, 140–1, 147, 149–50; of posted workers 46–50, 92, 174, *175*, 178–9, 186–7; pressures on 2, 15, 84, 169, 228, 230–2; regulation of 47, 49–50, *175*, 177, 234; of seasonal workers 178; and social dumping 2, 4, 25, 76, 80, 88, 90, 93, 98, 212–13, 227–8, 231–2; at supplier and subcontracting companies 157–61, 163–9; of temporary (agency) workers 47–8, 68, 149, 166–9; *see also* flexibility; health and safety; labour standards

World Works Council 133, 164

zero-hours contracts 55, 144, 149, 170n1

For Product Safety Concerns and Information please contact our EU representative GPSR@taylorandfrancis.com
Taylor & Francis Verlag GmbH, Kaufingerstraße 24, 80331 München, Germany

www.ingramcontent.com/pod-product-compliance
Ingram Content Group UK Ltd.
Pitfield, Milton Keynes, MK11 3LW, UK
UKHW010959180926
475701UK00004B/466

* 9 7 8 1 1 3 8 7 1 6 6 7 4 *